REPUBLICAN IDENTITIES IN
WAR AND PEACE

REPUBLICAN IDENTITIES IN WAR AND PEACE

Representations of France in the Nineteenth and Twentieth Centuries

ANTOINE PROST

Translated by
Jay Winter with Helen McPhail

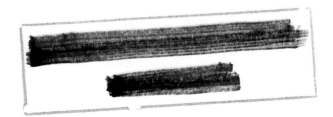

Oxford • New York

First published in 2002 by
Berg
Editorial offices:
150 Cowley Road Oxford, OX4 1JJ, UK
838 Broadway, Third Floor, New York, NY 10003-4812, USA

© Antoine Prost 2002

Berg is the imprint of Oxford International Publishers Ltd.

Library of Congress Cataloging-in-Publication Data
A catalogue record for this book is available from the Library of Congress.

British Library Cataloguing-in-Publication Data

Prost, Antoine, 1933–
    Republican identities in war and peace : representations of France
in the nineteenth and twentieth centuries / Antoine Prost.
        p. cm. – (The legacy of the Great War)
Includes bibliographical references and index.
        ISBN 1-85973-621-1 (cloth) – ISBN 1-85973-626-2 (pbk.)
        1. France–History–1914-1940 2. France–History–German
occupation, 1940–1945. I. Title. II. Series.
    DC389 .P76 2002
    944.081–dc21

                                                            2002011458

ISBN 1 85973 621 1 (Cloth)
        1 85973 626 2 (Paper)

Typeset by JS Typesetting Ltd, Wellingborough, Northants.
Printed in the United Kingdom by Biddles Ltd *www.biddles.co.uk*

Contents

Contents

III. Identities and the Discourse of Political Conflict

List of Maps and Figures

Preface

These essays are the fruit of Antoine Prost's scholarly work over four decades. Three – Chapters 6, 10, and 13 – have been written or substantially rewritten for this volume, and have not before appeared in print in this form. All the others have been amended or extended from earlier French drafts and for an English-language audience. In some cases, this has meant translating them for the first time; in others, there was an effort to bring out Prost's contribution by reworking texts that have appeared in English. In effect, all these essays are new, either in form, content or title.

The effort to produce an English rendering of Prost's style has been both difficult and an education for me. I have had the assistance of Helen McPhail, a historian of the First World War and a translator of many books on the subject. Together with Antoine Prost, we dealt with the art of translation as a conversation, across linguistic and national frontiers. Antoine's courtesy, patience and care have been essential to this exercise, as has been the hospitality of Pembroke College, Cambridge, the Maison Suger in Paris, and the Prost household in Orléans. A grant from the research centre of the Historial de la Grande Guerre at Péronne, Somme, helped us finish this task.

Thanks and acknowledgement are due to the following editors for permission to reproduce or use earlier versions of these essays:

Chs 1–2: Gallimard and Columbia University Press for 'War Memorials of the Great War: Monuments to the Fallen', originally published as: 'Les monuments aux morts. Culte républicain? Culte civique? Culte patriotique?', in Pierre Nora (éd.), *Les Lieux de mémoire. 1. La République*, Paris, Gallimard, 1984, pp. 195–225; and for 'Verdun: The Life of a Site of Memory', originally published as 'Verdun' in Pierre Nora (éd.), *Les Lieux de mémoire, 2. La Nation*, Tome III, Paris, Gallimard, 1986, pp. 111–41.

Preface

Ch. 3: Kluwer Law International for 'The Contribution of the Republican Primary School to French National Identity', originally published as: 'La contribution de l'école primaire républicaine à l'identité française', in H.-G. Haupt, M.-G. Müller and S. Woolf (eds), *Regional and National Identities in Europe in the XIXth and XXth Centuries*, Boston, Kluwer Law International, 1998, pp. 255–74.

Ch. 4: *Vingtième siècle*, for 'Representations of War in Inter-War France', originally published as: "Les représentations de la guerre dans la culture française de l'entre-deux-guerres", *Vingtième siècle, revue d'histoire* (janvier–mars), 1994, pp. 23–31.

Ch. 5: Cambridge University Press, for 'The Algerian War in French Collective Memory', originally published in Jay Winter and Emmanuel Sivan (eds), *War and Remembrance in the Twentieth Century*, Cambridge, Cambridge University Press, 1999, pp. 161–76 .

Ch. 6: Editions de l'Atelier, for parts of 'The People of Paris: The 18th Arrondissement in 1936', originally published as 'Structures sociales du XVIII° arrondissement en 1936', in Jacques Girault (dir.), *Ouvriers en banlieue XIX°–XX° siècle*, Paris, Ed. de l'Atelier, 1998, pp. 50–64.

Chs 7 and 11: Publications de la Sorbonne, for 'Celebrating Joan: A Feast of Collective Identity in Orléans since the French Revolution', originally published as: 'Jeanne à la fête. Identité collective et mémoire à Orléans depuis la Révolution française', in Christophe Charle, Jacqueline Lalouette, Michel Pigenet et Anne-Marie Sohn (éds), *La France démocratique, mélanges offerts à Maurice Agulhon*, Paris, Publ. de la Sorbonne, 1998, pp. 379–96; and for 'Workers, Others, and the State', originally published (with Manfred Bock), as 'Les ouvriers, les autres et l'Etat. Comparaison des paroles ouvrières', in Jean-Louis Robert, Friedhelm Boll, Antoine Prost (éds): *L'invention des syndicalismes. Le syndicalisme en Europe occidentale à la fin du XIX° siècle*, Paris, Publ. de la Sorbonne, 1997, pp. 219–35.

Ch. 8: *Annales E.S.C.*, for 'Marriage, Youth and Society in Orléans in 1911', originally published as 'Mariage, jeunesse et société à Orléans en 1911', *Annales E.S.C.*, 1981-4, (juillet–août 1981), pp. 672–701.

Preface

Ch. 9: Verlag Neue Gesellschaft for 'Youth in Inter-War France',
originally published as: 'Jeunesse populaire et jeunesse bourgeoise
dans la France de l'entre-deux-guerres', in D. Dowe (ed.), *Jugend-
protest und Generationen-konflikt in Europa im 20° Jahrhundert*,
Bonn, Verlag Neue Gesellschaft, 1986, pp. 189-98, and reprinted
in *Vingtième siècle, revue d'histoire*, n° 13, janvier–mars 1987,
pp. 35-43.

Ch. 10: *Revue française de science politique*, for 'Votes and Words',
parts of which appeared in Antoine Prost and Christian Rosenzveig,
'La Chambre des députés (1881-1885), analyse factorielle des
scrutins', *Revue française de science politique*, févr. 1971, pp. 5-50,
and in Louis Girard et Rémy Gossez : *Vocabulaire des proclamations
électorales de 1881, 1885 et 1889*, Paris, PUF, publ. de la Sorbonne,
1974.

Ch 13: *Le Mouvement social*, for 'The French Contempt for Politics:
The Case of Veterans in the Inter-War Period', originally published
as 'Combattants et politiciens. Le discours mythologique sur la
politique entre les deux guerres', *Le Mouvement social*, n° 85,
(octobre–décembre 1973), pp. 117-54.

Jay Winter
Yale University

xi

Introduction: Antoine Prost and the History of Civil Society

Jay Winter

Antoine Prost is a historian of civil society, perhaps the historian *par excellence* of civil society in France. This is more of an unusual achievement than may appear at first sight. For he is one of the few historians fully aware of the power of the state who has nonetheless in his scholarship managed to resist its aura.

I understand the notion of civil society in the way the Scottish Enlightenment did, as denoting that field of social, cultural and economic life that spans the space between the family and the state. Both associational activity on the local level and the market are pillars of civil society, and both have left voluminous records of their negotiations and overlap with families and the state. The challenge is to integrate the contours and conflicts within civil society into the broader history of the state.

In a host of publications over four decades, Antoine Prost has shown how that can be done. He has made fundamental contributions to historical study, not by ignoring the state or displacing its significance to some marginal terrain, but by resisting the temptation to what might be termed a centralist's perspective of the history of France.

The French state has spawned an enormous historical literature, and, given the archival richness of the departments and the central authorities, rightly so. But what Prost has done is to redress the balance in social and economic history away from a fascination with, or even an obsession with, state power by showing that there is nothing anaemic or fundamentally flawed about civil society in France. In other words, no French *Sonderweg* here; as elsewhere in Europe, state and civil society in France have been locked in an inextricable embrace since the French Revolution, and the dialectical

1

relations between the two are comprehensible in part because of the work that Prost has done. This is one reason for bringing these essays together for the first time in an English-language edition. Born in 1933 to a middle-class Catholic family, Prost was educated in Paris, passed his *agrégation* – the entry ticket to an academic career, as it happens in the company of the distinguished editor Pierre Nora – and served as a soldier in Algeria. Hearing the 'ping' of a bullet hitting sand in uncomfortable proximity to him during his military service was not an uncommon occurrence; many others went through this dark period of French military history. What was more unusual was how his military service informed his understanding of the mental and cultural world of French soldiers of the First World War, the men whose veterans' organizations he analysed in his *thèse d'État*, published in 1977.[1]

This work marked a turning-point in the cultural history of the Great War. Alongside Jean-Jacques Becker's authoritative study of attitudes to the outbreak of war in 1914,[2] Prost's study enabled French historical scholarship to present a fusion of military and cultural history that has transformed our understanding of the Great War and its aftermath. Remote from 'war enthusiasm' in 1914, French soldiers fought stoically for four years, and then, after a victory purchased by the blood of 1.5 million of their brethren, they formed organizations dedicated to honouring their dead comrades and to telling the truth about the abominations of war. Anyone who wants to understand why fascism failed in France in the inter-war years must consult Prost's magisterial volumes.

What Prost shows in this and other studies is that French soldiers created their own discursive field surrounding the war and their search for meaning in the midst of the slaughter. His essays on 'Verdun' and on 'War Memorials', written for Pierre Nora's celebrated collection of essays *Les lieux de mémoire,* as well as his essay on 'Representations of War in the Inter-War Years', written for the inaugural conference of the Historial de la grande guerre at Péronne,

1. *Les anciens combattants et la société française, 1914–1939,* avec sept hors-texts de Philippe Billois (Paris, Presses de la Fondation Nationale des Sciences Politiques, 3 vols, 1977).
2. *1914: comment les Français sont entrées dans la guerre: contribution a l'étude de l'opinion publique, printemps–été 1914* (Paris: Presses de la Fondation Nationale des Sciences Politiques, 1977).

2

Somme, all included in this book, point to a de-centred, multivocal cultural history of the war and its aftermath. The state had its diction and symbols, to be sure, but veterans had others, and insisted upon their right to speak out on the meaning of the war. After all, they had the moral authority to pronounce on this issue, an authority no one who had not put on a uniform could claim.

This emphasis on moral reasoning as the focus of civil society is revealed in similar ways in his study of the ambivalent remembrance of the French war in Algeria, Chapter 5 in this book. Without widespread agreement as to the moral validity of the French war effort to suppress the Algerian liberation movement, and with uncomfortable and still vibrant echoes of the war of the French resistance against the Nazis, but with the moral sides reversed, French soldiers and French society as a whole have had an uncomfortable time constructing a discursive field around the war. That helps explain why there is no date in the calendar marking its end; such an anniversary would imply a moral consensus where none existed.

What a difference between the lessons of Algeria and those of the war of 1914–18. Then the *anciens combattants* came home with a pedagogical mission. That is, they brought out in unforgettable images the horrors of war so that their children could be spared what they had gone through. Their associative life was lived outside the state – indeed, in direct opposition to what they saw as the cesspool of Parisian politics. Their task was to mobilize civil society against the politicians, that breed of self-serving pigs muscling their way to the trough. Chapter 13 in this book shows how the history of civil society is by no means subordinate to the history of the state: the two live together, sometimes antagonistically, sometimes symbiotically, but never in a simple vertical, top-down relationship.

We see here in high relief another major theme of Prost's historical work: the study of education as moral instruction in what it means to be a citizen in a Republic. Through numerous pioneering studies of the French school system,[3] Prost thus outlined one of the pillars of the set of Republican representations discussed in this volume of

---

3. *Histoire de l'enseignement en France, 1800–1967* (Paris, A. Colin, 1968); *Éloge des pédagogues* (Paris: Seuil, 1985); *L'enseignement s'est-il democratise?: les élèves des lycées et collèges de l'agglomeration d'Orléans de 1945 à 1980* (Paris: Presses universitaires de France, 1986); *Education, société et politiques: une histoire de l'enseignement en France de 1945 à nos jours* (Paris, Seuil, 1992).

essays. As he shows in the fourth essay in this collection, the way of life the men of '14 fought to defend was infused with a notion of Republican values grounded in the primary school. But Prost does more than this; he enables us to see how this outcome was achieved and what kind of patriotism the schools inculcated in their pupils.

The study of schooling is linked to another fundamental contribution Prost has made to modern cultural history. The history of youth is a complex matter, requiring forays into demography, the labour market, anthropology, and social movements. It is only at the local level that we can see the fine differentiations that separated the period of youth of the working population from that of more privileged social formations. This Prost has accomplished in the case of Orléans, a city he knows intimately as resident, and for the last decade as vice-mayor and Socialist councillor. From this research, presented in Chapter 8 here, he developed an interpretation of youth in the first half of the twentieth century (Chapter 9) of relevance to historians of the twentieth century as a whole.

The focus on the city is another major component of Prost's approach to the history of civil society. The nature of urban sociability is extremely difficult to pinpoint, and its evolution has largely been left to impressionistic accounts of a romantic kind. Not with Prost. In his essay on the Feast of Joan of Arc on 8 May in Orléans (Chapter 7) he shows how urban identities are performed. Different facets of sociability appear in his essay on Paris. In his study of the social structure of the 18th *arrondissement* of Paris (Chapter 6), here published for the first time, Prost ingeniously uses marriage registers to show how complex and fluid were social relations in this very mixed part of the capital.

One of the key features of Prost's work emerges in these exercises in quantitative social history. He shows the utility of statistical analysis when put to the task of reducing huge historical categories to the texture of lived experience. At the end of his study of the 18th *arrondissement* there is a discussion of the way in which such analyses can enable us go beyond the categories of social class imbedded in the literature of censuses and statistical offices. Using other sources enables Prost to show that class formations did not precede or inform the appearance of the Popular Front in the mid-1930s.

The implications of this finding are profound. If social class position does not by itself create the language contemporaries use to understand their place in the world, then the door is open to the opposite proposition, namely that political movements create social categories or identities that do not predate them. This argument is very close to what we now call the 'linguistic turn', that view of history that is predicated on the belief that there are no facts outside the language in which they are expressed. This fashionable position in historical study is one we recognize in Prost's work long before others arrived. What Prost has managed to do is to anticipate and to a degree to help shape a fundamental transformation in the way historical study is conducted. Twenty years before the 'linguistic turn' became a subject of historical inquiry, Prost was there. Before the notion of 'representations' displaced *mentalité* as a key to cultural history, Prost was there. Before labour history expanded to incorporate the life histories of workers in the domain of sociability, of family life and education, Prost was there. It is as if, over time, the rest of us in the profession had caught up with him. One of the signs of pioneering scholarship is the capacity to chart the direction of a scholarly field before others move that way. Prost has accomplished this conjuring trick not once but several times.

Let me provide two instances. In his 1973 article in *Le mouvement social* entitled 'Combattants et politiciens. Le discours mythologique sur la politique entre les deux guerres', here revised and entitled 'The French Contempt for Politics: The Case of Veterans in the Inter-War Period' (Ch. 12) Prost presented an analysis of discourse as rigorous as any to come out of the numerous studies of language in the 1990s. He did so by a quantitative study of usages and syntactical practices in a specified set of sources, pointing in one direction towards the social scientific character of the social history of the period, and then in another direction towards the representations of war and politics that informed the veterans' movement. In this one article, social history, with a quantitative bent, turned into cultural history, with a poet's flair. In a brief space of scholarly work, Prost had sketched not only where social history was at that time, but where it was to go in the subsequent decades.

Another instance of his prescience is a 1995 contribution to a comparative study of workers' discourse in France and Germany, here presented as Chapter 11. Once again, he explores the intricacies of language, but, through comparison, shows the imaginative gap that separated different labour movements. The implications are far-reaching. On the one hand we can appreciate how remarkable were those steps taken by the pioneers of international socialism, Jaurès and Liebknecht among others, to create a European or even an international working-class movement. But on the other hand, the fragility of these efforts arose out of the conceptual, perhaps even the temperamental differences imbedded in the political vocabulary of these different workers' movements. Here comparison opens up a field of inquiry that can inform political history through the study of language. Once more social history and cultural history are linked in a creative dialogue, leading to a deeper appreciation of the cultural fissures within the European labour movement.

Prost's contribution to labour history, in particular, to the history of working-class movements in the period of the Popular Front, is equally far-reaching.[4] As director of the *Centre d'histoire sociale du xxème siècle* of the Sorbonne, he spawned an entire generation of work on French labour history. Here, as an *apéritif,* we include in Chapter 13 his study of the struggle against deferential subservience manifested in the occupation of factories in 1936.

The link between words and deeds is a perennial conundrum in various forms of political history, and, in his studies of the early Third Republic, Prost has found ways to deepen our understanding of the inflections of political affiliation. Through a sophisticated statistical analysis of terms used in electoral manifestos as compared to votes in the Chamber of Deputies in the 1880s, Prost is able to show how political formations cluster prior to the existence of party discipline (Ch. 10). Part of the force of this argument brings us back to the linguistic turn, which Prost insists must be taken to its destination. If language matters centrally in cultural history, then the terms contemporaries use in their pronouncements must be analysed just as rigorously as their votes. Cultural historians must be numerate in order to be literate.

In sum, these essays present an agenda for the future of cultural history that spans the history of representations, quantitative analyses of the life cycle, social movements, and urban society, and the sophisticated study of discursive fields. What ties them together is, among other things, their centrality in the task of creating a history of civil society in parallel with and in dialogue with the state.

Antoine Prost has shown us how this can be done. But there are other reasons why his work has been so seminal. Perhaps a personal reminiscence will go some of the way towards an answer. While

---

4. *La C.G.T. à l'époque du Front populaire, 1934–1939; essai de description numérique* (Paris, A. Colin, 1964).

Introduction: Antoine Prost and the History of Civil Society

Antoine Prost was a visiting scholar at Pembroke College, Cambridge, he addressed the Cambridge Historical Society. We arrived at Christ's College a bit early, and found a piano in the anteroom of the meeting hall reserved for the talk he was to give. In the few minutes available, Prost sat down and had a brief musical conversation with Mozart. The geometry of music has always struck me as beyond the reach of those who deal with mere words – the prosaic, in the literal sense of the term. But with Antoine Prost, I wonder if part of the explanation of his gifts lies in the mixture of the musical, the abstract and aesthetic exploration of sound, and the analytical, the concrete exploration of experience. Put in other terms, he has given us the fruits of Cartesian precision, and then expressed his findings in lyrical, allusive writing of immense power and range. Of how many of our colleagues can we say the same?

I. National Identity

1

War Memorials of the Great War: Monuments to the Fallen

The idea of treating war memorials as important sites of republican commemoration may seem paradoxical. In ceremonies at war memorials, men festooned with decorations parade, and the tricolor flaps in the breeze above the strains of *La Marseillaise*: symbols such as these might seem more appropriate to a meeting of right-wing nationalists than to a republican memorial.

The ambiguity is longstanding. On 11 November 1923 in Choisy-le-Roi, near Paris, a contingent of veterans marching to the cemetery behind their banners encountered a group of protesters singing *The Internationale* and shouting 'Down with war!' The local veterans' organization objected that there had been a 'distressing misunderstanding': 'The purpose of these parades is to eliminate war by remembering its victims, whom the marchers wish to mourn and honour.'[1] In Grenoble, on 11 November 1932, the socialist mayor ordered veterans' groups to join with the rest of the crowd at the inauguration of a war memorial and asked them to leave their banners at home, on the grounds that these were 'militaristic warrior symbols'. The outrage of the former *poilus* (trench soldiers) forced the mayor to back down.[2]

Thus there are two ways of interpreting the cult of which war memorials serve as altars, and in order to decide between them we shall first look at their origin and then study the associated ceremonies and speeches with an anthropologist's eyes and ears.[3]

The Building of War Memorials

The idea of raising monuments to those who die in war did not originate with the First World War; but no other war spawned so many. Even the smallest village in France erected a monument to those who died in that conflict.[4] To be sure, the Great War was the 'greatest' of all French wars. The entire nation was mobilized. Eight million men – one-fifth of the population – served in the military; 1,450,000 died, and virtually every family suffered at least one death. The proliferation of monuments reflected the depth of the nation's trauma, and it is doubtful that so many villages would have erected monuments if they had not been obliged to mourn several of their sons. After the Franco-Prussian War, by contrast, only some cantons and *départements* erected monuments.[5] Perhaps the outcome of the war was also a factor. Conceivably, the defeat of 1871 did not lend itself to commemoration as easily as the victory of 1918. Should the monuments therefore be interpreted as nationalist symbols? Were they monuments to the fallen or monuments to victory?

We can begin to answer these questions by looking into who decided that these 38,000 monuments should be built, and when. The monuments to those who had died in the Franco-Prussian War were the result of belated private initiatives. They were not built in the throes of national mourning, but twenty or thirty years later, after the Boulangist episode and at the beginning of the twentieth century, when the Republic seemed to avert its eyes from the blue line of the Vosges. They were built by committees that raised the necessary funds from public subscriptions and by an association, *Le Souvenir français*, that was founded especially to preserve the memory of those who had fallen in the Franco-Prussian War by dedicating monuments to them in cemeteries and on the battlefield. The monuments thus expressed the views of that segment of the public that nursed thoughts of revenge. They did not involve the nation as a whole or its official representatives at either the local or the national level.

The monuments of the First World War were quite different. Their construction involved citizens and local as well as national authorities in close cooperation. A law of 25 October 1919, on 'the commemoration and glorification of those who died for France in the Great War' established subsidies for local governments 'proportionate to the efforts and sacrifices they are willing to make to honour heroes who died for their country'. Thus there was no legal obligation to build a monument: only an official recognition coupled with a relatively modest financial incentive.[6] But the existence of the subsidy obliged local governments to take an active role in filing applications with the prefecture: the initiative could not be purely private.

In fact, many municipalities enlisted the support of the population in building their monuments. Some municipal councils handled the matter on their own, but most created a committee for the purpose. In some cases government simply offered its backing to privately organized committees. In others, officials may have sought additional financing or a broader consensus by appealing to persons outside the council, such as a parish priest. Some private committees clashed with local authorities, who of course had the last word.[7] What one had, then, was not a purely private initiative or a purely governmental enterprise, but a convergence of municipal actions. The decision to honour the war dead was taken not by a citizens' group or by the national government but by individual communes, that is, by citizens in their most fundamental civic unit. Evidence of this can be seen in the inscription most commonly engraved on the monuments: 'The commune to its children, [who] died for France'. This established a precise relationship among three terms: the commune, which asserted its collective initiative; the dead citizens, recipients of the people's homage; and France, which received and justified the sacrifice of its soldiers

The building of war memorials proceeded rapidly, as if in response to a contagious necessity, which everyone took for granted. The law providing subsidies was passed before the election of the 'Sky-blue Chamber' (so called because such was the colour of the French uniforms that many deputies had been wearing a few months before), and communes had initiated their efforts even before the law was passed. Most village monuments were inaugurated before 1922, as each township vied with its neighbours. By contrast, there was less of a consensus in the cities, where opinion was more divided, monuments were more complex, their meanings were contradictory, and construction took longer: inaugurations were still being held in the early 1930s. But the fact that the cult of the fallen that spawned the monuments preceded their actual construction is of the utmost importance for comprehending their meaning. Even before the armistice the dead had already become the object of such a cult, with demonstrations in their honour by maimed and incapacitated comrades. These took place in cemeteries on November 1 or 2, the traditional day of the dead. They continued until monuments were built, and sometimes longer.[8] Could a cult born when it was still possible that the war might end in defeat have been a cult of victory?

Clearly, then, to interpret these war memorials as nationalist, when they were built not as a result of a cold official decision or a partisan effort but in response to a broad and deep popular movement that preceded the victorious outcome of the war, one would have to assume that the whole of France was nationalist, except for a handful of socialists.[9] Does the visible reality of the monuments bear this out?

Typology and Semiology of War Memorials

It is difficult to combat prejudices. One of the most tenacious of prejudices on the left, even among historians, is that the war memorials are an expression of jingoistic nationalism. To see this, we are told, one has only to look at the statues of heroic *poilus* (infantrymen) that crown many of these sculptural ensembles.

But is there any truth to this? Just how many monuments feature triumphant *poilus?* Research has conclusively demonstrated that the claim is false: *poilus* occupy only a small minority of France's village squares.[10] What is more, no simple catalogue of war memorials can do justice to the complexity of the matter. They embody an intricate system of signs, and to concentrate on the statuary alone is tantamount to deciphering a long sentence by focusing on a single word: mis-readings are inevitable. The significance of the monuments stems first of all from the fact that the space in which they stand is charged with meaning. The choice to build in a schoolyard, in the square in front of a town hall or a church, in a cemetery, or at a busy crossroads was not an innocent one. To be sure, village space was not always clearly marked (here, I leave aside cities, where monuments were much more complex, and often polysemic). Often the church and the town hall were located on the same square, which might also be the busiest place in town. Thus the significance of the location cannot always be clearly defined. In some cases, moreover, one has to allow for changes brought about by an evolving road system.

Usually, however, location was significant. Other signs complemented this fundamental choice. The nature of the monument, and above all the presence or absence of statues, constituted a second set of signs. Monuments with statuary are clearly in the minority, whether because they inevitably cost more than monuments without statuary or for ideological reasons. Although the most common statue was indeed the *poilu,* it was by no means the only possible choice. Eliminating the composite monuments from our sample, we find 91 *poilus* all told (16 per cent) compared to 224 bare steles, 19 steles topped by a funerary urn or torch, and 30 steles topped by a *croix de guerre* (soldier's cross).[11] When the statue was that of a *poilu,* its meaning depended on whether the sculpture was realistic or idealistic, on any allegories with which it might have been associated, and so on. Elsewhere, statues of widows and orphans or elderly parents expressed the grief of survivors more explicitly than did statues of weeping or proud women that might equally well stand for wives, mothers, France, or the Republic.

Finally, inscriptions on the monuments constitute a third group of signs. Little is to be gleaned from the lists of names, arranged sometimes in alphabetical order, sometimes in chronological order of death; in only about 4 per cent of the monuments in the sample were the names arranged hierarchically by rank. But the frontal inscription and accompanying commentary was often explicit or easy to decipher, from the laconic 'To our dead' to heroic epigraphs such as 'Glory to our heroes', to say nothing of the many pregnant quotations, ranging from the high-toned to the grief-stricken and moralistic.

By combining these three sets of signs, one can establish a typology of memorials that points to a range of local sensibilities. The most common type of monument – the 'canonic' form, in a sense, accounting for 60 per cent of the cases in the sample – was the naked stele, erected in a space symbolically dominated by the town hall, listing the names of the dead together with a time-honoured inscription: 'The commune of . . . [or simply the name of the town] to its children, [who] died for France.' There was also a closely related variant: 'died for the Fatherland *(la Patrie)*'. Indeed, the first formula was the 'official' one; it was inscribed on death certificates for soldiers killed in the war, and thus had a recognized legal significance. To use it was to speak the official language of the Republic, not the language of local tradition and sentiment. Indeed, that was why one leading veterans' group asked that any other formula be prohibited.[12]

Monuments of this type were typically quite bare. The stele featured no allegorical emblem except perhaps the *croix de guerre,* the decoration awarded to soldiers who died for France. The ultimate simplicity was achieved in certain Protestant villages in the Cevennes, where a plain plaque was affixed to a wall of the town hall.[13] Emphasizing the source of the homage, namely, the commune, that is, living citizens in their local organization, as well as the recipients, namely, the dead, in their concrete individuality, attested by their names and in some cases movingly reinforced by photographs placed in glazed medallions – that went straight to the heart of the matter.[14] Both civic duty and the duty to remember were affirmed, and each

Figure 1.1: Magny-le-Freule (Calvados). An example of a 'civic' type of war memorial, the most frequent commemorative form. (*Courtesy of Michel Petzold*)

individual was then free to do as he or she wished with grief or patriotic pride. The monument did not prejudge the opinions of the town's citizens: in that respect it was republican and secular. Religious symbols were indeed avoided.[15] These were *civic* monuments, defined as such by a double denial, and they took on their full meaning in contrast to monuments of other types. In fact, it took very little to inflect a monument's meaning from civic to patriotic or funerary.

Like the civic monument, the *patriotic* monument was erected on a public square, at a crossroads where it would be in plain view. Its iconography and inscriptions set it apart, however. The formula *morts pour la Patrie* already indicated a timid tilt from the civic toward the patriotic. The shift could be accentuated by adding phrases from the semantic realm of honour, glory, and heroism: 'Glory to the children of . . .', 'To our heroes . . .', 'To the children of . . . gloriously [or *heroically*] fallen on the field of honour'. Sometimes there was insistent repetition: 'Glory to our heroes.' Or a patriotic inflection could result from inscriptions engraved on the sides of monuments, including perhaps excerpts from celebrated poems:

> Ceux qui pieusement sont morts pour la Patrie
> Ont droit qu'à leur cercueil la foule vienne et prie.
> Entre les plus beaux noms, leur nom est le plus beau,
> Toute gloire près d'eux passe et tombe, éphémère
> Et comme ferait une mère
> La voix d'un peuple entier les berce en leur tombeau.
> Gloire à notre France éternelle!
> Gloire à ceux qui sont morts pour elle!
> Aux martyrs! Aux vaillants! Aux forts!
>
> [Those who have died piously for their *Patrie*
> Are entitled to have crowds come to pray beside their coffins.
> Theirs is the most beautiful of all beautiful names.
> Compared with them all glory is ephemeral,
> And the voice of an entire people
> Is like a mother's lullaby to them in their graves.
> Glory to eternal France!
> Glory to those who have died for her!
> To the martyrs! To the valiant! To the strong!]

These lines do not take us outside the republican tradition, however. Indeed, we are at its heart. Their author is Victor Hugo, one of the fathers of the Republic, which laid him to rest in a national funeral.[16]

The poem was taught in all public schools and even sung to music by Hérold, another great republican. Above all, the poem glorifies, not victory over the enemy, but the defeat of monarchs. These lines were written for the first anniversary of the Revolution of 1830. The dead celebrated in the poem fell not at the border defending French soil but on the barricades for love of liberty.

Figure 1.2: Saint-Jacut-de-la-mer (Côtes d'Armor). The French cockerel trampling on a helmet with a spike designates the republican patriotic-nationalist type of monument. (*Private collection*)

Further signs were therefore necessary to mark the difference between republican patriotism and out-and-out nationalism. The most common of these were allegorical in nature: the Gallic cock, for example, which we find atop 6 per cent of the steles in our sample. Or the triumphant *poilu,* brandishing a crown of laurels, as in Eugène Benet's widely copied statue, or waving a banner in the wind in imitation of Delacroix's allegory of the Republic.[17] Some statues depicted a soldier trampling on a spiked helmet or an imperial eagle. Others went still further, portraying a Victory with wings outspread and holding a crown. Such signs could be combined with others to create a whole spectrum of superlatives. In Brissac (Maine-et-Loire), for example, a monument features a *poilu* surmounted by a cock, brandishing a flag and kicking a spiked helmet. It was not uncommon, moreover, for a winged Victory to crown a *poilu.*

Nevertheless, the language of allegory was less explicit than the language of inscriptions, and ambiguity was possible. The crown and even the palm could indicate mourning rather than victory. Female images were particularly polysemic. Victory was identifiable by her

Figure 1.3: Creuilly (Calvados). Triumphant *poilu* brandishing a laurel wreath. Between 800 and 1000 local authorities chose this statue by Eugène Benet for Patriotic-nationalist type of monument. (*Courtesy of Michel Petzold*)

wings; but a woman without wings could represent France or the Republic.[18]

The same was true of statues of the *poilu*: not all were patriotic. Some appeared in purely civic monuments, like the sentinel who appears to be standing guard, his rifle at parade rest beside him, in front of the wall on which the town of Maisons-Alfort engraved the names of its dead in the town hall square. These were descriptive, realistic statues. Patriotism came with idealization. A step in that direction was taken by C. Pourquet, for example, in his statue of a *poilu* that bears the title *Résistance*.[19] At first glance it seems to be an accurate likeness. All the details are correct: the haversack, the cartridge pouches, the open collar, the pulled-up overcoat. Nothing is missing except the canteens. But the attitude seems posed: the jaw juts out too forcefully, the look is too proud, and the stance, at parade rest blocking the path of an imaginary enemy, is hardly the pose of a combat soldier. This is not a realistic image of the *poilu* but an illustration of the celebrated formula 'They shall not pass'. The monument is on the borderline between republican patriotism and nationalist exaltation. A brandished crown or an unfurled flag is all it would take to push it over the line.

Among the many variations of the *poilu* with flag, care should be taken not to confuse two distinct families. Beside the triumphant *poilus,* there are also the 'aggrieved', as one might have said in the sixteenth century: mortally wounded, they fall clutching the flag in their final agony or even using it as a winding sheet.[20] These are undeniably patriotic monuments: they proclaim the legitimacy of the sacrifice called for by the nation, which is sometimes represented as a woman bending over the dying man to gather in his last breath. But these monuments also signify that the dead are indeed dead: they are not only patriotic but also funerary.

There are enough such monuments to treat them as a distinct type. Other iconographic features also distinguish funerary from republican patriotic memorials. The former are often located in cemeteries or close to churches, outside the civic space dominated by the town hall. Crosses appear on many of them. Indeed, they glorify not the victorious Fatherland, the grandeur of France or the triumph of the *poilu* but the sacrifice of the dead. Their lesson is that of the conservative tradition: man is great and can realize himself fully only in total, unconditional obedience to transcendent realities. Hence it is not enough simply to do one's duty; love of country and devotion to duty are also essential. Like religion, patriotism is a school

Figure 1.4: Grugies (Aisne). *Poilu* standing guard. A monument of the republican-patriotic type. (*Private collection*)

Figure 1.5: Pleumeur-Gauthier (Côtes-d'Armor). *Poilu* with flag. A monument of the patriotic-conservative type. (*Courtesy of Michel Petzold*)

of self-denial and sacrifice, through which man fulfils his destiny and is saved. In this conservative tradition, the Fatherland, like God, becomes a transcendent reality, which justifies the sacrifice that becomes martyrdom, witness, and act of faith. This is a long way from the republican spirit, for which the individual is the ultimate end of society and which proclaims a message of individual and collective emancipation.

These *funerary-patriotic* or *conservative-patriotic* monuments are found mainly in Christian regions, and the 'dying *poilu*' is not the only form they take. The most elementary version is the flag laid on a tomb or draped over the arms of a tombstone cross. One also finds busts of *poilus* kissing a flag, a variant suitable for poorer communes. Elsewhere, religion is emphasized: the monument features a large cross, a soldier, and a flag. An extreme form of this alliance of patriotism and religion is the statue of Joan of Arc, combining martyrdom for both faiths, the very symbol of 'Catholic and French for ever'.

Eliminate the reference to *la Patrie* and the funerary monuments take on a different meaning. To fail to signal explicitly the legitimacy of sacrifice was to admit the possibility that it might not be entirely legitimate. This was a step toward pacifism. One finds evidence of this in monuments that realistically depict dying or dead soldiers, as at Fay-de-Bretagne at the foot of a calvary in a cemetery: here, faith in God is the only recourse. The resources of classical funerary statuary could be mobilized, with recumbent figures and weeping women; but these representations were a little too conventional to express the pain of survivors. The dead had to be mourned by real people. In rare cases this might be a comrade-in-arms overwhelmed by the horrors of war. More commonly, it was a woman plunged into grief, a wife or mother (or both at once), reminiscent in some instances of the *Mater dolorosa* of the Catholic *pietà*. In Brittany and the Basque region it was not uncommon for this woman to be dressed in a regional costume as a way of emphasizing local roots – and bestowing concreteness on a universal figure. Elsewhere it might be a widow flanked by one or two children or an elderly father and mother or a grandfather and grandson meditating over a grave. In the Saint-Étienne region the local sculptor Joanny Durand did several statues that expressed the grief of survivors in concrete and moving fashion.[21]

Funerary war memorials did not necessarily feature statues. They could derive their meaning simply from their location in a cemetery,

JARNAC (Charente) — Monument des Soldats Morts pour la Patrie

Cliché Lévêque   B. Rousseau, éditeur

Figure 1.6: Jarnac (Charente). A mother and a brother – or a friend – in mourning. A monument of the funerary type. (*Private collection*)

reinforced perhaps by a frontal inscription omitting any reference to France or the Fatherland. One frequently finds epigraphs such as: 'The commune of . . . to its dead children' or 'to its dead' or even 'To the soldiers killed in the war' or, more laconically, 'To our dead', as on the remarkably sober stele in the centre of the cemetery in the tiny village of Oison in the Beauce.

In rare cases the pacifism was made explicit, more through inscriptions than iconography. The monument in Levallois-Perret is a case apart. It became an object of polemics when someone claimed that it featured a soldier shot for mutiny in 1917. The mutinous soldier was scarcely identifiable, but the monument does indeed portray a worker breaking a sword, an allegory for the proletariat putting an end to war. The best-known pacifist monuments are those of Saint-Martin-d'Estreaux (Loire), whose rear facade bears a long and interesting moralistic inscription,[22] Gy-l'Evèque (Yonne): 'War on war', and Gentioux (Creuse), in which a child raises his fist before an inscription that reads 'A curse on war'.

Pacifist war memorials are too rare to count as a distinct type. They represent an extreme form of the purely funerary monument without patriotic justification. We thus have four main types of war memorial: civic monuments, the most common and the most secular, and fully republican; patriotic-republican monuments, which often celebrate victory as well as sacrifice in a more or less overt fashion; funerary-patriotic monuments, which glorify sacrifice; and purely funerary monuments, which emphasize the depth of grief without offering any justification for it, and thus tend toward pacifism.

This diversity, which corresponds fairly closely to the range of local political climates at the time the monuments were built, obviously rules out treating the triumphant *poilu* as the typical form of war memorial. The reality is more complex, more fruitful, and more profoundly republican. Apart from patriotism, most monuments gave voice to republican civic sentiment, with its rather cold, bare, and dryly secular spirit. Not even the most patriotic monuments honoured the army, moreover – there were no officers here – and they remained faithful to their essential function, which was to preserve for ever the name of each of the town's war dead. In this respect for individuals (not found in the cantonal monuments to the dead of the Franco-Prussian War), we see a fundamental feature of .the republican spirit, which held that citizens are equal before death as before the law, and hence equal too in the memory of future generations.

QUE MAUDITE SOIT LA GUERRE

AUX ENFANTS D·ÉQUEURDREVILLE

MORTS

PENDANT LA GUERRE

1914 – 1918

Figure 1.7: Equeurdreville (Manche). A pacifist monument. A desperate widow with her two young orphans are shown, with the explicit comment 'a curse be on war' and the implicit denial of patriotism : the dead are simply the fallen, and not for France. (*Courtesy of Michel Petzold*)

The significance of war memorials does not lie solely in their material reality, however. It also resides in what history has made of them. As we see them, they reflect the intentions of the municipalities that built them at the time when they were built (if we ignore later modifications: changes of inscription, additional inscriptions for the dead of the Second World War and the colonial wars, changes of location, etc.). But citizens have subsequently used the memorials in a variety of ways, thereby bestowing new meanings on them, just as *La Marseillaise* is no longer a revolutionary song. The ceremonies that have unfolded around the monuments have invested them with a significance they did not originally possess.

Ceremonies and War Memorials

Investigating the history of ceremonies at war memorials is a particularly tricky business. For one thing, what we can observe of ceremonies today does not tell us all we need to know about the ceremonies that took place between the two world wars. For another, the ceremonies were probably no less diverse than the monuments themselves, and there were not insignificant differences between villages and large cities.

This double uncertainty pertains in particular to the role of the army in these ceremonies. The unveiling of the monuments was a civil ceremony; in the whole department of the Loire-Inférieure, for instance, the army took part in the ceremony only in Nantes, and in two smaller cities.[23] On Armistice Day, 11 November, the army had no role outside garrison cities, and even in such cities it was not as large as it is today. As survivors of the First World War died off and the survivors' grief subsided, Armistice Day became less of a popular holiday, and the crowds at memorial ceremonies thinned. To some extent the government stepped in as popular emotion waned, and this had an effect on the role of the military.

In order to get a better idea of the original significance of these memorial ceremonies, we must look to the interwar period, for which certain interesting sources are available. The early Armistice Day celebrations led some veterans to reflect on how they were organized, and the veterans' press contains articles that set forth their expectations and desires and justify their views. In addition, certain local veterans' papers reported on Armistice Day ceremonies, especially in the period 1930–34. Finally, every local or national veterans' convention included a memorial ceremony of some sort:

some of these ceremonies were described, and these descriptions are particularly interesting because they establish a standard of reference.

The first point to make is that these memorial ceremonies were not originally official government occasions. They were organized not by the government but by veterans' groups.[24] Indeed, Armistice Day almost failed to become a national holiday. In 1919, of course, the first anniversary of the armistice was celebrated. And in 1920, November 11 was the day that Gambetta's heart was laid to rest in the Pantheon, after which the same procession moved on to deposit the remains of the unknown soldier beneath the Arc de Triomphe. Hence the date was once again a holiday. But in 1921 the 'Sky-blue Chamber' worried more about work than about the fatherland, postponed the commemoration of the armistice until Sunday the 13th. This provoked an outcry among veterans, who boycotted the official ceremonies and eventually secured passage of the Law of 24 October 1922 declaring Armistice Day a national holiday. The commentaries at the time were explicit: the veterans had forced the legislature to make *their* holiday a *national* holiday. And it was their holiday in two senses: because it was they and not the government that had won the war, and because they had come out of it alive. This was the point of a poster hung by the Mutilés des Hautes-Pyrénées in advance of Armistice Day 1921: 'OUR HOLIDAY, Armistice Day, is none other than November 11! Our dignity obliges us to pay homage to our cherished dead on the *anniversary* of the day the vile slaughter ended!' In another poster the following year the same group declared: 'If the morning of 11 November 1918 was our only day of happiness . . .'. They had won, and they were alive: what deliverance, but at what a price![25]

A second feature of these ceremonies was that they were not military. On this point the veterans' groups were unanimous. The Union Fédérale, radical-socialist in its leanings, issued a categorical demand at its 1922 convention: 'The national holiday on 11 November shall not be observed by any military ceremony',[26] and the same demand was echoed by a doctor of a more rightist stripe, soon to be elected to the Chamber, Marcel Héraud. On the right, the Union Nationale des Combattants was of the same opinion, even though it was headed at the time by a general: in an article offering the group's views on how the 1922 Armistice Day celebration should be organized, one official suggested that the army should have no place in the event except possibly at the head of the procession, where there might be 'a delegation of generals, officers, non-commissioned officers, and ordinary soldiers who took part in the war'.[27] A 'delegation' rather than a 'detachment' of any sort: this was to nullify the army as an organized force. Deliberately, and not by oversight: at the end of the ceremonies, the president of the Republic was to review, not troops, but a group of war victims. Not only was the army not honoured, it was not even recognized. If further corroboration that this was a unanimous attitude is needed, it can be found in an article by the editor of the *Journal des mutilés,* the most important of the veterans' papers and the only one sold at newsstands: 'What matters ultimately is that the celebration of 11 November be free of any military pomp. No armed salutes, no reviews, no parades. We are celebrating a "festival of peace, not a festival of war".'[28]

Thus the ceremonies were neither official nor military, but funerary in nature. The monuments were graves, and the ceremonies were funeral services. This was especially clear in regions of robust Catholic tradition such as the Loire and the Vendée, where the clergy played a central role in the ceremonies. After the Armistice Day mass, the priest remained in his robes, and a parade, or rather procession, formed up to proceed to the monument, led by choirboys in surplices bearing the processional cross and carrying lighted candles. If the procession was lengthy, canticles were sung. At the war memorial the chorus might sing another canticle or the *De profundis.* In some cases, the priest even absolved the war memorial while the *Libera* was sung: the monument thus occupied the place of the empty catafalque in the service for the anniversary of a death, and the priest walked around it and sprinkled it with holy water. To be sure, such ceremonies took place in only a few regions. They nevertheless reveal a broader climate of emotion.[29]

Other details confirm the funerary character of these ceremonies. One frequently attested practice was the reading of the names of the dead: before or after a minute of silence (the secularized form of prayer) it was customary to read all the names, perhaps as many as a hundred. After each name, a schoolchild or veteran would respond: 'Died for France' or 'Died on the field of honour'.[30] This reading, also taken from the Catholic liturgy, gave the ceremony its meaning: to commemorate the anniversary of those killed in the war.[31]

The laying of wreaths or flowers had a similar significance. Wreaths were more common, and the mortuary connotations are interesting. Since Armistice Day came shortly after All Saints' Day, when families visited the graves of their dead and laid flowers on the graves, the meaning of the gesture was plain: if people placed flowers or wreaths on war memorials, it was because they regarded them as tombs. In some towns, moreover, the procession stopped first at the cemetery, where flowers were laid on the grave of each individual soldier buried there. In many villages, the school pupils, led by their schoolteacher, went together to the monument, where one after the other, they deposited flowers at its foot. The decoration of monuments was a way for the community to emulate the individual acts of piety of its members.

But what about the singing of *La Marseillaise*? Care is in order here, for it is easy to jump to the conclusion that the singing of the national anthem at war memorials was inevitable. It was not. To be sure, singing often began at the end of the ceremony, but this was not a strict rule or a general practice. Indeed, uncertainty about what it was appropriate to sing and play on these occasions persisted for some time, and often the decision depended on what local resources were available. If someone had to sing, the job usually fell to the church choir, to 'kind ladies',[32] or frequently to schoolchildren. It may be that *La Marseillaise* was sung but not mentioned in our reports; but we have accounts detailed enough to be certain that in some villages, at least, it was not sung, perhaps because it was feared that too few of the participants would be able to sing along, perhaps because schoolteachers had been reluctant to teach it to their pupils for the occasion, or perhaps because it would have seemed too aggressive and triumphal. In its absence we find the psalms and canticles mentioned earlier, funeral marches played by a brass band, the 'Hymn to the Dead' of Frédéric Bataille or Victor Hugo, Maurice Bouchor's 'For Those We Mourn' and various hymns to peace.[33]

Given this diversity, it is striking that there was eventually almost universal agreement about the playing of a bugle call 'To the Dead' during the minute of silence that was the high point of the ceremony. Indeed, this particular bugle call was unknown in the French army. In the 1920s the minute of silence was preceded and followed by two bugle calls, 'To the Field' or 'Attention' at the beginning and 'To the Flag' at the end. 'To the Dead', as we know it today, was composed by the musical director of the Republican Guard and was officially adopted in 1932. It slowly but surely gained in popularity until by the eve of the Second World War it had become the standard bugle call for war memorial ceremonies, never played on any other occasion but always played on that one. Here, then, is still further proof that what we are dealing with is a funerary ritual.[34]

But that ritual contains only part of the meaning of the memorial ceremonies. These were complex affairs involving several protagonists in a structured, oriented space. The meaning of the ritual depended on the placement and gestures of the participants.

After mass, everyone marched in procession to the war memorial, sometimes by way of the cemetery. The schoolchildren marched in rows, shepherded by their teachers. In many villages, when the children reached the monument, each would place a flower or small bouquet on its pedestal. Then they would take up a position to one side, ready to sing like the choir in a church. Other villagers, content merely to watch the ceremony, would also take up places alongside the monument, leaving a substantial area open in front. With the stage now set, the ceremony could begin.

On the morning of Armistice Day, veterans would gather at the town hall and prepare to walk in procession with their banners. They marched at the tail end of the procession – the place of honour in religious processions, in which the officiant always came last.[35] Just as the clergy always entered the choir last to begin the service, the veterans would then march around the monument and array themselves in a semicircle behind it. If there were too many, some of them, bearing their flags, would stand there to represent them. Opposite them, and some distance away, thus creating an empty space in front of the monument, stood the authorities, the mayor and the municipal council.

What was particularly significant about the location of the veterans was that they remained in place throughout the ceremony, while others (the authorities always and the children if they had not already placed flowers upon arrival) left their places to place flowers on the monument. The veterans thus occupied the place next to the monument, just as the family in a funeral ceremony sat at the graveside and received the condolences of other mourners. Their position in the ceremonial space silently affirmed the solidarity of the living and the dead. In presiding over the ceremony honouring the dead, the veterans received the indirect homage of the entire community in its direct manifestation. Hence the presence of many members of the community along with its official representatives was essential; it would have been unthinkable for the authorities not to pay their respects.

The Armistice Day ceremonies were perhaps the only successful republican cult in France, and they enjoyed widespread popular support. Republican ceremonies have always had a problem with the difficulty of personifying the Republic. Crowds simply do not respond to the goddess Reason or even Marianne: everyone knows that these are just symbols. The Bastille Day celebration has become fairly popular, but it took a great deal of work before it caught on, as well as the fortuitous timing of the summer vacation.[36] It is a national holiday, but an impersonal one.

The fundamental innovation of Armistice Day, which set it apart from all other republican ceremonies, was that it celebrated not abstract principles but palpable citizens. The monuments, as we have seen, respected the individuality of each soldier and bore the name and sometimes the picture of each of the dead. Each man's name was read during the ceremony. Thus the event honoured citizens who had done their duty, and the survivors, who had also done their duty, took up their place alongside the dead.

What was celebrated at the war memorials was thus not the army or the fatherland. Instead, the fatherland paid its respects to its citizens, as the function of the flags suggests. It is a serious mistake to ignore the importance of these flags. When the flag was raised on the parade ground of a military base, at a scout camp, or at an elementary school under Vichy, it was a patriotic act not because the flag was there but because it was to be honoured, saluted. There was only one flag because there was only one France. In military parades with regimental flags, the troops first formed up in ranks, and then, when the colours were brought in, the troops presented arms. Finally, the troops marched past the colours, paying their respects to the unique symbol of the fatherland. Once again, the flag was honoured.

The Armistice Day ceremony was very different. Often there was more than one flag, representing not only the nation but various groups as well. No one marched past the flags. Instead, the flags marched to the monument. During the minute of silence the flags were dipped as a sign of respect for the dead, just as flags were dipped in church before the consecrated bread and wine at their elevation. To argue that the presence of the flags made the memorial ceremony a homage to the nation rather than to the dead would be as absurd as arguing that the presence of flags at mass meant that the purpose of the mass was not to honour God. At the war memorial, as in church, the flags were instruments of the ceremony, not its objects.

Thus the Armistice Day ceremonies were originally republican, not patriotic. Of course, all the participants agreed that the sacrifice of the dead was legitimate and that citizens have the duty to die for their country if the country demands it in a just cause. But the occasion was not to honour the fatherland; it was not held out as a supreme value or a self-sustaining divinity. On the contrary, it was the fatherland that honoured its citizens, and it was this that made the occasion republican, for the Republic held precisely that its citizens were the supreme value and ultimate end of society.

The Armistice Day celebrations were also republican in that they were educational. The Republic did not stand for unconditional obedience and submission to natural authorities such as the family, the army, or the monarchy. Through universal suffrage its citizens chose certain of their number to lead it. In order for the Republic to function well, it therefore needed enlightened and virtuous citizens who internalized the constraints of the social contract. Without instruction and education the Republic was therefore inconceivable. Hence it needed to ensure that each citizen acquired the knowledge necessary to fulfil his role as a citizen of a democracy. And it needed to make sure that every citizen shared its norms and values. As a liberal regime, based on elections and the rule of law, the Republic required citizens who accepted the need for collective discipline and respect for others. This resolved the classic problem of liberty: if republican education succeeded, liberty would have no enemies. Thus when the Republic paid its respects to those citizens who died in the line of duty, having 'freely consented', it was said with slight exaggeration, to a necessary discipline, it hoped to make better citizens by touching and moving those who survived. The civic cult was also a lesson in ethics.

That is why the participation of schoolchildren was so important. Being young, they were open to influence. They had yet to comprehend what the Republic was. It was essential that they subscribe to its principles: respect for all citizens, respect for the law, civic duty. That is why they were asked to attend the ceremonies, to deposit flowers, to sing, and to answer in place of the dead before a grave and emotional audience. The ceremony was supposed to impress them and thereby influence them. In some places they were rewarded for their participation with a brioche, while their elders drank the ceremonial wine. The Republic was a regime that obtained social conformity by inducing its citizens to subscribe individually to its fundamental values. For this it needed a civic cult and a method of moral education, which it found ultimately in the memorial ceremonies for the dead of the First World War.

Ceremonial Speeches

The civics lesson did not come entirely from the orchestration and staging of the Armistice Day ceremonies. It was also delivered explicitly in the form of speeches; for people spoke at these monuments, and it mattered who spoke and what they said.

Two groups of people had a claim on the right to speak in these ceremonies: elected officials, because they embodied the entire community, and veterans, because only those who had fought in the war were entitled to draw its lessons. In fact, the two groups often overlapped, and compromises were always possible: perhaps the mayor had fought in the war, or perhaps there could be two speeches instead of one. For the veterans, however, the very idea of delivering a personal speech was shocking. Whoever spoke on Armistice Day must not speak in his own name but in the name of all veterans, living and dead. In 1921 the *Mutilés du Loiret* drafted an address that they sent to all their sections to be delivered at their respective monuments. In 1935 the Union Fédérale, the largest of the national veterans' groups, adopted this practice nationwide, and ultimately it became universal.[37] Indeed, the republican Armistice Day cult did not need to single out individuals. The Republic was a regime whose citizens were supposed to learn how to serve in a disinterested and impersonal manner.

The very form of the Armistice Day speech was the first significant thing about it. The medium reinforced the message. Neither the victorious army nor its leaders were mentioned. Not a word was said about Foch or Joffre or Pétain. The spirit of the occasion was hostile to militarism or any cult of personality. Revanchist demands and Alsace-Lorraine were rarely mentioned. Defeated Germany never figured as a nation or people: it was always imperial or militarist Germany, and France, fighting for right and freedom, stood ever ready to respond to militaristic and imperialist aggression.

Most Armistice Day speeches were constructed in two parts. Part one: the past, the war, the dead; Part two: today, peace, the living. The first part invariably consisted of a panorama, which could be more or less lengthy and detailed, of the horrors of war: victory was never mentioned without a reminder of what it had cost. For the veterans present, this would have been a grave omission, for it would have meant overlooking both the death of their comrades and their own suffering. It was repeatedly stated, therefore, that war kills, that war is carnage, slaughter, massacre, and butchery.

The fact that these dark portraits drew some protest only confirms their importance and frequency. Listen, for example, to Sergeant Tapin, the secretary general of the *Office des Mutilés de la Meuse:*

> Read the programmes for the Armistice Day celebrations. . . . What will you find eight times out of ten? Nothing but visits to the cemetery, parades in front of memorial monuments, and the laying of palms on graves. . . . No, gentlemen, no! That is not what Armistice Day is all about! . . .
>
> On November 11, I would like to see *La Marseillaise* sung loudly at every crossroads. I would like to see all our kids jumping, shouting, and cheering for Foch and Pétain. I would like to see our gymnastics, soccer, and rugby clubs in work clothes showing their biceps, and I would like to see our theatres and concert halls bursting with shouts in honour of the *Poilu* . . .
>
> You heat up a race, gentlemen, you don't give it chrysanthemums to sniff for two weeks. That is dangerous, and it is too much.[38]

Here, the writer has allowed himself to be carried away, but elsewhere he himself went in for terrifying tableaux, because he felt the need to root out any remaining vestiges of foolish pre-war patriotism, which wished for nothing better than invigorating, joyous war. The dark vehemence of certain Armistice Day speeches was a way of settling scores with the pro-war jingoists of 1911 and with those who preached war during the fighting from safety behind the lines. These dark passages also served to heighten the optimism of the speeches' conclusions.

Armistice Day speeches, as has been said, were often in two parts. The first part stressed the need to keep the memory of the war alive. The second part was introduced by a transitional passage, which could take two forms: the speaker might ask his listeners to behave today in such a way that yesterday's sacrifices would not have been in vain, or, in a related strain, he might exhort the living to show themselves worthy of the dead. The first transition placed the accent on the meaning that the combatants themselves gave to their sacrifice: they were fighting the war to end all wars, and this justified a pacifist conclusion. Organizing the peace was the citizen's duty for two reasons: it would help preserve society from the scourge of war, and it was also the right thing for a 'citizen of humanity' to do, for, just as villages were organized into provinces and provinces into states, states themselves, it was argued, must seek a superior form of union. Republican patriotism thus found purity and fulfilment in subscribing to a League of Nations that would work toward a 'universal republic'.

The second transition placed greater emphasis on the virtues of the dead, whose example justified every moralistic appeal. The lesson to be drawn from their sacrifice varied from orator to orator and moment to moment, but it was also civic in nature. For some it was the need for absolute devotion to public affairs, for giving precedence to the general interest over any special interest, for loving and obeying the law and the duties to the community that were created by the rights the law guaranteed for every citizen. For others it was the concrete equality that citizen-soldiers experienced in their miserable living conditions and in their equality before blind death that revealed the true meaning of the formal equality of citizens before the law. From this came a concept of discipline freely accepted and of leaders recognized because they were the most meritorious of their fellow citizens. Not authoritarian and distant leaders, like the frequently reviled officers of the regular army, but familiar and humane leaders, basically identical to the men they commanded, who like themselves were mobilized citizens, leaders who exercised authority only briefly and who confronted suffering and death along with their men. Last but not least, there was the fraternity of the trenches, no doubt somewhat polished up for the occasion, but at times felt with sufficient conviction to rekindle memory. Keeping sufficient faith with that memory implied tolerance and respect for one's fellow citizens, which meant an end to sterile conflicts like the religious disputes of the turn of the century and to politics in so far as it created artificial divisions. Shaken by the death of many citizens once mutually hostile to one another, the Republic now signified reconciliation.

'Thus there is a purely civil profession of faith, the terms of which are to be set by the sovereign, not like the dogmas of religion precisely but like sentiments of sociability without which it is impossible to be either a good citizen or a loyal subject.' In the last chapter of the *Social Contract* Jean-Jacques Rousseau argued the need for a civil religion. 'It is important to the State that each citizen have a religion that causes him to love his duties. But the dogmas of that religion are of interest to the State and its members only in so far as those dogmas relate to morality and to the duties that he who professes it is required to fulfil toward others.'

The republican cult of the war dead, as constituted and practised between the two world wars, is perhaps the only example in history of a civil religion in Rousseau's sense; and it emerged at a specific point in time. With the separation of Church and State, the state could no longer call upon organized religion to foster love of its laws. The war, moreover, had been a terrible calamity, and the sacrifices it required went beyond what could be expected from mere civic obedience. The need for citizens with a love of duty was widely felt. Finally, death had come indiscriminately to republicans and conservatives, freethinkers and clericals alike. The Republic ceased to be a party: it had become France itself, and that reconciliation needed to find expression for the purpose of consolidation.

War memorials thus became the centrepiece not of a memory of the Republic (that was the role of republican sculpture) but of a republican cult, a civil religion, whose distinctive features we shall review by way of conclusion. It was first of all an open cult. Its ceremonies took place not indoors, in enclosed spaces, but in public places, places with a centre, an axis, but belonging to no one in particular because they were the property of all.

Secondly, it was a secular cult, without gods or priests. Or, rather, gods, priests, and believers were all one. In truth, this was a religion in which citizens celebrated themselves. It was a cult in which citizens paid heartfelt homage to those of their fellow citizens who had done their civic duty. In preserving their memory, the monument became a civic site. The purpose of the memorial was not to deify the army or the fatherland. Recording the names of citizens killed in the war and reading them out one by one was a way of indicating that the Republic was nothing but its citizens. The dead were honoured by citizens like themselves: the living were exactly the same as the dead, one might say, only luckier. They were the ones who had escaped the slaughter and who could speak of it in the language of soldiers, as well as those who had not been called upon to serve: women, old men, and children. The initiative for the monument as well as the holiday came not from the government or social authorities: it came from municipalities, committees, and veterans' groups. If, moreover, those groups played a major role in Armistice Day ceremonies, it was not because of their character as groups but because of the duty that their members had individually fulfilled. We have seen how they tended to merge into a single collective actor speaking an impersonal rhetoric: since all citizens are equal before the law and have the same civic duties, one cannot step forward from the ranks to speak in the name of all unless one has been mandated to do so, and even then one's words must have been scripted by the group.

To celebrate those citizens who had done their duty was to exhort others to do theirs. In one form or another, the memorial speeches repeated what the memorial ceremony had already said through its minute of silence and lowered flags and what the monument itself affirmed throughout the year by its mere presence: because it was profoundly good to do one's civic duty, those who paid the supreme price in doing theirs must never be forgotten; and conversely, to honour those citizens who died for the Republic was to uphold the importance of civic duty.

This commemoration was therefore at the same time a form of civic proselytism and pedagogy. Armistice Day was a time for citizens to celebrate themselves. It strengthened their civic spirit and passed it on to the younger generation. Where a cold official initiative coming from above, from the state, might have failed, this anonymous collective enterprise succeeded. It depended on broad popular support and on the sincere conviction of its participants, a conviction that was itself the fruit of the republican elementary schools, for that was where republican dogmas were taught. To those dogmas the cult of the dead added the power of shared collective emotion. To that end it mobilized religious customs borrowed from a Catholicism that was still familiar to most Frenchmen, creating a distinctive ritual that orchestrated movement and immobility, silence and song, symbols, gestures, and words. In itself the republican ideal was abstract and legalistic. In the grave and contemplative atmosphere of Armistice Day, it shed its austerity and dryness and became a vital bond among human beings. The republican cult can of course be looked at sceptically, and it is no more immune to irony than other religions. Its goal was not simply to improve the standard of living or make people happier: it embodied values and offered a kind of salvation. It therefore required a cult in which its ideals could be celebrated, that is, recognized and shared. Without the republican cult, there is no longer a republican faith or republican virtue. What reigns in their stead is a disenchanted regime, in which the social contract is overshadowed by functional necessities. A Republic that does not teach itself and does not celebrate itself is a dead Republic, that is, a Republic for which people are no longer willing to die. This was apparent in May 1958, and even earlier in 1940. But if the Republic is not already alive in the hearts of its citizens, then teaching is sterile and celebration artificial. Under those conditions one can sustain the memory of the past, but it no longer has any impact on the present or meaning for the future. This has happened to the monuments to the dead and the Armistice Day ceremonies. Today abandoned by the popular fervour that created them, they are merely war memorials, and it is easy to forget that barely half a century ago the confident French Republic invited all its citizens to gather around them as celebrants and objects of their own republican cult.

Notes

1. *La Voix du combattant* (3 Dec. 1923).

2. *Le poilu dauphinois* (Dec. 1932) and *ibid.* (Jan. 1933) for the mayor's response.

3. See my *Les anciens combattants et la société française, 1914–1939*, vol. 3. *Mentalités et idéologies* (Paris: Presses de la Fondation Nationale des Sciences Politiques, 1977), or the English translation of my shorter book: *In the Wake of War: Les "Anciens Combattants" and French Society* (Providence, RI and Oxford: Berg, 1992). See also Monique Luirard, *La France et ses morts* (Le Puy-en-Velay: Imprimerie Commerciale, 1977), and June Hargrove, 'Souviens-toi', *Monuments historiques*, no. 124 (Dec. 1982–Jan. 1983). Further research has been done since this article was first written and published in French: see in particular the special issue on war memorials in the French journal *Guerres mondiales et conflits contemporains*, no. 167 (July 1992), for comments on recent work.

4. Fewer than 2 per cent of the 38,000 French communes have no war memorial. In those cases there is at least a plaque in the church, and the quick initiative of the clergy made the erection of a monument seem pointless to the overwhelmingly Catholic population: see Luirard, *La France*, p.19. Sometimes, also, the social unit is not the commune but the parish, which includes several communes, and one finds an inter-communal monument, as in Fraroz, La Latette, and Cerniébaud (Jura), where the monument is in any case next to the church.

5. In addition to the examples mentioned in Luirard, *La France*, pp. 13–14, and in Prost, *Les Anciens combattants*, pp. 38–9, there is also the monument to the *mobiles d'Allier*, built by public subscription in Moulins, in the Place d'Allier.

6. The schedule of subsidies was established by the law of 31 July 1920. The main subsidy ranged from 4 to 15 per cent of the total expense, depending on the number of war dead relative to the size of the population. There was also an additional subsidy determined by the wealth of the commune, ranging rom 11 per cent for the poorest to 1 per cent for the

richest. Mme Luirard, who was apparently unaware of the practice, points out that there were also departmental subsidies, and in some cases she is able to cite the share of the expense raised by subscription and the share drawn from municipal funds (p. 24). For 128 monuments, she cites the total cost: 28 under 5,000 francs, 48 between 5,000 and 10,000 francs, 39 between 10,000 and 25,000,and 13 above 25,000. According to one foundry catalogue, a cast bronze statue of a *poilu* cost at least 4,800 francs, a simple bust around 2,000. See price list, May 1921, of Fonderies et Ateliers de Construction du Val d'Osne.

7. These disputes generally involved the priest's insistence on adding a religious symbol of some kind to the monument, and the council's refusal to do so. See Prost, *Les Anciens Combattants*, pp. 39–40.

8. In Lyons, at the cemetery of La Guillotière, 1 Nov. 1916 (minutes of the *conseil d'administration* of the Union des Mutilés et Anciens Combattants du Rhône, 5 Nov. 1916); in Nîmes, 1 Nov. 1917 (*Après la bataille,* Nov. 1917); in Orléans, the same (minutes of the *conseil d'administration* of the Mutilés du Loiret, 20 Oct. 1917.

9. The minority formed two associations: the *Association Républicaine des Anciens Combattants* and the *Association ouvrière des mutilés,* associated with the C.G.T., which later became the *Fédération Ouvrière et paysanne des mutilés*. The A.R.A.C. and the F.O.P. were the only organizations to refuse to join in the celebrations of Bastille Day 1919 after the government agreed that they should be preceded by a memorial vigil in honor of the war dead. But the demonstrations organized at Père Lachaise cemetery drew about a thousand people. The A.R.A.C. was a very small association before 1940, while the F.O.P.was larger, but still much smaller than the major veterans' groups. In 1927, moreover, it pulled out of the (Communist) Veterans International.

10. The sample was chosen to cover all regions of the country and designed to be exhaustive in each area looked at. I personally viewed 306 monuments, and colleagues viewed 51 others. In addition 500 questionnaires were sent to teachers in eleven regional groups of communes. I received 201 responses , so that in all the survey included 564 monuments in 35 different departments. See Prost, *Les Anciens Combattants*, p. 42.

11. In very republican departments like the Nièvre, there are fewer *poilus*: 24 out of 325 monuments (7.4 per cent). See Hervé Moisan, *Sentinelles de pierre, les monuments aux morts de la guerre de 1914-1918 dans la Nièvre*, Saint-Pourcain-sur Sioule, Ed. Bleu autour, 1999.

12. The request came from the *Mutilés du Loiret* (minutes of the *conseil d'admnistration*, 5 Nov. 1931), one of the first associations of disabled veterans, whose president, Henri Pichot, was probably the most eminent veterans' leader between the two wars and for a long time the president of the largest national veterans' group, the *Union Fédérale*.

13. In Ayhere, for example.

14. Saint-Martin-d'Estreaux (Loire), Brassac (Tarn), etc. Luirard, *La France*, p. 27, mentions four communes in her department, but not Saint-Martin-d'Estreaux.

15. The law on the separation of Church and State prohibited affixing religious emblems to memorial monuments, but not to funerary monuments. War memorials were considered to be funerary if they were located in cemeteries. In some communes, however, monuments were planned for public squares without crosses, only to have crosses added later. See Prost, *Les Anciens Combattants*, p. 40.

16. Victor Hugo, 'Hymne', *Les chants du crépuscule*, p. 3.

17. This statue was produced by the Durenne Foundries and is referred to as model EE in their catalogue (Établissement métallurgiques A. Durenne, *Statues et ornements pour monuments commémoratifs* (Paris, Imprimerie Puyfourcat, 1921, p. 5). Unfortunately we do not know the price. This statue is found in 2.6 per cent of the war memorials in our sample. If the sample is representative there would be 900 similar statues in French village squares.

18. It would be interesting to extend this study by systematically analysing the imagery of females in these monuments. Maurice Agulhon, *Marianne au combat* (Paris, Flammarion, 1979), contrasts the popular Republic, wearing a Phrygian cap, the symbol of liberty, and the moderate Republic, robed and sober, crowned with ears of wheat or laurels. I found few Republics with Phrygian cap on any war memorial. Luirard, *La France*, reproduces a photograph of one, in La Ricamarie in the Loire. Agulhon saw one in Provence. I found mainly women in ancient garb, which I am inclined to interpret as symbols of the Republic even when wearing helmets, as in Boën-sur-Lignon and La Courneuve. Agulhon, p. 211, also notes a helmeted Republic, the bust by Clésinger in the Senate. If my impression is correct, the First World War marked the triumph of the sober, moderate, conservative Republic, which then became identified with France, for it was subsequently accepted by all the French, who had been willing to die for it regardless of their political views; the Republic was no longer associated with one party. This was already the theme of de Marcère's speech upon the inauguration of the statue of the Republic on the Champ-du-Mars, 30 June 1878: see Agulhon, p. 218. The feminine representations of the *Patrie* and the Republic have also been studied by Maurice Agulhon, *Les metamorphoses de Marianne: l'imagerie et la symbolique républicaines de 1914 à nos jours,* Paris, Flammarion, 2001.

19. No. 854 of the Catalogue of the Fonderies du Val d'Osne, this statue cost 5,300 francs in cast bronze. It was not very common (only four appear in our sample), but other sculptors treated the *poilu* in similar terms, as a sentinel or lookout.

20. The most common statue of this type appears to have been that of Gourdon, which turned up seven times in our sample; but it was apparently copied frequently.

21. See Luirard, *La France*, for the monuments of Chazelles-sur-Lyon, La Fouillousse, Leigneux, and Sorbias.

22. The inscription is a triptych. In the centre: 'Results of the war: more than twelve million dead! An equal number unborn! Still more maimed, wounded, widowed, and orphaned. Billions of francs in damages. Scandalous fortunes built on human suffering. Innocent people hanged on the gallows. The guilty rewarded. The disinherited plunged into misery. A huge bill to be paid. Has war at last caused enough suffering and misery, killed enough men, that men may find the intelligence and will to kill war itself?' And the last panel on the right reads: 'A curse on war and those responsible for it'.

23. Yves Pilven Le Sevellec, 'Une étude des monuments aux morts de la Loire-Atlantique', *Visions contemporaines, revue d'histoire,* n° 4, mars 1990, pp. 9–131, especially pp. 89ff. The minister of War asked the municipality to call out the *gendarmerie* for these ceremonies; however, in this quite conservative department, the *gendarmes* participated in only four inaugurations.

24. This was easy when there was only one veterans' group. When there was more than one, their presidents generally formed a committee.

25. *Le Combattant* (Tarbes; 10 Nov. 1921, and 1 Nov. 1922).

26. *Compte rendu* of the Clermont-Ferrand conference (Paris: Presses Universitaires de France, n.d.), p. 291.

27. F. Malval (Hubert-Aubert), *La Voix du combattant* (30 July 1922).

28. A Linville (A. L'Heureux), 'La Fête du 11 novembre', *Le journal des mutilés et réformés* (14 Oct. 1922).

29. For the Loire, see for example, *Le Poilu du Loire* (Dec. 1934) – *De profundis* at the monument: Chuyer, Montregard, Saint-Maurice-de-Lignon, Chassigny-sur-Dun; absolution: Arthun, Saint-Victor-sur-Loire, Sevelinges, Chazelles-sur-Lavieu. For the Vendée, see *Le Combattant vendéen* (Dec. 1930). There were similar ceremonies in the Ardennes (see *Le Combattant sanglier* [Dec. 1933]) and in Normandy. At Henqueville (Seine-Maritime): 'After the mass the procession formed, led by the clergy, and proceeded to the monument singing the *Libera*. At the war memorial there were the usual prayers, a blessing, the laying of a wreath, the reading of names, and a speech by President Levasseur [a summary is given]. Return to the church singing *Te Deum*' (*La Flamme* [Nov. 1934]).

30. The reading of the names of the dead is explicitly mentioned in 11 of 29 communes in the Ardennes in 1931 (*Le Combattant sanglier* [Dec. 1931]). It was common in Isère, Aveyron, etc.

31. In many parishes at this time the sermon began with a necrology: the priest read a list of names of the dead and at the end the Lord's Prayer was said for them. Then came the sermon proper. Similarly, at the war memorials, the speech generally came after the reading of the names.

32. Williers (Ardennes), 1930. 'Kind ladies sang a canticle for the occasion', *Le Combattant sanglier* (Dec. 1930).

33. Prost, *Les Anciens Combattants,* p. 59.

34. C. Vilain, *Le Soldat inconnu, histoire et culte* (Paris, Maurice d'Hartoy, 1933).

35. Manent is explicit about this in *Le Combattant* (Tarbes; 1 Oct. 1921).

36. Rosemonde Sanson, *Les 14-juillet, fête et conscience nationale* (Paris, Flammarion, 1976) explains how this ceremony was organized.

37. On the initiative of the *Mutilés du Loiret,* see *La France mutilé* (29 Oct. 1922), *Le Journal des mutilés et réformés* (4 Nov. 1922), *Le Combattant du Pas-du-Calais* (9 Nov. 1922). See also the advocacy of speeches by veterans rather than elected officials in Linville, *Le Journal des mutilés et réformés* (14 Oct. 1922), and Bruche, *Le Combattant du Pas-du-Calais* (9 Nov. 1922).

38. In *Le Béquillard meusien* (Nov. 1926).

2

Verdun: The Life of a Site of Memory

Great battles linger in every nation's memory, especially battles in which the national identity asserts itself in an effort to halt the advance of an aggressor. Thermopylae in antiquity and Stalingrad in the Second World War are good examples. Hence the case of Verdun is not exceptional. It is nevertheless an interesting case to study for anyone who wishes to understand how events are transformed into symbols and how national memories are crystallized in historic sites.

1916: A Battle and Its Aftermath

The military history of the battle of Verdun is well known. The configuration of the terrain played an essential role. Northeast of the Meuse River the land rises gently toward a plateau known as the Meuse Heights, from which there is a rather abrupt descent to the Wöevre plain. At the beginning of 1916 the front stretched in a wide arc around the city of Verdun. From the Argonne and Vauquois it ran north of the city from west to east, crossed the Meuse, and touched the Meuse Heights at the Caures forest. It then descended into the Woëvre plain, where it first veered toward the southeast and then turned southwestward until it once again crossed the Meuse Heights south of Eparges and the Meuse River at Saint-Mihiel, which the Germans occupied.

The German offensive began on 21 February on the right bank of the Meuse in the sector of the Caures and Haumont forests, and was directed toward Verdun. It quickly met with success. On 24 February the French abandoned the Woëvre plain and fell back on the Meuse Heights. On 25 February the Fort of Douaumont fell without a fight. Pétain took command that night and reorganized the front. His major fear at this point was that the Germans might attack on the left bank of the Meuse northwest of Verdun, because, if they

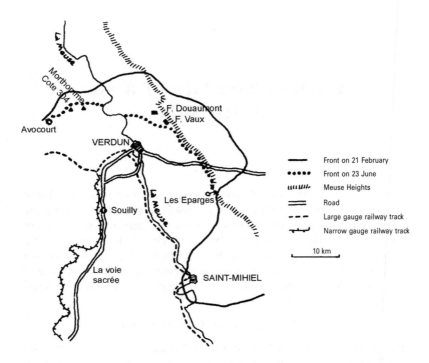

Map 1: Map of the Site of the Battle of Verdun

broke through in that sector, the troops committed on the right bank
were vulnerable from the rear. He therefore set up a blocking
position along a line that ran from Hill 304 to the Dead Man, another
prominent hill, and beyond. The feared attack came on 5 March, and
on 7 March the Germans also moved on the fortress at Vaux on the
right bank. On 8 March, a French counterattack on the left bank
restored the front. The danger was not yet over, however. Additional
German offensives were stopped on 10 April, the date of Pétain's
famous order to his troops ('Courage! . . . On les aura!'), and in early
June (the fortress at Vaux fell on 7 June). The German advance
attained its ultimate point of penetration in early July: an offensive
launched on 23 June threatened to seize the last ridges before
Verdun, which then would have come under direct German artillery
fire. On 1 July, however, a Franco-British offensive on the Somme
relieved the pressure, and on 12 July the Germans suffered a serious

defeat at the fort of Souville. Now the initiative was with the Allies: a first French offensive on 24 October resulted in the recapture of Douaumont and Vaux; a second offensive, in mid-December, restored the front to the line covered by the fortresses.

This bare summary raises a number of questions. To begin with, why did the Germans choose to attack Verdun? The military reasons are obvious: the objective was difficult to defend, because artillery was to play an important role in the battle and the French supply lines for men, *matériel*, and munitions consisted of just one narrow-gauge railway line and one small country road. Furthermore, if one examines the front from the German side, the Verdun salient constituted a permanent threat, from which an offensive could be launched at any time; hence it made sense for the Germans to try to eliminate it. But why, in that case, attack the salient head-on rather than try to envelop it with a pincers movement by launching attacks at two points on the left bank of the Meuse? The German tactics may have been designed to pin down the French forces around Verdun; but other possible reasons have been suggested as well. The Germans may have been trying to 'bleed' the French army by luring it into a battle of attrition in which it would be obliged to make a full commitment of its forces.[1] Or they may have chosen Verdun rather than Belfort for strategic reasons: Verdun was more centrally located and offered a broader front to attack. Above all, they may have been striking at 'France's moral main line *[le boulevard moral de la France]*'.[2]

The problem with this thesis is that it was formulated *after* the battle. It assumes that Verdun already occupied a central place in French national memory *before* 1916. It is not obvious that this was so. A city such as Rheims, where France's kings were once anointed, would probably have been a more potent symbol. To be sure, Verdun appeared in all pre-1914 French history books because of the treaty signed there in 843 to divide up the Carolingian Empire. Already a fortified city in the time of the Gauls, Verdun was further fortified in the twelfth century and again in the seventeenth century by Vauban. In the nineteenth century its defences had been beefed up with a triple ring of fortifications stretching all the way to the Meuse Heights. Verdun thus became the centre of a veritable 'fortified region'. The last of the new forts, Douaumont, was an awesome citadel of reinforced concrete. Yet these vestiges of Verdun's important military past did not count for much in 1915: the fortresses around Verdun had been disarmed, and their cannon had been removed in order to reinforce the French army's inadequate heavy artillery. If Verdun had actually been a 'symbol' for France and the entire world, as General Dubail said it was in 1919, why, when he commanded the army group in charge of the area in 1915, had he not been more concerned with its defence?[3] Furthermore, pre-war textbooks attached no special significance to Verdun, the last of the 'three bishoprics' annexed to France in 1552 (along with Toul and Metz). For the pedagogues of the late nineteenth century, Verdun was no different from many other cities.

Thus to say that the Germans attacked Verdun for its symbolic value is probably to mistake effect for cause. It is to grant the city a place in French national consciousness that it assumed only as a result of the battle. The very anachronism of the alleged reason points up one of the most indubitable consequences of the battle: before 1916, Verdun was surely not a central element of France's national memory, but after the war it was *the* central element. So the question then becomes, When did this change take place?

The very first days of the German offensive were undoubtedly the moment when Verdun became more than just a military objective, indeed a national symbol. The force of the enemy onslaught, the French retreat, the disorganization of the front, and the fear that it would collapse lent dramatic intensity to the weeks from 21 February to 9 March. The memoirs of President Raymond Poincaré give evidence of this: he wanted to go to Verdun from the moment the battle broke out but was obliged to postpone his trip first to 26 February and then again to 29 February; he did not actually depart until 1 March.[4] Serrigny has told the story of the president's meeting with Pétain. The front on the left bank of the Meuse (between Hill 304 and the Dead Man) was still in flux, and Pétain was afraid that a German success in this sector would jeopardize the rear of his troops on the right bank. He therefore envisioned a possible withdrawal of French forces to the left bank and told the president that he would not hesitate to abandon Verdun if it seemed necessary to do so. 'Don't even think about it, General,' Poincaré immediately responded. 'It would be a parliamentary disaster.'[5]

Of course Serrigny wrote with the intention of injuring Poincaré, and he failed to recognize that, for a lawyer like Poincaré, the National Assembly and the Nation were one and the same. Yet the anecdote still points up the crucial issue of those critical weeks: should Verdun be held regardless of the cost? The strategists who pored over their topographical maps were not dogmatic about defending the city:

neither Pétain nor the young officers of the general staff ruled out a strategic withdrawal.[6]

Politicians, however, sensed that the fall of Verdun would have a tremendous impact on public opinion. For reasons of morale, they wanted the army to dig in on the right bank. This was the president's position, as we have just seen. It was also the position of the prime minister, Aristide Briand, who on 22 February made his view clear to General Joffre, the supreme commander, whose detractors accused him of planning a retreat to the left bank. Joffre in fact gave orders to defend Verdun on the right bank, both for reasons of morale and because of military suspicions about the terrain. On several occasions he ordered Pétain to counterattack in order to recapture lost ground. An exasperated Pétain offered this reply on April 9: 'I ask for your confidence and beg you not to be misled by a few calculated partial withdrawals.'[7] But the concept of a defensive position in depth was neither understood nor accepted at the time. Pétain was regarded as a pessimist without backbone. On 1 May, moreover, he was promoted to the position of commander of the Army Group of the Centre, and Nivelle, a 'fighter' who dreamt of taking the offensive, assumed command of the Second Army. Pétain was still in charge at Verdun, but from a distance; he was seen to wipe away a tear when he received the news.

In June, when Verdun was in danger of coming under direct German fire, debate flared up anew. Pétain's staff studied the possibility of falling back to the Meuse; this would have left a portion of Verdun in French hands, so that political leaders could still plausibly maintain that the city had not fallen. From this small hypocrisy we can gauge the state of public opinion: Verdun had become a symbol.

By this point, however, a split had developed: the symbol was not the same for the troops at the front as for people in the rear. Behind the lines the battle quickly took on heroic proportions. Was this because the defence of Verdun was purely a French, as opposed to an Allied, affair? Be that as it may, the battle rapidly achieved a special status. *L'Illustration* devoted an extraordinary amount of space to it, publishing countless drawings and photos of remarkable documentary value. They portray the battlefield as a lunar landscape, completely covered with shell craters. The articles discussed the trenches at length. The realistic images were contradicted by the commentary. In fact, a process of euphemization had begun. The weekly magazine portrayed the entire nation as united behind the soldiers of Verdun, modest heroes all and unflaggingly confident. The wounded smiled courageously; the more seriously wounded were not shown. A reader of *L'Illustration* would never have known that anyone died at Verdun. Gérard Canini, whose work I am drawing on here, has shown that the magazine actively misled its readers: it published photographs of impressive stocks of heavy artillery shells, when in fact there was a shortage of shells at Verdun.[8] And on 13 May it identified a group of fresh reinforcements as a unit just returning from the front lines.

This idealization of the battle misled some people into describing the event in all sincerity in terms of the sort generally found only in official citations. On 11 July 1916, for example, the Académie Française sent the Second Army a message of 'admiration, gratitude, and respect'. The president of the Republic visited Verdun six times in 1916. His last visit, on 13 September, was to bestow six decorations on the city of Verdun, which thereby became a symbol of heroic resistance: 'The name Verdun,' he declared, 'which German dreams turned into a symbol now represents . . . all that is purest, best, and most beautiful in the soul of France. It has become synonymous with patriotism, bravery, and generosity.'[9]

With all France's attention riveted on Verdun and all its people anxious about the battle's outcome, the stubborn resistance of French troops there elicited wholehearted and sincere admiration. Less noble sentiments also emerged, however. Verdun became not just a national symbol and site of memory but, incredible as it may seem, a fashionable place to visit. For five months Verdun was the place to be. We are still a little shocked by Serrigny's accounts of important guests and members of learned academies invited to lunch by Pétain at his headquarters in Souilly. Such frivolous diversions may seem improper at such a time and place. Many decorations were awarded behind the lines at Verdun, to the dismay of soldiers at or on their way to the front.

Take Louis Barthas (an anti-militarist, to be sure), *en route* to Verdun on 3 May 3 1916. His entire division was ordered to form up in a vast meadow so that Joffre could award Pétain the Grand Cross of the Legion of Honour. Joffre reviewed the troops and awarded various decorations, after which the troops went on parade. 'When the parade was over, Joffre, Pétain, and their entourage of brass jumped into their automobiles and set off for Bar-le-Duc, where they probably gathered at a sumptuous table to celebrate a medal earned with the blood of thousands of poor chaps.'[10] A month later,

Joffre came to inspect the division of a Captain Garnier, who found the general 'friendly and generous' and quick to pass out watches and cigars to the troops: 'This distribution of gifts reminded us of the cigarette and glass of rum that the executioner generously offers the condemned man.'[11]

For the combatants, Verdun was indeed a place rife with symbolic significance, but symbolizing chiefly death and sacrifice. They knew that the troops sent to the front were sustaining terrible losses. When a unit found out that it was going to the line, the soldiers knew at once that many of them would not be coming back. 'At six one night, we were just sitting down to supper when the news came and took away our appetite. The orders were that the regiment and in fact the entire division were to move out in buses at seven.'[12] A little later, in the autumn, this song was sung in the trucks carrying replacements to the front:

> Adieu la vie, adieu l'amour, adieu les femmes,
> C'est pas fini, c'est pour toujours de cette guerre infâme.
> C'est à Verdun, Douaumont ou Vaux
> Qu'on va laisser sa peau
> Car nous sommes tous des condamnés
> C'est nous les sacrifiés.[13]

Verdun's reputation turned it into a prize worthy of immeasurable sacrifice. This image owed a great deal to the collective anxiety of the first few weeks: from the way civilians looked at them *en route* to Verdun, the soldiers were in no doubt as to the gravity of their situation, and the sounds of endless shellfire, which could be heard from great distances, left them under no illusion about what to expect.[14] But Verdun's reputation also owed a great deal to conversations among soldiers and to encounters between troops from different units who met in the course of the vast manoeuvres occasioned by the battle.

This brings us to a very important point: if Verdun is not just one battle among others, but *the* battle that sums up the whole of the First World War, it is because nearly the entire French army took part in it. On the German side, the divisions committed to Verdun were not relieved; they ensured their own supply of fresh troops by rotating regiments in and out of the front lines. By contrast, Pétain tried to commit each major unit to Verdun only once. He himself called his system a 'bucket-chain or relay [*noria*]': French divisions were sent up to the front one after another. On 15 July, seventy of the ninety-five existing army divisions were committed to Verdun along an active front some twenty miles long, from the Avocourt forest west of Hill 304 to the La Laufée forest south of the fortress of Vaux. Only twenty-three divisions were sent to the line more than once in this sector in 1916, and that was because after 1 July the Battle of the Somme made it more difficult to rely on the relay system.

For Pétain, the relay system served the needs of military efficiency. More than any other general, he was aware of the ordeal that a week on the front lines at Verdun represented. At Souilly he often watched as replacement troops marched by. Ten years later, he described the fate of those troops in measured and moving words. He portrayed them as they reached their destination on the far side of the Meuse and came under shelling, hindered in their march by the evacuation of the wounded and the movement of supplies, shivering with cold at every stop, seeking in vain the guides who were supposed to show them the way forward, taking up their positions on their own, at random, and suddenly encountering the enemy. 'Our men suffered and toiled beyond the imaginable,' he wrote.[15] Hence he believed that to force soldiers who had already been through this hell to return to the front would undermine their courage and persuade them that he wished to see them dead: if the objective was to hold out at all costs, then it was better not to have demoralized troops on the front lines.

Inspired by military considerations, the relay system had important consequences for morale. It made the battle of Verdun the battle of the entire army. As a result, the stakes changed. The soldiers who went to the front advanced through terrain that was unfamiliar but not entirely unknown: they had heard about it from those who had preceded them. Before experiencing the battle, they had imagined it, and that experience later fed the collective imagination. Verdun thus became a sacred place: a place of sacrifice and consecration. Going to Verdun was a kind of initiation anticipated, vaguely foreseen, feared, and inevitable. The names that marked this ascent to martyrdom became familiar to everyone, and no soldier's memoir fails to mention them: the Faubourg Pavé, the Sainte-Fine chapel, the ravine of Froideterre, the shelter at Quatre-Cheminées. The shared memory of a great and ultimately triumphant ordeal was thus inscribed in the names of places that everyone recognized.

Two collective memories of Verdun thus took shape simultaneously in 1916. The first was a national memory – national in two senses: it was the memory of the entire nation, a memory structured by the press, the authorities, prominent local citizens, and daily conversation; and it was also a memory filled with patriotic pride, and hence national in that sense too. Alongside this memory, and linked to it through letters from the front and through the partial, bowdlerized tales of men on leave, was the memory of the combatants, which was narrower, denser, more vivid, and more intimate in its pride, as well as laden with emotion, anguish, and grief. In 1916 these two forms of memory were still bound together by the proximity of the event. But once the battle was over, by 1917, the only links that remained were Pétain, whose stature thereby took on extraordinary proportions, and the very sites in which the heroic action and sacrifice had unfolded. Those sites then became a symbolic battleground: how would they be commemorated, and what enduring significance would be bestowed on them as a result?

The Cults of Memory

At first the memories of those who had witnessed the battle with gratitude and admiration from a distance were more powerful than the memories of those who had participated in it directly. The number of people behind the lines exceeded the number of soldiers at the front. What is more, those in the rear were not kept busy fighting the war, which raged on even after the battle ended. In 1917 and 1918, only noncombatants were in a position to commemorate. The most common form of commemoration consisted in bestowing the name Verdun on squares, streets, and boulevards. Further study will be needed before we can give an exact chronology of this process, which probably followed hard on the heels of victory. There is no doubt that it was widespread: there is not a city in France without a Rue de Verdun.

This form of commemoration is neutral: it recalls the event without imposing any particular interpretation on it. Similarly, the battle of Verdun was taught in both primary and secondary schools, but the history books did not turn the story into a legend.[16] The battle of Verdun was treated in the same way as the battle of the Marne, and, although the portrait of Pétain was always associated with it, it was often flanked by portraits of the two other marshals of the First World War, Joffre and Foch.

The first attempts to etch the memory of the battle into the very soil of Verdun were a very different matter.[17] The very sincerity of those efforts inevitably reflected an interpretation of the battle, one of patriotism and heroism. Although that interpretation may have sounded rather hollow to many veterans of Verdun, they were reluctant to refuse the conventional homage to their valour.

The first commemorative initiative came from the city of Verdun. From its refuge in Paris, the municipal council decided in July 1917 to erect a monument to commemorate the battle. Proposals were accepted in August 1919, the first stone was laid on 23 June 1920, and final plans were approved in March 1921. Construction took several years, and it was not until 23 June 1929 that the monument was inaugurated, with the president of the Republic in attendance. Built adjacent to the twelfth-century ramparts and integrated into the city whose resistance it symbolized, this was a monument to victory, not a memorial of the battle. It was also a municipal monument, and hence not an embodiment of national memory.

A second monument was begun later, in 1919, but built very quickly and inaugurated, also in the presence of the president of the Republic, on 8 December 1920. It offered a conventionally heroic view of the battle as people behind the lines imagined it. Behind this monument was an actual event: the resistance of two platoons of the 137th Infantry Regiment, almost wiped out by withering artillery fire. Unfortunately there was nothing unusual about this slaughter, which was duplicated elsewhere on the battlefield. The site, now known as the Trench of Bayonets, was originally called the Trench of Rifles, either because the dead men's weapons, which had been placed on the parapet of the trench, remained visible even after shells had obliterated the trench itself, or because other soldiers had planted rifles in the ground to mark a mass grave, a common practice at the time.

This incontrovertible fact was soon embroidered until it became a legend: the soldiers of the two platoons had allegedly been buried alive while standing erect with fixed bayonets awaiting an enemy attack. The change from rifles to bayonets seems minor, but was in fact of great significance. The bayonet evoked a whole series of stereotypes in which rear-echelon patriots delighted. Of such images the artist Georges Scott would later write: 'What you saw in *L'Illustration* . . . is mere imagery. What I am doing for myself, for afterward, . . . is very different, as you will see.'[18] The bayonet conjured up a comic-book ideal of heroism, a false idea of courage and the sublime according to which soldiers quivering with patriotic emotion and joy yearned for nothing better than to attack the enemy. The reality was more sombre: Pétain quite rightly noted that soldiers did their duty simply and without bravado. An anecdote will suffice to illustrate their state of mind. The event took place in 1916. A young lieutenant, facing his baptism by fire, tries to make a 'patriotic speech' to his men in the trenches. A veteran of the Marne interrupts him: 'Stuff it, shavetail. Shut up and give some orders.'[19] Pierre Mac Orlan puts it succinctly: 'A patriotic death was the death of a novice in war.' [20]

The legend of the Trench of Bayonets was a pious fraud, but a fraud nonetheless. A howitzer shell could not fill up a trench in the sense in which noncombatants understood the word 'fill'. Shells dug craters even as they collapsed structural supports.[21] When a trench was pounded by shells, the soldiers did not quietly stand their ground waiting to be killed. They took cover in the shell craters. Bayonets were rarely used, and only for attacking, not for defence. On 12 June 1916, the 137th Infantry Regiment was under attack. Why would the men have fixed bayonets? To drive the attackers back? But the attack came mainly in the form of shelling rather than an infantry assault. Norton Cru is right to think that the legend of the Trench of Bayonets reflects the absurd ideas that the earliest tourists to visit Verdun had about the battle.[22]

What is more, no historian nowadays believes the story as it was told. Ducasse, Meyer, and Perreux deem it highly unlikely that soldiers could have been buried alive while standing up. They argue that the bayonets were 'probably attached to the dead men's rifles after the fact'. The legend is one 'whose implausibility the general public is not in a position to appreciate'. Yet having demystified the story, they repudiate their own criticisms and declare the legend to be authentic. The difference between edifying patriotic imagery and reality is obliterated: 'Here, legend rejoins history.'[23] One finds the same formula and the same reconciliation in Jacques-Henri Lefebvre's book.[24] Today's official guidebooks reveal the truth, yet still justify the deception: 'In the Trench of Bayonets, history and myth are ultimately indistinguishable . . . It is likely that some men of the 137th were buried alive, as unfortunately often happened. Others lay dead or gassed in the bottom of the trench, on whose parapet lay their rifles . . . The Germans finished filling in the grave.'[25]

Nowadays we may refuse to choose between history and legend: we are barely aware of what was once at stake in the debate. Immediately after the war, however, things were different. The commemoration of a myth like this one meant that the memory of the rear echelon was silencing that of the combatants. Veterans of the war were too scattered and too glad to be back in civilian life to make their voices heard. Verdun became a central site of national identity, but of what nation? At stake were not merely two images of the battle, Nivelle's and Pétain's, or two conceptions of military valour: the nature of the combat had implications for understanding why France had gone to war and what it had fought for.

In the end, however, the veterans' memory won out. In fact, the condition of the battlefield at the end of the war forced the nation to accept their interpretation. They did not have to mobilize to impose their view.

By 1919, places like Douaumont, Vaux, and the 'Dead Man' hill were nothing but shell craters, shrapnel, and bodies. Tourists walked off with bones and skulls. Scrap metal dealers, who collected wagon loads of copper and steel, frequently dug up the remains of both French and German victims. Things could not be left as they were. The bodies had to be gathered up, rescued from curiosity seekers, and suitably honoured. The need for a collective burial place was obvious.

It was at this time that the idea of building an 'ossuary' at Verdun was first proposed. The word itself is worth pondering, for it indicates a symbolic shift. The people who first propose building a commemorative monument at Verdun used the more literary and heroic term *mausoleum*. The association of *mausoleum* with death was attenuated by a certain architectural splendour. By contrast, the word *ossuary* plainly evoked anonymous mass burial. By 1917 the idea of a mausoleum was in the air. The library at Verdun contains plans for a 'National Mausoleum for French and Allied Heroes Fallen on the Field of Honour'. These were drawn up in 1916 by the secretary of the Société Nationale des Beaux-Arts. It was perhaps in reaction against such monumental proposals that *L'Illustration* on 23 February 23 1918 published a drawing with this caption: 'The most beautiful mausoleum for the dead of Verdun: the ruins of the Fort of Douaumont.'

It was Msgr. Ginisty, the bishop of Verdun, who first proposed building an ossuary at Douaumont. The idea supposedly came to him on 22 November1918, as he travelled through the districts of Fleury, Vaux, and Douaumont on his way home to Verdun. In any case, he announced it publicly at a meeting at the Trocadero on 16 February 1919. In that same year, a temporary ossuary in the form of a wooden barracks was built on the site. Remains retrieved from each sector of the battlefield were stored there, and tourists were invited to come and 'pay pious homage to the relics of our glorious defenders'.

The Ossuary of Douaumont was thus the work of a private group, which was soon declared a war charity, with the bishop of Verdun as its chairman. Interestingly, religion played a major role in transforming Verdun into a site of memory. It was religion that made Verdun a peaceful place of reverence for the dead, and veterans were able to accept the religious interpretation of the site. In the past, the Church might have done more to extol the victory and demonstrate its patriotic commitment. But Church and State were now separated, and France was a country whose president felt that he could not personally attend the victory mass and sent his wife to represent him: religion therefore had no officially recognized place except to honour the dead. Since commemorative structures had to be secular in character, only a burial vault of some sort could be openly religious. The ossuary was therefore designed as a funerary and religious monument open to all religions: the technical specifications given to the architects indicated that there must be room for Protestant, Jewish, and Muslim facilities alongside the Catholic sanctuary. Given the large number of Catholics who died, however, it was further specified that the Catholic portion of the building was to be the largest and most centrally located.

Construction of the ossuary took twelve years. The corner stone was laid on 20 August 1920, well before final plans were approved on 24 March 1923. The first part of the edifice was inaugurated on 18–21 September1927, in the presence of the president of the Republic, and his successor returned to Douaumont for the final inauguration ceremonies, which ran from 6 to 8 August 1932.

The project drew the support of many people beside its initial promoters. It might be more accurate to say that those promoters could not have completed the project without mobilizing widespread public support. Building the ossuary cost fifteen million francs, only one million of which was contributed by the state, when the structure was already nearly complete. The ossuary committee mounted an extensive publicity campaign to raise the remaining fourteen million francs. Many communities offered support: 122 French cities and 18 foreign cities made contributions. Local committees were set up throughout France to collect money by organizing 'days in honour of the dead of Verdun', 'patriotic evenings' and 'solemn concerts', reviving age-old traditions of communal festivals and charity sales. Catholic participation was extensive: the national committee chairman was the bishop of Verdun; the most active propagandists were Msgr. Ginisty and Canon Lombard; the chaplain of Douaumont gave unstintingly of himself; and the treasurer, a man of shrewd skill as an investor, was also an ecclesiastic, Abbé Mouton. Nevertheless, the Ossuary Charity followed in the footsteps of the Union Sacrée by calling on prominent citizens from all parts of the political spectrum. In Avignon, for example, the local committee was chaired by an elementary school inspector, and his board included the principal of a girls' boarding school, the vice-president of a disabled veterans' organization, the principal of another school, a municipal stenographer, and an employee of the treasury department. The secular middle class was thus quite involved in the project. Elsewhere, for example in Tourcoing, the committee was more bourgeois: its board included an entrepreneur, two merchants, an industrialist, an official from another veterans' group, and a war widow. Thanks to the work of these countless volunteers, tens of thousands of anonymous contributors provided the funds for the burial of tens of thousands of unknown soldiers.

If the financing for the Ossuary of Douaumont was truly national, its architecture set it apart from all the other war memorials of the First World War. It is nothing like the churches of Notre-Dame-de-Lorette or Dormans. Still, it cannot be called beautiful. Indeed, the jury that selected Leon Azéma's proposal in 1923 was impressed by its functional qualities: its interior was spacious enough to accommodate major ceremonies; the religious parts of the edifice were separate from the parts that would receive the remains of the dead and welcome visitors; and the modular structure lent itself to construction in several stages as funds became available (and allowed doing away with roughly one-third of the original plan when contributions dwindled).

The Ossuary of Douaumont is no different today from what it was seventy years ago: it is unclassifiable, neither religious nor civilian nor military in character. Its squat structure is intended to evoke the dyke that the defenders of Verdun hoped to erect against the invading German forces, but it also looks rather like a pillbox. As for the tower, which rises more than a hundred and fifty feet above the plateau, it is neither a beacon nor a bell-tower. Each of its four faces has a cruciform structure, in keeping with its funerary intent. Indeed, the tower is like a gigantic cemetery stele: the Ossuary is an immense monument to the dead.

Various kinds of religious services are held at Verdun. Long ago there were private services: grieving widows and parents came to honour slain husbands and sons. In the period between the two world wars, greying veterans also came to visit a site that still haunted them. Pierre Mac Orlan describes men who brought their families on their first visit to the battlefield but, realizing that other family members soon became bored, returned alone to pursue their private memories. Each veteran explored on foot the sector he knew best and noted every change in the terrain since the great battle. In the 1930s, the issue of whether or not to replant the former battlefield with trees provoked a great debate among veterans.[26]

Before long more formal services were also organized. These generally ended with a solemn visit to the Ossuary. For a long time veterans' groups made pilgrimages to the site. By 1927 or 1928 such groups had become powerful, and many sponsored excursions for their members. Veterans liked to get together and talk about old times, and battlefields, especially the battlefield at Verdun, were a natural destination. These pilgrimages often featured silent marches ending at the Ossuary. Silence had always been the rule at the site: the statue of Resignation that had stood in front of the temporary ossuary indicated the need for quiet with a finger across its mouth. It would have been unseemly to speak in the presence of the dead, and here the dead were everywhere. Veterans who marched together could share memories more easily than those who made solitary visits to places significant only to themselves. When troops went to the front in 1916, they started out in groups and dispersed as they came closer to the line. By contrast, the Ossuary was a common objective for all, bringing together remains collected from all parts of the battlefield. Pilgrimages culminated inside the cloister in silent meditation, as if keeping vigil over the dead.

The most organized of these veterans' pilgrimage were known as Fêtes de la Bataille, which one veterans' group began organizing in February 1927. The memorial service included a vigil in the Ossuary's cloister. At dawn a procession made its way around the cloister and laid wreaths on each burial vault. The national day of mourning on 12 July 1936 was somewhat different: at eight in the evening, 20,000 veterans, including German and Italian delegations, marched from the Sainte-Fine chapel to the cemetery of Douaumont, where each man took up a position in front of a grave. Together, they took an oath to preserve the peace, and then laid wreaths on the steps of the Ossuary. These veterans' services were memorial services, civilian and pacific in character. *La Marseillaise* was not sung; there was no military parade or presentation of arms, and there were no official speeches. Participants were expected to meditate in silence. Given the immensity of the sacrifice being commemorated, peace was the supreme value, taking precedence over individual and national pride.

Different in tone were the Fêtes de la Victoire organized from 1920 on by the city of Verdun. These ceremonies sustained the 'national memory' of Verdun as opposed to the 'veterans' memory'. The date chosen, 23 June, was rather arbitrary, since the final German offensive launched on that date was finally turned back on 12 July; but the latter date was too close to Bastille Day, 14 July. Spread out over two days, the ceremonies included a parade in which battle flags were carried into the city, a religious service, a review of the troops, official speeches, and a military parade, ending with a memorial vigil at the Ossuary. The inauguration ceremonies of 1927 and the even more spectacular ceremonies of 1932 belong to the same tradition as the Fêtes de la Victoire: although the dead were not forgotten, the focus was on celebrating France and its victory.

There is no better indicator of the character of the Fêtes than the personalities chosen to preside over them. Two-thirds of the ceremonies through 1952 were presided over by generals and marshals. In the interwar years Marshal Pétain officiated at Verdun on four separate occasions, and President Poincaré twice. Clearly, this was an official and patriotic commemoration.

After the Second World War, however, the climate changed. In 1954, Germany joined NATO. In 1956, Germans visiting the battlefield were officially received by the municipal authorities of Verdun. Franco-German reconciliation and the construction of Europe were the order of the day. Civilians now presided over the Fêtes de la Victoire. The difference between official commemorations and veterans' rites dwindled. On 22 September 1984, the president of France and the chancellor of West Germany went to the cemetery of Douaumont and stood hand in hand in a moment of silence.

The character of pilgrimages to the site also changed. As veterans grew older, it became increasingly difficult for them to explore the battlefield. As the years went by, their numbers dwindled. Nature reclaimed the site, and forests soon covered the shell craters. Tourists, who had been coming to Verdun since 1919, grew more numerous as vacations were democratized and the automobile made travel easier. Half a million people visited Verdun every year. Many knew only that a memorable battle had taken place there, but they had no idea how the battle had been waged or when or over what terrain. They needed explanations, guides, and signs. As the last survivors of the battle carried their emotion-laden memories to the grave, it became increasingly necessary to organize commemoration: history was substituted for fervour.

In 1939, a veterans' group from the Meuse decided to build a 'veterans' bureau' at Verdun as other groups had done in Le Havre, Orléans, and elsewhere. The plans called for a huge library and diorama, but the Second World War forced the project to be abandoned. The Comité National du Souvenir de Verdun, which had existed since 1926, was revived in 1951. Under the leadership of Maurice Genevoix, the author of five remarkable books on his war experience, and then a member of the French Academy, who had been wounded on the battlefield of Verdun in 1915, the group decided in 1959 to build a memorial on the battlefield; it was inaugurated in 1967.

At the veterans' memorial visitors can obtain maps, photographs, and documents of all sorts concerning the battle. There is also a museum where one can view the types of weapons used in 1916, along with historical reconstructions that make it easier to imagine what the battlefield was like. The memorial is an educational rather than a religious institution. Now that the last veterans are gone, teaching visitors about the battle of Verdun is the only way to perpetuate its memory.

From Memory to Symbol

The commemorative ceremonies that take place at Verdun thus offer three distinct and complementary memories of the battle: the official, patriotic one; the veterans' meditative, testimonial memory; and the historical memory that is imparted to tourists. But Verdun is not a national symbol solely by virtue of these local commemorations. Just as the 'relay system' meant that large numbers of soldiers experienced the hell of the battlefield, the interwar pilgrimages and commemorations made hundreds of thousands of French people aware of what had happened there. Other discourses have also shaped the nation's collective consciousness: Verdun has been spoken of constantly since 1916. What have people said about it?

There is no single answer to this question. What people said changed over the years. Broadly speaking, one can distinguish three successive waves of books about Verdun.[27] The first began at the time of the battle and culminated in 1922 or 1923. By then the field was saturated, and there was no outpouring of new works to mark the tenth anniversary of the event. In this first period, two discourses with which we are already familiar were juxtaposed. The official, patriotic discourse was promoted by early historians of the battle such as Henry Bordeaux, who told the story from the point of view of the general staff, in which generals and colonels play a more prominent role than ordinary soldiers.[28] Books in this category naturally emphasized the heroic and moved easily in the narrative space defined by staff communiqués on the one hand and feats of arms on the other. The veterans' discourse took precisely the opposite tack: it highlighted the testimony of individuals, who claimed to give not an overview of what happened but an authentic account of the typical soldier's experience. Some of the best war memoirs appeared in this period, including those of Delvert, Gaudy, Jubert, and Daniel Mornet.[29] The brass had no place in these remembrances of mud, fear, misery, and death.

In the late 1920s people began to take renewed interest in books about the war and especially about Verdun, as if Verdun had begun to epitomize the entire war. A second wave of publications appeared at this time and continued until 1939. The two discourses that had characterized the earlier period remained but now merged into one. It was no longer possible to ignore the horror of the battle or to paper it over with patriotic homilies. There were too many bodies buried in the Ossuary, and too many films, such as *Verdun, souvenirs d'histoire* (1928) and *Les Croix de bois* (1931), showed unforgettable images of the daily shelling.[30] Emblematic value can thus be ascribed to the two books that mark the beginning and the end of this period: Marshal Pétain's *La Bataille de Verdun* (1929), which struck just the right tone in its moving description of the soldier's plight, and Jules Romains's *Verdun* (1938), which represented an impressive effort to synthesize diverse points of view.

The most characteristic feature of the period lies elsewhere, however: in the attempt by veterans to regain control of their own history, the history of their war. More than a decade had passed since the end of hostilities. Memories had faded; nightmares had subsided. Veterans claimed an increasingly important role in national life. André Tardieu became the first veteran of the Great War to head the government, and the Chamber of Deputies expressed the belated gratitude of the nation by approving veterans' pensions. Writing the history of the war was no longer a task that could be left to men who had not fought in it or who had served only behind the lines. The moment for a combatants' history had arrived.

André Ducasse led the way with his introduction to *La Guerre racontée par les combattants,* a collection of excerpts from the best published war stories that Flammarion brought out in 1932. But Verdun was not the only subject of this work. In 1933, Jacques Péricard published his monumental *Verdun,* a work of 534 large-format pages copiously illustrated with contemporary photographs. This book sold extremely well, and left its mark on subsequent writing about the battle. Péricard had solicited the testimony of veterans, more than 6,000 of whom responded to his queries. Roughly half of these unpublished eyewitness accounts found their way into the text, which wove a detailed chronological narrative around them: here was the story of the battle told sector by sector, day by day, in some cases hour by hour. In addition, each chapter included appendices dealing with general questions such as replacements, medical services, and so on. Based on the most pertinent individual accounts, these digressions kept the chronological narrative from becoming monotonous.

Péricard's *Verdun* was important for more than just the richness of its documentation. The text succeeded in combining official, patriotic history with the testimony of combatants. It attempted to bring the broad view of the battle, the staff view of the generals, colonels, and majors, who were abundantly cited, together with the soldier's viewpoint. But the two vantage points were very different, and the battle that one saw from each was not the same battle. Rather than a synthesis, this *Verdun* was a compromise.

In fact, the book embodied the very contradiction that many combatants, including Péricard himself, knew from their own experience. Péricard had fought at Verdun as a lieutenant and in 1918 had published a controversial book entitled *Debout les morts.* The central episode of this vibrant tale of patriotism is the moment when Péricard, whose position has been overrun by the enemy, galvanizes his men by shouting 'Debout les morts! [Dead men arise!]'. A stereotypical tale of heroism, in other words. Still, the book did not deserve the stinging criticism that Norton Cru levelled at it. In fact, it is an interesting example of how the combatant's memory was transformed by the memory of the rear, for it was not Péricard himself who had shouted 'Dead men arise!'; it was Maurice Barrès, who, in his preface, had used the phrase in commenting on Péricard's narrative. To be sure, Péricard had authenticated it, as it were, by accepting it as the title of his book. He believed in glory, in heroism. In *Verdun* he expressed outrage that Norton Cru had cast doubt on the authenticity of the Trench of Bayonets, as if the criticism were tantamount to a denial of the immense sacrifice that was made at Thiaumont. But Péricard was also a soldier of the ranks, who knew what the battle was really like and had experienced its true misery. He saw courage in the routine events of the soldier's life, and had no use for patriotic bluster or showpiece offensives designed to impress people in the rear. He encouraged the myth even as he sought to win a hearing for the authentic voice of the soldier.

It was probably about this time that the public image of the battle became established. In the national imagination Verdun was noted above all for the most monstrous shelling of any war – monstrous in both intensity and duration (six months). The Germans had massed more than 1,200 artillery pieces, or one gun for every twenty-five yards of the front. On 1 July, they had fired twenty-one million howitzer shells larger than 120 mm in calibre since the beginning of the battle, and no doubt even more shells of smaller calibre, or roughly one shell for every square yard of the battlefield. This heavy shelling is what made the site look like a piece of lunar landscape. Verdun was equated in people's minds with shell craters.[31] Other characteristic features of the battle were also consequences of the heavy shelling. Moving reinforcements up to the front was incredibly difficult. 'Every night,' Pétain later wrote, 'one watched small columns climb the slopes toward the smoke of battle on the plateaux: lines of grave, silent men, conscious of the fate that lay in store for them.'[32] All lines of communication converged on the few points where it was possible to cross the Meuse. The communications trenches were crowded with supply details and replacement troops and of course with the wounded who were being evacuated. Pinpointed by the enemy, they were subject to frequent shelling, and many men were killed or wounded on their way to and from the front. The closer the exhausted troops came to the front, the shallower the trenches became, until they were little more than shallow depressions flanked by shell craters. 'We stepped over the dead and wounded. Not a tree in the forest remained intact. Here and there a section of trunk was left standing. The rocky ground was strewn with grenades, ammunition, weapons, overcoats, corpses, and bodies that were still breathing.'[33] At night replacement troops tried to rendezvous with guides from the units they were relieving. If they missed the rendezvous, the men on point could suddenly find themselves face-to-face with the Germans. Or else, 'by the light of exploding shells and flares, the relief troops might discover the remains of the unit they were supposed to replace at the bottom of a shell crater'.[34]

Once a unit reached the front lines, it was in for four to six days of living hell. Replacements were repeatedly given the simple order to move into 'vaguely organized lines of shell craters' and to hold their ground at all costs.[35] Although there might be intense but intermittent skirmishes with rifles or, more frequently, grenades, what most soldiers remembered about Verdun was the systematic, persistent, unrelenting, and merciless shelling. They came away with images of bodies pulverized or torn to shreds or buried alive. Shells crashed down on comrades in the next crater. Troops went hungry because the supply details rarely reached their destination. During the first few months of the battle they also suffered from the rain and cold, because there was no shelter and it was obviously impossible to light a fire. And the men became so terribly thirsty that they drank the foul water from shell craters, in which all sorts of debris lay rotting.

Like Auschwitz in the Second World War, Verdun came to symbolize a breach of the limits of the human condition. Defenceless soldiers were forced to lie on the bare, ravaged, devastated earth and were subjected to endless shelling. Cut off from human society, abandoned to the elements – rain, snow, wind, and cold – and unable to satisfy the most basic human needs, they found themselves shorn of the last vestiges of civilization. To be sure, these were tough, hardened men, used to sleeping on the ground, to working themselves into a stupor, to living without heat, and to surviving on the most meagre rations: the age of modern comforts and mass leisure had not yet arrived. Nevertheless, a week at Verdun was a journey to the outermost reaches of the human condition, beyond the imaginable.

And yet, despite their exhaustion, 'amid this living hell and against all probability, our men held out', Pétain wrote. The losses were terrible: some regiments returned from the front reduced to the size of a company. Most units suffered casualties of at least 50 per cent. The troops looked forward to the arrival of their relief as to a deliverance. Soldiers who returned from the front in the pre-dawn hours reeling with fatigue, their heads still pounding from the shelling, looked like nothing so much as ghosts:

> They marched with bowed heads and sad looks, bending beneath the weight of their packs and holding their mud-caked rifles by their slings.

The colour of their faces was almost the same as the colour of their over-coats. Mud had covered everything and dried, and new mud had caked upon the old. Their clothing and skin were covered with it . . . They did not have the strength to complain. They were like convicts just released from the prison of war, and when they looked up at the roofs of the village one read in their eyes unspeakable depths of pain. As they raised their faces, their features seemed trapped in the dirt and twisted by suffering. Their mute faces seemed to cry out in horror at the incredible awfulness of their martyrdom.[36]

The public image of the battle that predominated in the period 1929–1939 thus achieved a sort of balance. It reflected an accurate and realistic idea of how soldiers had lived and died, and did not equate their courage with ignorance or contempt for danger. Pétain wondered whether the soldier of Verdun had been touched by some special grace that had made a hero of him. He answered, rejecting the official military line: 'We who knew him, we know that he was quite simply a man, with his virtues and his weakness, a man of our people, whose thoughts and emotions remained attached to his family circle, his workshop, his office, or the farm where he grew up.' In doing his duty conscientiously, 'he went to the front without enthusiasm, to be sure, but also without faltering'.[37] The hero of Verdun was not the soldier who charged the enemy with fixed bayonet out of love for the fatherland or hatred of the Boche. He was rather the ghost who returned from the line muddy and haggard, but having held his ground. What France remembered about Verdun was that the nation had survived because men had been willing to endure an inhuman, dreadful, and murderous ordeal.

The Second World War buried the memory of Verdun and replaced it with memories of still more dreadful atrocities. Histories of Verdun ceased to be runaway bestsellers. It was not until the late 1950s that new works on the battle began to appear, and these were joined by still others on the occasion of the fiftieth anniversary of the battle in 1966.[38] These were shorter than the works that had appeared in the 1920s and 1930s, and addressed to a public that counted fewer and fewer veterans of the battle among its number. The crucial need was no longer to defend a particular interpretation of what had happened at Verdun, but to keep people from forgetting about it entirely. The new texts were therefore both more didactic and more general. They aimed at giving an overview of the battle to readers who knew very little about it, rather than a blow-by-blow account directed at men who had been there. J. H. Lefebvre's book, published by Durassié in 1960, is a richly detailed narrative history, yet still far from the book by Péricard that it replaced: it was not a pious monument to the memory of those who had died at Verdun. Just as the veterans' memorial and museum supplanted the Ossuary of Douaumont, history supplanted the age of comradely commemoration.

'Anyone who was not at Verdun was not in the war.' These words, spoken while the battle still raged, suggest a lasting identification with the experience on the part of those who shared it.[39] For me and my contemporaries, Verdun epitomizes the whole of the Great War. It was not only the war's climax, but also its essence. It was not only the decisive battle that determined the outcome of the conflict, but the battle that exhibited the features most characteristic of that particular war.

Verdun was also a 'pacific' battle. It is remembered all the more vividly because it was neither a humiliating defeat nor an act of aggression. Nations remember their defeats, but bury them in the depths of their unconscious: where are the commemorations of the debacle of 1870 or the disaster of June 1940? On the other hand, peoples are reluctant to perpetuate the memory of their conquests: to do so would be to remind former enemies of their humiliation and to boast of having been a predator state. Verdun was a defensive victory: the German advance was turned back. In a broader sense, the memory of Verdun thus coincides with the memory of the Great War as a whole: it was a war brought on by German aggression, and waging it was legitimate because France was merely defending its own soil. Winning the war did not mean taking anything away from the enemy; France simply remained France. With Verdun the nation affirmed itself, but not at the expense of anyone else. This was a flattering idea, in which national pride was coupled with international morality. France could be seen as the unvanquished warrior fighting on behalf of justice and liberty. It could flaunt the banner of Napoleon alongside the principles of 1789: hence it offered what can be called *une certaine idée de la France.*

Finally, Verdun was the memory of a terrible and supremely deadly ordeal. Even if few French people today can fully appreciate what the suffering of the soldiers at Verdun was like, most people have at least a vague idea that hundreds of thousands of soldiers (roughly 270,000 in fact) died there under dreadful conditions. The details of this enormous sacrifice may have faded from memory, but the lesson has been piously preserved: that it is life which is sacrosanct, not death, and no matter how legitimate or necessary some wars may be, peace is worth more. In the memory of the French people the soldiers of Verdun live in grave and respectful silence as exemplary heroes, to be sure, but also as innocent victims whose lives might better have been spared. By making Verdun a key element of its national memory, France is saying not only that the greatest victories are defensive, but that the price of victory may surpass all measure.

The transformation of the event into a symbol has erased many of its details, however. It is receding ineluctably into the past, and our national memory is the poorer for it. For French people today, Verdun is not a clear and vital memory, but a vague idea. People know that it was horrible, and that in the end it was a victory; but it is no longer part of today's world. With each passing day the ordinary men who suffered and died at Verdun sink deeper into another universe, into a past that is gone for ever.

Symbolically, therefore, Verdun marks the boundary between two worlds. The cold world in which men were capable of enduring conditions that have become unimaginable and of sacrificing their lives for the sake of duty ended at Verdun in a blaze of glory. The new world is one in which the nature and meaning of patriotism have changed. The spectre of war remains, and slaughter on a vast scale is still possible, but now it is mankind as a whole that is threatened, and not France as such. With today's tanks, missile, and nuclear weapons, war no longer means a slow accumulation of individual deaths through a lengthy ordeal of suffering. The world may again experience horror, but in new, more brutal, more rapid and massive forms that do not require the inner consent of their victims.

Because of this, Verdun occupies a unique place in France's national memory. It is not one episode among others, one element in a series, but rather the apogee of nineteenth-century patriotism, which culminated in an immense sacrifice, a sacrifice that was at once superhuman and supremely inhuman. Thus the collective imagination can neither forget it nor truly comprehend it. The memory of Verdun includes an irreducible share of sacred mystery, which is what infuses it with the glow of a legend.

Notes

1. So said Falkenhayn, and the Crown Prince worried about it: 'What worried me was the idea often expressed by the head of the general staff

that in this way we would succeed in 'bleeding' the French army, regardless of whether or not the city fell': Hohenzollern, Crown Prince William, *Souvenirs de guerre*, Fr. Trans. (Paris, Payot, 1923), p. 205.

2. The expression was used by Marshal Pétain in *La Bataille de Verdun* (Paris, Payot, 1929), p. 9. Pétain did not accept this interpretation, and believed that the Germans were trying to break through France's front lines. The alternative between Belfort and Verdun is mentioned by the Crown Prince.

3. Speech by General Dubail at the Trocadéro to mark the anniversary of the battle, *Le Temps*, 24 Feb. 1919. The lack of defensive preparations at Verdun is well known. General Herr, commander of the fortified region, issued numerous warnings, which were relayed in December by his deputy, Col. Driant, who would later die in the Caures Forest at the beginning of the battle. On 16 Dec. 1915, Gallieni warned Joffre of gaps in French defences at Verdun.

4. Raymond Poincaré, *Au service de la France*, vol. 8, *Verdun 1916* (Paris, Plon, 1931), pp. 87ff.

5. General Serrigny, *Trente ans avec Pétain* (Paris, Plon, 1959), p. 64. Pétain also alluded to the difference between himself and Poincaré, but without going as far as Serrigny, in *La Bataille de Verdun*, p. 68.

6. Jean de Pierrefeu, *G.Q. G. secteur 1* (Paris, Éditions G. Grès, 1922), vol. 1, p. 127, and Pétain, *La Bataille de Verdun*, p. 68.

7. Pétain, *La Bataille de Verdun*, p. 71.

8. Gérard Canini, *'L'Illustration* et la bataille de Verdun', in *Verdun 1916: Actes du colloque international sur la bataille de Verdun* (Verdun, Association Nationale du Souvenir de la Bataille de Verdun, University of Nancy II, 1976), pp. 175–85.

9. Poincaré, *Au service de la France*, vol. 8, *Verdun 1916*, p. 350.

10. Louis Barthas, *Les Cahiers de guerre de Louis Barthas, tonnelier (1914–1919)* (Paris, Maspero, 1978), pp. 280–1.

11. Captain Albert Garnier of the 52nd Infantry Regiment, as cited in Jacques Péricard, *Verdun* (Paris, Librairie de France, 1933), p. 278.

12. Barthas, *Les Cahiers*, p. 282.

13. The song is well known. Private Élie Vincent of the 107th battalion of *chasseurs* confirms that it was sung in this context at this date. See Antoine Prost, *Les Anciens Combattants et la société française, 1914–1939*, vol. 3, *Mentalités et idéologies* (Paris, Presses de la Fondation Nationale des Sciences Politiques, 1977), p. 10.

14. See Ch. 12 of Jules Romains, *Verdun* (Paris, Flammarion, 1938).

15. Pétain, *La Bataille de Verdun*, p. 39. A little later, he returns to this subject and contrasts reality with imagery. The country 'imagined them as veritable supermen, always ready to perform prodigious feats. These exalted popular images included their share of exaggeration, as the public, believing in the intervention of mysterious forces, was apt to neglect our soldiers' true misery and the limits of what they could accomplish' (p. 86).

16. Roland Andreani and Jules Maurin, 'La Bataille de Verdun enseignée aux jeunes Français à travers les manuels d'histoire des classes terminales', in *Verdun 1916: Actes du colloque international*, pp. 199–218. The authors rightly point out that elementary school textbooks devote too little space to the battle to permit extensive analysis. This very brevity, I find, indicates an absence of heroization.

17. I wish to take this opportunity to express my deepest gratitude to Prof. Claire Andrieu, who was kind enough to do research for me at Verdun and to whom I am indebted for all of my local information and much additional documentation as well.

18. Letter preserved in the Bibliothèque Nationale, Fonds Barbusse. The artist was inviting the author of *Le Feu* to come to his home to see his drawings.

19. Testimony of M. Abel Cruchard: see Prost, *Les Anciens Combattants*, vol. 3, p. 81.

20. Pierre Mac Orlan, *Verdun* (Paris, Nouvelle Éditions Latine, 1935), p. 31. The book is part of a literary tourist collection.

21. Tourists who visit the famous trench are presumably surprised to discover that there are no shell craters in the ground beneath the protective roof.

22. Jean Norton Cru, *Témoins: Essai d'analyse et de critique des souvenirs de combattants édités en français de 1915 à 1928* (Paris, Les Étincelles, 1929), pp. 33–6. Some people felt that Cru, himself a veteran, was unduly critical. Among them was Jacques Péricard, the author of *Verdun*, who expressed his views on pp. 272–5. But Cru's arguments are difficult to refute. What is more, Péricard does not even attempt to refute them, but merely dismisses them out of hand, as when he objects that it simply doesn't matter whether the trench was initially referred to as the 'trench of rifles' rather than of 'bayonets'. He concludes by saying that the Trench of Bayonets 'is neither more nor less entitled than any other trench at Verdun' to symbolize the tenacity of French forces. Mac Orlan, who has harsh words for Cru in passing, says nothing at all about the trench, although he does discuss other battlefield monuments.

23. André Ducasse, Jacques Meyer, and Gabriel Perreux, *Vie et mort des Français 1914–1918* (Paris, Hachette, 1959), pp. 166–7.

24. Jacques-Henri Lefebvre, *Verdun, la plus grande bataille de l'histoire racontée par les survivants* (Paris, G. Durassié, 1960).

25. *Voir et comprendre. Verdun: Champ de bataille – Environs*, 5th ed. (Drancy, Éditions Mage, 1985), pp. 79–80.

26. This debate was extensively reported in the weekly *Journal des mutilés et réformés*. See especially the issues of 7 and 28 Sept. 1930, 19 Oct. 1930, and 2 Nov. 1930.

27. The incomplete but homogeneous catalogue of the Bibliothèque de Documentation Internationale Contemporaine includes 46 works in French

on Verdun published between 1916 and 1922, 9 between 1923 and 1928, 42 between 1929 and 1939, 2 between 1945 and 1958, and 27 between 1959 and 1969. This pattern is consistent with the publication of war narratives in general in the interwar years; but the second period includes more works about Verdun. See Prost, *Les Anciens Combattants*, vol 1. *L'Histoire* (Paris, Presses de la Fondation Nationale des Sciences Politiques), p. 133.

28. Henry Bordeaux, *La Victoire de Verdun* (Paris, 1916); *La Chanson de Vaux-Douaumont*, 2 vols (Paris, 1916 and 1917); *La Bataille devant Souville* (Paris, 1920).

29. Captain Charles Delvert, *Histoire d'une compagnie: Main de Massiges, Verdun, novembre 1915–juin 1916* (Paris, Berger-Levraut, 1918), part one of Delvert's *Carnets d'un fantassin*, published in their entirety by Albin Michel in 1935; Georges Gaudy, *Les trous d'obus de Verdun* (Paris, Plon-Nourrit, 1922); Raymond Joubert, *Verdun, mars, avril, mai 1916* (Paris, Payot, 1918); Daniel Mornet, *Tranchées de Verdun, juillet 1916–mai 1917* (Paris, Berger-Levrault, 1918). Mornet was a well-known professor of French literature in the Sorbonne.

30. In addition to the two films mentioned in the text, one could also cite *La grande parade* (1928), *À l'ouest rien de nouveau* (1930), *La patrouille de l'aube* and *Les anges de l'enfer* (1931), and *No man's land* (1932). I am grateful to Yves Blavier, the author of a master's thesis on Léon Moussinac, for making this list of films available.

31. From which Gaudy took the title of his work, *Les trous d'obus de Verdun*.

32. Speech delivered at the Ossuary of Douaumont on the occasion of the first inauguration, as printed in *Le Temps* (19 Sept. 1927). I thank Claire Andrieu for making this remarkable text available to me.

33. Henri Nicolle, 408th Infantry Regiment, quoted in Péricard, *Verdun*, p. 276.

34. Pétain speech, see Note 32.

35. These words can be found at the beginning of Canon Polimann's account of the Trench of Bayonets in Péricard, *Verdun*, p. 273.

36. Gaudy, *Les Trous d'obus*.

37. Pétain speech, see Note 32.

38. The success of the book by Ducasse, Meyer, and Perreux in 1959 suggests a renewal of interest in the First World War.

39. 'April 17: At midnight we reached a deep ravine that I will call the "ravine of flashes", for it was continually, repeatedly, uninterruptedly illuminated by shell explosions during the endless minutes that we spent in it. The noise in this ravine was as extraordinary as the illumination. Alongside me, motionless, an officer stood with his back to the explosions and carried on a conversation with a ghost: "Anyone who was not at Verdun", he said, "was not in the war"': Lieutenant Jacques d'Arnoux, 62nd Infantry Regiment, in Péricard, *Verdun*, p. 276.

3

The Contribution of the Republican Primary School to French National Identity

The republican school as a school for patriotism, and its dissemination throughout the great mass of the nation of a powerful source of shared identity, is both observable fact and a commonplace. Every analysis of the mobilization in 1914, for example, invokes the real patriotism of the primary school to explain why the revolutionary trade union militants went to their barracks and put on their uniforms instead of launching a general strike, as they had decided to do. Perhaps it is time to have another look at the well-known history of patriotism in primary schools, the school battalions with their wooden rifles from Déroulède's *Clairon* or the map of France 'wearing violet-coloured mourning for the lost provinces',[1] or the legendary primary teacher who concluded his final class by writing on the blackboard, 'you will become a soldier'. These stereotypes retain their impact, but we learn nothing from them: it is not news that the republican school was patriotic. The question that remains, however, is to ascertain by what means this objective was realized effectively, and precisely what kind of patriotism it disseminated.

George Mosse's *Fallen Soldiers*,[2] remarkable in many respects, gives new weight to this question. In effect, Mosse sees the war of 1914 as one of the sources of fascism. By making men accustomed to mass death, by naturalizing death – even taming it – the war, in his eyes, was a root cause of a brutalization of political life. What had been applied to external threats was now used against internal enemies. Mosse's thesis plays down the differences between France and Germany: the war had very different consequences for the two countries, for reasons that relate to differences in political cultures.[3] This contrast sends us back to the analysis of the particularities of national identity as it has historically been constructed in France. It is then less a matter of explaining the national cohesion which enabled France to pass through the ordeal of the war without falling apart than of understanding why French patriotism did not lead to a form of fascist nationalism. And this leads us back to the republican primary school and its achievements.

Geography

We can call on one of the finest experts on republican education, and one of the pioneers of cultural history in France, Maurice Crubellier, to act as guide. In a sensitive book[4] he considers primary-school teaching as a cultural undertaking and first interrogates, rightly, not how the French language is taught, but the 'general frame-works of school culture', that is the way in which it defines space and time through geography and history.

What is at stake in teaching geography far exceeds national identity; in reality it sets out a radical inversion of perspectives. For centuries mankind was the measure of the universe: geography and the metric system present pupils with a universal reference system, complete with a homogeneous and uniform rule. It proceeds from cosmography, 'the earth in space',[5] to address familiar landscapes. These it describes through general terms: mountains, plateaux, plains, lakes, rivers and streams, oceans. This apprenticeship in 'descriptive language' is also a 'conceptual style of analysis'. Such 'grammar of the landscape' removes specificity from concrete geographical realities and detaches them from the close familiarity that they represent for pupils.

There is here, without question, a desacralization, a de-romanticiz-ing of space. In this area as in many others, the primary school is on the side of areas of rational knowledge, of ideas that are susceptible to generalization. It is an attempt to locate space that is concrete, lived in, within abstract universal settings: but at the same time it moves towards the resacralization of one part of space – the national territory. Geography as it is taught, within a conceptual framework valid for the whole world, is that of France, the country on the map on the wall of every classroom.

Eugen Weber clearly appreciated the significance of this teaching when he raised the question of the image of 'the Hexagon',[6] but his reflections focused more on the Gallicizing of the peasants than on school geography. The Hexagon is an obvious concept for the French, because it returns to schools' usual educational patterns. Every schoolchild learned to draw maps of France and, to help them, teachers habitually used a simple geometric template – the hexagon – and then identified reference points such as the Cotentin peninsula or Lake Geneva half-way down one of the sides, thus simplifying the task of locating characteristic features that are otherwise inevitably imprecise. Geometry was a useful tool of map-making.

The use of geometry was not however purely an instrumental aid. It unified the representation of the national territory. France was drawn in its entirety, with the curves of its mountains and the twisting lines of its rivers. The message emphasizes the merits of this sweetly proportioned space, its temperate climate, the variety and richness of its natural resources. Above all, the geometric figure consolidates the concept of 'natural' frontiers, despite its complete lack of foundation. With the exception of Alsace-Lorraine, to which we shall return, the national identity is put forward for interpretation as complete, fully achieved. Other nations exist beyond the frontiers, equally legitimate nations, though less perfect and less fortunate. The geography of the primary school, the preparatory course for national identity, arises from no territorial claims, other than those implied by a 'civilizing' mission to the colonies. In this sense, it encourages no claims against neighbouring nations.

But hexagonal France is also the France of its *départements*. The republican school requires its pupils to recite the names of all the departments, with their prefectures and sub-prefectures, potential staging posts along the civil servant's peregrinations.[7] Insufficient thought has been given to the cultural significance of this systematic memorization by generations of French schoolchildren. It involves a political reading of the space. The France of the schoolroom is not only a country of mountains and rivers, it is the France of the State in a double sense: the State as the unified arena of the careers that education can offer in administration, the railways, and business – and also the State as Republic, with its rational and egalitarian administrative basis. The equality of the citizen begins with the equality of the *départements* within the State.

What the republican school accomplished in this respect made sense both scientifically and politically. Yet it could not succeed in educational and political terms without local reference. Emphasizing the geographical unity of the nation and the equivalence of its parts would not provide much room for local realities. The pre-1914 school ignored natural regions: yet to have meaning in a rural France it needed something concrete to offer schoolchildren in their village schoolrooms.

The republicans set great store by this, first out of concern to establish the Republic securely in each village: an unanchored school, a kind of colony, would turn the Republican state into a distant foreign power. Republicans had to cope with the strength of local identities, constructed by the communities and the Church and imbedded in folklore centuries old. Secondly, they feared a rural exodus, and saw urbanization as a major factor in social unrest. Politically, it was not enough for them that the school itself was securely established; it must also create a deep attachment to one's village.[8]

School geography was therefore required to present the discourse of both national identity and local roots. This significant tension was resolved through the deep attachment of the teachers to their origins. Recruited locally, they knew their own terrain and, moreover, they wrote detailed monographs about their villages for the universal exhibition of 1889. They were expected to know their local surroundings perfectly, and around 1882 they contributed information about their villages to the national mapping of France.[9] In their teaching, specific examples taken from their immediate surroundings were used to illustrate more general questions. It was an effective approach when it was a matter of explaining the adaptation of human activity to the natural constraints of the landscape, climate and soil; but this vision of France ignored differences in social or economic status, and even more in cultural matters, when it focused on physical geography. Conceived primarily for a nation of rural inhabitants – and on this point Eugen Weber[10] was entirely accurate – it treated natural features such as climate, relief or soil types as the only real reason for local differences.

Attention to local factors intensified on the eve of the 1914 war[11] – perhaps an indication that the primary aim underlying the construction of a national identity was under threat. In nearly half the departments the society for local studies offered dictation exercises in local history and geography. In 1920 regional geography was introduced into official school curricula. The department, however, is obviously not a geographical unit, and the definition of 'regions' is very difficult. Regional geography was therefore limited generally to the neighbouring countryside, defined as a limited extension of the familiar village setting.

School geography was successful in implanting national identity in this way and, because of this, in making this national identity the property of every Frenchman. It was not enough to teach the existence of a land called France: it was further necessary for pupils to take possession of this land as their own. The appropriation of 'my' country could only be expressed on the proven basis of the continuity linking local attachments to national ones.[12]

History

The republican educational culture also depended on a structured pattern of time that is familiar today but that was profoundly unfamiliar to the peasants and workers of the nineteenth century. The time-scale by which they lived differed very greatly from that of our own period. It was still the era of natural time, running from sunrise to sunset, not the time of hours and minutes as shown on the face of clocks and still-rare watches; they listened for church bells ringing the angelus to be aware of mealtimes and the end of the day's labour. In the cities factory sirens played a similar role. In the country-side, the passage of the days was part of a series of cycles, immutably renewed from year to year: the cycle of crops, ploughing, sowing and harvest; the liturgical cycle punctuated by the great seasonal festivals: Christmas, Easter, the Assumption, All Saints; the cycle of traditional folklore, with feast days, carnival, Saint John's or Mart-inmas.[13] This cyclical calendar moulded a sense of time as slowly flowing, repetitive, immutable. It was a time-scale that shaped human communities and individual lives, outside personal control; the time of tradition and ancestral experience, permanent, not a pattern of transformation nor of human efficacy.

The teaching of history in the primary school proposes a different temporal framework: a universal time, a common form of reference for the whole of humanity – above all an orientated pattern, with meaning, direction, movement. This time-scale is to some extent creative, making the present different from the past, announcing a future that in its turn will differ from the present.

Schools did not, however, reject the cyclical calendar of tradition: they came to terms with it or, better, adopted it within their own school cycles, articulated around the opening of the school year, the school fête, prize-giving, the students' Certificate. The time of seasons, of works and of days, or failing that of the liturgy, appears in all the dictation exercises. We find here the spirit of compromise that ensured the success of the Republic. Time with direction does not exclude cyclical time; it superimposes itself on it and soon takes over, like the true calendar of a higher reality.

Much has been made of the patriotic aspect of history teaching in the primary school. Historians have shown how it established something like a collective set of legends, with a gallery of genuine or imaginary heroic figures such as Jeanne Hachette and the soldier Barra.[14] All this is accurate, but does not point out the true originality of such teaching. There was undoubtedly a shift in emphasis, with an imagery of religious faith yielding to an imagery of patriotic heroes. Yet apart from this change of intentions, what the Republican school would inculcate in its pupils when presenting them with illustrious figures was not different from what the catechism proposed: courage and virtue remained models of personal behaviour. The novelty came partly from lining up these great figures in an ordered chronological series and partly from including a criterion of social utility in their selection. Beyond the contrast between explicit objectives, the difference between republican history and sacred history is profoundly cultural. It lies in the chronological ordering by which it advances, on the nature of the evidence and the inclusion of benefactors of humanity, inventors or scholars, in its pantheon.

Before validating the Republic, the teaching of history thus operates to instil a new temporal framework. It constructs the civic, political, economic and technical temporality of human activity within society. This linear and directed time of history bears a name, imbued with a strong political and ideological charge: the name of Progress.

While analysing the electoral manifestos of 1881 I was struck by the observation that the most discriminating lexical contrasts opposed the vocabulary of the threat on the right with that of the long march of the left. To propose to 'step out boldly along the road to the future' was to proclaim oneself a republican, without equivocation. 'Progress' is a key word in the republican vocabulary.[15] The expression is electorally powerful because it is more than propaganda; it refers to a concrete reality, based above all on economic evolution but visible to all, a factor of which the republican school takes pains to create awareness in order to use it for the credit of the régime.[16] On the eve of 1914, the French no longer doubted that they lived in an era of progress. At Mazières-en-Gâtine, for example, progress lay in objects as it did in attitudes; this, to quote Roger Thabault's subtitle, is the 'rise of a people':

All the land is cultivated. The houses are clean and spacious. Vehicles and bicycles fill the area round the town hall. In the public hall, men in substantial and comfortable working clothes or in their Sunday best [. . .] listen to one of their number, a former worker who is now a legislator. Everyone understands and speaks French [. . .] A revolution was achieved around 1880, in objects, habits and minds [. . .] A new faith was born, creating efforts and happiness, a feature both of progress and of social stability that proved capable of arousing the finest devotion.[17]

Naturally, this sense of time as progress was the red carpet that the school spread at the feet of the Republic. Economic and material progress was inseparable from progress in science and culture. It was the work of men such as Gutenberg, Palissy, Parmentier and Pasteur, and institutions such as the school. The ascent towards affluence and well-being, comfort and hygiene, is simultaneously a historic rise towards civic equality and liberty, towards the abolition of feudal rights and privileges, towards the right to vote. Here the Revolution appears as the inaugural and founding break that the Republic alone extends and completes.

The proof of progress achieved in every domain gives the French a feeling of superiority over other nations, yet without any sense of rejection or exclusivity. Here, I feel, lies the core of a national identity that is inseparable from republican pride.

The Republic

On the eve of the 1914 war French people were deeply conscious of the originality of living in a Republic. Germany, Austria, Italy, Spain and Great Britain were monarchies. France was the only republican regime, with the sole exception of the United States. Other exceptions, such as those of Latin America, were ignored. French national identity merged with republican identity.

This association of ideas was so powerful that in the statuary of war memorials – the French reference is specifically to 'monuments to the dead', *monuments aux morts,* and not to victory – the two figures of the Nation and the Republic are often indistinguishable. This confusion does not date from the war. Maurice Agulhon observed among the 1870 war memorials around a dozen figures of France or the Nation crowned with the republican Phrygian bonnet, out of a total of around fifty monuments. France is indeed, as he said, 'this land in which the same mythic figure symbolizes simultaneously the

Republic as the ideal of democracy and Justice, the national State confronting the foreigner, and the administrative State confronting the dissenter or the taxpayer.[18] In the minds of most French people, France and the Republic are a single entity.

History teaching spread the belief that the Republic was the inevitable end-result of any national evolution, and towards which the whole of humanity was bound to move. The Republic is not in fact one particular regime, specific to France, a unique and historically explicable phenomenon: it is also, within the domain of rationality – that of political philosophy – the best possible regime, because it is the only one to treat humans as full citizens, and because a man is not fully a man unless he is a citizen. The Republic is not therefore valid only for the French: it has a universal value. Hence the claims, difficult to understand today, that were frequently voiced in France in the nineteenth century: 'Everyone has two countries, his own and France.'

The Republic means primarily civic equality, the same law for all, protection against arbitrariness. This feeling undoubtedly includes an element of illusion, for the Republic does not eliminate all illegitimate favour. It also contains an exaggeration, for other regimes are equally capable of respecting human rights. *Habeas corpus* was not a French invention. Nonetheless, in these popular aspects republican rule conforms profoundly to the egalitarian aspirations of the French. No royal court, no uniforms, few *ex officio* privileges. We can understand the heartfelt remark of the soldier from the Meuse who, on 2 August 1914, encountered his parliamentary deputy André Maginot in his barracks: 'To see a former Under-Secretary of State for War turned into an ordinary private soldier upsets all ideas of hierarchy. Fundamentally, that is pleasing to egalitarian tastes, and he makes no secret of it . . . "After all, the Republic is something fine" he remarked after a moment.'[19]

Egalitarian aspirations provided an umbrella for powerful interests. The arbitrariness of princes had long been perceived as a very real threat. The peasants had not forgotten that part of their land came from the national estate, seized by the Revolution from the clergy or the nobility, and they feared that the former owners would take it back. In one place the rumour ran that the marquis had more than a hundred yokes in his château to which he intended to harness the peasants.[20] In another, at the end of the Second Empire a bishop who made a display of personal insignia derived from aristocratic tradition harboured the fantasy of an imminent return of the tithe.[21]

But egalitarian aspiration was also, and above all, a matter of dignity. In the eyes of the peasant who aspired to independence, any superiority that did not depend on merit was felt as a humiliation. This was one of the reasons for valuing education: there are only two sources of legitimate superiority – education and election. Egalitarianism rests on the assertion of the absolute value of the individual, who does not acquire his rights from his membership of one or another specific community; moreover, the French Republic, still today, alone in Europe, does not recognize any community within itself.[22] The rights of the individual are part of his essence as a human, a rational being and, as such, imbued with an absolute value. As part of this culture, individualism and egalitarianism are one and the same.[23]

The *locus classicus* of this individualism is the Declaration of the Rights of Man and of the Citizen, which is taught in primary schools. The Republic stands on these principles and guarantees that they are respected. It ignores all titles of nobility and makes public appointments through competition. Above all, it definitively abolishes privileges,[24] because it subjects power to universal manhood suffrage. Equality as a citizen is the basis of individual equality within French society. Setting women aside, the French learn that they are all electors while the British are not, and that the suffrage in Germany is unequal. That all men have the vote is a source of collective pride.

It is true that part of the working class sets little store by formal democracy in the state, at least in its discourse. This de-valorization arises partly because, unlike their British and German equivalents, they had not had to fight to win the right to vote. But among revolutionary syndicalists, such views also stem from republican egalitarianism pushed to its ultimate consequences: the rejection of any directing agency whatever, perceived as a challenge to the liberty of the citizen. This point of view was expressed clearly by Pelloutier in 1895: '*It is not our intention only to prepare for a revolution consisting of a simple transmission of powers. We wish to accustom the proletariat to doing without governors. We should therefore advise, instruct but not direct.*'[25] It is not a question of reneging on the gains of the Revolution, but of superseding them. This would be apparent when the principles of 1789 appeared in danger, as after the right-wing demonstrations of February 1934 for example: working-class mobilization was prompt at such moments.

Patriotism or Nationalism?

It is in this cultural context that we must consider the question of French patriotism on the eve of war in 1914. At this time, France was not nationalist: it was patriotic and pacific. This was not a natural trait; it was the result of a construction, of a presentation of history. France was not a pacific nation throughout its history: it conquered Europe under Napoleon I, and derived some pride from this. This tradition had not completely disappeared, and there was something of a revival immediately before the war. However, this revival occurred mainly among literary circles, whose position was defined precisely in reaction to the overwhelming majority of Frenchmen, who rallied to the Republic.[26] Republican national identity won the day over militarist or nationalist currents at the end of political confrontations throughout the nineteenth century.

Originally the Nation – with a capital N – acquired self-consciousness in the face of royal power, confronting the king in the Revolution rather than confronting foreigners in conquest. For revolutionaries, and for republicans who take possession of their heritage, in the powerful words of Saint-Just at the trial of Louis XVI: 'No one can reign in innocence; all kings are tyrants and usurpers.' Historically, the Nation, in France, is primarily the whole body of citizens in that they hold sovereignty; the Nation is the true and only legitimate sovereign.

This founding discovery subsequently validated expansion in Europe: it was a matter of setting up sister republics. Then came a slide under Napoleon into conquest pure and simple. Yet in one way the alibi of the emancipation of peoples was not a matter of indifference; it came to be taken seriously. France adopted the cause of national independence in Italy, Greece and Poland, heart and soul; Napoleon III was never so warmly applauded by the people of Paris as in 1859, when he went off to fight for independence in Italy. And in another way, revolutionary tradition was still very much alive: this was clear in the 1840 crisis with Lamartine's *Marseillaise de la Paix*.[27]

The republicans began by cultivating revenge. This was the time of Déroulède's *Chants du soldat*, of school battalions and the little book of history by Lavisse (1884),[28] although the Boulanger crisis and then the Dreyfus Affair showed how nationalist and militarist dangers threatened the Republic. Nationalists challenged universal suffrage: the well-being of the nation was for them the supreme law, the end which justifies all means. What was the value of citizens in such a case? For republicans, nationalism is the negation of the State of right, the ruin of citizenship, that is to say both of liberty and the right to choose who governs. To eliminate this threat they must build an identity creating a true attachment to the nation as a whole, while at the same time preventing this link from justifying an authoritarian regime. The pedagogy of Republican national identity is but a means of achieving this goal.

Yet it is not enough to present the France of *départements* and of the Rights of Man, not as a people, a race or a language. It is not enough to inculcate the conviction that France is a Republic, meaning that it obeys the only regime consonant with reason, and the only one founded on right and equality. It is not enough to ask pupils to love France because it is a Republic. They must also be protected against nationalist impulses.

The first antidote is a moral one: the same principles operate for those who govern and for the citizen, for States and for the individual. I have stressed elsewhere the significance of this point: the republican catechism, like its Catholic counterpart, asserts the uniqueness of the moral element. There are not two sets of moral values, one appropriate to ordinary people and another that could enable governors to violate their promises and to act immorally, even in the defence of the general interest: the end does not justify the means. Nor is there one moral standard for individuals and another for a community, of whatever kind. The school that teaches its strong pupils not to beat the smaller ones in the playground is also teaching them the mutual respect that nations owe each other.

The republican school finds a second antidote in the relative intermediary position that it accords to love of one's country, placing it between love for one's local 'country' and love for the whole of humanity. Patriotism is part of an ensemble of solidarities that strips it of any exclusivity. It is difficult to make it evident in English, for the translation necessarily uses different words when French stresses continuity by using the same word (*Patrie*) with different adjectives (*petit patrie, grand Patrie*). A guide known and followed by all primary-school teachers ends by prescribing: 'Taking the family home and the school community as your starting point, you will extend the domain of human solidarity from the locality, *la petite patrie*, to the homeland, *la Patrie,* and to Humanity.'[29] On the one side, the love for the 'country' – physical, concrete, in which pupils live: '*To love the homeland, begin by loving the locality. Study the land where you live, its products, its wealth. Ask which great men came from your village, your town, your province.'*[30] On the other, the love of humanity: in 1904 the congress of the *Ligue de l'enseigne-ment,* the Education League, facing the mounting tide of pacifism among elementary schoolteachers, adopted the resolution '*that secular and republican education should develop patriotic and humanitarian sentiments simultaneously, duty to the nation being the leading form and the most concrete of duties towards hum-anity*'.[31] The interlocking of successive and mutually compatible loyalties implies the continuity of attachments and the similarity of patterns of social organization. Arbitration in the conflicts that inevitably arise between nations is thus deflected into the sphere of right rather than that of power, as also is that of conflict between social groups within the nation or between individuals in a village. Progress consists of reaching beyond love of the Nation to that of humanity, as it used to consist of reaching beyond the love of modest local 'countries' *(petites patries)* to the love of France.

The Republic is therefore, by definition, a peaceful state. The message here is ambiguous, even contradictory. On the one hand the educational pantheon is populated with military heroes: even if they are honoured for their loyalty and courage, Du Guesclin, Joan of Arc, Vercingetorix and Bayard distinguished themselves in war. Gambetta leaving Paris in a balloon to continue the battle is offered as an example. On the other hand, however, war is presented as the source of wretchedness and grief. Louis XIV is severely criticized for having loved war too much. Admiration for the Napoleonic epic, the stuff of dreams, brings with it the realist's reminder of the cost of war – economic, political and above all human: the Emperor was respons-ible for too many wars, and they were too blood-soaked.

As war is the scourge of the common people but not of the powerful, the Republic is the finest guarantee against it. It not only protects against the arbitrariness of governors and against inequality: it places power in pacifist hands. The people, in fact, cannot want war. They have nothing to gain from it, contrary to the princes who pursue their personal or dynastic glory even when they are not seeking military prestige to recover wavering popularity. War exists because tyrants exist.[32] The French are convinced that had they not been ruled by an Emperor, the disastrous war of 1870 would not have happened. Revenge then ceases to constitute a national aim. Although they always see the annexation of Alsace and Lorraine as a crime, the textbooks of the early twentieth century, as opposed to those of 1880–90, do not see it as justification for a war. Some even evoke occasionally the hope of a peaceful settlement: 'A reasoned patriotism dictates both the vigour of attachment to the lost provinces and the preference for a peaceful solution.'[33]

The 4,000 primary school teachers of the pre-1914 period, who responded to Jacques and Mona Ozouf's enquiry in the 1960s, were well aware that on this point they differed from the generation that preceded them.[34] Patriots but not thirsty for revenge, they no longer wished for the return of Alsace to France at the price of a war. One example was the primary schoolteacher who called herself 'chauvinist' and who none the less 'believed too strongly in the unfailing progress of humanity to accept the idea of Revenge'.[35]

And yet war remains a possibility that must be faced with determination. The school must therefore reconcile two contradictory messages: 'Love France' and 'Hate war'. It achieves this by distinguishing between just and unjust wars. The first are defensive, wars of threatened rights undertaken by nations that refuse to be enslaved. The second are wars of conquest, which end in annexations achieved in disregard of the right of people to govern themselves, a popular principle in France, as we have seen. Colonial wars were certainly the exception, justified by a claim to be a civilizing force. But France must be only the soldier of Right. The government understood perfectly this defensive patriotism when in 1914 it decided to withdraw its troops ten kilometres inside the frontier, to make German aggression obvious: this step was the price the government paid to ensure the *Union sacrée*.

On the eve of war, primary education had thus drawn close together patriotism and love for Humanity. In the interwar years, veterans were to take up this theme time and time again. It raised the question of the very identity of the nation and of the regime. Because it is a Republic, France could not be other than pacific.

Nothing illustrates this profound consensus better than Roger Thabault's description of the 1914 electoral campaign in Mazières-en-Gâtine, in the west of the Poitou. In the public hall an old senator is campaigning for the Radical candidate, a peasant of humble background. He himself is a former tannery worker: the Republic is not lying when it claims to make political responsibilities available to the children of the ordinary people. The old senator is speaking of the possibility of war with Germany:

I can still hear his voice, I can see his gestures: 'Yes, it is possible that we will have war with Germany . . .'. A halt, stirrings in the audience. 'You must understand, Germany lacks the good fortune of being a Republic; it is governed by an Emperor who does what he likes.' There was a little laughter. How could you be civilized and not be a Republic! 'What we want, we who are Republicans, is peace. But if war were to come, we would tell the Germans after the victory to be Republicans like us, and the German Republic would be a sister to ours . . .

No one applauded; not a gesture, not a murmur. But the audience was held; an old man next to me had tears in his eyes. Young people beyond him, young peasants, were listening with a serious expression, their gaze tense and alert . . .[36]

This remarkable document raises the question of the link between these young people, these young peasants, their Republican convictions, and their experience of primary schooling.

Generally the efficiency of the French primary school in making Frenchmen, as Weber put it, has been taken for granted. Most testimonies come from teachers, and one might suspect that they would not conclude that their teaching was futile. Other evidence is needed in order to document this point of view more fully. However, the image of the golden age of the French Republican school is so overwhelming that, in itself, it can be taken as a kind of indirect evidence about the political success of this Republican project. Probably part of the difference between French and German political culture lies in the contrasts between early primary schooling in the two countries.

Conclusion

At the end of this investigation, two questions remain. The first is that of the nuances that such an overall picture requires. A number of chronological variations have appeared along the way; there are many others to be analysed, some of them regional – Lorraine is not the same as Brittany or Languedoc – and others social. We have no space here to go into greater detail in this study; but we must point out the risks of the generalizations we have offered here.

The second and even more difficult question concerns the impact of the war of 1914 on national identity. In overall terms, I feel that the war strengthened rather than weakened republican identity. The French hardly questioned the justice of their cause and the responsibility of Germany, confirmed by the Peace Treaty. But what is a just war, if the human cost is so high? Experience disturbed the naïve belief in the progress of civilization, for this positivist optimism carried little weight in the face of so many dead. It reinforced the rejection of war already present in primary education at the beginning of the century. Yet, through the same movement, it fed the conviction that it was necessary to create a League of Nations to avoid new horrors. The war thus gave a credible horizon to the progress of right and of civilization, a possible shape to the universal Republic of Victor Hugo. Faith in the advance of Humanity was too fine and too deep for primary teachers to give it up: rejection would require more and even greater horrors.[37]

Probably the decisive fact in the evolution of French national identity was the popularization of the Republic as a regime and as an ideology. The United Kingdom was increasingly acquiring the appearance of a Republic whose president was a king. Germany had adopted the Weimar Republic, emperors were disappearing; to some extent it was the end of French exceptionalism. The French saw themselves strengthened in their conviction of having been the first to be right, and in the unbelievably presumptuous idea that their country was the beacon for the whole of humanity.

The decisive break came the defeat of 1940, the creation of the Vichy regime, and the occupation. This series of humiliations led to a major revision. The breakdown of both the Republican tradition and the patriotic tradition undermined national identity itself. For, on the one hand, the republican tradition was rejected by the Vichy regime. Even if the vote of 10 July by both Chambers conformed to the constitution, by seizing power the very next day, and by suspending the Chambers, thereby suppressing any kind of election, Pétain introduced a hierarchical and authoritarian regime that was the opposite of a Republic. And how could the republican spirit be maintained in an occupied country, with no free press, and no elections? The French people were very critical of the Republic, but they remained attached to democratic freedom, which was the very legacy of the Republic. And, on the other hand, the national interest was confused. Who was the incarnation of the Nation: the Marshal, the defender of Verdun, remaining in France, deprived of military forces and political independence, and collaborating with Nazi Germany, or the General, continuing the war against the enemy, but from Great Britain, a country hated by many Frenchmen, and through whose subsidies he survived? Ordinary political cleavages were entirely blurred.

After the war, French national identity had to be rebuilt. The core of this reconstruction was the interpretation, supported both by the Communist Party and the Gaullists, of the dark years of the war as a betrayal of the French people by a minority of 'collaborators' who had to be punished. The *épuration* – the purge – was not a mere formality; it was rather severe: ten thousand people were executed, and more than 150,000 persons were prosecuted.[38] However, after some years, a consensus emerged that it no longer made sense to emphasize the divisions of the war. It became possible to occupy prominent political positions, even after having been a former supporter of the Vichy regime. For instance, M. Pinay, head of the 1952 cabinet, was a former member of Pétain's National Council. Then, the idea that the whole people of France had not been involved in the crimes or even the compromises of the dark years prevailed. The symbol of this unity of French people against the authoritarian regime of Vichy and the Nazi occupation, as well as of the unity of Resistance both outside and inside France, was the burial of Jean Moulin's ashes in the Pantheon in 1965.

This reconstructed unity was rather fragile. At the same time, France was involved in colonial wars, where atrocities were committed not only by regular troops but by conscripts as well. France was denounced in each session of the United Nations as opposing the peoples' right to freedom and the rights of mankind. Was this the behaviour and the stand of a Republican nation? The commemoration of Jean Moulin in the Pantheon happened just after the end of decolonization, during a short period where France felt that it had recovered its international standing and power and de Gaulle stood for challenging the United States' international power. Unfortunately, upholding the image of France as the incarnation of Republican ideals depended on the evasion of the fact that many more Frenchmen than it was commonly admitted had found a way to accommodate themselves to the Nazi occupation. This became evident in 1971, when the well-known movie of Ophuls, 'The Sorrow and the Pity' appeared, and when the history of the genocide emerged from the shadows. Hence it was necessary to include in the memory of what France was some qualifications. National identity was not again as brilliant and robust as it had been before the war; it included elements of uncertainty and of weakness.[39]

From this perspective, French acceptance of the European idea, which was rather rapid and deep, reflected both these weaknesses and the force of a revived Republican identity. On the one hand, national identity was not sufficiently strong to contest the development of a new collective identity. On the other hand, the power of the traditional French identity resided in its openness to embrace humanity as a whole. France had no need for adversaries, but found in itself its self-definition and its own sense of legitimacy. Joining Europe thus appears as the very continuation of French Republican identity.

Notes

1. As charmingly expressed by one of the witnesses quoted by Jacques and Mona Ozouf, *La république des instituteurs*, Paris, Hautes Etudes, Gallimard, Le Seuil, 1992, p. 136

2. George Mosse, *Fallen Soldiers, Reshaping the Memory of the World Wars*, New York, Oxford, Oxford University Press, 1990.

3. Antoine Prost, 'The Impact of War on French and German Political Culture', *The Historical Journal*, 1994, 1, pp. 209–17.

4. Maurice Crubellier, *L'école républicaine 1870–1940, esquisse d'une histoire culturelle*, Paris, Editions Christian, 1993.

5. Maurice Crubellier, ibid., p. 51. This is the title of the first 'talk' in the preparatory course.

6. Eugen Weber, 'La formation de l'Hexagone républicain' in François Furet (ed.), *Jules Ferry, fondateur de la République, actes du colloque organisé par l'EHESS*, Paris, Ed. de l'EHESS, 1985, pp. 223–41.

7. Benedict Anderson, *Imagined Communities. Reflections on the Origin and Spread of Nationalism*, London, New York, Verso, 1983. Anderson rightly stresses the importance of these civil service routes in the construction of nationalism.

8. Jean-François Chanet, 'L'école républicaine et les petites patries. Enseignement primaire et sentiment d'appartenance en France sous la Troisième République (1879–1940)', thesis at the University of Paris I (directed by M. Agulhon), 1994, published under the title, *L'École républicaine et les petites patries*, Paris, Aubier, 1996.

9. Jacques Gavoille, *L'Ecole publique dans le Departement du Doubs (1870–1914)*, Paris, Les Belles Lettres, 1981.

10. Eugen Weber, *Peasants into Frenchmen: The Modernization of Rural France, 1870–1914*, Stanford, CA, Stanford University Press, 1976.

11. Chanet, *L'ecole republicaine*, pp. 346ff., mentions that in 1911 there was a Ministerial instruction about the teaching of local history and

geography, and the foundation that year of the Society for Local Studies within public education. This paragraph is based upon evidence cited in this work.

12. In French one could put this link as the continuity between the *petite* and the *grande patrie*.

13. On these points, see Arnold Van Gennep, *Manuel de folklore français contemporain*, Paris, Picard, 9 vols, 1943-1958, and Maurice Crubellier, *Histoire culturelle de la France, XIXe–XXe siècle*, Paris, A. Colin, 1974.

14. Christian Amalvi, *Les héros de l'Histoire de France, recherche iconographique sur le panthéon scolaire de la troisième République*, Paris, Ed. Phot'oeil, 1979; Dominique Maingueneau, *Les livres d'école de la République 1879-1914, discours et idéologie*, Paris, Le Sycomore, 1979.

15. Antoine Prost, *Vocabulaire des proclamations électorales de 1881, 1885 et 1889*, Paris, Publications de la Sorbonne, PUF, 1974, p.38. The significance of the term 'progress' in the vocabulary of republicans of the day reappears in the pejorative expression 'progressistes' thought up by their detractors to designate them.

16. As in this dictation text used in the Certificat d'études at Pithiviers-Ville on 12 July 1894 (*Bulletin de l'enseignement primaire du Loiret*):
Progress in France since the revolution:
Workers have an easier and a wider life. They have higher wages; they eat and dress better; they have an ever-growing share of the remuneration in the profits of a business.

(. . .) They are citizens of a free State, they learn in a school that is now free for everyone; they can, through their voting paper, operate in a serious manner on the market and on governmental control. Through work, through the dignity of life, through saving, the humblest workers can attain the highest fortune; through intelligence and talent, the son of the peasant and the worker can aspire to reach the highest ranks in the army, the most eminent positions of State. In this lies true equality: equality in the face of labour; that is where true social progress lies. No doubt many reforms will still be attempted; many improvements will be brought to the destiny of the greatest number. And yet it can be asserted confidently that nowhere is general freedom greater than in France.

17. Roger Thabault, *Mon village, ses hommes, ses routes, son école*, Paris (1st edition, Delagrave, 1938), Presses de la FNSP, 1982, p. 232.

18. Maurice Agulhon, *Marianne au pouvoir. L'imagerie et la symbolique républicaines de 1880 à 1914*. Paris, Flammarion, 1989, pp. 128-36 and 345.

19. André Maginot, *Carnets de patrouille*, Paris, Fédération nationale André Maginot, 1964, p. 28.

20. The Marquis de Gourgues, in 1849, in the Lalinde region (Dordogne). Cf. Alain Corbin, *Le village des cannibales*, Paris, Aubier, 1990, p. 19.

21. Eugen Weber, *Peasants into Frenchmen*, p. 364 et seq.

22. This makes it impossible, for example, to approach the problem of regional languages in France as in the other countries of the European Community. The term 'the Corsican people' was censured by the Conseil constitutionnel, in a recent proposal for a law, as incompatible with the Constitution.

23. Louis Dumont, *Essais sur l'individualisme. Une perspective anthropologique sur l'idéologie moderne*, Paris, Le Seuil, 1983.

24. To illustrate this development, see a significant passage in the *Lectures choisies d'auteurs français*, by Martin and Lemoine (1905, p. 273, quoted without further reference details by Maingueneau, *Les livres d'école*, p. 109 (italics in the text):

> In France there is no *privilege* whatever except that conferred by services rendered, devotion to public affairs. *Honour* goes to the most worthy. Each one is the son of his works: the liberty of all is protected by vigilant and impartial laws. Sovereignty, moreover, belongs to the people through its freely chosen representatives. The government of the *Republic* is the government that offers the best guarantees of strength, security and freedom.

25. Quote by Jacques Julliard, *Fernand Pelloutier et les origines du syndicalisme d'action directe*, Paris, Le Seuil, 1971, p. 225. (J. Julliard's italics).

26. This right-wing current is exemplified by the well-known inquiry of Alfred de Tarde and Henri Massis, *Les jeunes gens d'aujourd'hui* (published under the pseudonym of Agathon, 1912). On the subject of the evolution of the right, see Jean Francois Sirinelli (ed.), *Histoire des droits en France*, Paris: Gallimard, 1992, 3 vols, esp. vol. 2 (*politique*), the chapter by Gilles Le Beguec and Jacques Prevotat, '1898–1919: L'éveil a la modernité politique', pp. 213–87.

27. Nations, a grandiose way of saying barbarity.
Does love stop where your footsteps stop?
Tear up these flags: another voice cries out to you:
Egotism and hatred alone have a nation.
Fraternity recognizes none.

28. On this point, see Pierre Nora, 'Lavisse, instituteur national' in Pierre Nora (ed.), *Les Lieux de mémoire, I, La République*, Paris, Gallimard, 1984, pp. 247–89.

29. *Code Soleil*, article 115. Quoted by Bertrand Geay, 'La fin de l'univers primaire. Les instituteurs français et la représentation syndicale', EHESS thesis [P.Bourdieu], 1994, p. 306. Although this text dates from the 1950s, it is so firmly rooted in the continuity of the republican school that I cannot deny myself the pleasure of quoting it.

30. *Bulletin de l'Enseignement primaire du Loiret*, dictation used for the *certificat d'études*, the certificate at the end of primary education, at Chécy, Beaugency, Beaune-la-Rolande, Châteaurenard, Sully-sur-Loire, 18 June 1888.

31. Jean-Paul Martin, 'La Ligue de l'Enseignement et la République des origines à 1914', Thesis at the Institut d'Etudes Politiques de Paris [directed by Jean-Marie Mayeur], 1992.

32. This formula, which so effectively condenses the consensus of republican schoolbooks, is from Jacques and Mona Ozouf, 'Le thème du Patriotisme dans les manuels primaires', *Le Mouvement social*, no. 49, October–December 1964, p. 18.

33. See in full the demonstration of Jacques and Mona Ozouf, ibid., who quote several examples of this double rejection of the renunciation of Alsace-Lorraine and of a war of revenge, such as: 'Between France and Germany only a free and peaceful agreement, which it is unfortunately difficult to foresee for a long time ahead, could settle on the Rhine as a lasting frontier.'

34. Jacques and Mona Ozouf, ibid.

35. Ibid., p. 138. These authors show in full the nuances of positions that I summarize here in inevitably truncated form.

36. Roger Thabault, *Mon village*, p. 230.

37. On the evolution of schoolteachers' thought on this point, see Olivier Loubes, *L'Ecole et la nation d'une guerre à l'autre en France'*, Ph.D., Universite de Toulouse Le Mirail, 1999, Paris, Belin, 2001.

38. Henry Rousso, 'L'épuration en France. Une histoire inachevée', *Vingtième siècle, revue d'histoire,* n° 33, janvier–mars 1992, pp. 78–105 ; Peter Novick, *The Resistance versus Vichy: The Purge of Collaborators in Liberated France,* Londres, Chatto and Windus, 1968.

39. Henry Rousso, *Le Syndrome de Vichy*, Paris, Le Seuil, 1987.

4

Representations of War in the Cultural History of France, 1914–1939

What difference did the Great War make in the cultural history of France? This question is surprisingly difficult to answer today, in part because of the multiple meanings now associated with the terms 'culture' and 'cultural history'. In brief, I take cultural history not as the history of cultural, literary or artistic creation, nor as the history of those who create these forms. I take cultural history to be the evolution of social representations. In this context, cultural and symbolic products are certainly relevant, but only as traces, among others, of representations that give them form and meaning. In addition, linguistic forms merit attention, because even the most colloquial modes of speaking often disclose implicit representations.

From this point of view, what the 1914–18 war did was to discredit one set of representations and replace them by another set. The consequences of this shift were profound. In this sense, the conflict between before the war and after the war was, while the conflict was still going on, a conflict of social representations. Before 1914, war was associated with images, words, values incapable of describing the reality of the war that unfolded between 1914 and 1918. It was no exaggeration to claim that the words did not exist to describe the war that actually took place. The sense soldiers had, and expressed with considerable force, of having lived through an incommunicable experience, was not restricted to the subject of death, inflicted or suffered. It also arose out of a discordance between two kinds of representations. On the one hand, there were those expressed by civilians, representations well known to the soldiers, who knew what their family and friends were thinking; and on the other hand were the representations the soldiers themselves fashioned to comprehend the experience through which they had lived.

Representations of War: Before 1914

Before 1914, there were three central elements in representations of war: they concerned representations of combat, of the soldier who fights, and of his adversary. On the eve of 1914, combat was imagined in terms of *imagerie d'Épinal*, of cavalry charges (Reischoffen), of decisive battles, the character of which determines the outcome of war (Sadowa, Sedan), of war to the bitter end. This was not the sole property of Ardant du Picq or of the general staff, but of a more universally shared sense of what war was. The men mobilized in 1914 would have been exposed as schoolboys to texts infused with these representations. One such passage, from J. Payot's discussion of morale, is entitled: 'Victory goes to those who advance'; in it, the reader is told that 'Bravado and joyous audacity diminish casualties; to go forward is [the soldier's] duty, whatever the cost'[1].

This dynamic representation of combat was linked to a moral portrait of the soldier, which emphasized his courage, his virile enthusiasm, or at least his initiative. The next paragraph in this manual is entitled 'Gaily and courageously'. It concludes that 'we have nothing to fear from an invasion if we know how to do our duty courageously'. It is not enough just to accept duty; one must embrace it fully. Here is the source of the emphasis on the gaiety of the soldier, his songs, his spirit of doing his duty voluntarily and joyously. In its popular version, this is the clarion call of Déroulède. And, from a different political perspective, it is also present in Péguy's *Victor-Marie, Comte Hugo*. It is to the young men of Agathon, and in particular to Ernest Psichari, that Péguy dedicates the last pages of this work: 'young man, with youthful blood, a man of pure heart; who in a secular home had reintroduced that antique glory, the first glory, the glory of war'.[2] This same hymn to sacrifice and to death freely embraced was expressed by Victor Hugo in his *l'Hymne* of 1831: 'To those who piously died for their country . . .', and by Corneille, in his *Polyeucte*: 'To die for one's country is a dignified exit/many clamour for such a beautiful death.'[3] This is the stance, at once ethical and aesthetic, that informed a letter to the Head of the Cabinet: 'the undersigned, future soldiers, want to assure you that they are ready joyously to sacrifice three years of their youth for the life and glory of France'.[4]

This dynamic representation of war and of the soldier coexisted, before 1914, with another representation, more static, but also more civic in character: that of the city besieged. War was a matter of assaults and sieges. Frenchmen before the war were well aware of the spirit of the siege of Paris of 1870–71. Many had lived through it and could talk about it; others learned about it at school.[5] In any event, the urban landscapes, with their fortifications, suggested the eventuality of siege and of a resistance for which they had to prepare. Here we encounter another representation of the soldier, partially civilian in character: the armed city-dweller, who stands guard and endures the hardships of a prolonged siege, particularly hunger.

The representation of the enemy, the German, or earlier the Prussian, is a subject that merits further study. There is some recent research on German atrocities committed in 1870. John Horne is right to point out that the discourse of German atrocities in 1914 arose out of those of 1870. We could go further still and locate the reception of stories of 1914–15 about children with severed hands in already existing representations of Prussians as capable of such acts of barbarism. A full survey of images of the Germans in school-books of the Third Republic remains to be done; but in it one would encounter the kind of thinking illustrated by L. Brossolette, who provided one etching of the maltreatment of French prisoners by Uhlans, and another of 'Bavarian vengeance' after the seizure of Bazeilles: 'To take their revenge, they burned 360 houses in the town; they shot one hundred inhabitants, and among them an 86-year-old man; and they threw a woman and her two children down a well.'[6]

One remains astounded, in any event, by certain negative representations of Germans before 1914. An author like Barrès at times became so extreme that today the reader is left dumbfounded. Here he is talking with his young son Philippe, who remarks: 'Listen, I want to ask you something. . . . Since German dogs do not have souls, isn't it true that German people don't have souls either?' To this Barrès hugged his son, and replied, 'What you say is a bit foolish, but if you keep it a secret, I will tell you that I am of the same opinion.'[7]

Representations of War During the War

This representation of war could not resist the shock of experience. 'At a single glance', wrote de Gaulle, 'we could see clearly that all the courage in the world could do nothing against firepower.' Lived experiences destroyed prior representations. Or rather most of them. When we look carefully at the testimony of the veterans of 1914–18, we find significant passages completely distorted by the persistence of elements derived from earlier representations. It is as if, in

telling of 'their' war, the soldiers simply drew on earlier and distort-
ing images, without even noticing the contradiction with their direct
experience. Here are but two examples, taken from Péricard's
collection of soldiers' memoirs.[8] The first is an account of an attack,
an account embedded in the pre-war imaginary universe. Attack is
always described as rapid and filled with movement. One closes with
the enemy. One of Péricard's correspondents tells of how his captain
charged 'with a reckless fervour that carried the whole company
through knee-deep mud'; as if such a thing were possible. Another
writer continued to view German soldiers through pre-war stereotypes, and described 'goose-stepping soldiers, engaged in a bayonet
charge among the shell holes . . .'.[9]

Overall, these stereotypes did not last long. They were scoffed at
as 'eyewash'. The trench journals studied by S. Audoin-Rouzeau
contain many examples of such denunciations. Consider this satirical
description of an attack: 'Since dawn the men were there. They
waited impatiently for the order to attack, an order that would arrive
any minute. They did not want to sleep that night, filled with joy that
they were about to get their hands on the Boche . . .'.[10] One could
repeat these examples. The point here is not so much that representations of combat and of the soldier were inadequate to the task
of describing the 1914–18 war, as that there persisted in wartime
representations pre-war elements that soldiers recognized perfectly
well, and clearly saw as inadequate, but of which they did not totally
succeed in ridding themselves. In effect, some common elements,
some familiar *topoi*, reappeared irregularly in the trench journals
themselves.

The same was true with respect to representations of the Germans.
Trench journals portray them simply as men, and not, certainly from
1915 on, as brutes or barbarians. However, hostility did not really
vanish, and the term 'hatred' still appeared. We can see here a composite representation where the personality of the adversary at the
front seems to resemble that of his French brothers facing the same
hardships.

Post-war Representations

Representations of war in French culture in this period, termed
significantly, the 'inter-war years', flow directly and progressively
from the experience of war as seen by the men who fought it. In
the early 1920s, in effect, pre-war representations persist here and

there. But veterans constituted a considerable part of the population, and their voices are everywhere. In 1930, they represented 45 per cent of men aged 20 and over.[11] This figure is below that of 55 per cent in 1920; but those cohorts too old to have gone to war were progressively replaced by those of children raised during or after the war, in such a way that, paradoxically, the new representations spread more generally as the war receded in time.

At the same time, the representation of the enemy became more human. Certainly, bad memories of the German occupation of the north of France persisted. The image of atrocities did not disappear. But, in general, the most negative traits faded away. The German ceased to be a brute and instead became a soldier who had done his duty, just as the French soldier had done his, but in the German case with a discipline, a submission, of which Frenchmen did not approve. The most widely circulated texts, such as schoolbooks, abjured all hostility.[12]

The representation of combat is above all that of trench warfare and of shellholes. This is what pours out of literature, caricature, teaching, as well as tourism.[13] It refers back to the old imagery of siege, by its static character and by the attendant suffering it entails: hunger, thirst, rats. But it adds some new elements so widely known that they constitute a primary point of reference, less emotive than that associated with bombardment, or fear, or the loss of comrades. In certain respects, post-war representations are a kind of enlargement of the idea of a siege, extended to the terrain of the nation as a whole. It is noteworthy, in any event, that this notion is materialized in the construction of the Maginot line precisely at the same time as the zone of urban fortifications is dismantled and handed over to urban development.

Other images of war were evidently discredited. The assault and the offensive became symbols of futility – indeed, of murderous futility. The notion of the assault may have given some degree of gratification to the general staff; but that merely demonstrated their absence of imagination. Victory arrived when the enemy was broken by the failure of his own offensives, and when the counterattack was launched at an opportune moment. From here it is difficult even to conceive of an offensive that could be fruitful, let alone one that is not too costly in human lives. Such a representation of combat made it very difficult to draw clear lessons from the Spanish Civil War.

In the new representation of combat, death takes pride of place. Prior representations never denied the possibility of death in combat;

but one did not dwell on it. After 1918, death is at the core of representations: the objective, even the very definition, of combat. To make war is not to capture prisoners, take cities, conquer territory; it is to kill and to be killed. The semantic landscape is arranged around terms such as: 'killing', 'butchery', 'carnage', 'bloody horror'. This set of representations is in war memoirs, in soldiers' stories, in war memorials and in the ceremonies on 11 November, culminating in a vast funerary cult and pilgrimages to war graves and cemeteries at the front. The Ossuary of Douaumont, for instance, is a kind of cemetery of cemeteries for those whom the war had not only killed, but had reduced to a state of dispersed bones impossible to identify. The physical site of warfare matters because there one can see how in a crucial, more, in a carnal or charnel way, death is at the core of perceptions of what war is. War and death become inextricably embraced: so much so that, on the eve of war in 1939, it was impossible to imagine a war where losses would be relatively limited, a war such as the one waged by the Germans in France a year later, or by the Americans after 1944. War became murderous catastrophe *par excellence*.

Evelyne Sullerot provides an indirect, but particularly moving, instance of this sinister representation of war. She grew up in a 'big and happy family', in the 1930s. 'Constantly', she remembers, 'I was struck by my mother's friends telling her: "Don't you fear having children in these times?" And I still hear my mother on 3 September 1939, distraught, telling us: "Forgive me for having brought you into the world." She felt guilty.'[14] No doubt there is a reflection here of some sources of the decline in French fertility, a decline that took place at a time when a war was on the horizon, a war that one could not image otherwise than as long and bloody.[15]

This dark representation of war changed the image of the soldier as well. Evidence for such a shift may be found even in official language. Prior images of the soldier, filled with the joyful courage of Péricard's story of the rising of the dead, or of Jean des Vignes Rouges (the pseudonym of Jean Taboureau),[16] no longer have a place, even in official military discourse. Consider, for instance, these remarks of Pétain about the soldier of 1914–18 (he spoke at the inauguration of the Ossuary of Douaumont): 'We who knew him, knew him simply as a man, with his strengths and his weaknesses, a man of our people, whose thoughts and affection remained attached to the family circle, to the workshop, to the office, to the village, to the farm where he grew up.' Conscientiously doing his duty, 'he went up to the line, certainly without enthusiasm, but without weakness'.[17]

This reserve in the tone of military homage, expressed precisely at a place where one might have expected a certain bravado, suggests strongly that a certain type of elegy to the soldier had become impossible. To boast about his courage, his initiative, is to applaud mass death. Post-war culture is in part a critique of pre-war values. One of the most influential philosophers of the period, Alain, is joined here by someone whose success came later, but who also was a veteran of 1914–18, Jean Giraudoux. Alain's *Mars ou la guerre jugée* says nothing that varies on this points from Giraudoux's *La guerre de Troie n'aura pas lieu.*

One of the salient ideas of *Mars ou la guerre jugée*, is that what pushes men towards war, and what those in power exploit, are not base instincts or vulgar interests, but, on the contrary, noble sentiments:

> The sentiment of honour is the true source of wars. . . . The free man feels he must prove that the most terrible menace will not shake his will. This is why he goes into combat as a trial; and his father and mother do not think of dissuading him, but consider that fear, anxiety, grief, are their lot, another kind of trial, one they bear as well as they can, wanting to prove that they too choose the worst rather than accept slavery.[18]

Here is the source, says Alain, of the power of propaganda, which plays on the finer sentiments of a man, so central to public life: 'Here the man who turns away from violence is called a coward and a traitor. Here anger is prepared at a distance; men are "fanaticized", as they dared to say; or better still, let us say that they are intoxicated systematically and in every sense of the word. The excess of violence is raised to the level of beauty by the visible order, by music and by speech.' And here one recalls the contemporary novel of Céline, *Voyage au bout de la nuit:* 'Almost all poets and thinkers add their rhythms to it, their proof, their systems. Love smiles. Shame, scorn and rocks are hurled at the man who resists or even argues.'[19]

In private life, there is no point to such heroic posturing. The encomium on courage, even when indirect or implicit, sentences men to death. Referring to 'admirable' letters he had received from his students, Alain imagined replies he never sent:

> I see that you want to die with grace. But I do not demand this of you. Such beauty is too much. . . . I would rather you had averted your lips

from the cup and that you had not drunk its bitterness. But you drank the bitter draught. . . . You were forced into it, forced like the meanest recruit and under pain of death. . . . You ran faster than your fate, summoning your manly courage and cutting a fine figure of condemned innocence, marching to your punishment. But why do you want to console me?

And perhaps you did not have the right to console us, or to lie even to the women. This lie may kill yet another million men in the next ten years.[20]

Giraudoux denounces propaganda just as firmly. In his play, written in the same period as was Alain's essay, and as were two works of Jules Romains on Verdun, it is the old who praise war, and the women who answer them. To her father-in-law Priam, for whom 'peace will give you feeble husbands, layabouts, shifty men, while war will make of them true men', Andromaque responds: 'Leave us our husbands as they are', and later, 'It is the brave who die in war. To stay out of death's way, you need great luck or great judgement. You must keep your head down, or bow on your knee at least once before danger. Soldiers who stride under the arch of triumph are death's deserters.' And the President of the Senate, the poet, Demokos, part Poincaré and part Déroulède, filled with pre-war banalities, said: 'Cowardice is not to prefer deaths on every hand over the death of one's country.' To this Hecuba responds: 'I was expecting poetry at this point. It never lets us down.'[21]

Even on the political right, the traditional home of those who celebrate sacrifice and moral qualities, the pre-war cadences of *Action française* became impossible to sustain. This is how it was that the right of centre *Union National des Combattants* reacted harshly to a declaration of Mussolini, a man they normally saluted as an example and a friend. 'War and only war can fully valorize human energy and set the seal of nobility on those peoples who have the courage to face it', said the Duce. The journal *L'UNC de Paris*, the organ of the association that 18 months later would call the demonstration of 6 February 1934, responded thus: 'Over 13 years, no one had dared to return to the theme of holy war, of war the regenerator. . . . M. Mussolini has decided to break the fast. With fervour, he has poured a libation to the gods of catastrophe.'[22] And the national voice of the national UNC was no less severe:

It is with such lies that war is provoked. It is with such solemn stupidities that one fools the people, that one brainwashes them and prepares them for the next butchery. No, a thousand times no, war is not a school of nobility and energy [. . .] War is a worse affliction than leprosy, plague, cholera, cancer or tuberculosis. War kills not only men but also consciences. War unleashes the lowest human instincts and leaves moral ruins still worse than material ruins and more tragic than the slaughter itself.[23]

Here we can see the appearance of a negative representation of the soldier. His courage, his tenacity, his sacrifice are not denied, but what war does, without his knowing it, is to insert inhuman instincts within these very qualities. It is not only the absence of heroes: 'We know the vocabulary', says Hecuba in Giraudoux's play. 'In time of war, men are called heroes. But if they are among the brave, they cannot survive with all their limbs. It is not less heroic to flee.'[24] But behind every hero, there is also a brute, without whom the hero would not exist. The representation of the soldier as a death-giver, without a troubled soul, without remorse, and sometimes even with troubled pleasures, is not a secret that veterans kept to themselves. They spoke openly about it. It is inscribed in the personality of Captain Conan in Roger Vercel's novel.[25] Or in a principal of a school in Bayonne, a disabled man, who received the Legion of Honour in 1936 and who, instead of saying trivial things as was expected of him, made a painful admission:

War made of us, not only corpses, impotent, blind. Also, amidst honourable acts of sacrifice, war awakened in us, to the point of paroxysm, ancient instincts of cruelty and barbarism. It so happened that I never stabbed anyone . . . out of the pleasure of killing. When, in the course of an attack, we crawled towards the enemy . . . fear twisted our entrails, and yet an ineluctable force pushed us forward. To surprise the enemy in his trenches, to leap upon him, to terrify a man who doesn't believe in the devil and who suddenly sees him fall upon his shoulders! This barbaric moment, this atrocious moment had for us a unique flavour, a morbid attraction . . .[26]

This text is perhaps a bit excessive in its desire to offer counter-testimony. Given the fact that they would be published in the organ of the most important veterans' organization, these remarks would reach a wide public. What is important here is the character of these words as the opposite of the moralizing elegy in the manner of pre-war patriots like Déroulède or Agathon. The war had produced evils well beyond the deaths of so many men; it had done more than create a world of bereavement and of suffering among so many survivors. The war had also perverted the very humanity of man. The soldier was a man whom war dehumanizes.

Thereafter, in an understandable reversal, the desire to save men from war could easily lead to a sacrifice of honour. The pacifism of the schoolteachers or the postal workers of the CGT is certainly an extreme case, and the slogan 'better servitude than death' cannot be taken entirely literally. But many Frenchmen, without going so far, went some of the way and were ready to accept distortions of the notion of national honour in order to preserve peace. Here we are at the opposite end of the spectrum from the Corneillian notion of honour expressed by Péguy in 1910.

La guerre de Troie n'aura pas lieu (creatively entitled in English *Tiger at the Gates)* by Giraudoux allegorically and prophetically justifies all the evasions Frenchmen concocted in response to Hitler's Germany. Let us recall that the author was a diplomat, and that the play was written at the moment when Hitler decided to rearm Germany. His hero, Hector, twice sacrifices honour for peace. To preserve the peace, Hector denies having been slapped by the Greek Ajax, who in turn slaps Demokos, thereby bringing war about. Then Hector slaps Demokos to silence him, and to show that no affront had been committed by a slap, and thereby to preserve the peace. A little later, he denies against all the evidence that something had happened between Paris and Helen on the boat, thereby provoking the indignation of the spectators, who see Hector's statement as a slight to Trojan virility. It is not just that Hector refuses to be provoked. It is the very de-valorization of honour that is at stake. Peace is worth the sacrifice. Insults, aggression have none of the significance given to them. The same is true in international law, a point made by the expert Busiris, under the insistent pressure of Hector that the embarkation of the Greeks did not constitute aggression against Troy: it was simply a question of how it was presented. And Ulysses, who ends up trying to thwart fate, concludes his dialogue with Hector with cynical lucidity: 'I have more than sufficient eloquence to convince a husband of a wife's virtue. I will even persuade Helen to believe it herself.'[27]

In their heart of hearts, though, Alain and Giraudoux, like the majority of Frenchmen in 1935–36, knew well enough that a war was going to take place. The act of will of Alain has an air of desperation about it. The refusal to accept war, the duty to say 'no', [28] led to these precepts:

> . . . in the face of all warlike declamations, silence; and if an old man manages to rekindle the idea of the massacre of youth, a cold contempt.

In the face of warlike ceremony, a refusal to go. If one is forced to stay, think of the dead, count the dead. Think of those blinded in war, that will cool their passion. And for those who are in mourning, instead of revelling and drowning in glory, have the courage to be sad. [29]

These are civic virtues in a Republic. And, Alain added, 'What is sufficient is an act of will . . . not to consent, not to admire evil; not to accept it in spirit'.[30] These moral precepts force us to admit 'that it is complete prejudice to see war as inevitable'. If we do not want to make it inevitable, we have to fall back upon 'faith, the queen of virtues'. 'There lies unhappiness, but not evil.' And Alain's book ends with an appeal to the reader to come around to his renunciation, and to say: 'No – not perhaps without war, but at least without the consent of our spirit.'[31]

When we consider Giraudoux, we need to consider the heavy weight he put upon the title in French, since he knew that another Trojan war would indeed take place. The efforts of Hector were thwarted by destiny. He was right to kill old Demokos, who wanted to block the return of Helen to the Greeks, and yet who, while dying, claimed falsely that it was a Greek who had killed him, thereby making war inevitable.

Here we are very much in the landscape of *entre-deux-guerres*, of between the wars. These authors tried in vain to exorcize or to avert war by opposing to it the moral force of their will, their refusal, their concessions, and even the sacrifice of their honour. But they still saw war at one and the same time as a bloody catastrophe *and* as their destiny. This system of representations did not enable them to prepare for war – that would have been to consent to it – nor even to accept the risks of war. French policy with respect to Germany between 1933 and 1940, through the Armistice, the defeat and the submission to Nazi rule by Vichy, are inscribed in this system of representations. One can always place responsibility on the shoulders of politicians. But at the same time we must not ignore the weight of these inter-war representations, which made it impossible to construct another policy. After 1940, the Resistance would emerge from those who did not share these inter-war representations, from those who stuck to pre-1914 representations, or who elaborated new representations, within which liberty and respect for human rights played a critical role. But for those whose representations of war were formed in the shadow of the 1914–18 war, to make war again was unthinkable. Here the arrival of Marshal Pétain as head of state in France in 1940 was more than just the result of circumstances: it was a symbol of a constellation of thought, a set of social representations, arising in one war and haunting the French throughout another.

Notes

1. Jules Payot, *La Morale à l'École*, Paris, A. Colin, 1907, p. 226.
2. Charles Péguy, *Victor-Marie, Comte Hugo*, Paris, Gallimard, 1934 [1st edn 1910], p. 227.
3. Ibid., p. 62 and p. 87.
4. Cited by Raoul Girardet, *La société militaire dans la France contemporaine (1815–1939)*, Paris, Plon, 1953, p. 239.
5. This literature was filled with heavy associations with patriotic resonance. Cf. G. Bruno, *Le Tour de la France par deux enfants*, Paris, E. Belin, 1877, p. 136: 'Alésia, assiégée et cernée par les Romains comme notre grand Paris l'a été de nos jours par les Prussiens, ne tarda pas à ressentir les horreurs de la famine.'
6. Christian Amalvi, *Les héros de l'histoire de France*, Paris, Ed. Phot'Oeil, 1979, p. 236.
7. Maurice Barrès, *Les Amitiés françaises. Notes sur l'acquisition par un petit lorrain des sentiments qui donnent un prix à la vie*, Paris, Plon, 1924 [1st edn 1903], p. 85.
8. Lt Jacques Péricard published a very patriotic memoir during the war, *Debout les morts*, with a preface by Maurice Barrès (Paris, Payot, 1918). In 1933 he published *Verdun* (Paris, Librairie de France), the originality of which lies in unedited recollections of soldiers who had responded to his request in the press for soldiers' testimony. These citations are from this collection, which is less a correspondence than an exchange of soldiers' memoirs.
9. Philippe Glorennec, 'Le fonds Péricard', in Gérard Canini, *Mémoire de la Grande Guerre. Témoins et témoignages,* Nancy, Presses universitaires de Nancy, 1989, pp. 313–24, citation at pages 321 and 322.
10. Stéphane Audoin-Rouzeau, *Les combattants des tranchées*, Paris, A. Colin, 1986, p. 108.
11. Cf. Antoine Prost, *Les Anciens combattants et la société française 1914–1939*, Paris, Presses de la FNSP, 1977, vol. II, p. 7.
12. Roger Andréani and Jules Maurin, 'La bataille de Verdun enseignée aux jeunes Français à travers les manuels d'Histoire des classes Terminales

(1920-1962)', in *Verdun 1916, Actes du Colloque international sur la bataille de Verdun 1975*, Verdun, 1976, p. 211.

13. The iconography of the *Guides illustrés Michelin des champs de bataille* is strikingly realistic.

14. Evelyne Sullerot, in Alfred Sauvy, *Histoire économique de la France entre les deux-guerres*, vol. III, Paris, Fayard, 1972, p. 431.

15. Jean-Claude Deville has established that the birth-rate of the 1930s is inflected by a delay of increasing magnitude in reaching completed fertility: 'Analyse harmonique du calendrier de constitution des familles en France. Disparités sociales et évolution de 1920 à 1960', *Population*, (Jan.-Feb. 1977), pp. 17-64.

16. Jean de Vignes Rouge, *Bourru, soldat de Vauquois* (Paris, Perrin, 1916), one of the best instances where an active soldier's representations were remote from the reality of combat.

17. Maréchal Pétain, discours d'inauguration de l'Ossuaire de Douaumont, *Le Temps*, 19 Sept. 1927.

18. Alain, *Mars ou la guerre jugée*, Paris, Gallimard, 1936, p. 57. [Trans.: The translation varies slightly, when I thought fit, from the English translation, entitled *Mars or the truth about war*, trans. By Doris Mudie and Elizabeth Hill (London, Jonathan Cape, 1930), p. 77.]

19. Ibid., p. 174. [See the English translation cited above, pp. 215-16 - Trans.].

20. Ibid., pp. 93-94. [See the English translation cited above, pp. 108-9. - Trans.].

21. *La guerre de Troie n'aura pas lieu*, I, 6.

22. *L'UNC de Paris*, novembre 1932.

23. *La Voix du combattant*, 13.8.32 (Archives, p. 115)

24. Giraudoux, *La guerre de Troie*, I, 6.

25. Roger Vercel, *Capitaine Conan* (Paris, Albin Michel, 1934).

26. *Cahiers de l'UF*, 15 août 1936.

27. Giraudoux, *La guerre de Troie*, I, 6.13.

28. 'Refus' et 'Dire non' are the titles of two parts, numbers CV and CVIII, of *Mars, ou la guerre jugée*.

29. Ibid., pp. 241-2.

30. Ibid., p. 248.

31. Ibid., pp. 253-4.

5

The Algerian War in French Collective Memory

From November 1954 to March 1962 French troops fought in Algeria, in order to keep Algeria a part of France. This was a conflict which, in France, was not officially termed a war at all. The end result was the independence of Algeria under the control of the FLN (National Liberation Front), and the departure for France of one million French people who thought life would be impossible in Algeria under the new regime.

This war was arguably the longest war of decolonization, and although French forces undoubtedly were better equipped and more numerous than the Algerian *fellaghas*, it still cost 35,000 French soldiers their lives. However, it has disappeared from collective memory. No agency of remembrance did work to commemorate the memories of this war. Jean-Pierre Rioux pointed out this fact effectively in a paper published in 1990: 'Since 1962', he wrote, 'there is no French national memory of the Algerian conflict; this un-named war never received the honours of memory.'[1] This chapter deals with the reasons why in France there is no public memory of the Algerian war.

The Algerian War

Algeria was an integral part of France. During the Second World War, de Gaulle's provisional government moved from London to Algiers, for it was on French territory. It was divided into three *départements* that had roughly the same administration as others in metropolitan France. When needed, bureaucrats and teachers were appointed by Algerian selection boards and schools as well as by committees in metropolitan France. Many civil servants began their career there and later went back to France.

During the early 1950s, approximately ten million people living in Algeria were French full citizens; they were termed the *pieds noirs*. They were settlers, workers in the public services, teachers, merchants and so on. Some of them were wealthy and arrogant *colons*, but many of them were lower-middle-class people, very ordinary people. Their families had migrated to North Africa during the nineteenth century or later. Some came for political reasons after the Paris Commune, for instance, or for reasons of national sentiment, as in the case of Alsatians arriving after German annexation in 1871. Some of them had Spanish or Italian origins, but it did not matter that much, because they were all French-speaking people and they had exactly the same rights as people living in France. They participated in the legislative elections as French citizens and sent MPs to Paris.

Alongside the *pieds noirs*, there were nine million people who were termed 'Frenchmen of North-African origin'. These natives spoke Arabic or Berber rather than French, and only about one in five had been to school. Most of them were Muslims. They understood French and spoke a kind of French. Some of them were fully educated and constituted a native elite: there were native lawyers, doctors, chemists, teachers, civil servants. However, even this elite was not given equal citizenship; for local affairs, the local council was composed of two parts, one elected by the *pieds noirs*, the other by the natives. For the national legislative elections, the voters were similarly divided in two parts, electing the same number of MPs. But since the government illegally manipulated the results of the native electoral college, this dual regime gave full power to the *pieds noirs*. Attempts to reform this inegalitarian and undemocratic system had been tried, but they had been unsuccessful. The *pieds noirs* opposed them in order to preserve their own control of public affairs and their social superiority. Here are some of the sources of the emergence of an Algerian nationalist movement. It was heavily repressed and had no hope of achieving its political goals except by violent confrontation with the French police and army.

The Algerian war began in November 1954, when small groups of Algerian partisans made attacks on several places in the Algerian countryside and killed eight people.[2] For French public opinion, the appropriate policy was to send police forces to Algeria and to maintain order. However, the nationalist rebellion expanded, and it was necessary to send military units in Algeria in 1955. The legislative election of January 1956 was won by a socialist–radical coalition after a campaign focused on the Algerian war. The socialist Guy Mollet, the leader of the party, had said that he would make peace in Algeria. But he went to Algiers and was confronted by a *pied noir* demonstration that impressed him so much that he changed his policy and gave 'pacification' priority over 'negotiation'. Hence he decided to send conscripts to Algeria.

From 1956 until the end of the war, in 1962, there were permanently in Algeria 500,000 young conscript soldiers from France. These conscripts were not as strongly committed to the cause of French Algeria as were the officers. Active officers were convinced that the Algerian rebellion was a communist one, inspired and supported by Nasser. They had applauded the Suez expedition in November 1956 and opposed any French government that they supposed eager to negotiate with the FLN. Hence the upheaval of 13 May 1958, which led to de Gaulle's coming back to power and to the advent of the Fifth Republic.

However successful, the military conflict against the FLN did not open the way to a political solution. De Gaulle progressively withdrew from his policy of keeping Algeria French. He moved to the policy of self-determination (September 1959), and later to negotiations with the FLN that resulted in the Evian treaty (18 March 1962) and to the recognition of an independent Algerian republic.

To French public opinion, the Algerian war was a much more important matter than the Vietnamese war which had ended with the Geneva agreement of 1954. First, Vietnam was quite far from France, and French vital interests were not at stake there; very few people from France were living there, and French people with family in Algeria were much more numerous than those with kin in Vietnam. Algeria was just the other side of the Mediterranean sea, and it was viewed as a part of France; it was impossible not to help the *pieds noirs*, these not-so-distant cousins, against the threat of the Algerian 'rebels' who were fighting for a new Algeria, free from colonial – i.e. French – control.

However, French public opinion was reluctant to support fully the *pieds noirs*' stance in Algeria; in a confused manner, French people felt that the *pieds noirs* were responsible for the Algerian situation and that 'French Algeria' was very difficult to maintain. Defending the status quo would lead to a deadlock, but no alternative policy was clearly conceivable; hence, from very early on, there emerged, amid the perplexities and hesitations of public opinion. the thought that negotiations with the FLN would necessarily occur.[3]

There was a second reason why French opinion, although indecisive, was concerned with the Algerian conflict much more than with the Viatnemese one. The Vietnam war had been fought by an expeditionary force, including many troops from the French Empire, and Moroccan and Algerian Muslim soldiers; only volunteers had gone from metropolitan France to the Vietnamese battlefields. General Giap's army was actually an army, with guns and heavy weapons; against it, the French army had fought a war similar to ordinary wars, with battles such as that of Dien Bien Phu, with winners and losers. On the contrary, the Algerian war was fought by conscripts from France against small groups of rebels, and not against an army. The FLN *fellaghas* never became an army, with heavy weapons and large battalions. The 'un-named' war was termed an 'operation to maintain public order'. It consisted of a succession of small-scale fights with dozens of rebels, not battles in the full meaning of the word. Rather than a war, it was a series of guerrilla clashes.

Actually, in Algeria the crucial issue was to keep a tight control of the Muslim civil population, an objective that made it necessary to have French troops in almost every village. For this *quadrillage*, a huge number of soldiers was needed. The French government sent to Algeria the whole of the conscript army, month after month, and for the entire span of their military service, which was lengthened from eighteen to twenty-four, and later to twenty-seven, months.

During the six years that the war lasted, there were permanently nearly 500,000 soldiers from France in Algeria. In total, near three million young Frenchmen crossed the Mediterranean sea to campaign in the Algerian *djebels*, far from their family and their loved ones. They belonged to all sections of French society: they were white-collar workers, workers, peasants, students; they had postponed their personal projects, left their jobs, their young brides or their fiancées, sometimes newborn children. They suffered losses, injuries, separation from their families and so on. Inevitably millions of French people worried about their fate.

This is the context in which to place France's very strong concern for the Algerian war. Many highly emotional issues were intermingled: considerations of national prestige, solidarity with the *pieds noirs*, worry for sons, husbands and friends fighting in Algerian *djebels*. These reasons made it difficult to envisage either an independent Algeria or a never-ending war.

It seemed to French public opinion that only a few activists were involved in the rebellion on the *fellagha*'s side, and it was inconceivable that a powerful army would be unable to win a war against so weak an enemy. But it was clear too that it was impossible to maintain the privileges of the *pieds noirs*. Time was needed for the idea to surface that there was no alternative to entering into discussions with the FLN (Algerian national liberation front), leading to an independent Algeria. Potentially, ex-soldiers and *pieds noirs* had the ability to present themselves as victims of the Algerian war. We will discuss later the reasons why they did not fulfil this potentiality.

Let us begin briefly with a third group of potential victims, of whom we have not yet spoken: the *harkis*. The *harkis* were soldiers from the native Muslim community of Algeria, enrolled as complementary forces to supplement French army. They did not form regular units enrolled in the French army; they rather formed a kind of civil militia with light weapons for night patrols around the villages. The *harkis* helped the French army to flood the countryside, in the tactic they called *quadrillage*.

At the end of the war, the *harkis* were in a critical position. They were volunteers, committed to the French and the perpetuation of colonial domination. They were deemed traitors by the Algerian National Liberation Front, and it was clear that many of them would be murdered after independence. Actually, between 55,000 and 75,000 of them were killed.

Notwithstanding contrary orders, some officers thought it was impossible to abandon them when they left Algeria, and approximately 85,000 of them came to France.[4] Unfortunately, it was difficult to integrate them into French society. They had no family in France, no relations; most of them were unskilled, and only some of them were educated, French-speaking people. When in France, they were put in camps. Progressively, their conditions of living and housing became better, their children went to French primary schools, they found casual employment.

But the difference between them and Algerian immigrants was not evident, and in France they encountered the same difficulties as immigrants in renting a flat or finding a job. They were perceived as a burden on the army and on French society as a whole. They did not even form a sub-sections of veterans' associations. They remained second-class Frenchmen. They did not count in the public debate until recent years, when mass unemployment precipitated nationalist, racist or xenophobic movements. Then, the sons and daughters of the *harkis*, more educated than their parents, unemployed and socially excluded, no longer saw their deprivation as acceptable, in the light of their fathers' commitment to France and of their own Algerian origin. Some of them joined in violent demonstrations in

several small towns of southern France. They won some improvements; but they are insufficiently numerous to create more than local
difficulties.

Much more puzzling is the case of the two other groups : neither
the *pieds noirs* nor the ex-soldiers found ways to commemorate
collectively their experience and their losses. They never formed a
community of victims. Why?

The Pieds Noirs: A Restricted Memory

The first reason was the division of these two groups. Had they united
their forces, they could have been more successful. But the fact is
that they were divided. The relationship between the ex-soldiers and
the *pieds noirs* had been ambiguous during the war. A recent study
in oral history among ex-non-commissioned officers shows the
resentment of these young Frenchmen from France against the *pieds
noirs*. Although they came to fight the Algerian rebellion and protect
the *pieds noirs* at great personal risk, they were not given a very
warm welcom by the *pieds noirs*. They felt that the *pieds noirs*
thought it was natural that French soldiers would protect them, and
that the locals did not value highly enough the sacrifices they had
made.

Small anecdotes still vivid in these ex-officers' memories illuminate their sense of frustration and deception. One of them says they
were never invited to dance with the daughters of the *pieds noirs*.[5]
Another remembers that once a *pied noir* settler asked him to pay
for a glass of water. A poll among 533 soldiers coming back to France
in 1959 presented similar evidence. Such little incidents, and their
significance to French soldiers, are revealing. They help account for
the fact that in a 1959 poll 61 per cent of the respondents expressed
more antipathy against the *pieds noirs* than against the 'Arabs'.[6]

On the other hand, the *pieds noirs* resented the distinction made
by many non-commissioned officers and conscript soldiers from the
other side of the Mediterranean sea between the interests of France
as a nation-state and the interests of the *pieds noirs*. They found that
at times the French army did not share their point of view. This
friction turned into open opposition when renegade French army
officers formed a clandestine organization, the OAS, dedicated to
keeping Algeria French. The OAS directly confronted the army, and
so did the *pieds noirs*. French soldiers opened fire on *pieds noirs*
demonstrating against the French government; several demonstrators

were killed. The fusillade on the rue d'Isly in Algiers on 26 March 1962 was the climax of this kind of internal war. In the light of such events, one can understand why it was very difficult for ex-soldiers and *pieds noirs* to constitute any kind of community after the war, let alone act as a 'fictive kinship group'.

The one million *pieds noirs* living in Algeria were full French citizens. After independence, most of them had the right to live in Algeria, with joint Algerian and French nationalities. However, there was a clear and overwhelming consensus within Algerian public opinion and among officials that their only choice was between leaving and being killed. They chose to go – for some to return – to France, abandoning in Algeria everything they could not take with them.[7] They lost their land and property, their houses, their furniture, and sometimes their savings. As they were numerous and had suffered heavy material losses, they had grounds to claim reparations from the French state.

After a few months in France, the *pieds noirs* formed specific associations of *rapatriés* (people returning to their homeland) in order to express their demands for compensation from the state. The main association, with perhaps 200,000 members in the late 1980s, is the ANFANOMA (National association of Frenchmen from North Africa, from overseas and of their friends). This organization had been founded in 1956 after Tunisia and Morocco had declared independence. After 1962, it was there for the *pieds noirs*. Many other associations were formed in later years: RECOURS (Rallying point and unitary coordination of *rapatriés*); and FURR (Federation for the unity of *rapatriés*, refugees and their friends), among others.[8] These associations operated as pressure groups urging Parliament and the government to pass laws to compensate *rapatriés* for all that they had lost. But, as such indemnification would have been costly, the government was very reluctant. The law of indemnification was passed only in 1970, after the events of May 1968. Payments were spaced over a long period, after claimants had submitted documentation that was often difficult to obtain. This unsatisfactory and deceptive law was modified in 1974 and further improved in 1987, but many *pieds noirs* still believe that they have never been compensated for the losses they suffered.

The *pieds noirs* movement was and still is weakened by political rivalries. Many associations opposed the Gaullists in the presidential or legislative elections, since de Gaulle remains in their opinion the man who abandoned and betrayed them. RECOURS alone supported

Jacques Chirac. The resentment against the Gaullists, responsible for the Algerian disaster, opened the way for more radical tendencies. The nationalist Front National of J.-M. Le Pen is very active in some associations such as the JPN (Young *Pieds Noirs*). By and large, as the *pieds noirs* were not united politically, the associations they founded are politically diverse.

However, claiming benefits is only one of the functions of these associations; they have cultural and emotional aims too. Beside the major associations, there are smaller ones grounded on local affinities of origin or of destination – *pieds noirs* from the city of Jemmapes, or of Beni-Saf, or living in the Val d'Oise *département*, for instance). Other associations have cultural objectives, keeping alive songs, folklore and theatre. There is a *pieds noir* culture, with its jokes, its tales, its particular *argot*, its traditions. The memory of lost Algeria is still alive in these small local groups, as it is alive in the very large families where cousins, aunts, uncles and their kin meet together regularly for baptisms, weddings, and funerals, or sometimes for birthdays or feasts.

This *pieds noirs* memory is built on the divide between before and after.[9] What matters are the good memories of Algeria before the war. These are memories of particular places: the landscape, the orange trees and the vineyards, the light and warmth of the sun, the aromas of the market places and of the wine cellars. Memories of a homeland where life was simple, easy and cheap. Memories of a kind of community with the 'Arabs': the children playing football together; with their parents on good terms in business or in the neighbourhood. It conjured up a kind of sociability that made it impossible to understand why the story ended in a tragic way. The *pieds noir* memory of Algeria is that of a Paradise lost, from which their exclusion remains an inexplicable misfortune. This nostalgic reverie is still strong and vivid among them.

However, it is not a set of memories expressed or directed to French society as a whole. They never argued that France had a 'duty of remembrance' about lost Algeria; it is only 'their' memory, a memory restricted to the initiate population.

What are the reasons for this restriction? A first reason is their physical location: they did not form homogeneous communities. Most of them migrated to southern France, where the land, the climate and the kind of agriculture were similar to those of Algeria; others went to the Paris region or elsewhere. But, even in the Garonne valley or in Provence, they never built new villages or settlements. They were living among a long-settled population, and had to cope with local customs. More than this, they wanted to become Frenchmen like anyone else, not to distinguish themselves from the population at large. After 1962, they worked passionately to be integrated into French society.

This was no simple task, for they had to find jobs and homes, to form new friendships and bonds within their neighbourhood. Many of them had no money, no support. They helped one another very frequently, but their success depended upon their constant effort and the fortuitous conditions of a booming economy. Working so hard to become integrated into the French community prevented them from claiming that they were victims of that very community. These aims were contradictory.

From this point of view, their cultural institutions or traditions, such as theatrical companies, choirs and so on, can be seen as a means of integration; for other groups, from various provinces of France, or from various countries, have similar activities. These ethnic associations are more integrative than distinctive. Hence it is difficult to avoid the conclusion that the *pieds noirs* are a progressively vanishing community. Their cultural difference remains, but it does not operate as giving ground for a kind of outward political or social movement. Their restricted memory is for internal use only.

On that point, two qualifications must be made. One could ask whether hostility to immigrants in contemporary France is fed by the *pieds noirs*' trauma. Possibly, some *pieds noirs* think that, since they have once already been forced to quit their beloved country and their familial environment 35 years ago, now they want to keep this country as their own. One can understand their propensity to take an active part in the nationalist movements such as the Front National of J.-M. le Pen, himself a former activist in the cause of French Algeria.

A second qualification concerns Jewish *pieds noirs*. Was not the new strong Jewish identity of French Sephardi Jews, whose fathers were not threatened by the Nazi genocide, a kind of substitute for an alternative identity, that of victims of Algerian independence, a population in exile, forced to leave their homes and go to metropolitan France? These victims could chose their victimizers. Supporting this statement, one could underline the double relationship between the *pieds noirs* and the Jews of Israel, and between the Algerians and the Palestinians.

The Ex-soldiers: An Impossible Memory

The second group of potential victims of the Algerian war were the ex-soldiers. Like the *pieds noirs*, although for different reasons, they too were unable to convert personal memories of that war into a collective memory. First, they were deeply divided politically. Their veterans' association, the FNACA (National federation of *anciens combattants* of Algeria), was controlled by the French Communist Party. This made it impossible for more conservative veterans to enrol in that association. Hence the rightist association of 'anciens combattants' of the First and Second World Wars, the UNC (National union of combatants) organized a particular sub-section for Algerian veterans. These two associations opposed each other on every issue, especially on symbolic ones. Therefore it was impossible, for instance, to find an agreement on the date on which to commemorate the end of the war. It would make sense for people of this forgotten generation who participated in the Algerian war to have a day in the year devoted to rituals of remembrance, parades, talks, banquets and so on. However, for one ex-soldiers' association, the leftist FNACA, the appropriate day is the nineteenth of March, which is not exactly the date of the treaty between France and the FLN (18 March), but the day when the struggle ceased; for the rightist association, this is unacceptable, for this treaty is considered as a kind of betrayal. They tried to make 16 October the date for commemoration because on that day, in 1977, one unknown soldier of the Algerian war was buried in the cemetery of Notre Dame de Lorette.[10] This conflict over dates made commemoration impossible. Commemoration enforces unity; but it first needs some unity to begin with.

The second reason is more profound. This war was meaningless for the soldiers who fought it. The conscripts hated it. Armand Frémont, a geographer who himself went to Algeria as a non-commissioned officer, underlines this point. The untranslatable slogan: 'La quille, bordel!', was the strongest, the most profound and the most popular epithet of this period. 'Said with anger, violence or derision, it sums up fairly well the attitude of nearly all the conscripts. They did not accept the task they had to fulfil, even when they did their duty. The death of every one of them was seen as a double scandal: dead aged twenty; dead for nothing.'[11] They never thought that French national interests were at stake: the Algerian war was not the beginning of something; only the end of colonial times. It was a closure, not an opening.

A final reason is probably the most important of all: it arises out of the absence of a generally accepted sense of the legitimacy of the Algerian war itself. This war was not legitimate from many point of views. The French army committed many crimes, including torture and killings in Algeria. One of the best-known cases was that of Maurice Audin, a junior lecturer in mathematics at Algiers university, who was a communist. He was arrested by French paratroops, led to the villa Susini, the well-known headquarters of the investigation section of the army, tortured by French officers whose names are known, and finally killed. Torture was an ordinary practice, and one general, General Paris de la Bollardière, was dismissed for not accepting it. These facts were covered by an amnesty; hence they have not been discussed in the courts. It is possible to charge Mr Papon for the role he played as general secretary of the Gironde prefecture in 1942–43 in the deportation of Jews, but not for what he did when he was prefect in Constantine during the Algerian war, or later in October 1961, when he was responsible, as the Prefect of Police in Paris, for the killing of dozens of Algerians demonstrating in the street against an illegal curfew.

Papon's case is quite interesting, because it leads to my central point: the link between the non-remembrance of the Algerian war and the remembrance of the Second World War. On the one hand, the illegitimacy of the Algerian war was due to the means and practices of the French army. But on the other hand, the entire war was illegitimate in itself; its goals were not acceptable. Opposing Algerian independence was not legitimate, as the United Nations said openly. The Algerian people had the right to become an independent nation-state. The French government claimed that Algeria was France, and a part of the French nation supported that position. They said that this war was not a war, but only an operation to maintain order, with the legal consequence of excluding ex-soldiers of that non-war from war benefits. However, in their soul and conscience, most of the French people knew perfectly well that the kind of domination imposed on the Algerian people had to come to an end.

Confusedly, French society did not feel that this war was a fully legitimate war. This lack of legitimacy was rooted in the obvious, although impossible, comparison between the Algerian situation and that of France occupied by the German army from 1940 to 1944. Undoubtedly, there are a myriad of differences between those two historical situations. But there are similarities too. French soldiers fighting the *fellaghas* were they entirely different from German soldiers fighting the *résistants*? Were their methods so different? The debate over torture posed the question anyway: was the villa Susini different from the Gestapo's cellars? It was impossible to avoid the parallel; and, even if merely confronted openly, such a debate would have been devastating.

However, French soldiers in Algeria still had the question in mind. Some of the ex-officers interviewed by B. Kaplan say it openly : 'We were doing *quadrillage* as the Germans did. Others [the *fellaghas*] were fighting as guerrillas as the *maquis* were. We knew that very well; we had seen the *maquis*, we had seen the Germans. It was memories of our childhood. And we were the Germans, with our heavy weapons. They, they were the *maquis*, and we were the German occupation troops.'[12] For these soldiers, the Algerian war was and remained a dirty war; the indisputable legitimacy of the Resistance against the Nazis undermined the legitimacy of the Algerian war.

Hence, as B. Stora has suggested, the soldier's memory of the war remained a merely private memory. Soldiers without victory, without good causes and without enthusiasm cannot become positive figures.[13] Many books were published about the war – more than one thousand, reflecting every angle of opinion. However, most of them were only narratives of individual experience, given and read as such. There was no collective work of remembrance, and the memory of the Algerian war was covered over by that of other events. This un-named war was and still is an un-remembered war. And for the same reasons.

The Second World War : Resistance And National Unity

This is precisely what makes the memory of the Second World War a kind of necessary memory. The principle of legitimacy is fully alive here: it works to support and deepen the memory of this war. However, such a principle tends to distort memories in some respects.

The victims were many. Prisoners of war, for instance, numbered 1,800,000 in 1940. No doubt they were victims of the war, but not entirely legitimate ones. They had not fought enough. According to the military system of values which was shared by the elder part of French population, mainly by First World War veterans, surrendering was shameful. The POWs were not welcomed by the existing associations of *anciens combattants de* '14,[14] which contested their status as combatants. Was not surrendering the opposite of fighting? Hence the POWs were obliged to create their own association in order to claim benefits. They meaningfully entitled it the 'Federation of combatant prisoners'.[15] It is now the largest association of veterans (300,000 members), and it succeeded in making the prisoners legitimate victims of the war. But by the time it had achieved this goal, it was too late: the individual prisoners had succeeded too in achieving their own goals – to recover their civilian condition, their occupation and their family life. The time when the ex-prisoners were accepted by French society as legitimate victims of the war was the time when they had ceased suffering the consequences of the war. They did not constitute or perpetuate a sense of the kinship of victims of war.

The most legitimate victims, at the very end of the war, were the *résistants*, especially those who had been deported by the Nazis to the concentration camps. The predominant legitimacy of having fought the Nazis had many consequences. The major crime was collaboration with the Nazis: this was the main focus for the work of memory. Pétain and the Vichy officials were tried for having offered aid and assistance to the enemy. Otherwise, their judgment would have been a political, not a national event. Hence the original features of the *Épuration* – the cleansing of collaborators – in France.

Some people have argued recently that the *Épuration* in France was relatively mild. They are wrong: on the contrary, France had a very broad and tough *Épuration*. The civil courts opened more than 300,000 files for inquiry; 150,000 cases were judged; more than 25,000 civil servants were punished; nearly 10,000 people were executed.[16]

However, it is true that the main point was whether the person charged had had some kind of relation with the Germans or not. When the general secretary of the anti-Jewish office, Xavier Vallat, was prosecuted before the High Court, he said in his defence that he was proud that his own anti-Semitism was purely French and existed long before the Nazi regime. In the circumstances of 1945, being an anti-Semite through personal initiative was less culpable than being one in response to Nazi orders.

This paradox is still alive. Paul Touvier was sentenced in 1994 for having sent to death seven Jews in 1944. According to French law, it is impossible to try someone 50 years after the deed, except in the case of crimes against humanity. But the definition of such a crime implies collaboration with the Nazi genocide. Hence the Court justified its pronouncement by stating that Touvier had obeyed Nazi orders, although it was perfectly evident in the proceedings that the

Gestapo had had nothing to do with these seven murders, which were the sole responsibility of Touvier himself. A just sentence is founded on an unjust argument.[17]

Conceived on these premises, the *Épuration* had the function of uniting the French people: the evil was outside. That made it impossible to face the fact that this war had been a civil war in some respects. The work of remembrance was made of lies, pious lies – well-meaning lies, but lies nonetheless. For instance, let us consider the case of Jean Zay. He was a very young and brilliant, talented politician, and the Minister of Education from 1936 to the war. He was murdered by the French *miliciens* (French collaborationist police) on 20 June 1944, because he was a freemason, a left-wing member of the hated Radical Party, a minister of the Popular Front and supposedly a Jew. On his gravestone, one reads: 'Killed by the enemies of France'. Before the door of the high school that has been named after him, there is written: 'Victim of Nazi barbarity'. Both statements are wrong: the right one would have to be: 'Victim of Frenchmen who thought themselves more French than he was'. The work of remembrance has tried to hide the fact that Frenchmen murdered other Frenchmen. Remembering was a way of preserving this kind of secret. The victims were rightly identified; the executioners were not.

Eight years later, it became somewhat difficult to preserve this hypocrisy. In 1953, the Court of Bordeaux had to judge the German SS soldiers who had burnt the little village of Oradour, near Limoges, in June 1944, burning inside the church most of the inhabitants of this village, including women and children. This martyred village was and is a strong symbol. It was a good case for remembering: the victims were French, and the executioners German. Unfortunately, it appeared that among the SS soldiers prosecuted, fourteen out of twenty-one were not Germans, but Alsatians, conscripted into the German army. Undoubtedly, they had contributed as much as the purely German soldiers to the slaughter. Meanwhile, Alsace was now part of France again, and there was an outcry in that part of France when it became clear that the Alsatians were guilty and would be sentenced. The government suspended the proceedings and found a compromise: they were sentenced first and immediately received full pardons.[18]

This attitude toward resistance and collaboration had two consequences for ensuring that the Algerian war would be un-remembered. As noted above, the legitimacy of the resistance made the *fellaghas'* fight somewhat legitimate, and undermined the legitimacy of the war on the French side. Furthermore, the incapacity to face what had been a kind of civil war inside the World War made it quite difficult to acknowledge that part of the evil that lay in the behaviour of the French army, if not of all French soldiers in Algeria. The distinction has to be made, for torture is spontaneously spoken of by many veterans of the Algerian war, although no one says he was actually involved in the torture business. Everybody knows something that nobody did.

The emphasis put, after the World War, on fighting the Nazis as the basic principle of remembrance had a second consequence: only those who had actually fought the Nazis were real, legitimate victims. Those who had not, were not worth remembering.

Such was the case of the few Jews (2,500 out of 75,000) coming back from the concentration camps. As they had not been deported for fighting the Germans, but 'only' for being Jews, they were not true victims. This point is widely documented. For instance, the former minister Simone Veil was evacuated from her camp to Birkenau at the end of the war. A few days after entering Birkenau, she heard voices speaking French in a shed. She entered and tried to take part in the conversation. After she had said she was a racial deportee, something was broken; she felt the political deportees despised her and she gave up.[19] Another example of that attitude is to be found in the main agencies of remembrance, the associations of ex-deportees. They accepted as members only resistance deportees, not racial ones. There were painfully few racial deportees who had come back from the camps. The survivors were obsessed with reintegrating into the French community, and as many of them were ill and depressed, they did not succeeded in making themselves a community of legitimate victims. They were not seen as a distinctive group. More books about the deportation of the Jews were published between 1945 and 1950 than during the twenty-five following years; but they were not read. As Annette Wieviorka put it, Buchenwald hid Auschwitz.

Things changed one generation later, around 1968–70. There were many reasons for this change: the Middle Eastern wars and the Eichmann trial; the coming to the fore of the generation of deportees' children, such as Serge Klarsfeld; a new intellectual mood, inspired by '68 and the Foucauldian spirit of demystification. Undoubtedly, some agencies of remembrance were at work. The results are clear: the issue of genocide has become the crucial one for the memory of the Second World War. The specifically French question of collaboration with the enemy has been replaced by that of co-operation in genocide.

Thus there has emerged progressively, forty years after the war, a community of victims of genocide. This community was constructed less by the victims themselves, survivors of the camps, than by their families and sometimes by people whose families had not been threatened by the Nazi genocide.

And here we have to cope again with the *pieds noirs* : the *Sephardi* Jews from Algeria contrast their condition to that of the victims of genocide. The *Ashkenazi* Jews deported from France to the death camps have a legitimacy as war victims that the Algerian Jews never had as victims of the Algerian war. Here is another link between the very weak collective remembrance of the Algerian war and the much stronger remembrance in France of the Second World. One could not win on every table: the memories of the résistance occluded, indeed precluded, remembrance of the Algerian war. The memories of the good, noble war hid the memories of the dirty one, which remains un-named.

Here we see how the social framing of individual memories is a decisive element. Individuals can form groups with the aim of transforming their collective memories into social action only when these memories are compatible with social norms and values accepted by the larger community. On the contrary, it is as implausible for ex-soldiers as it is for the *pieds noirs* to claim their rights as victims of war. The war itself lacked the legitimacy necessary for this claim.

Victims are victims only when being in no sense guilty of complicity in their suffering. Suffering and losses are necessary, but not sufficient, conditions for victimhood. Innocence is needed, too.

Notes

1. Jean-Pierre Rioux, 'La flamme et les bûchers', in Jean-Pierre Rioux (sous la dir. de), *La guerre d'Algérie et les Français* (Paris, Fayard, 1990), p. 499. This important book arose out of a colloquium organized by the Institut d'histoire du temps présent, 15–18 December 1988.

2. The best history of the war remains Bernard Droz and Evelyne Lever, *Histoire de la guerre d'Algérie* (Paris, Ed. du Seuil, 1982). A much shorter

account is given by the well-known specialist, Charles-Robert Ageron, in his article 'Guerre d'Algérie', in Jean-François Sirinelli, *Dictionnaire historique de la vie politique française au XX siècle* (Paris, PUF, 1995), pp. 462–70.

3. Charles-Robert Ageron, 'L'opinion française à travers les sondages', in *La guerre d'Algérie* Rioux, ibid., pp. 25–44.

4 . Benjamin Stora, ibid., pp. 200–3 and p. 261.

5. Benoît Kaplan, 'Une génération d'élèves des grandes Écoles en Algérie. Mémoire d'une guerre', mémoire de maîtrise d' histoire, Université de Paris I, 1994, published as winner of a prize by the FEN, *Cahiers du Centre fédéral*, no. 18, (November 1996), p. 110.

6. 'De jeunes militants dans le contingent: l'enquète des organisations de jeunesse de 1959–1960', in Jean-Pierre Rioux (sous la dir. de), *La guerre d'Algérie et les Français*, p. 90.

7. About 930,000 *pieds noirs* came to France from Algiers in 1962. See Benjamin Stora, *La gangrène et l'oubli, la mémoire de la guerre d'Algérie* (Paris, La Découverte, 1992), p. 256.

8. See Joëlle Hureau, 'Associations et souvenir chez les Français rapatriés d'Algérie', in Rioux, *La guerre d'Algérie*, pp. 517–25. As these associations' names are meaningful in French, let me explicate their acronyms. ANFANOMA means Association Nationale des Français d'Afrique du Nord d'Outre-Mer et leurs Amis; RECOURS means Rassemblement et Coordination Unitaire des Rapatriés et des Spoliés; FURR means Fédération pour l'Unité des Rapatriés, Réfugiés et de leurs amis.

9. See the excellent analysis of some interviews by Anne Roche, 'La perte et la parole: témoignages oraux de pieds noirs', in Jean-Pierre Rioux, *La guerre d'Algérie*, pp. 526–37.

10. See Claude Liauzu, 'Le contingent entre silence et discours ancien combattant', in Jean-Pierre Rioux, ibid., pp. 509–16.

11. Armand Frémont, 'Le contingent: témoignage et réflexion', in Jean-Pierre Rioux, ibid., p. 84.

12. Benoît Kaplan, ibid., p. 176 et seq. Many years later, Claude Bourdet, who had been one of the leaders of the resistance movement 'Combat' and an ex-deportee to Buchenwald, stated the point: 'I saw what the Nazis did. Was it worth it to defeat the Nazis by doing the same things as they did?' Cited in Benjamin Stora, ibid., p. 110.

13. 'Des soldats sans victoire, sans cause juste ou sans enthousiasme ne peuvent devenir des figures positives', Claude Liauzu, ibid., p. 515.

14. Antoine Prost, *In the Wake of War: 'les Anciens Combattants' and French Society* (Providence/Oxford, Berg Publishers, 1992).

15. Christophe Lewin, *Le retour des prisonniers de guerre français* (Paris, Publications de la Sorbonne, 1986), tells the story of the formation of the Fédération nationale des combattants prisonniers de guerre.

16. Henry Rousso, 'L'Épuration, une histoire inachevée', *Vingtième siècle, revue d'histoire*, no. 35 (January–March 1992), pp. 78–105; François

Rouquet, *L'Épuration dans l'administration française*, (Paris, CNRS Editions, 1993).

17. See Eric Conan and Henry Rousso, 'Touvier: le dernier procès de l'Épuration', in *Vichy, un passé qui ne passe pas* (Paris, Fayard, 1994), pp. 109–72.

18. Henry Rousso, *Le syndrome de Vichy de 1944 à nos jours* (Paris, Ed. du Seuil, 1987). See also 'La Seconde Guerre mondiale dans la mémoire des droites françaises', in Jean-François Sirinelli, *Histoire des droites en France, tome 2, Cultures* (Paris, Gallimard, 1992), pp. 549–620.

19 . See Annette Wieviorka, *Déportation et génocide, entre la mémoire et l'oubli* (Paris, Plon, 1992), p. 249.

II. Identities and Civil Society: Urban Space, Social Identities and Youth

6

The People of Paris: The Eighteenth *Arrondissement* in 1936

The population of nineteenth-century Paris has been much more extensively studied than has that of the twentieth century.[1] Actually, we do not know very much about the composition of this population between the wars, its origins, its social structure; hence the idea of launching the first detailed investigation of this subject in the social and demographic history of Paris. This aim, however, is not the only purpose of the present essay. By describing the population of an *arrondissement*,[2] we aim to show how profoundly any social description is shaped by the categories and tools it uses in analysing its subject. It may be helpful to offer a number of introductory remarks on this methodological issue.

As do all social scientists, historians need to construct a relevant taxonomy in order to describe any given society or social formation. They have to determine what groups the society they study is composed of, and how to denominate these groups. Collectively, the array of these groups should give a picture of that society; and within it, each social group is taken to be separate from any other. Generally, historians borrow the taxonomy they use from sociologists, demographers and other statisticians, so that their results can be compared with a set of observations and conclusions arising in the work of these colleagues. It is for this reason that historians rarely discuss the character of the social classification on which their own analysis depends. Many historians are like theatrical directors: they direct plays in which collective characters are on the stage: 'workers', 'the bourgeoisie', 'peasants' and so on, as if these entities existed as such in a 'real' world. However, the relevance of such entities to historical situations and the adequacy of such taxonomies are crucial determinants of the scientific value of such research. Social analysis of this kind is only as valuable as the taxonomy it uses.

The point is not a minor one, for social classification systems are historical artefacts, which are marked by arbitrary elements. At times they appear in periods of social confrontation, which leave their traces on the classifications framed at the time. One illuminating example is, in France, the construction of the category of 'cadres' in 1936–38 and 1945–47, during periods of intense social conflict.[3] It is crucial to note that social taxonomies are not outside history: they are themselves historical in origin. This is the reason why each society sets up its own social taxonomy according to its own practices, its constituent circumstances and the self-representation it wants its own members to internalize. Underneath the scientific patina of any taxonomy, some historical contingency rests.

The social taxonomy used today in France is quite different from its Anglo-Saxon counterpart. In France, the framework of social classification was elaborated by the French statistical agency, INSEE,[4] for the 1954 census.[5] Surprisingly enough, in this supposedly Cartesian country, this exercise in social classification was not based on a theory, but arose from a very pragmatic approach. Several criteria were taken into account, such as the level of income and social prestige, the level of qualification required for a job, the employment status (independent, salaried and so on). And the words chosen for naming the groups resulting from this statistical elaboration were very close to vernacular language shared by most people. Everybody knows what they mean. These features explain why the socio-professional categories (CSP) constituting this social taxonomy were easily accepted and naturalized as obviously true. The social classification used in Great Britain is quite different, more theoretically-based and hierarchical in character.[6]

Although it is empirically constructed, the French grid of socio-professional categories – farmers, farm-workers, industrial and commercial employers, the learned professions and senior managers, middle managers, salaried staff and wage-earning employees, service personnel – does not fit all populations. Two objections must be noted.

The first one is particularly relevant to the study of the Parisian population. The INSEE taxonomy, developed for national surveys, cannot match the multiplicity of local hierarchies with all their intricacies, whether urban or rural; it inevitably loses in depth what it gains in breadth. Of course it can be refined, and it allows for precise distinctions, between office and shop staff, for example, or between small and large employers. However it postulates that all office staff are alike, in banks or in insurance offices, in Paris as in Lyons, in Aurillac or elsewhere: a uniformity that can be questioned, especially in the case of Paris.

The second objection is less about observations than about what they mean to the people whose lives are described by them. Although empirically constructed, this taxonomy concentrates on objective indices of social position to establish relatively homogeneous groups by income or social position. Yet the rational and the real do not necessarily coincide: we do not know whether these logically constructed statistical entities correspond to the realities as they are experienced and perceived by individuals, i.e. the social groups consisting of individuals who create networks of relationships.

For these two reasons, it is impossible to give an adequate picture of what was the social structure of the Parisian population between the wars by using the officially accepted INSEE taxonomy. Instead, we have tried to construct an alternative: one based on social relations. Our ultimate aim will be to compare the description produced by this classification of social networks with that produced by the INSEE format, and to show how different are the pictures these two approaches provide.

Data and Method

In order to elaborate a Parisian taxonomy based on social networks, it was necessary to select a limited set of data that would make such an exercise feasible. We decided to concentrate our investigation on the restricted area of one Paris arrondissement. We selected the 18th arrondissement because of its size and the diversity of its population: in 1936 its 280,000 inhabitants represented 10 per cent of the Paris of the day, and included relatively middle-class streets and districts alongside popular or working-class quarters. Within this territory we try to give a precise description of social networks, to identify individuals who encounter each other and thus to identify groups that are based on relationships knitted together by individuals, and from this, ultimately to construct a social taxonomy consistent with lived experience.

But how can one observe relational networks? Sixty years after the Popular Front of the mid-1930s, a direct survey is impossible; hence the idea of looking at a unique archival source: marriage certificates. At this special moment in their lives, spouses indicate clearly some of their significant social relationships. Alongside the occupations of the two people being married, the civil record indicates with scrupulous care the occupations of their parents and of both their witnesses. The result is a documentary record of eight different occupations, including four (those of the spouses and their witnesses) that are the result of mutual social selection.

Of course, the occupations listed in these registers arise from the participants' statements, and naturally they are more precise about their own details than about those that relate to their witnesses – which no doubt explains why more employees are shown as 's.a.i.' (*sans autre indication*, no further information) among the witnesses than among the brides and bridegrooms. It is also possible that these statements were occasionally influenced by the spouses' wish to appear more important than they were. It is even more probable that this very wish can be seen as socially significant and worth taking into consideration. The statements are also somewhat vague: is an electrician a worker or a craftsman? Is a *chauffeur* a boiler-man, or the driver of a steam engine, or does he drives a delivery lorry? These are problems that we have not underestimated, and that would repay more extensive consideration than is possible here. Essentially, however, what we use are the words selected by the participants to describe themselves and their witnesses. They are expressions of self-designation, and this is precisely what makes them particularly valuable statements.

To make use of these self-designations they must be handled with care; in other words they must not be folded into more general expressions such as 'middle managers'. No spouse or witness ever described himself as a 'middle manager' (*cadre moyen*) or even a 'senior manager' (*cadre supérieur*). We must avoid assuming that the employee who described himself as an insurance office worker should be considered the same as the one who gives the description of 'office worker', or the furniture salesman the same as the shoe-salesman or the shopkeeper. This methodological precaution, which means using the marriage certificates without any preset coding, is the only way of avoiding the surreptitious introduction at the beginning of the analysis of the taxonomy that the analysis specific-ally sets out to construct empirically.

This entails fairly severe constraints that would be unmanageable on a larger scale. Even the limited scene of the 18th arrondissement is too large, with 2,473 marriages celebrated in 1936. In order to facilitate the analysis we have reduced the field through a double exclusion. First, we have excluded the parents. The large number of parents who were already dead (from 27 per cent of mothers of brides to 46 per cent of fathers of bridegrooms) or without any trade or occupation (more than 50 per cent of the mothers) means that we cannot know the occupation of more than a minority of parents (45 per cent at best, for the husbands' fathers, 17 per cent for their mothers), thus depriving the analysis of part of its point. Further, the parents' occupations appear more like a survey of social mobility than an analysis of networks of contemporary relationship, particularly because a significant minority of these parents lived neither in Paris nor in its outlying suburbs. We have therefore concentrated on the spouses and their witnesses. Furthermore, we have sought to eliminate witnesses closely related to the bride or bridegroom, whose marriages provide evidence of networks more familial than social. But since the marriage certificates do not reveal any degree of possible family connection between witnesses and spouses, there is no alternative to considering witnesses who bear the same family name as one or other of the parents as connected to the spouses through a familial link. This is a reasonable exclusion, though no doubt unjustified in some cases, and inadequate in others: the sister's husband does not have the same family name as her father or mother.

To analyse these uncoded data,[7] we have exploited a software program developed by the Historical Demography group of the École des Hautes Études en Sciences Sociales. This programme uses links to define connections between the occupations.[8] In this way we have analysed 3,633 bridegroom/witness pairs and several hundred bride/witness or bridegroom/bride pairs; to make these configurations readable, we have set up relatively homogeneous groupings by retaining the pairs where either the bridegroom or the witness represented the same group of occupations. Thus a mechanic/engineer pair is located once under engineers and again under mechanics. This avoids the risk of unilaterally recreating networks of social relationships. The annexed diagram (Figure 6.1) shows the results produced by this method for the artists.[9]

Social Networks

The first fruits of this investigation can be found in precisely this intertwining of links that unites occupations as remote from each other in prestige as in type. Among the draughtsmen's witnesses, for example, one can find a company director, a manufacturer, an engineer or a judge as easily as a labourer, a butcher or a clerk. Thus

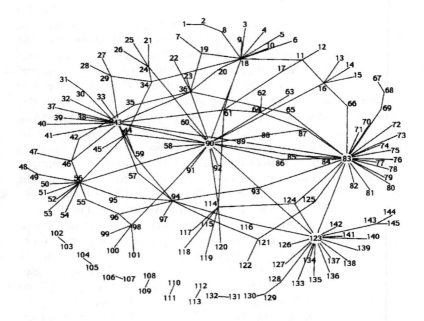

1 Furrier	25 Draftsman	50 Banker
2 Female student	26 House painter	51 Shop employee
3 Toolmaker-fitter	27 **Acrobat master**	52 Bank director
4 Female hotelkeeper	28 Dress maker	53 Manufacturer
5 Chemical engineer	29 **Acrobat**	54 Saleswoman
6 Telephonist	30 Engineer	55 Sailor
7 **Piano teacher**	31 **Ballet master**	56 **Actor**
8 Insurance employee	32 Insurance under-manager	57 **Phographer**
9 Railway employee	33 Dentist	58 **Violinist**
10 Postal employee	34 Shopkeeper	59 Shop worker
11 Police superintendant	35 Baker	60 Musician artist
12 Translator	36 **Film actor**	61 Sales representative
13 Town councillor	37 Stationer	62 Fitter
14 Baillif	38 Decorator	63 Foreman
15 Pork butcher	39 Interpreter	64 **Music composer**
16 Jockey	40 Taxi-driver	65 Representative
17 Stockbroker	41 Agent	66 Plumber
18 Student	42 **Man of letters**	67 Panel beater
19 Secretary	44 **Artist**	68 **Tuner**
20 Administrative employee	45 **Assistant**	69 Mechanic
21 Female shopkeeper	46 No indication	70 Bank employee
22 Chamber maid	47 **Male dancer**	71 Female cashier
23 Lawyer	48 Rabbi	72 Female property owner
24 **Cinema projectionist**	49 Book-keeper	73 Sewerman

132

74 Café manager	98 **Orchestral conductor**	122 Underground employee
75 Broker	99 Ironmonger	123 Soldier
76 Controller	100 Warehouse woman	124 Driver
77 Cashier	101 Cook	125 Dry-cleaner, dyer
78 Typesetter	102 Photo-engraver	126 Fitter-toolmaker
79 Female retailer	103 **Female dancer**	127 Cement worker
80 Central heating installer	104 **Film director**	128 Male hotelkeeper
81 Joiner	105 Mechanical designer	129 **Cinema worker**
82 Restaurant	106 Insurance draftsman	130 Cinema/Theatre manager
83 **Male musician**	107 **Male singer**	131 Sleeping-car attendant
84 Shoe maker	108 **Bandmaster**	132 **Clown**
85 **Music teacher**	109 Postal controller	133 Female hairdresser
86 **Female musician**	110 Stock exchange employee	134 Butcher
87 Male employee	111 **Model**	135 Female barkeeper
88 **Boxer**	112 **Cinema assistant**	136 Clerk
89 Pastry cook	113 Male nurse	137 Male hairdresser
90 No occupation	114 **Lyric artist**	138 Wholesaler
91 **Pianist**	115 Architect	139 Manservant
92 **Dancing teacher**	116 Tailor	140 Earth-worker
93 Shorthand-typist	117 Intermediate broker	141 Electrician
94 **Fine-art painter**	118 Inspector	142 Gardener
95 Draughtsman	119 Female employee	143 Insurance inspector
96 Concierge	120 **Engraver**	144 **Wardrobe master (male)**
97 Bootmaker	121 **Sculptor**	145 **Wardrobe mistress**

Figure 6.1: Networks of witnesses to marriages of people in artistic occupation, 18th *arrondissement* of Paris, 1936 (the artistic professions are put in bold characters).

the pattern of most of the pairs over most of the sample was strictly speaking unreadable: even enlarged into formats of nearly a metre long, the diagram shows thousands of tangled lines from which no network emerged.

This result was surprising, for it invalidated our original hypotheses. The reason for highlighting the links between spouse and witness was that they suggested both the bringing together of two occupations and their social inequality. William Sewell was the first to draw attention to one feature: the witnesses usually represented more prestigious professions than the spouses.[10] We have confirmed this finding for the 18th arrondissement in 1936.[11] It is easily explained: spouses sought witnesses who would bring them credit, such as the pilot who invited the director of Air France for this purpose (no. 2695),[12] or the mechanic who sought an engineer (no. 2161). We decided therefore to show relationships of order between the occupations, in the mathematical sense, which would make it possible, we thought, to define hierarchies: occupation A inferior to occupation B, which was in turn inferior to occupation C, and so on. We also thought that the occupational worlds were relatively enclosed, that workshop staff did not mix with shop staff, that the fitter would be linked with the mechanic, the draughtsman or the engineer but not with the teacher, while the latter would mix with other civil servants, or book-keepers, but not shopkeepers. These two hypotheses led to the idea of a Parisian society structured in socio-professional sub-groups that were both relatively clear-cut and fairly strictly ordered.

The truth was entirely otherwise: neither of these theories was accurate. Even though we found that not everyone mixed with everyone else, no pairing, even the most unlikely, was excluded. Thus we find a journalist and an editor acting as witnesses for the marriage of a labourer and a house-maid (no. 1831), and there were many such examples. Sometimes, hierarchies were reversed: one could also find an engineer taking a mechanic as a witness (no. 1432), while others were supported by a cutter, a film-projector, a ballet-teacher, an office worker (2 cases), a primary-school teacher, a manufacturer, a shopkeeper, a dentist. This first finding deserves emphasis, since sociologists too often consider social groups as entities closed to one another, as stable and clear-cut things. Urban society is much more fluid and permeable than is generally supposed.[13] The great city is indeed, as its apologists maintain, the place for multiple encounters and intense social mixing.

For these reasons we ended with a much more open taxonomy, far less clear-cut in its hierarchies, than that of INSEE. We have had to be satisfied with a fairly summary hierarchy, achieved by distinguishing between three classes: upper, middle and lower. With further internal subdivisions we were able to identify seven hierarchical levels, but these precise hierarchies remain partial: the occupational designations do not always make it possible to assign an individual to a precise level. In certain cases we have therefore retained a lack of precision which is shown in the attached image by cases 'astride' two hierarchical levels, such as those of manufacturers and merchants in the upper class. We thought it better to accept this imprecision as a significant feature of the occupational structure than to make an arbitrary decision. In this way certain occupations create a continuity between the middle classes and those above and below them.

The frontiers between professional worlds made it possible to distinguish six major sectors. The first three correspond to three concrete styles of production and also to three types of product: (1) the factory and the workshop, which is the world of the mechanic and of metals; (2) construction and its elements, building sites with their stone, cement, zinc and paint; and (3) the world of craftsmen or men and women home-workers who work with wood, fabrics, leather and furs. (4) The fourth is the world of shops with their street access, their deliveries and their customers; a specific place must be identified here for food shops and cafés. Finally, the two last sectors are (5) those of offices and (6) public services. A number of residual categories have been excluded. Farmers, the unemployed and the deceased have been separated out and given a separate code to make it possible to continue the survey at a later date on the parents.

Excluding these residual categories, we are left with a taxonomy of 57 self-ascribed occupational categories (see Figure 6.2 below). To define the groupings in greater detail would have meant losing the diversity of social groupings that the analysis has the great virtue of bringing out. What is the social landscape that it describes?

The Upper Classes

The top of the social hierarchy in the 18th arrondissement is undoubtedly occupied by the members of the liberal professions, in particular lawyers – often chosen as witnesses, followed by insurance underwriters, doctors, architects and, among the less prestigious, accountants and dentists. Senior government officials are rare: what one might call the State *bourgeoisie* is represented only by a magistrate of the Court of Appeals, witness for a judge together with a lawyer (no. 260), an ambassador, a vice-consul and a few generals and colonels.

The bourgeoisie of the business world is represented by merchants, company managers and manufacturers. It seems that the first of these stood a little higher on the social scale than the two other categories. In fact the spouses who sought a manufacturer as witness appear more modest: they include a dentist and some engineers, while the bridegrooms supported by a merchant include a doctor, a communications engineer and an officer. The difference would not be significant if they were equally numerous; but since manufacturers produce many more witnesses than merchants (35 against 19), if they were equal one should find more of the higher professions among the husbands whose marriages they witnessed. With respect

LOWER CLASS			MIDDLE CLASS		UPPER CLASS	
1	2	3	1	2	1	2
			40 Foreman		16 Engineer, Plant manager, Manager (unsp)	
80 Labourer, Day-worker	70 Fitter, Assembler, Turner	60 Tool-maker, Mechanic, Printer	41 Draughtsman, Quantity surveyor		12 Manufacturer	
	71 Mason, Stove setter, Painter, Plumber	61 Electrician		20 Contractor		
		62 Joiner, Cabinet maker, Locksmith				
	72 Laundress	63 Dressmaker	42 Craftsman			
		64 Tailor, Furrier, Leather worker, Hatter, Cutter, Upholsterer				
		65 Hairdresser, Milliner				
	76 Baker's boy	66 Baker, Butcher, Pork butcher				
	77 Café waiter, Restaurant staff	67 Café manager, Wine merchant		21 Hotel or restaurant manager		
85 Greengrocer, Street vendor			44 Shopkeeper (spec) such as Stationery, Hardware, Clocks	22 Dealer (unsp)	13 Trader, Company manager or director, Sales manager	
86 Musician			45 Broker, Travelling salesman	23 Salesman		
	75 Caretaker	68 Warehouse keeper, Shop assistant	47 Shop assistant, Salesperson, Unsp. employee		18 Owners, Leisure class	
				30 Actor	19 Student	
88 Domestic staff	74 Driver, Delivery-man, Taxi-driver	59 Concierge	48 Shorthand-typist, Typist, Cashier	31 Clerks	14 Dentist, Accountant, Journalist	10 Lawyer, Doctor, Insurance agent, Architect
			49 Book-keeper, Bank staff, Office staff	32 Secretary, Draftsman, Insurance staff		
		55 Postman, Telephonist	50 Postal worker	33 Manager of office, service, accounting	15 Officer, Teacher	11 Judges, Senior civil servants
		56 Conductor, Gasman	51 Railway or Metro employee			
		57 Policeman	52 Unspecified supervisor	34 Tax inspector, Police inspector		
		58 Caretaker (public)	53 Nurse, male nurse, Pharmacist	35 Primary school teacher		
			54 Non-comm. Officer			

0 Farmer, 1 Wine grower, Truck farmer etc., 2 agricultural labourers, 95 No occupation, 96 Occupation unknown, 97 Missing, 98 Unknown person, 99 Deceased

Figure 6.2: A sketch of the social structure of the 18th *arrondissement* of Paris, 1936.

to those who took the category of 'contractor', building contractors, with one exception (a lawyer witness), have more connections with the world of craftsmen and labourers, which places them a little below the manufacturers, astride the upper and middle classes.

There remain those who would today be called managers, and who constitute a sort of business upper class: sales managers, factory managers, engineers. We find here the same slight difference as between the industrialists and the merchants. The social horizon of the sales managers is broader, more highly ranked than that of the directors of industry or factory, which was more focused on the workshop world. Everything seems to indicate that production was of a lesser social status than trade.

This is confirmed by the case of the engineers. Taking all designations overall, engineers represent 43 of the new husbands. They are older, for nineteen of them are over 30. Their network of relationships is very varied, and touches all the sectors of our sample. We may be looking at a very heterogeneous category: what is the common link between an electrical engineer who marries a women without an occupation, with an ambassador and a factory manager as his witnesses (no. 866), and another electrical engineer who marries a shorthand-typist with the support of a quantity surveyor and a shoe-mender (no. 1158)? Or the engineer – no further information given – who marries a bride without an occupation, with a film director and a ballet teacher as witnesses (no. 520)? In fact only the engineers from the school of Arts and Crafts and the École Bréguet indicate their origin explicitly, though that does not mean that no one came from the École Centrale des Arts et Manufactures; there was even a graduate of the École Polytechnique accompanying the chief engineer of the École des Ponts – though it is true that he was 43, his bride did not work and his two witnesses were engineers (no. 2760). On the other hand, nothing indicates the professional branch of the majority of the engineers, and a large proportion of them were probably in-house engineers; the distinction of the title of graduate engineer was then very recent (1934), and the homogeneity of the occupational group reflects this.

Overall, the *bourgeoisie* was not strongly represented in the population of our arrondissement, and it seems both less prestigious and less prosperous than that of the grander districts. For a detailed survey of those circles, a survey of the 16th or the 7th arrondissements would be very instructive. On the other hand, for the middle and lower classes the 18th is extremely informative.

The Middle Classes

The most debatable point, and the most delicate for a social taxonomy, lies in the middle classes. Their intermediary location makes any precise assignment uncertain: does the construction contractor or finishing trades contractor belong to the upper fringe of the middle classes, or is he already part of the upper classes? This could be discussed at length, and, as noted above, we have chosen to embrace this very lack of precision by placing them astride two levels. Similarly, should one place craftsmen and skilled tradesmen such as cabinet-makers or upholsterers in a superior stratum of the lower class or a lower stratum of the middle class? One may well hesitate. For a long time INSEE considered foremen as workmen, before they were classified, in its new nomenclature, among the intermediate professions.

If there is one sector of activity in which social hierarchies are clear, it is however that of industrial production, the world of the factory or the workshop. The social horizon of the foreman, the head of the workshop or the site, like the draughtsman or the quantity surveyor, is very broad: it is as open towards engineers and secretaries as to workmen. One may find foremen as witnesses for an architect, a music composer, a bar-keeper, a printer, etc., and draughtsmen as witnesses for a dealer as well as for a mechanic, for an accountant as well as an actor, etc. These professions are to some extent transitional. The breadth of their social horizon locates them in the middle class.

More hesitation arises over trades, sometimes very widespread, such as that of electrician or joiner, the tasks of which can be undertaken either by a craftsman or as a wage-earning employee, or again over trades such as working with fabrics or skins. It is impossible to know if the tailor, the furrier, the leather-worker, the hatmaker or the carpet-layer, or even the dressmaker, had his or her own shop or studio, if they were employed by a craftsman or whether they worked to order for a trader. Sometimes we are on the lower edges of the middle classes here, which is why, while respecting this ambivalence, we have given these professions codes in the same series as those of other professions in this stratum.

Most of the middle classes are clearly shopkeepers and those who today would be described as middle managers: a group of rather vaguely defined occupations for which an analysis of social relationships sketches out a hierarchy. First, there are the food trades:

butchers, pork butchers, bakers. Their network of relationships contains virtually no members of the upper classes and relatively few of the lower class. Many of their witnesses come from other food trades and the world of employed staff. Here, people tend to marry younger and to be less Parisian in origin than the average. This picture suggests young men, both geographically and socially mobile, who marry before becoming established. It seems logical to consider them as astride the line between the lower and the middle classes.

The picture of café owners, bar-keepers, licensed victuallers, wine merchants, restaurateurs and hoteliers is similar but clearer. Here, the lower class of café waiters and chefs is clearly designated. Café owners, strictly speaking, appear only as witnesses and not as bridegrooms, as if it were impossible to run a café without being married. However, it is worth noting for whom the café owners stand as witness: they are people who form part of a more modest group than the hoteliers and restaurateurs – who clearly represent the upper level of the middle class and can be seen among the witnesses of *bourgeois* marriages. Café owners represent the lower level, and sometimes the upper levels of the lower classes. Between these two professions, the difference may be explained by the amount of capital at stake and by a stronger element of *bourgeoisie* among the clientèle.

Among other traders, self-descriptions are not without hidden meanings. As a general rule, traders, merchants or dealers in a specific sector are lower on the social scale than those who give no further indication. The reason for this distinction escapes us. Perhaps it represents the contrast between speciality and generality? Or the emphasis tending towards the product being sold, as opposed to the merchant activity itself? Similarly, the hierarchy is clear between representatives without specific indication and, a notch lower, salesmen, but this is no doubt easier to explain: the representative who moves around little and enjoys the exclusivity of well-known businesses no doubt occupies a more respectable position than the travelling salesman obliged to dash from one customer to the next.

Most commercial or office staff also come from the middle classes, but with revealing divisions. The analysis here covers not only the bridegrooms but also their brides, for women employees are numerous in this grouping. Male and female bank and office staff, like book-keepers, are a little below secretaries; but insurance staff, for example, have more flattering witnesses: two manufacturers, an engineer, two students, a hospital doctor, and only one mechanic and one day-labourer, compared to the mechanics, fitters and electricians who came forward at the side of the bank staff; conversely, the latter served as witness to the same working trades, while an insurance inspector and an inspector of public works called on insurance office staff as witnesses. The same asymmetry can be seen between secretaries and book-keepers. This is because at the time book-keeping was very limited – the first book-keeping plan dates from 1942 – and book-keepers primarily added up figures, while bank staff checked counterfoils, particularly in the 18th area close to large bank headquarters. Secretaries and insurance staff enjoyed less monotonous occupations involving greater responsibilities.

In the public services the hierarchies are often explicit, and examination of relationship networks confirms them. The heads of something (of an office, a service, etc.) represent the upper level of the middle classes, and ordinary staff the lower level. Supervisors without any further indication come from the lower level, like NCOs, pharmacy dispensers and nurses. Primary-school teachers, on the other hand, belong to the upper level; none of them had a witness from a labouring occupation, indicating a certain social distancing. The distinctive feature here is their strong endogamy – half of them marry women teachers, which suggests a group that tends to be inward-looking.

The situation is similar for workers in postal communications and railway or metro staff. This very distinctive world of those who wear uniforms is striking in the significance of its sector divisions; each public body forms a separate world, with internal relationships frequent within the group, but where external relationships appear to avoid the most closely neighbouring public bodies in favour of the more distant ones. Railways and the post office meet only once in our sample: a postal inspector who took a railway employee as his witness (no. 2792). On the other hand, railway workers appear widely as witnesses for labourers, mechanics or electricians in particular and as witnesses to their marriages we find traders, two property-owners, a dealer and an engineer, which places them in the middle class.

The Lower Classes

The prestige of a uniform, and the status that it represents, confer benefits on the most humble employees of public administration and services. This explains the place in the upper stratum of the lower class of policemen, post-office staff and postmen. Telephonists and telegraphists have workers as witnesses (a winder, an electrician). Postmen generally recruit their witnesses from offices. Policemen choose teachers, a police inspector, office staff. It would be unwise here to attempt any introduction of hierarchies: we are above labourers or messenger boys, but these circles meet on a relatively egalitarian footing.

On the other hand, hierarchies are very clear in factories and workshops. Labourers, like day-workers, are more often bridegrooms than witnesses; they act as witnesses for other labourers or day-workers, for drivers or delivery men, for a lorry-driver, a taxi-driver and to manual workers, particularly in the building trade: carpenter, joiner, roofer, roofer-plumber. In their world the building site is better represented than the factory: no doubt mechanization has reduced the demands for factory hands, while the building trade, more traditional in its structures, continues to demand labourers in large numbers.

Among workers we can be fairly clear on the differences that divide the well-represented occupations – adjusters, winders, assemblers, toolmakers, electricians. Two convergent criteria enable us to draw up a hierarchy here: on the one hand the barrier against the working-class world, on the other, the relative numbers of husbands and witnesses. Adjusters and winders take witnesses from the worker group more often than mechanics and electricians: one in three or four adjusters and winders, no more than one in five electricians, locksmiths and mechanics. The former are much less in demand as witnesses than the second group: among the individual representatives, the first group of occupations, taking witnesses and bridegrooms together, provides one witness compared to two husbands, while in the second group we find two witnesses for three husbands. This is what leads us to classify the first in the median stratum of the working-class world, between labourers and the upper stratum of toolmakers, mechanics and electricians.

A similar situation can be seen in what one may call street people and casual workmen, these trades whose distinctiveness too often disappears behind labels such as 'worker' or 'service staff'. Here, for example, we see the many waiters in cafés, hotels or restaurants, waitresses, greengrocers, drivers, delivery men and taxi-drivers. Here too are domestic staff and concierges, who often appear as witnesses. Can we discern a pattern among these occupations?

Café waiters are younger than the average bridegroom. They choose their witnesses primarily from among their equals and their employers, but also in the working-class world (labourer, fitter, winder, mechanic), from sales representatives and office staff, and similarly from male and female shopkeepers, or even dealers. Restaurant waiters follow the same pattern. Female restaurant staff, who one might wrongly imagine with dish-cloth in hand, have socially superior witnesses: a lawyer, an insurance agent, nine male or female shopkeepers. The social boundaries of these professions are very broad, no doubt because of the multiple encounters that take place in cafés and restaurants. Domestic staff represent a more modest world, largely working-class, where the escape to other worlds is limited to the middle class and not to the upper class, as for café waiters. Chambermaids find their witnesses among their close companions at work or among craft workers (joiners, upholsterers). Children's nannies marry modest husbands, and only one can be found among the witnesses: it is not a profession that raises the tone of a marriage. Thus we can class domestic staff in the lower stratum of the lower class, while café waiters and similar categories come into the middle level.

Drivers, delivery-drivers and delivery men represent the group of professions with the highest numbers. The network of their relationships shows slighter links with factory workers than with those of the street, shops and offices, confirmation that they are genuinely drivers of lorries or other automobiles and not of steam engines. The group is very probably heterogeneous, and it no doubt includes some private chauffeurs, successors to the former category of coachmen, like the driver whose witness is a parliamentary deputy (no.1091). Among their witnesses we find around ten workmen, some craftsmen, shopkeepers and wine-merchants, office staff, and even some members of the middle classes. Conversely, they are chosen by workmen, shopkeepers and craftsmen, by café waiters and domestic staff. We are not at the bottom of the social scale here, but in the heart of the lower classes.

Then there are the occupations that are particularly well represented in the Pigalle district and around the Rue Francoeur – artists. Our population includes numerous musicians, musical or dramatic performers, acrobats, orchestral conductors, music composers, film directors, film staff, etc. Where should we locate these occupations, marginal on the national scale but an essential feature here? Their networks are particularly enlightening (see Figure 6.1 as an example). Musicians have unimpressive witnesses: central-heating installer, typesetter, cashier, supervisor, dyer; on the other hand, they are chosen by a bank employee, a drains worker, a driver, a pastry chef, a republican guard, a joiner. The contrast with actors is striking: their witnesses are a banker, a bank director, an manufacturer. Orchestral conductors and music composers are ranked alongside musicians, like singers, artists, jockeys and acrobats.[14]

A New Picture of Parisian Society?

This detailed survey was crucial for highlighting the diversity of the population of this arrondissement; however, it does not permit us to draw a synthetic global picture. Consequently, grouping of categories at a second level was necessary. We tried to draw relatively relevant aggregates – i.e. those that implied the stronger contrasts – while still maintaining a reasonable balance of people included in each grouping. After several trials, the most relevant course seems to be to construct 11 social groups from the 57 primary categories. These social groups are the following :

1 The bourgeoisie (professionals, senior managers, higher civil servants, engineers, manufacturers and company managers).
2 The entrepreneurial middle class (employers, hotel and restaurant managers, dealers, salesmen).
3 The educated middle class, the *capacités* as they were termed under the July Monarchy, people whose occupation depends on the education they have (personal secretaries, chief clerks, managers of offices, schoolteachers, NCOs, police inspectors and so on).
4 Craftsmen and lower managers (foremen, draughtsmen, quantity surveyors, toolmakers, electricians, cabinet-makers), people whose very wealth lies in their skills and competence and who are sometimes independent workers, sometimes salaried workers.
5 Shopkeepers, travelling salesmen, butchers, pork-butchers, bakers, wine merchants.
6 Shop assistants, sales employees, warehouse keepers.
7 Office staff.
8 Employees protected by specific statutes[15] and lower civil servants.
9 Dressmakers, tailors, furriers and so on. These occupations are mostly feminine. People work mainly at home and are paid for the work done, not for the time spent. The very small numbers of domestic workers have been included in this group.

10 Unskilled workers, daily workers and labourers, including fitters, assemblers, masons, painters and so on.
11 People of the street.

Obviously, these social groups are not strictly hierarchically ordered. The bourgeoisie and the middle class are clearly identified, as is the upper stratum of the lower class, but the main interest of this classification is in the way it delineates diverse groups among the popular classes, the people of Paris.

However, to draw up a social taxonomy is not an end in itself; it is a means to describe a given society. The point here is to know whether this classification establishes a different and better picture of the Parisian population than the INSEE's grid. If the proposed classification outlines a description that is not so far from the traditional occupational analysis, it will be useless, however scientifically valid. This is the crucial question.

In order to answer this question, we can simultaneously apply the social relation-based classification and the INSEE grid to the same population. Two sub-populations can be analysed here. The first one is the population of spouses: 2,473 brides and 2,473 bridegrooms, married in the 18th arrondissement during the year 1936. The second is the population listed in the March 1936 census, from which we have drawn a sample of one household out of twenty, which makes more than 13,600 individuals.[16] The following tables show the results of that comparison.[17]

The results of this double comparison are clear enough: the social picture that emerges from the relation-based taxonomy differs from that drawn using INSEE categories. The description given through the INSEE format is that of a working-class district (30.6 per cent workers and labourers in the male population) with a strong presence of small shopkeepers and craftsmen (20.7 per cent small 'patrons'). Applying the relation-based taxonomy breaks the occupational clusters of workers evident in INSEE statistics into a set of social groups distinct from one another. Consequently, it substitutes for the implicit worker/employee/middle manager hierarchy a more subtle ranking, in which employees and labourers can be found on the same social level, and sometimes even alongside shopkeepers. One may question these results, pointing to the exceptional nature of relationships between spouses and witnesses: the landscape would no doubt appear different if we could analyse hospitality given and received, shared café visits, etc. Yet it seems to us that the equality

Table 6.1: Occupations of marriage partners, 18th Arrondissement of Paris, 1936 according to data on social networks and according to INSEE statistical categories.

Social Groups	Husbands	Wives	Husbands	Wives
Bourgeoisie	167	17	7.0%	1.0%
Businessmen and women	127	4	5.3%	0.2%
Middle class (educated)	148	92	6.2%	5.6%
Middle management and professions	432	21	18.0%	1.3%
Merchants (small)	250	126	10.4%	7.6%
Shopworkers, salesmen	169	244	7.0%	14.8%
Office workers	158	375	6.6%	22.7%
Public employees (lower ranks)	197	56	8.2%	3.4%
Dressmakers, tailors, domestic servants	101	375	4.2%	22.7%
Manual workers	342	184	14.3%	11.1%
People of the streets	309	157	12.9%	9.5%
Sub-total	2400	1651	100.0%	100.0%
% of Total			97.0%	66.8%
Other	21	0	0.8%	0.0%
Inactive	52	822	2.1%	33.2%
Total	2473	2473	100.0%	100.0%
INSEE Occupational Categories				
Large proprietors (commerce and industry)	50	11	2.1%	0.7%
Small proprietors (commerce and industry)	511	142	21.5%	8.6%
Higher management and free professions	123	8	5.2%	0.5%
Middle management	296	93	12.4%	5.6%
Office workers	293	450	12.3%	27.3%
Commercial workers	138	215	5.8%	13.0%
Skilled workers and foremen	605	399	25.4%	24.2%
Manual workers	67	62	2.8%	3.8%
Service personnel	175	230	7.4%	14.0%
Army, clergy, police	122	38	5.1%	2.3%
Sub-total	2380	1648	100.0%	100.0%
% of Total			96.2%	66.6%
Farmers and farm labourers	19	0	0.8%	0.0%
Inactive	74	825	3.0%	33.4%
Total	2473	2473	100.0%	100.0%

Identities and Civil Society

Table 6.2: Alternative sketches of the social structure of the 18th arrondissement of Paris, from a 1 in 20 sample of households taken from the Census of 1936.

Social Groups	Husbands	Wives	Husbands	Wives
Bourgeoisie	248	56	5.3%	2.0%
Businessmen and women	186	175	4.0%	6.4%
Middle class (educated)	248	59	5.3%	2.2%
Middle management and professions	586	27	12.6%	1.0%
Merchants (small)	404	226	8.7%	8.2%
Shopworkers, salesmen	439	390	9.4%	14.2%
Office workers	297	395	6.4%	14.4%
Public employees (lower ranks)	446	102	9.6%	3.7%
Dressmakers, tailors, domestic servants	261	666	5.6%	24.3%
Manual workers	854	284	18.3%	10.4%
People of the streets	690	362	14.8%	13.2%
Sub-total	4659	2742	100.0%	100.0%
% of Total			88.3%	43.9%
Other	8	3	0.2%	0.0%
Inactive	612	3503	11.6%	56.1%
Total	5279	6248	100.0%	100.0%

INSEE Occupational Categories

	Husbands	Wives	Husbands	Wives
Large proprietors (commerce and industry)	103	48	2.3%	1.8%
Small proprietors (commerce and industry)	937	331	20.7%	12.1%
Higher management and free professions	149	20	3.3%	0.7%
Middle management	508	149	11.2%	5.5%
Office workers	810	682	17.9%	25.0%
Commercial workers	208	217	4.6%	7.9%
Skilled workers and foremen	1126	555	24.9%	20.3%
Manual workers	257	106	5.7%	3.9%
Service personnel	316	597	7.0%	21.9%
Army, clergy, police	205	74	4.5%	2.7%
Sub-total	4516	2731	100.0%	100.0%
% of Total			87.5%	44.5%
Farmers and farm labourers	5	2	0.1%	0.0%
Inactive	655	3465	12.4%	55.5%
Total	5279	6248	100.0%	100.0%

of social setting that can be seen, for example, among foremen, draughtsmen and quantity surveyors, traders, travelling salesmen, book-keepers, nurses and non-commissioned officers – in short, the lower level of the middle classes – is not an arbitrary construction. The same appears to be true with respect to fitters, drivers and café waiters.

The population of the 18th arrondissement is then characterized by three features on the eve of the Second World War. First, a weak bourgeois presence (5.3 per cent).[18] Secondly, a middle class not very robust (around 10 per cent), the educated middle class being a bit stronger than the entrepreneurial middle class. Thirdly, an overwhelming and very differentiated 'people', with street traders, people working at home such as dressmakers or tailors, and a rather small group of industrial workers – 18.3 per cent of the male and 10.4 per cent of the female population. Between these groups and the middle class, the pivotal group, astride the lower middle class and the upper level of the lower class, is a large group of craftsmen, shopkeepers, office staff, open to the most highly skilled working trades and towards a still remote bourgeoisie. The social barrier appears more permeable downwards than upwards. Upwards, the bourgeoisie and the middle class are clearly distinct. Downwards, the frontier is somewhat blurred. The joiner or the electrician who sets up business on his own account, the café-owner who is success-ful, remain very close to the people from whom they have emerged. The shopkeeper, and particularly the dealer, provide them with a social horizon that is virtually beyond attainment. From this point of view, the social discourse of the Popular Front on the union of the French nation against the great or the wealthy corresponds to a plausible representation of society.

Conclusion

There are three main conclusions that arise from this study. The first conclusion is methodological. The example of the population of the 18th arrondissement illustrates how much the description of a given society depends upon the tools of analysis applied. What one sees depends upon the glasses through which one peers. It would be absurd to deduce from this statement that all glasses or lenses are equivalent, for some people need glasses to see at a distance and others to take a closer look. Good lenses are appropriate to both the thing observed and the person who observes. As the conceptual tools used by the historian or the sociologist are responsible for the construction of any historical category, their relevance to the material analysed and the questions asked must be at the core of any rigorous historical discussion.

Secondly, it appears that the Parisian population on the eve of the Second World War still remained very close to that of the nineteenth century. Probably the 18th arrondissement was less modern than others like the 15th, close to the Citroën plants. However, what emerges from our registers is a people consisting of waitresses and waiters, greengrocers and musicians, drivers and concierges, a still surviving pre-industrial population in both workplace and pay: men and women who work in the street or its terraces, who are not permanently subject to rigorous patterns of life and who retain a certain level of independence in the use of their time, who sometimes put money in the till and send out bills for payment, or who receive tips. All in all, this nation of the streets and of tips, so close to the skilled worker, was more numerous in the 18th arrondissement in 1936 than was the genuinely industrial proletariat. Strikes and factory sit-ins were remote from these people. At the time of the *Popular* – not *workers'* – Front, the society portrayed in the films of Jean Gabin and of Marcel Carné still occupied the pavement and streets of Paris.

This society predates the social recasting of the Popular Front. The representation of the people of France that prevailed at this time put to the fore such emblematic figures as the metalworker of the Renault plant at Billancourt. In the 18th arrondissement, this character was not totally missing, but he played but a supporting role. The working-class hierarchies codified in collective conventions that sprang up after the May–June 1936 strikes had not yet supplanted those of trades. There are already specialized workers, professionals and highly qualified workers; but the nomenclature has not been adopted uniformly. Designations of skill or trade retain their full force, their full social import and identifying value. There is as yet no talk of *cadres*, or managers: these concepts will develop as part of the great confrontation between bosses and workers beginning with the strikes of May–June 1936 and extending beyond the Liberation in 1944. We know that the engineers and salaried company directors fought to confirm their place as third parties in social negotiation, and that they sought to expand their representation in granting the label of *cadres*, managers (middle, admittedly), to wage-earners who did not wish to be confused with manual staff.[19] It is hardly surprising if the concept of the 'middle manager' does not appear in our social taxonomy: it is premature.

Here we arrive at one last point. It is the point with which we began, namely the profoundly historical character of collective identities. The identity 'worker' of the Popular Front does not emerge out of a sociological reality. The Popular Front did not speak for a 'working class' that was there before it was born. The contrary is true. The historical movement we call the Popular Front constructed this collective identity in ways that went beyond these objective social differences, even when it is apparent that the social barrier between the upper and the lower middle class in itself gave force to the project of the Popular Front: the rallying of the people of France against the '200 families'.[20] In this cultural and political movement, what distinguishes the people of the 18th arrondissement from the workers in large factories begins to fade away, and instead there emerges a powerful social identity. Perhaps this is what defines great historical movements: their capacity to construct social identities that draw people together, despite their objective differences, into a common social formation. History here prevails over sociology, while never denying its significance.

Notes

1. We refer to a number of well-known studies, e.g. Louis Chevalier, *La formation de la population parisienne au XIX° siècle,* Paris, PUF, 1950; Charles Pouthas, *La population française pendant la première moitié du XIX° siècle,* Paris, PUF, 1955. See also, for more specific insights, Gérard Jacquemet, *Belleville au XIX° siècle. Du faubourg à la ville,* Paris, Ed. de l'EHESS, 1984, and Jeanne Gaillard, 'Paris, la ville (1852–1870)', Lille, Service de reproduction des thèses, 1975, x-665 p.

2. Paris is divided into twenty *arrondissements* of uneven size.

3. Luc Boltanski, *Les Cadres. La formation d'un groupe social,* Paris, Ed. de Minuit, 1982. Sociologists such as Pierre Bourdieu and his followers have put the emphasis on social conflicts about the very process of definition of social groups.

4. Institut national de la statistique et des études économiques.

5. The history of social classifications in France has been studied by Alain Desrosières, "Histoire des formes: statistiques et sciences sociales avant

1940", *Revue française de sociologie*, 1985, 26-2, pp. 277-310, and 'Les nomenclatures de professions et emplois', in Joelle Affichard (ed.), *Pour une histoire de la statistique*, Paris, INSEE/Economica, 1987, tome II, pp. 35-56.

6. John H. Goldthorpe, *Social Mobility and Class Structure in Modern Britain*, Oxford, Clarendon Press, 1980; Robert Erikson, and John H. Golthorpe, *The Constant Flux. A Study of Class Mobility in Industrial Societies*, Oxford, Clarendon Press, 1992. The question of revising the French CSP is a recurrent one. A modification was adopted in 1982, giving a new social classification, mostly similar to the preceding one. On this point, see the little book by Alain Desrosières and Laurent Thévenot, *Les catégories socio-professionnelles*, Paris, La Découverte, 1988 [4th edn 2000], and the detailed comments of Baudouin Seys, 'De l'ancien code à la nouvelle nomenclature des catégories socio-professionnelles', Paris, INSEE, ronéogr., 1986 [Archives et documents n° 156]. With European unification, this point is now widely discussed.

7. As it was impossible to enter into the computer such professions as 'supervisor of indirect contributions' because of the length of such titles, we have reduced them to sets of eight characters at most, such as CTRL_CI.

8. We are grateful to Maurizio Gribaudi for his permission to use this software, devised by André Mogoutov and named *Reseaulu*.

9. For more details of our results, see the report presented to the PIR-Villes of the CNRS, which financed this research: 'Relations et structures sociales dans le XVIIIe arrondissement: le peuple de Paris à l'époque du Front populaire', Paris, CRHMSS, March 1996, 87 p. typescript and appendices.

10. William H. Sewell jr., *Structure and Mobility. The Men and Women of Marseille 1820-1870*, Cambridge (UK), Cambridge University Press, 1985.

11. In the group of witnesses assumed not to belong to family or business, workmen and service workers represent 32.5% against 37.5% among the husbands, while owners of factories or commercial undertakings represented 27.3% against 23.1%, and middle and higher managers 31.1% against 10.8%.

12. The reference is to the marriage number in the official register. These numbers are not allocated in strict numerical order, and their order includes gaps and irregularities, for unknown reasons. It appears that several registers were in use at the same time.

13. People are not assigned to one social group forever. In a survey of retired people from Paris, Françoise Cribier found that 42% workers at the beginning of their career before the Second World War, against 24% when they retired, in 1972; 75% had been employed as workers during one stage at least during their professionnal life. See Françoise Cribier, *Une génération de parisiens arrive à la retraite*, Paris, CNRS, Laboratoire de géographie humaine, 1978.

14. One occupation is missing in this survey: for evident reasons, prostitutes as such are neither brides nor witnesses.

15. In my book, *La CGT à l'époque du Front populaire, essai de description numérique,* Paris, A. Colin, 1964, I showed how differently workers behave in ordinary factories and in sectors where a statute defines the rules of the trade, such as mining, railways, gas and electricity utilities. This difference has been shown in many cases.

16. The list of individuals, ordered by streets, houses and households, is retained by the Archives of Paris, under the cotes D2M8, n° 668 to 684. The database constituted from these registers includes 13,681 individuals. All the individuals living in the selected household have been captured in a format such that the analysis of household size and structure will be feasible.

17. We put aside here the comparison between the spouses and the entire population, although it would show how the social structure changes from one generation to the following. Let us stress that the relation-based classification shows a wider evolution than the INSEE CSP.

18. The use of the CSP framework gives the same result – unsurprisingly, for the differences between the two classifications concern mainly the lower classes, the people.

19. Luc Boltanski, *Les Cadres*.

20. The expression 'the two hundred families' comes from the fact that the governing Board of the Bank of France was elected by the two hundred largest shareholders, and symbolizes from the time of the financial crisis of 1924–6 onward the control of politics by 'money power' and the bourgeois establishment.

7

Celebrating Joan: A Feast of Collective Identity in Orleans Since the French Revolution

Every year, on 8 May, inexorable fate brings an assortment of generals and archbishops, athletes and town councillors out on to the streets of Orleans. Closely watched by a double row of soldiers standing at attention, these unfortunate victims trail their dress uniforms and ermine-trimmed gown over the uneven stones, without hope of escape. What fame could survive such an ordeal? The crowd sees its masters filing past, brows gleaming yellow with sweat, collars wilting, feet weary and painful; it savours the primitive delights of the Punch and Judy show with wronged husbands and disappointed plaintiffs satisfying old resentments by knocking down the cardboard cut-out bride and judge.[1]

In a few words, the young Jean Zay, born in Orleans, and later elected Deputy for the constituency of Orleans in 1932, then Minister of Education during the Popular Front, and murdered by the Vichy Militia in 1944, depicts the distinctive nature of the Joan of Arc celebrations in Orleans, as though he were an outside observer. None of the modern organizers of collective festivities would dare to suggest to a town council that the civilian, military and religious authorities should parade through the town for over five kilometres between rows of cheering or whistling idlers. Yet this is how the Orleans celebration is run. Heir to a remote medieval world, it brings together authorities and the people in a complex relationship in which the authorities confirm their power by offering it to the popular gaze and to their licensed challenge; and the popular festival becomes fully legitimate as being part of acknowledged history, played out according to traditional ritual in its designated space, and marked out with powerfully symbolic reference points. This is where the city's identity is performed.

Sites

The feast of the Maid (*La Pucelle*), as it was known until 1840,[2] was very different from the national celebration decreed in 1920, or even the version created at the same time in Rouen.[3] Even older than the appearance of nationalism, this centuries-old tradition dates back to the founding moment of Orleans' identity: the English siege of the city and its relief by Joan of Arc. The first festival was the procession of thanksgiving organized on the day that the siege was lifted, 8 May 1429.

At this time the city was still protected by its Gallo-Roman wall, except on the west. The *cardo* ran from the cathedral to the River Loire, and the Roman *decumana*, running east–west, became the Rue de Bourgogne, the main trading street. The medieval bridge had been built immediately to the west of this enclosure, leading to the development of a new district between the river and, at the north-west corner of the wall, the Place du Martroi, site of the gallows (*martyrorum*) and also the place for carts and trade. This extension from Le Martroi to the bridge was in turn protected by a later wall.

When the English besieged Orleans, the buildings outside the walls were razed to the ground, including venerated churches, such as St Aignan, dedicated to the saint who halted the hordes of Attila the Hun. The English set up wooden towers, particularly to the west, from where French reinforcements might be expected to come. They stormed the Tourelles fort, which marked the southern end of the bridge, and reinforced its defences with a strongpoint on the bank behind the Tourelles, in the Augustinian monastery.

Joan of Arc crossed the Loire from the east of the city and entered Orleans through the Bourgogne Gate on 29 April 1429. Thursday 5 May was Ascension Day. The decisive battles took place on 6 and 7 May, ending with the capture of the Tourelles fort by the French. Next morning, Sunday 8 May, the French army formed up to confront the English: they, however, lifted the siege. A procession to the cathedral was arranged immediately, to thank God for the relief of the city.[4] The following year a procession of thanksgiving was organized on 8 May at the site of the battle, in particular at Les Tourelles. This was the start of a commemoration that was interrupted only by the Calvinists in 1562, the French Revolution and the two World Wars.

The route of the 'procession' or *cortège* through the city has of course changed since 1429. The first stage was the construction of a new ditch-lined wall, in the late fifteenth century. This new wall lay along what is now the mall, created in the nineteenth century by filling in the ditches. It followed approximately the line of the English wooden towers, and added generous space to the city, which gradually expanded to fill it during the ensuing centuries. Later suburbs were established along the main roads. At the northern point of the wall the Paris road entered through the Porte Bannier. The two streets leading up to it, the Rue Bannier from Le Martroi and the Rue de la Bretonnerie from the cathedral and the Place de l'Etape, soon acquired a degree of importance. Then three major road developments reshaped the city. In the second half of the eighteenth century the ruinous medieval bridge was removed and replaced by a new bridge a few tens of metres further downstream. To serve this new bridge the royal superintendent created a street from Le Martroi, the Rue Royale, which formed part of the processional route in 1772. In 1840 a second new street, the Rue Jeanne d'Arc, linked the Rue Royale to the Place Sainte-Croix in front of the cathedral. Finally, fifty years later, the Rue de la République was built between Le Martroi and the railway station, built in 1843 close to the mall.

Four foci mark out the space of the Orleans commemorations: Les Tourelles, the site of the victory, to the south of the river; Le Martroi in the city centre; the cathedral; and the neighbouring city hall. The two latter sites are relatively late additions: the city hall was established in a large Renaissance house, in the Place d'Étape close to the cathedral, in 1790. The cathedral itself suffered such severe damage in the Wars of Religion that it was rebuilt in the seventeenth century, acquired its façade (by Gabriel) under Louis XV and the crowning of its towers by Viollet le Duc in the nineteenth century. These four locations are linked, Les Tourelles to Le Martroi by the bridge and the Rue Royale, Le Martroi to the Place de l'Étape by the Rue d'Escures, with its fine seventeenth- and eighteenth-century houses. The cathedral is linked to the Rue Royale by the Rue Jeanne d'Arc, but not directly to Le Martroi.

Early Nineteenth-century Vicissitudes

Under the *ancien régime*, the festival was a religious event. It took the form of a solemn Mass in the cathedral with a eulogy of the saint, followed by a procession that featured the relics of St Aignan and St Euverte and of the True Cross, the banners of St Michael, St Aignan and St Euverte, and those of Saint Catherine and St Margaret, Joan of Arc's two saints. This pattern places it outside the traditional May

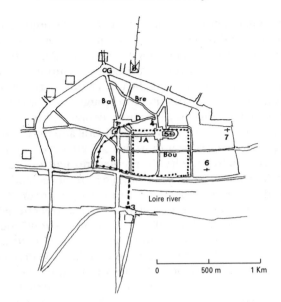

Key:
1. Martroi
3. Les Tourelles
4. City Hall, Place de l'Etape
5. Cathedral
6. Church of St Aignan
7. Church of St Euverte
8. Railway station
Ba. Rue Bannier
Bre. Rue de la Bretonnerrie

Bou. Rue de Bourgogne
D. Rue d'Escures
G. Place Gambetta
JA. Rue Jeanne d'Arc
R. Rue Royale
☐ Sites of English wooden towers
••••• Roman wall
••••• Wall of the medieval extension of the city

Map 2: Plan of Orleans in 1950.

cycle,[5] although it incorporates traditions taken from youth festivals.[6] Each of the city parishes had a maypole carried on a table by young girls. The banners had their own guard of honour of young boys. The Maid's banner was carried by a very young boy, the little *puceau* (or Master), who represented the saint in the procession from the sixteenth century onwards. This religious festival may have been in decline by the end of the eighteenth century. Because of bad weather the procession was held in the cathedral in 1776 and 1779;[7] this may be the reason for the addition, in 1786 and 1789, of two impressive weddings in the cathedral, each one of a virtuous young girl, richly endowed by the Duke of Orleans.

The Revolution brought a break with tradition: festivities were celebrated until 1792[8] and then abandoned. Orleans then had revolutionary festivals and a ceremony of the Supreme Being, following the same routes and in particular crossing the bridge. This demonstrates how the pattern and setting of the festival endured, even though it no longer referred to the deliverance of the city. National symbols superseded local identities.

After the return to normal times, the festival was re-established in 1803 by the First Consul and a statue of Joan of Arc was erected in Le Martroi the following year. The 1803 celebration was a tremendous success: a troop of more than two thousand soldiers, all the clergy, every magistrate, judge and court usher; one contemporary thought it was the finest procession that Orleans had ever experienced.[9] The authorities fought to claim credit. Bernier, the Bishop of Orleans and negotiator of the *Concordat*, took matters in hand with the agreement of the Prefect. Despite the mayor's protests to the Minister of the Interior, the bishop sent out invitations to the religious ceremony and designated the orator for the eulogy, although this was the mayor's prerogative: and further, the municipal officers came after all the State officials in the procession led by the clergy.[10] In 1805 the Prefect considered that, since the festival was entirely municipal, State officials should not take part in the procession; the bishop therefore invited them independently to the religious service. This led to an officially registered protest from the mayor, whose decree organizing the festival, countersigned by the prefect, charged him to issue all the invitations to the secular and ecclesiastical bodies and to organize all the details of the festival: 'At all times this festival has been considered as specific to the city of Orleans [. . .] and the ceremonial has always been regulated by the mayors of Orleans and at their specific invitation'.[11] Then a compromise appeared to win the day: in 1806 the mayor appeared in the procession after the chairmen of the courts but ahead of the military commander, and the town officials ahead of the military officers. Nonetheless, it was at the seat of the Court of Appeals and not at the City Hall that the authorities came together to go to the service. Clearly, the State and the Clergy ranked ahead of the City.

The Restoration brought change. In October 1814, when the episcopal throne was vacant, the mayor claimed the right to designate the orator. With the support of the Prefect the head of the Cathedral's clergy rejected the claim; but for the festival of 1815 responsibility lay with the municipal body. In 1816 the new mayor, nominated in February, took up his predecessor's battle in the name of a return to pre-Revolutionary practices. In 1817 he won the right of selection of the orator. The procession moved to the Tourelles, where a cross was blessed. Above all, the mayor reinstated the custom of the little Master (*puceau*), whose costume and upkeep imposed considerable expenditure. This 'representative of Joan of Arc' was a child aged between 8 and 12, selected from the ordinary people (the sons of a cooper, a gardener, a roofer and a policeman have been recorded), dressed in the style of Henri IV's day and bearing the banner of Joan of Arc – the banner itself, too heavy for his strength, being put in the hands of his father, who walks with him. The little Master (*puceau*) attended all the church services on the eve of the procession, on the day itself and the next day. He ate and slept, however, with his father, in the prison. He took the head of the procession and, on reaching the southern end of the bridge, stood on a dais and saluted all the groups as they passed him.[12] Bimbenet, as a dignitary of this time, took a severe view of this addition, but noted that 'the people were delighted at the sight'.[13] No doubt we should see the little Master (*puceau*), a sexually neutral figure, as a symbol of youth who enabled this celebration imbued with worship to be accepted more readily by the people of Orleans.

The 1830 revolution brought a break in tradition: the clergy no longer left their churches. Instead of the procession, 'the bust of Joan of Arc, surrounded by the *Garde nationale* and the civilian and military authorities, would be borne in triumph to the sites of her glorious feats'.[14] Did this plaster bust on a litter look unsatisfactory in the procession? Certainly, in 1836 it was no longer carried in the procession, but was placed instead at the end of the bridge where the little Master (*puceau*) stood; the civilian and military authorities stood in ranks beside it and the troops paraded in front of it. Yet the festival lacked at its heart a living representation of the heroine or her symbol, consecrated by ancient custom, in the form of the banner, which was held by the clergy. In 1840, therefore, with the agreement of the minister, passed on by the Prefect, the banner formed part of the procession once more. Yet the State declined responsibility: 'This festival being essentially municipal and civic, he [the minister] notes that it is you who should send out the customary invitations.'[15] The procession left the cathedral through the great door, took the newly-opened Rue Jeanne d'Arc and returned from Les Tourelles through Le Martroi and the Rue D'Escures.

The Orleans festival's sensitivity to national political events, as seen in the ruptures of 1803, 1817 and 1830, reappeared in 1848: the religious ceremony continued, but the clergy no longer took part in the procession, which set out from the City Hall and returned to Le Martroi, where the town council and officials stood facing the statue to watch the parade. The government Commissaire reviewed the troops along the mall. Between 1849 and 1851 the procession returned to the City Hall; in 1852 the clergy took their place there once more, and the return route was extended to the cathedral, where a *Te Deum* was sung.[16]

Development of the Modern Festival

Despite political ups and downs, the festival has been held every year without interruption since 1803 and has been well established ever since. The 'popular rejoicings' (as the posters call them) provide an essential element. From 1803 greasy poles were set up in Le Martroi and fireworks set off; from 1841 these traditional games appear on the poster, with the city organizing running or sack races and awarding prizes to the winners, who sometimes joined the procession. Dancing was introduced. The procession ceased to represent only Orleans: in 1842 fire-fighting teams from the two neighbouring villages, Olivet and Saint Pryvé, were given permission to take part. In 1853, for the first time, a military band that did not belong to the garrison took part in the festival, with the city covering the cost of its accommodation. The festival was clearly expanding.

1855 was the key year. Foyatier's statue of Joan of Arc was inaugurated in the Place du Martroi, the result of a national fund-raising effort to replace the statue of 1803 which was considered to be 'of paltry size'.[17] This unique occasion gave the festival a particular – and costly – lustre:[18] the cathedral interior was freshly decorated, the sixteenth-century Joan of Arc banner was replaced by a new one – the fruit of 5-franc subscriptions from 558 ladies – the streets were decorated with flags, and a platform was set up in Le Martroi. The festival now opened on the eve of the anniversary. Since the Restoration, the Belfry clock had normally been rung each quarter-hour from midday on 7 May until sunset to proclaim the festival, but the only formal observance on the eve was the singing of Matins in the cathedral in the mid-afternoon, a service abandoned under the July Monarchy. Occasionally, for example in 1840, a band gave a concert in Le Martroi during the evening of 7 May.[19] Yet the quest for ritual continued. In

1855 a historical cavalcade in period costume took a complicated route throughout the city during the evening of 7 May, from Les Tourelles to the Place de l'Étape. Next day it joined the procession. The following year, however, this innovation was abandoned as too burdensome.

In 1860, possibly even in 1859,[20] a new pattern developed. A torch-lit retreat set off from Les Tourelles to the Place Ste Croix, where the mayor and town council joined it, led by Joan of Arc's banner and the city banner. The bishop then appeared with his clergy on the *parvis*, the pavement in front of the cathedral, to receive Joan of Arc's banner. The Place Ste Croix and the *parvis* were illuminated. The following year the poster specifies 'Bengal lights'.[21] In 1866, 110 500-gram Bengal lights were lit in the cathedral towers. Handing over the banner and illuminations in the cathedral towers thus became part of the festival ritual. Next, the retreat continued to Le Martroi, followed by the rue Bannier and the place Gambetta.

This festival pattern continued until the early twentieth century. It was arranged round three key moments: the retreat and present-ation of the banner in the evening of 7 May, the Mass and eulogy, regularly published as a leaflet by the city, on the morning of 8 May, and the ensuing traditional procession to Les Tourelles. The festival was thus indissolubly civilian, military and religious. To this could be added 'popular', for the afternoon of 8 May became devoted to games and the evening to fireworks and dancing.

An Impossible Secularization

The separation of Church and State broke the pattern, although it is impossible to specify here all the complexities that it created. In 1906 the festivities followed the usual ritual, but in 1907 Georges Clemenceau, President of the Cabinet and Minister of the Interior, banned state officials from taking part in the festival if it was religious in nature. The Mayor and the Radical deputy, Fernand Rabier, a sup-porter of the law of separation of Church and State, in the Chamber of Deputies insisted on concessions. Clemenceau agreed to the fiction of two processions, one civilian and the other religious, separated by a 'discrete space';[22] he accepted that the clergy could process in choir robes with their crosses. The question of the prayers at Les Tourelles remained; he accepted that the clergy could pray `as they passed'. In fact, with a good deal of hypocrisy, it was possible to avoid sacrificing local ritual to national politics. However, since the bishop had made public a letter in which he indicated that the clergy could not join the procession if freemasons were taking part, the latter, who did not usually take part, demanded a place in the parade. The mayor tried to refuse them, but since Clemenceau would not accept any exclusions, he finally suggested that the town council should organize the procession without the clergy. This was adopted by 14 votes to 14, with the mayor giving the casting vote in favour.[23]

The 1907 procession was therefore marked by the presence of 200 freemasons in top hats and the absence of the clergy, who refused to join in presenting the banner or the celebration of Mass on 8 May. A large part of the population was shocked, and a third of those present turned their backs on those town councillors who paraded.[24] In an indication that the secularization of the festival clashed with public opinion, the following year, in order to avoid any risk of losing the council elections, Radicals and freemasons did not persist, and the festival was organized with the clergy. In 1909 the same mayor refused to organize the ceremony without the clergy, and Clemenceau forbade officials to take part. In order to make the choice clear, he even arranged for the Prefect and the general to organize a military parade in Le Martroi at the time of the religious service. This time the festival took place without the participation of many neighbouring villages and their fire-fighting teams. In 1910 the mayor won a concession from the President of the Cabinet, Briand: officials would have the right to attend the religious service in their private capacity and not as a body, and the military parade was arranged after the procession.

This episode introduced three changes of varying importance. First, the organization of a separate military tribute, whereas hitherto the troops had taken part in the procession. Next, an alteration in the order of the procession, with the clergy coming at the rear instead of at the front. Finally, the evident lack of organization over places in the cathedral for the religious service: with the constituent bodies no longer taking part *ex officio*, their members found themselves seated wherever there was a place available.[25]

The splendour of the festival was much diminished, and the shopkeepers complained. Traders in the main commercial street of the day, the Rue de Bourgogne Street, invented an entirely new element to be added to the Joan of Arc festival: a commemoration of the liberator's entrance into the city through the Bourgogne Gate on the evening of 29 April. In 1909 they therefore organized a costumed commemorative procession from the Bourgogne suburb to the Place du Martroi. In 1910 a young girl on horseback took the role of Joan of Arc in this procession.

The 1912 election brought Fernand Rabier as mayor into the City Hall. Having tried in vain to come to an agreement with Monseigneur Touchet, he organized the festivities of 1913 and 1914, in contrast to those of 1909–1912, with the participation of public officials but without the clergy. They had reached stalemate. Then came the war, and the festivities were interrupted. Commemoration continued nevertheless, reduced to essentials: the council paraded to Le Martroi to lay a wreath at the foot of the statue of Joan of Arc before moving on to put flowers on the graves in the military cemetery. The same pattern was followed in 1919.

By 1920 the climate had changed, and a compromise was possible. The Republic prepared to introduce a national day in honour of Joan of Arc on the second Sunday in May (adopted in July 1920), and the Pope was to canonize the heroine. The Mayor issued an official invitation to the two masonic lodges which, satisfied with this formal recognition, declined the invitation – thus enabling the clergy to take part in the commemoration.[26] It was given added lustre by the presence of Marshal Foch, who thus inaugurated a new tradition: the participation in the festival of a personality from outside the city. The next year it was the Minister of Justice, who addressed the public alongside the Mayor in Le Martroi before the military parade.

The postscript to this reconciliation between civil and religious authorities for the Orleans festival was the 500th anniversary of the city's liberation, in 1929. The President of the Republic, Gaston Doumergue, agreed to come to Orleans on 8 May, accompanied by Poincaré and Painlevé. The Pope named a Cardinal Legate, who attended with six cardinals and ten bishops. The customary ceremonies took on an unusual splendour: commemoration of Joan's entrance into the city, in the evening of 29 April, with a historic *cortège* of 150 costumed participants including a Joan of Arc on horseback; evening torch-lit retreat on 7 May with the historic parade, presentation of the banner and illuminations of the cathedral towers.[27] Next morning, the cathedral service was followed by the eulogy: the President of the Republic attended a religious service *ex officio* for the first time since the separation of Church and State.[28] At the end of the morning came the traditional commemorative parade, in the rain; the officials joined in as far as the bridge, where they took their places on a platform. When the procession returned, they resumed their places in it. After the banquet, at 3.30 p.m., Marshal Pétain presided over the military homage in Le Martroi.

The ceremonial pattern established in 1920 has continued essentially unchanged until today with an interruption from 1940 to 1944, when the pattern of 1914–1918 was revived, with slightly greater decorum, in 1942. The traditional procession was revived in 1945, with a lasting innovation: the presence of a young girl playing the part of Joan of Arc on horseback. The other significant addition was the organization of a parade of groups representing people from various regions: from Britanny, the North, the Basque country, Burgundy, or other parts of Le Berry. The participation of 'provinces' in the commemorative parade is recorded before 1940, but now they paraded independently through the city, first in the late afternoon (1946) and then, from 1947 onwards, in the morning, during the religious service. The festival does not appear to have changed since 1947; but if we are to understand its significance, we must consider who takes part in the parade and in what order.[29]

The Participants

Originally, only corporate bodies took part in the procession. Under the July Monarchy, they seem to have followed behind representatives of guilds, including bargemen; but the participation of the National Guard enhanced the ceremony and brought a number of citizens into the *cortège*. Under the Second Empire the procession included mutual aid societies, winners of medals for life-saving from the city of Orleans, and neighbouring communities, represented by their firemen or their choral societies with their banner. In 1865, seven villages were represented in this way. The town schools sent representatives. In short, the procession attracted a whole series of delegations and clubs: military and naval veterans after 1870, winners of military medals, former soldiers and handicapped veterans after the 1914–18 war, Resistance veterans, internees and deportees from 1940–44, shooting and athletics clubs and church-based groups, secular and Catholic, Protestant scouts (in 1914), then boy scouts, drum majorettes in the 1960s, and of course the 'provinces'.

Significantly, the only ones missing were employers' organizations, trade unions, and political parties. One may perhaps pose the question whether the representation of class conflict is incompatible with the self-representation of the collective unity of the city, or

whether divisive politics are excluded from the ceremony, in order
to prevent its disruption.

The elements that made up the parade can thus be grouped in
four categories: civil society, the clergy, the town officials, public
institutions. The clergy always followed the same order: delegations
from the various parishes, bearing their relics or their maypoles; then
the cathedral clergy in liturgical order, with the celebrant last in line.
Joan of Arc's banner, symbol of the saint, was always part of the
clerical group, either leading them or borne between the parishes
and the cathedral chapter. The town officials were usually led by the
town banner, and by the municipal firemen or band. Their group
included the mayor, the assistant mayors, the town council, and also
the administrators of the city's institutions, the old people's home
and the orphanage, which often sent a group of orphans. The city's
executive officer was always present. The public institutions were
generally led by the Prefect, and appeared in the order determined
by protocol. For example, the academic group occupied a higher
place when it included the university rector and university professors
and not just the academic inspector and a delegation of schoolteachers. Among the public institutions, the Court of Appeals, the
Magistracy and the Commercial Courts accompanied the representatives of the Bar. All paraded in their gowns, like the academics.[30]

The sequence of these varied participants in the procession was
a matter of dispute among the authorities. Under the First Empire,
as has been noted, the group of city officials was dispersed among
the public institutions. It reassumed its form under the Restoration
and led the procession, behind the little Master (*puceau*) but ahead
of the clergy. Under the Second Empire, when civil society was added
to the parade, the organization became more sophisticated, and
various bands set the pace. In general terms, civil society came first,
followed by the city representatives, and then the clergy. Officials
and invited bodies closed the parade, in order of protocol. This
pattern was recorded in 1861 and reappeared in 1879 and 1899.

The crisis of the separation of Church and State before the war
of 1914–18 reversed this sequence and set the religious *cortège* last,
in order to dissociate it from the civil parade. Observed in 1908, this
order was retained for 1909 and 1910 despite the absence of state
officials and of public institutions. In 1913, when they returned, they
took their place behind the city representatives. In 1920 came a
return to the 1908 order, with civil society, city representatives,
officials and public institutions, and then the clergy – with the slight

Figure 7.1: Orléans' city council marching on the *rue Jeanne d'Arc,* 8 May 1955. The procession starts from the Cathedral. (*Courtesy of La République du Centre*)

alteration that the youth club athletes concluded the parade, and thus joined the clergy.

The presence of an official personality had no effect on this order. In 1939, for example, when the President of the Republic joined the festival, civil society was followed by the city officials: the city banner, mayor, assistant mayors, city council, the administrators of municipal establishments. Next came the General Council, the Prefect, the President of the Republic and the ministers, followed by the public institutions. The clergy, escorted by Scouts, came last. This order was repeated in 1947 when Vincent Auriol was present.

The addition of delegations from civil society and the complaints of the clergy, who felt their dignity impaired at having to parade after drum majorettes, then led to a change in parade order. Within civil society there was a distinction between the combatant or patriotic associations and other groups. The former retained a place in the official parade, while the latter, together with the 'provinces', formed a detached rearguard 'junior' group. In 1975 the processional sequence was as follows: war veterans, the municipality with the mayors of twinned towns, and then the guest of the year, Mme Giscard d'Estaing, accompanied by the Prefect, members of parliament, general councillors and ambassadors, followed by the official representatives of the armed forces, the magistracy, the university and the major administrative bodies. The clergy were at the rear of the official procession. Behind them came Joan of Arc on horseback with her escort, associations of young people including the drum majorettes, and the 'provinces'.

Joan of Arc's place in the procession is not fixed. This very popular innovation has developed its own traditions. The young girl who will play the part of the heroine is selected one year from a state school and the next year from a private school. However the logic of this performance differs from logic of the procession. Neither the clergy, the city nor the public institutions can adopt this young horsewoman as their own symbol. Sometimes, therefore, Joan on her horse may lead the procession (as was seen between 1960 and 1974);

Figure 7.2: The clergy, coming from the *rue Royale* (in the background) and crossing the bridge on the Loire river, 8 May 1963. (*Courtesy of La République du Centre*)

but she may also take her place as the link between the two elements, between civil society and the city officials in 1955 for example, and between the clergy and the youth associations in 1975 or 1980.

This pattern is becoming blurred, however, and the elements of the traditional procession are arranged according to a hierarchical logic that mingles the various corporate bodies. Thus the members of individual bodies appear alongside other members of other institutions, instead of being entirely separated in corporate blocs. This system appeared in 1981 and was confirmed in 1982, when the new President of the Republic, François Mitterrand, took part in the festival. Behind the war veterans and ahead of the clergy, the various public institutions thus formed a whole according to their hierarchical rank. In this arrangement, the body of city officials as such disappeared. This happened in 1981, when the municipal band and the city banner preceded the Chancellor of the *Légion d'honneur*, that year's guest, accompanied by the Mayor-Deputy, the Prefect and the members of parliament; next came the President of the *Conseil Général* and the general councillors, ambassadors, the first assistant mayor and the mayors of twinned towns, and then the city council. The military authorities, the magistracy, the university and the public institutions came behind, followed finally by the clergy. [31]

Certainly, the still 'traditional' parade is changing its meaning. In a conurbation of 250,000 inhabitants, the social visibility of the various public institutions is naturally reduced, and there can be few spectators capable of distinguishing a judge from an academic, or a mayor from a member of parliament. Attention is shifting from the public institutions to the more spectacular elements, notably the foreign brass bands with colourful uniforms and unusual music. The procession has become a parade.

The Festival in Urban Space

This evolution has required new space. The nineteenth-century festival was established in a civic and historic setting: the torchlit retreat in the evening of 7 May set out from Les Tourelles for the cathedral, via the bridge, the Rue Royale and the Rue Jeanne d'Arc: after the presentation of the banner it continued to Le Martroi, first along the Rue d'Escures and then, after the creation of the Rue de la République, along the Rue de la Bretonnerie and the Rue de la République. It ended with the Rue Bannier and dispersed in the Place Gambetta (see Map 2). The official procession advanced from the cathedral to

Les Tourelles and then the Croix St Marceau, and returned to Le Martroi along the Rue Royale to end at the cathedral – following more or less the same route as the torchlit retreat.

The locus of the festival is thus that of the official city: the Rue Royale and the Rue Jeanne d'Arc obey classical rules of monumental design – the mark of power over the city. The places where the festival comes to a halt, the cathedral *parvis*, Les Tourelles, the Place du Martroi, are official sites marked by monuments inaugurated in the grand style. The memory of the liberation of the city has been taken over by the civil and religious authorities, who make a pilgrimage every year to symbolic monuments that they themselves have set up.

The procession thus does not follow popular streets crowded with local residents: these are commercial streets, more middle-class, with large apartments. The popular city is not far away; but now it no longer forms part of the route. The expansion of the festival with the addition of supplementary features, is one way of restoring the equilibrium between the official city and the popular city; but the style of these new processions is very different: while the traditional parade sets off from the heart of the city, either religious or civic (the cathedral, the city hall) and returns to it, the other processions move from the exterior of the city to Le Martroi. The circuit of the traditional procession expresses the power of the authorities over the territory that they have marked out, while the two other processions represent incursions into the city, the outskirts taking possession of the centre.

The 29 April procession leaves from the Bourgogne district and follows the Rue de Bourgogne from end to end, to reach Le Martroi along an east–west route at right-angles to the traditional north–south processional route. The parade of the 'provinces' forms up at one of the city gates, the Porte Saint-Jean to the west, or Place Halmagrand, near the City Hall, and advances to Le Martroi, to which it returns after several loops within the city centre. Its composition confirms the significance of its route, for it specifically incorporates people from outside Orleans to honour them at the foot of the statue of Joan of Arc. The generic term 'provinces' in fact designates groups of people, each representing one region of origin: relatively numerous (already in 1947 there were ten, and 13 in 1960 or 1981), independent of the local authorities and lacking any social or political function, their purpose is purely convivial sociability, and they might perhaps disappear one day if they did not feel responsible for an element of the spectacle of the Joan of Arc celebrations. An assemblage of all age-groups, picturesque and highly colourful, they parade in regional costumes, and sometimes with their own bands, as the Bretons do, or dances, like the Antillese. Dressed in shepherd costumes, the people of the *Landes* criss-cross the town on their stilts. Miss Orleans, the new incarnation of 'La Rosière', takes the head of the 'provinces' procession. This is not merely a popular addition grafted on to the celebrations and invading other sections: it is very clearly the entry into the city of the non-Orléanais who assert their status as true Orléanais.

The festival is supposed to represent the whole city; this is the reason for its expansion throughout the city districts. For some years now, in the new city of Orléans-La Source, 10 kilometres south of the city centre, the drum-majorettes and various societies have paraded through their district on 7 May. The various invited bands give open-air concerts in several districts. The 'provinces' entry into the city is matched by the movement of some elements of the festival out into the peripheral quarters: a reciprocal shift that enables the festival to be assimilated within the expansion of the conurbation.

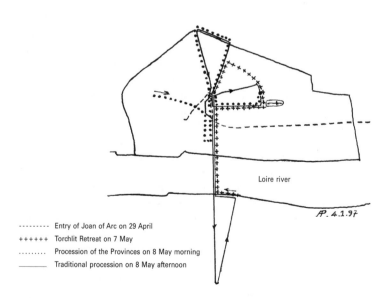

- - - - - - - - -   Entry of Joan of Arc on 29 April
+ + + + + +   Torchlit Retreat on 7 May
· · · · · · · · ·   Procession of the Provinces on 8 May morning
_____   Traditional procession on 8 May afternoon

Map 3: The Processional Routes in Orleans in 1981.

Identities and Civil Society

At the end of this brief examination we can see how, down the years, the festival of Joan of Arc has succeeded in assimilating commemorative or festive practices of varying origin and significance. The religious cult of the saint, the civic commemoration of the city's liberation, flow together in a single mould – the procession or parade, inheritor of the past and charged with tradition, but also sufficiently flexible to absorb the many groupings of unequal status and prestige, from war veterans to drum-majorettes, from the 'provinces' to academic bodies or boy scouts. This means that, apart from the invited brass bands, the visual spectacle is provided by the people of Orleans themselves: the dignitaries and members of corporate bodies do not parade in isolation; they hear applause or catcalls and above all are acknowledged by those close to them, friends or neighbours. It is said that one half of the city parades before the eyes of the other half. In this interplay between the representatives of power and the people, which on the one hand parades and on the other freely watches the parade, at the intersection between the institutional and the informal, it is essentially a matter of the city's self-celebration of its own identity.

In this self-celebration, geography counts perhaps more than history. Of the liberation of the city, most citizens of Orleans know only that it happened and, despite the long series of civil and religious eulogies, they see Joan of Arc only as a brave young girl with an extraordinary destiny. On 8 May, Orleans celebrates Orleans. But the fact that it does so in these ritualized forms creates a very strong spatialization of local identity: each Orléanais perceives the sites taken over by the festival as the heart of the city, and the festival as a way of appropriating them. The festival settings are simultaneously or successively invaded and cut off, open to all and consecrated, reserved as symbolic sites by the demarcating line of barriers and the marking out of names and statues. The crowd of pedestrians that wanders more or less freely in the city centre in the evening of 7 May is at home, like the crowd swollen with tourists arriving as spectators, massing together to see the procession pass in these same streets, which are suddenly transformed into the sites of an unusual cult. Symbolically, the procession is a taking possession of space by those who form the procession – from the authorities to the drum-majorettes – but also by those who watch them. It means that the centre of the city is taken over by the whole of the city.

Finally, this dramatic staging within the city itself of Orleans society, with its elements of varied associations and diverse powers, operates as a means of regulating conflict. Of some conflict at least, for the world of business remains formally absent from the festival: neither the employers' association nor the trade unions joins the procession. But, as we have seen, every great political crisis has had its effect on the festival, and the speeches pronounced are not detached from the passage of time. In 1860, for example, the Prefect regrets that the mayor has sent out 400 copies of the eulogy spoken by Abbé Freppel which contained references denigrating the government's policies, even though these references were removed from the text in its published form.[32] More recently, in 1993, in the midst of a discussion on the reform of the law of nationality on the square before the cathedral on the evening of 7 May, the bishop 'greeted with joy' the girl selected that year to incarnate Joan of Arc because she was 'a young Orleans girl of Portuguese origin': 'Something has changed, there is a step forward: I take pride in this'.[33] The history itself of the festival reveals encounters between the long term of local tradition and the shorter term of national politics. The commemoration is part of the present day, and the festival takes place in a here and now in which conflicts are still visible. But they are expressed here in a such a form as to reinforce consensus. This necessitates that the Mayor invite the President of the Republic in the year following his election, whatever their political differences. Thus it was that a mayor of the Right greeted François Mitterrand in 1981, and a mayor of the Left, Jacques Chirac in 1996. Failure to respect this tradition would undoubtedly be badly received by the population.

In these ways the history of the Orleans festival reveals several counter-balancing movements that give it its meaning: seeking equilibrium between the institutional and the informal, between official commemoration and popular celebration, between order and transgression. There is a balance between the authorities; who put themselves on show and establish the legitimacy of their power at the very moment that they allow its contestation, and the crowd, which creates its own festival, transgressing on occasion time and space, and even accepted practice. There is a balance between the sacred moment of the historic episode, recalled each year, and the present time of the political situation; between the symbolic consecration of the city-centre space and its appropriation by the crowd.

We are therefore equally remote from a cold official occasion and a pure and simple popular feast with nothing at stake. Nor is the festival of Joan of Arc the union of all Orleanais in a merging community, in which differences of social position and political views could be eliminated. Its very vitality stems from the many tensions that are expressed and balanced within it. In recognizing the differences, and even more by staging them, it subordinates them to the more fundamental affirmation of the enduring character of the city. The significance of the festival is that it is perpetuated from year to year, ritually occupying the same sites, with participants and gestures that are progressively renewed. A centuries-old tradition in a symbolic space reappropriated annually – here, I feel, are the foundations of a powerful collective identity. In this sense, the festival of Joan of Arc transforms the people of the city into citizens of Orleans. Here citizenship is performed.

Notes

1. J. Zay, *Chroniques du grenier*, Orléans, L'écarlate, 1995, p. 25. This text by Jean Zay was first published in the literary review, *Le Grenier*, in 1925.

2. The 1840 poster bears the title 'Fête de la Pucelle', the 1841 poster is missing, the 1842 version shows 'Fête de Jeanne d'Arc', Orleans Municipal Archives (AMO) 1 J 157.

3. I am grateful to Loïc Vadelorge, who kindly passed on information about the Joan celebrations in Rouen as described in pp. 459–502 of his thesis: 'Pour une histoire culturelle du local. Rouen 1919–1940', Paris, Université de Paris IV, 1996.

4. R. Pernoud, *8 mai 1429. La libération d'Orléans*, Paris, Gallimard, 1969, p. 145.

5. A. Van Gennep, *Manuel de folklore français contemporain*, vol. I, IV, 'Cérémonies périodiques cycliques, 2 cycle de mai – la Saint-Jean', Paris, A. and J. Picard, 1949. See pp. 1421–1726 for the May cycle.

6. Mona Ozouf, 'Du mai de liberté à l'arbre de la liberté: symbolisme révolutionnaire et tradition paysanne', *Ethnologie française*, 1975, V, pp. 9–32.

7. As noted by the corn chandler Sylvain Rousseau in his diary. See the *Bulletin de l'Association des amis du Centre Jeanne d'Arc*, no. 14, 1990, p. 35.

8. Nineteenth-century scholars, D. Lottin, *Recherches historiques sur la ville d'Orléans du Ier janvier 1789 au 10 mai 1800*, Part II, Vol. I, Orléans, Impr. D'Alexandre Jacob, 1838, pp. 139, 276 and 315, followed by P. Mantellier, adviser at the Imperial Court of Orléans, Director of the History Museum, *Le Siège et la délivrance d'Orléans*, fêtes du huit mai 1855,

Orléans, A. Gâtineau, 1855, pp. 96 et seq. note without identifying their sources the marriage of the young girl and a procession round the cathedral in 1790 and purely civilian and military festivals in 1791 and 1792. However, two accounts of the 1791 and 1792 festivals have been preserved, with expense accounts, (AMO I J 153); they appear to confirm the participation of the clergy in the festivals and the procession, which in 1792 was called a 'march'. More extensive research would be necessary to establish its precise nature.

9. Sylvain Rousseau, 'Diary', in *Bulletin de l Association,* p. 36.

10. AMO I J 154. See also E. Bimbenet, 'Le 8 mai à Orléans depuis le Consulat jusqu'à nos jours', *Revue Orléanaise*, Orléans, Alexandre Jacob, Deuxième année, 1848, pp.121–58. The Appeal Court deliberated before accepting the bishop's invitation and reported to the Minister of the Interior, who is said to have responded: 'This festival is public and religious, all the authorities established in the city should be invited by the Bishop, to whom it falls to arrange in the cathedral church places for the various officials [. . .] and to regulate the order of procession' (p. 134).

11. AMO I J 154. Relations between the mayor and the bishop appear poor. The bishop did not receive the mayor's representatives.

12. AMO I J 155.

13. Bimbenet, 'Le 8 mai à Orléans', p. 141.

14. AMO I J 157

15. Letter from the prefect to the mayor, dated 28 April 1840, ibid.

16. AMO I J 157.

17. P. Mantellier, *Le Siège et la délivrance*, pp. 96ff..

18. The cost rose to nearly 100,000 francs. See accounts in AMO 1 J 159.

19. AMO 1 J 157.

20. The 1860 poster (AMO 1 J 161) confirms the ceremony of presenting the standard in the evening of 7 May. The 1859 poster has not been preserved. A note to the mayor from a city councillor, A. Frémond, dated 27 March 1859, concerns deliberations on the organization involved in presenting the standard to the bishop (AMO 1 J 160).

21. Bengal lights are pots full of powder, which burns with an illuminating red light. They do not sparkle or ascend, but remain in place, illuminating the sculptures of the façade of the Cathedral, in the form of a stone filigree.

22. In French: 'un espace de raison'.

23. On this episode, see the local press and box AMO 1 J 166.

24. In 1909 the mayor recalled this episode: 'It was painful to see the people of Orleans turning their backs on their elected representatives, as with least one-third of them.' Deliberations of the town Council on 19 March 1909, p. 268.

25. See for example the general's reply to the invitation from the mayor to the cathedral ceremony in 1910: he would be delighted to attend the service 'but not in an official capacity that would include the allocation of a reserved seat' (AMO 1 J 167).

26. AMO 1 J 169. Letter from the Indépendance lodge to the mayor, dated 19 April 1920, demanding that the mayor should write to him that his participation would inevitably lead to the clergy's absention, so that the lodge could 'withdraw its acceptance' of the invitation. Minute of the mayor's response, same date.

27. An innovation that was not repeated: the young girl playing the part of Joan of Arc came to take her place on her horse on the open pavement in front of the cathedral during this ceremony.

28. On 8 May 1929, see the special number of the *Bulletin de la Société Archéologique et Historique de l'Orléanais*, Mgr. P.-M. Brun: *Jeanne d'Arc entre l'Élysée et le Vatican*, Orléans, Impr. Nouvelle, 1977: Mgr Brun, then assistant priest in the cathedral, reports that the President approached the Legate and said to him: 'Monsieur le Cardinal, my presence here and that of my government indicates that the French Republic is neither atheist nor antireligious but that it is traditionalist' (p. 9). It is known that in 1918 Poincaré, then President of the Republic, arranged to be represented by his wife in Notre Dame for the victory *Te Deum*.

29. This study suffers from a double gap in the documentation: we do not have the programme of festivities for every year, and the programmes themselves, often copied from the preceding year, do not give the whole story. More extensive research, impossible in the framework for this article, would bring out more information.

30. As a young teacher in the Lycée Pothier, I was therefore called to the director's office, where a costume hire company took my measurements and I paraded in my robe on 8 May 1961. That same year I was to give the address at the prize-giving. I offered as my topic: the sociology of the city of Orleans according to the decoration of houses for the Joan of Arc festival, but this was considered disrespectful and rejected by the Academy inspector; I fell back on a eulogy devoted to Pothier. Thus continued my apprenticeship into local identity!

31. In 1998, after the publication of this essay, and a public lecture on the conclusion of this subject, this order has been changed, and the City Council, and other public institutions, recovered their unity, and the City Council its precedence, in this procession. Thus history may lead to municipal politics.

32. Letter from the Prefect to the Mayor, AMO 1 J 161.

33. *La République du Centre*, 10 May 1993.

8

Marriage, Youth and Society in Orleans in 1911

Despite their narrowly demographic basis, marriage certificates are better than many other documents for offering a clear picture of a society's dynamism and diversity. They do more than supply elementary information on the civil status of the spouses' age, place of birth, domicile, profession, for they also show the domicile and occupation of their parents, if living. The result is a sort of survey of two successive generations, which is all the more significant because the sample created by the chance circumstance of the marriage cannot be distorted through the subjective selection of the historian's eye. With contemporary cities too heavily populated for the individual to be well known, such a survey appears particularly interesting. More easily than the census, in which the volume of information discourages analysis, marriage certificates enable us to establish a basic structural framework for a given population, its evolution and the phenomena of mobility – social as well as geographic – that arise within it. There is material here to attract the cultural and social historian.

This is particularly true if he has ethnological leanings, for from between the lines of the register of civil status he will glean a mass of information on the status of the young people to be married, on the social practices of youth and of marriage. A frontier between two periods in life, marriage marks the end of a period of independence and liberty with identifiable limits. It sanctions a mutual choice that is not the work of chance. In short, within the neutral sketch presented by the marriage certificates, details such as the consent of the parents, the existence of a marriage contract, the selection of one witness or another, of a date or a day of the week for the civil ceremony, encourage us to recreate the characteristic customs of various social circles.

And yet the following question tends to temper the historian's optimism as he approaches this source: does not the size of the sample constituted by the marriage certificates affect the validity of the conclusions? What can we assert with confidence, from such a small number of individuals? Surely a few special cases would be enough to affect our view of the conduct of groups of a dozen people? The objection is pertinent, and we considered increasing the size of our sample by examining the certificates from two years instead of one.[1] In the event, however, we chose not to do so, for lack of an overwhelming argument that would guarantee the validity of an analysis on this scale. Of course, two years would produce firmer conclusions than a single year; but then why not three or four years? In this respect, the temptation is considerable to yield to dizzying exhaustivity: it would undoubtedly be better to have an analysis concerning the whole of a population rather than surveys within samples.

As soon as one settles for a survey, its greater or lesser extent simply pushes back the question of the validity of results, without overcoming it. Whether one analyses 5,000 certificates or 500, there is no escape from questioning the degree of significance of the results obtained; better to face up to it squarely. The full question then becomes one of 'significant' differences. Whatever the sample studied, social history brings out differences between groups or sub-groups, each consisting of several dozen people. From what point can one trust these differences, and draw conclusions from them? It is a truly classic question of statistics – and psychologists as well as sociologists are used to resolving it by testing the zero hypothesis: they calculate the differences that chance alone could have produced in a group of the size under consideration, and compare them to what they have perceived. Why should not historians follow this discipline too? As soon as one works on the differences between small groups, this method is the only one that can enable a quantitative history of societies to avoid being buried in the mass of documentary series of figures on which it is based.[2]

Within the framework of a more ambitious research project on Orleans society in the Belle Epoque, we therefore turned to the marriage certificates, and we undertook the systematic examination of all the certificates from one year. The year chosen was 1911, which coincides with the last census before the war.

The town hall in Orleans recorded 528 marriages that year, out of a population of 72,096. This is relatively low,[3] but the marriage certificates in fact give us information on more than 800 young Orléanais: the 528 brides, to whom can be added those husbands – 398 – who lived in the city. Further, 1,502 parents were still living at the time of their children's marriage (including 710 fathers), and we know their trade and their domicile. There is material here to stimulate the historian's curiosity.[4]

Orleans Culture and Society: Change and Continuity

The survey met all expectations.[5] Quite apart from questions of local history, in fact, it posed questions of a far wider import concerning early twentieth-century urban societies in France.

Two different generations

It is tempting to begin the survey with the occupations of those concerned, since these are known with relative accuracy. We can expect it to provide an initial view, global and approximate, of social structures in Orleans. The marriage certificates contain information on two groups of Orleans men: the husbands and the fathers who lived in the commune. These two groups are very similar in size: 398 for the first, 425 for the second. Yet if we analyse the composition of the groups by socio-professional category, as displayed in Table I, we discover significant differences between them: there is less than one chance in a thousand that the gap between the two generations can be the result of chance.[6]

Table 8.1: Occupational structure of two generations of men of Orleans.

Profession	Fathers	Husbands
AGR (Farmers, winegrowers, gardeners)	13.4%	7.3%
JOUR (Day labourers, unskilled workers)	16.9%	8.8%
BTP (Masons, joiners, stone-cutters)	10.1%	10.3%
MET (Locksmiths, mechanics, metal-workers)	5.4%	9.5%
A/OUV (Other skilled workers)	12.0%	16.6%
DOM (Domestic servants)	0.5%	3.8%
CHF (Railwaymen)	11.1%	12.1%
ENQ (Employees, clerks)	5.9%	12.1%
EQ (Bookkeepers, chief clerks, NCOs)	2.8%	8.3%
ARCO (Shopkeepers, self-employed craftsmen)	6.1%	7.0%
BGS (Industrialists, salesmen, professionnals)	14.1%	4.3%
TOTAL NUMBERS	425	398

The comparison between one generation and the next obviously concerns different stages in individual trajectories. The husbands are beginning their life in society, for the greater part, while the fathers and stepfathers are ending theirs, if they have not already done so. We should therefore not be surprised at the relatively smaller number of *bourgeois* in the sons' generation, a lower number balanced by the large number of skilled employees and governmental officials: a dealer's son has no need to be ashamed of beginning as a bank clerk, any more than a notary's son of being a clerk in a professional colleague's office.[7] Conversely, the low number of domestic servants in the fathers' generation can be explained either by a move out of this category once wages have been saved sufficiently to constitute a basic capital or, as may be suggested by the presence among the fathers of several private caretakers, by installing older domestic servants, or those with children, in country properties.

Other differences, on the other hand, relate to the evolution of Orleans society. The reduced numbers of wine-growers, farmers and gardeners, for example, reflects the urbanization of the commune. Even though the population is not growing rapidly – 20,000 inhabitants more, a growth of 3.8 per cent between 1876 and 1911 – the area of the commune is closely limited by that of the surrounding communes, to which the vines, nursery gardens and market gardens have retreated. Similarly, in the working class, alongside the railway workers' stability, which tended to make Orleans in some respects a 'railway town', and the continuing presence of construction workers,[8] an evolutionary pattern can be discerned. Day labourers are becoming less numerous, and weavers and cap-makers are disappearing, while the numbers working in food trades (confectionery, chocolate, vinegar) are increasing. There is an air of a slow slide from work that requires purely physical strength towards more skilled employment.

A Stable Society

It is true that these differences have a greater effect on the internal equilibrium of the working classes than on that of society as a whole. The only true change is the decline in working on the land, which is balanced by the expansion in office work. The middle class (the *bourgeoisie*) and the lower middle class (the *petite bourgeoisie*) of craftsmen, traders, clerks or office managers represent nearly one-fifth of each generation: 23 per cent of fathers, 19.6 per cent of sons. Without railway workers and domestic servants, industrial workers make up slightly under one half of the population: 44.4 per cent of fathers, 42.5 per cent of sons. If we add the railwaymen to this, we achieve virtually the same results from the first generation (55.5 per cent) as from the second (57.3 per cent). Taking it in its overall mass, Orleans society appears to show a surprising stability.

It is moreover an urban society closer to the nineteenth century – or even the eighteenth – than the twentieth. Despite a real increase in numbers, office employees are still a small category in this city of garrison and *préfecture*, and the white-collar proletariat lies far behind the large majority represented by industrial workers. No doubt our sources underestimate the weight of the upper categories in society: four husbands of aristocratic origin (with a 'de' to their name), three of whom are marrying commoner wives from elsewhere – a very low number in relation to the nominative lists of the census in certain districts. Very probably their status as major landowners in their villages required them to marry their children in the country, at their châteaux. But these few exceptions should not make much difference in our study.

So, Orleans an industrial city? Certainly not. Tradition shows precisely the history of the local economy through its decline as a trading centre, linked to navigation on the Loire, even though the great number of railway workers in the city shows that railway expansion brought some compensation. Contemporary memory does not mention bustling industries in the Belle Epoque, and documentary evidence confirms this view. The list of commercial voters for 1911, for example,[9] shows around fifteen manufacturers of clothing, blankets, caps or corsets, a dozen making kitchenware or ironmongery, makers of files or pins, machinery builders, four carriage-builders, and four manufacturers of chemical products, paints, varnish and insecticide. Most of Orleans' contractors deal with construction (79), food production (often linked to trade, as with the 41 vinegar-makers, who are in most cases also wine or spirits merchants), and every kind of trade. Out of 325 commercial electors, first or second category, no more than fifty are industrialists; and even here it is a matter of minor industry.

This paradox of a workers' city without industry or factories is explained if we are alert to cases of misleading terminology. These locksmiths, carpenters, cabinet-makers, fitters, engineers, file-makers and others, whom we would classify as industrial workers, do not in fact make up an industrial proletariat. They are far more represent-ative of an urban population from pre-industrialization days. It is a poor population, with uncertain means of livelihood, threatened by illness, old age and seasonal unemployment, a hardworking and exploited population, industrious and badly paid, but without any of the features of the great factory centres, their discipline and anonymity. It is radical rather than socialist. The Catholic writer Charles Péguy came from this population, through his mother, a chair-mender, as well as through his father, who died young, the son of a gardener and a joiner by trade. No connection at all with the miners and glass-workers of Carmaux. At a time when France was experiencing the vigorous industrial expansion in which Jaurès's socialism could flourish, the example of Orleans is an opportune reminder that the nineteenth century was not over everywhere, and that the proletariat had not yet completely replaced the old urban population.

Local Rootedness

The endurance of an old-style urban population, like the overall stability of social structures, relates to Orleans' slow rate of growth. While other cities of similar size were overwhelmed by a tripling or quadrupling of their population, Orleans expanded slowly. Her population increased by only 5.8 per cent between 1851 and 1911, while most cities of the same size grew more quickly – for example, Rheims (152 per cent), Nancy (165 per cent), Grenoble (147 per cent) or Dijon (138 per cent). Even within the Loire region Orleans was now overtaken by towns that fifty years earlier had been her followers, such as Angers (+ 156 per cent) and Tours (+ 119 per cent), the direct rival of Orleans.

The counterpart of this low growth-rate was to be the deep-rootedness of the people, a factor reflected in the proportion of husbands born in the city or its suburbs. In Orleans the relevant figure in 1911 was 44.4 per cent of spouses born in the city, including its outlying areas: exactly 49.4 per cent of brides, and 39.3 of husbands. Six husbands and five brides out of ten were therefore born outside Orleans – a figure that appears high precisely where we would expect a solid local deep-rootedness.

In fact the lack of precise comparisons makes it difficult to appreciate the exact import of these figures. In Bordeaux, where since the early days of the Third Republic the population had increased at the same pace as in Orleans, as Pierre Guillaume shows, 44 per cent of husbands were local in 1913, a rate that appears relatively high compared with the 36 per cent of 1883 and 33.5 per cent of 1938.[10] Yves Lequin has calculated these rates in the Lyons region, but only for the working class: there are fewer local husbands in Lyons and Saint-Chamond, similar numbers at Givors and Vienne, and more at Saint-Étienne. Lequin sees this as the indication of a greater stability in the industrial working class compared with the middle of the nineteenth century, but he notes that the lowest rate of local-origin working class is at Saint-Chamond, despite its virtually static population. He therefore rightly warns against over-rapid summarization. The link between urban growth and the size of the migrant population is not straightforward, and the relative deep-rootedness of working populations is no guarantee of their social and political calm.[11] The demarcation between the people and the proletariat does not match exactly that of the rooted and the deracinated.

An index of significance difficult to evaluate, the proportion of husbands of local origin is also an ambiguous factor. Marriage is celebrated in the wife's home commune. Orleans shows only two exceptions to this rule in 1911, and for this reason wives of local origin outnumber the local husbands, some of whom live outside Orleans and its suburbs. The overall rate, a simple average of these two percentages, therefore reflects – but in proportions that are impossible to differentiate – both the rootedness of the husbands and the greater or lesser number of husbands who have come from elsewhere, in other words the openness of the marriage market.

If we wish to develop the analysis it is therefore safer to consider only husbands who live in Orleans. This enables us to bring focal points of stability, and others of immigration, into consideration. The least well-rooted women in Orleans are of course domestic servants: even so, one in six is locally-born, and three more come from the rural Loiret. Other departments supply only one in three (27 out of 79, to be precise). Similarly, women day-workers are often living away from their roots, with one in two born outside the Loiret. In all other social groups, Orleans is the home town for at least one in two, with the Loiret supplying a contingent containing in all between 8 and 27 per cent of wives, leaving around one-third of migrants. One particular group can be identified that is purely local in origin: women working in gardens or vineyards, who were all born in Orleans or in the Loiret.

For husbands, the situation is different, although three-quarters of them live in Orleans and its immediate surroundings (75.5 per cent). To them may be added the few husbands (3.5 per cent) who live in the Loiret, essentially the nearest regions of the department. In this group from 'greater' Orleans, two-thirds are of local – or, rather, departmental – origins (65.4 per cent), a proportion barely smaller than that of their brides (69 per cent), an insignificant difference in view of the numbers.[12] Between one trade or profession and another, the variations are considerable. The most firmly rooted are farmers, wine-growers and gardeners (89 per cent), followed by minor government officials and office employees (86 per cent): pen-pushers don't have itchy feet. Day-workers and construction workers are still locals, in three cases out of four, while other workers, such as craftsmen or traders, match the average, with external additions slightly over 30 per cent. The middle classes are the least rooted: out of 21 who live in the department, and among whom we should recognize the presence of officers and senior local government managers, eleven were born outside the area. Railway workers are, naturally, the least well-rooted – one in two comes from outside, followed by the white-collar workers whom we designate as 'skilled office employees', that upper fringe of the tertiary subdivision that today would be seen as 'middle management' (14 of non-local origin, out of 33).

The same differences appear in the fathers' generation. By comparing their current domicile at the time of the birth of the child who is to be married, it is simple to pick out from those who live in Orleans – and here we are concerned strictly with the commune – the men who were already living in the city or its suburbs twenty or thirty years earlier. Deep-rootedness is a feature of the same groups: farmers (42 out of 44), day-labourers and construction workers (71 out of 100), minor officials and office workers (22 out of 33). Conversely, mobility is a characteristic feature of railwaymen (27 of Orleans origins, out of 42 resident in the city) and for skilled employees (6 from Orleans out of 16 in the group).

From these figures a social geography emerges for the population of Orleans. The stable elements are on the one hand those who work the land and, on the other, those who have neither professional qualification nor training. Far from attracting labourers, Orleans to some extent retains unqualified manual jobs for its own citizens, and a further proportion as commercial or office staff. Mobility is linked to qualification: either in a craft, particularly in engineering, or in teaching. And it would be interesting to know if, from this point of view, Orleans is simply a city that takes people in or whether it is not at the same time a city that exports people. Paradoxically, the *bourgeoisie* appears less rooted than one would expect – but, also, because its rootedness is more complex: we are assessing it here according to the movements of the men, although it is undoubtedly the women who develop roots.

Measuring the rootedness of the various elements of the people of Orleans is not enough. One should distinguish the degrees of rootedness; however, we have limited ourselves to distinguishing the Orléanais born in Orleans, or who have lived there for some twenty years, from more recent arrivals. The reality is far less simple. What is there in common between the female day-labourer born in the Nièvre who left her parents to live in Orleans – via who knows where? – and the seamstress or female office worker, daughter of a railway worker, born in a remote railway settlement and brought to Orleans by her father's employment? In the first case, migration is a strictly personal matter; it implies isolation, and no doubt insecurity. The second case relates to family circumstances, and although the location of her life has changed she continues to live among the same familiar faces.

For the 710 fathers still living at the time of their child's marriage – and no matter where the latter is domiciled – we know how many lived in Orleans at the time, and how many were already living there at the time of the birth of the child who was to be married. Table 8.2 summarizes these figures.

Table 8.2: Rootedness in Orleans of spouses and their fathers.

Origins or status of the fathers of marriage partners	Husbands	Wives
Spouses living in Orleans or Orléans' suburbs	75.5%	100.0%
Spouses born in Orleans or Orléans' suburbs	39.3%	49.4%
Fathers living in Orleans in 1911, at time of their children's marriage	44.0%	67.7%
Fathers living in Orleans in 1911 and at time of birth of these marriage partners	32.6%	46.0%

The proportion of fathers living in Orleans since the birth of the son to be married is obviously lower than that of bridegrooms born in the city, for some have left Orleans to retire elsewhere. On the other hand, the number of fathers who live there is appreciably greater than that of bridegrooms who were born there, and markedly greater for the fathers of brides than for fathers of their bridegrooms. It appeared probable that the migration of young men was more individual and that of young girls more a matter of family: the figures in Table 8.2 offer proof of this surmise. Only 11.4 per cent of fathers had come to live in Orleans since the birth of the son who was to be married, and 44 per cent lived in Orleans. On the other hand, out of 100 new brides, all resident in the city or suburbs, half were born there and half had moved there since their birth. But among the latter, 21.7 per cent came with their families, leaving 29 per cent who moved independently. This is a very low total, and more than two-thirds of the young women getting married in Orleans had their family resident there.[13]

The survey thus brings out the limits of renewal in the population of Orleans. It does not imply either a city enclosed on itself or a substantial degree of movement. On a basis of stability, more marked in certain occupational sectors, a moderate level of immigration is represented in different forms for men and for women. The numbers in question do not enable us to identify particular regions supplying this somewhat diffuse type of immigration in any particular way. In any case, the neighbouring departments supply fewer new Orléanais than the rest of France, and the city's proximity to Paris is a significant factor. The picture is one of a city of sufficient size for the population to manifest relative mobility, but one that does not draw on any specific dependent rural area, and where growth remains too low to threaten fundamental stability. Social mobility here should therefore be equally low.

Social mobility

Marriage certificates offer a double study of social mobility: that of mobility between one generation and the next, through the comparison between fathers and sons, despite the difficulties due to the fact that the former are ending their working lives while the latter are beginning theirs; and that of matrimonial mobility in its true sense, which offers comparisons between fathers and fathers-in-law, husbands and wives, or husbands and fathers-in-law. Because of the large number of women without occupation we have not drawn comparisons between the circumstances of bride and bridegroom, and have retained the comparison between sons-in-law and fathers-in-law, which is based on fuller information. Tables 8.3 and 8.4 give, respectively, the distribution of bridegrooms in 1911 as a function of the situations of their fathers and their fathers-in-law. We can see in Table 8.3, for example, that out of 36 railway workers who married in 1911 in Orleans and whose fathers we can identify with precision, 12 are sons of land-workers and that out of 26 railwaymen whose sons were getting married, 10 had a son who was himself a railway worker.[14]

Table 8.3: Occupations of fathers and husbands.

Husbands' Occupation	Occupation of fathers									Total Husbands
	AGR	JOUR	BTP	A/OUV	CHF	ENQ	EQ	ARCO	BGS	
AGR	22	1	1			1		1	1	27
JOUR	4	5	3	2				1		15
BTP	2	5	12	6	1	1		2		29
A/OUV	13	23	12	30	9	7	1	4	5	104
CHF	12	4	3	1	10	1		4	1	36
ENQ	6	8	4	4	1	6	3	4	3	39
EQ	6	3	2	3	4	1	2	4	14	39
ARCO	3	1	2	3	1		1	8	6	25
BGS	1						1	1	23	26
All Fathers	69	50	39	49	26	17	8	29	53	340

Note: For meanings of occupational abbreviations see Table 8.1.

Table 8.3: Occupations of fathers and husbands.

Husbands' Occupation	Occupation of fathers-in-law									Total Husbands
	AGR	JOUR	BTP	A/OUV	CHF	ENQ	EQ	ARCO	BGS	
AGR	18	4	3	1					1	27
JOUR	4	10	5	4		2		1		26
BTP	2	4	1	8	2	5				22
A/OUV	14	19	13	29	9	5		5	2	96
CHF	4	9	4	5	12	2		1	2	39
ENQ	5	6	6	11	7	4	2	4	3	48
EQ	3	2	2	5	2	3	2	5	11	35
ARCO	2	2	2	1	4	1	2	6	2	22
BGS			1	1	1				29	32
All Fathers-in-law	52	56	37	65	37	22	6	22	50	347

Notes: For meanings of occupational abbreviations see Table 8.1. Differences in numbers are due to fathers who had died, fathers without occupation, or whose occupation is unknown.

Although these are classic tables they are not easy to interpret. This is the reason for using them to create Table 8.5 from them, which summarizes their data in a style that is more abstract but more accessible. If the index that appears at the intersection of a line and a column is greater than 1, this is the sign of a proximity, a preferential link.[15] Conversely, an index lower than 1 indicates a distance.[16] We have also undertaken the factorial analysis of the correspondences of these tables.

The strongest social heredity, like the strongest endogamy, occurs within the middle classes, marking out a veritable trench between them and the rest of the population that is shown up clearly by factorial analysis. The middle class, the world of the *bourgeoisie*, constitutes a separate and self-sufficient world, where endogamy is even stronger than social heredity. A settled *bourgeois*, a dealer, lawyer, officer or property-owner, virtually never marries outside his own circle. Conversely, the *bourgeois* does not give his daughter to someone who is not of his own world. We find *bourgeois* daughters married to representatives of our category of 'skilled employees' – office managers, clerks, accountants – but very few to craftsmen or shopkeepers, although it is not uncommon to find a *bourgeois* son running a shop. The significant fact is that marriage is permanent – at least it is intended to be so[17] – while jobs are impermanent. One's son may open a shop: with time – with a legacy? – he will return to his own rank, while giving one's daughter to an uneducated shopkeeper is an irretrievable step. The lack of manners and culture appears here to be more to be feared than the lack of wealth, and a misguided marriage is more serious than a modest professional beginning.

Skilled office employees are thus a little less remote from the *bourgeoisie* than craftsmen and shopkeepers. But, with them, they make up a minor *bourgeoisie* that shows features similar to those of the true *bourgeoisie*, but watered down, a semi-tone lower down the scale. The sons of this lesser *bourgeoisie* spread out through the ranks of subordinate office staff and even among railway-workers – at least for craftsmen and shopkeepers; but they do not go into exile in the world of labourers, nor do they find their wives in that world. It is true that this social group is somewhat more open than the *bourgeoisie*. Although no *bourgeois* comes from the common people, we can find skilled office employees, or craftsmen and shopkeepers, whose fathers are land-workers or manual workers, although they are very few. Upward social mobility remains very limited.

Table 8.5. An Index of social proximity between husbands, their fathers, and fathers-in-law (in each cell, the first line indicates proximity with fathers, the second line, proximity with fathers-in-law).

Husbands Occupation	Occupation of Fathers and Fathers-in-law								
	AGR	JOUR	BTP	A/OUV	CHF	ENQ	EQ	ARCO	BGS
AGR	4.01	0.25	0.32	–	–	0.74	–	0.43	0.23
	4.44	0.92	1.04	0.19	–	–	–	–	0.26
JOUR	1.31	2.26	1.74	0.92	–	–	–	0.78	–
	1.02	2.38	1.80	0.82	–	1.21	–	0.61	–
BTP	0.34	1.17	3.61	1.44	0.45	0.69	–	0.81	–
	0.61	1.12	0.43	1.94	0.85	3.58	–	–	–
A/OUV	0.62	1.50	1.01	2.00	1.13	1.35	0.41	0.45	0.31
	0.97	1.23	1.27	1.61	0.88	0.82	–	0.16	0.14
CHF	1.64	0.75	0.73	0.19	3.63	0.55	–	1.30	0.18
	0.68	1.43	0.96	0.68	2.89	0.81	–	0.40	0.36
ENQ	0.75	1.39	0.89	0.71	0.33	3.08	3.27	1.20	0.49
	0.69	0.77	1.17	1.22	1.37	1.31	2.40	1.31	0.43
EQ	0.76	0.52	0.45	0.53	1.34	0.51	2.18	1.20	2.30
	0.57	0.35	0.54	0.76	0.54	1.35	3.30	2.25	2.18
ARCO	0.59	0.27	0.70	0.83	0.52	–	1.70	3.75	1.54
	0.61	0.56	0.85	0.24	1.70	0.72	5.25	4.30	0.63
BGS	0.19	–	–	–	–	–	1.63	0.45	5.67
	–	–	0.29	0.17	0.29	–	0.91	–	6.29

Note: For meanings of occupational abbreviations see Table 8.1.

Between the workers' world and the petty *bourgeoisie*, railway-men and subordinate office employees constitute a particularly interesting intermediate group, resembling an upper layer of ordinary townsfolk. Once they have reached this level they appear to some extent to be protected against falling into the lower ranks of the proletariat. Sons of railwaymen or of office staff do not become day-labourers or navvies, bricklayers or joiners – open-air work that is severely looked down on. Some may gain entrance to the upper tertiary sector, particularly sons of railwaymen. Most follow their fathers – professional heredity is considerable here – or, by default, become craft industrial workers – locksmiths, engineers or carriage-builders.

This expanding group – numbers are larger in the sons' generation than among the fathers and fathers-in-law – clearly cannot supply all its own recruits; but it does not open its doors to all and sundry. Railwaymen above all welcome the sons of farmers, while office employees take on the sons of day-labourers. We may think here of the 'open sesame' that the *certificat d'études primaires* represented for many children anxious to escape from the over-burdensome conditions of their fathers lives, or simply exported from the countryside by the rural exodus.

Marriage certificates are unfortunately silent on the spouses' level of education,[18] to the extent that it is impossible to be sure of the role that this played in inter-generational mobility. Yet we should surely recognize the existence of two distinct lines of mobility through primary education: a rural network that led farmers' sons to become railwaymen, and an urban network that enabled the sons of day-labourers to penetrate the world of offices or shops without moving too far from home.

Nonetheless, some differences exist between railwaymen and subordinate office staff. Railwaymen seem more secure in their jobs than office staff or minor government staff. In contrast to the latter, their sons become skilled employees. Their daughters virtually never marry day-labourers or construction workers, although many daughters of the minor office employees marry into the lower ranks of the proletariat – but this is clearly not a homogeneous category: it encompasses shop staff such as the stock-keeper and also office staff similar to a head clerk, or to a primary-school teacher. Further, we find employees who are the sons not simply of craftsmen or shop-keepers – an equal number of railwaymen comes from this background – but sons of skilled office employees, who are never railwaymen. Here, undoubtedly, we have the sign of a social permeability. The category of office employee is one through which people pass, not one where they remain; men in this group may marry the daughter of a construction trade guild member or a girl whose father is a shopkeeper, a labourer or a senior office employee. No other group shows such diversity.

Land-workers appear slightly separate. As we are here not looking at men from Orleans alone, the rural exodus naturally expands the group of farming fathers into a substantial contingent of rural people of every type. To the vineyard workers and gardeners of the Loire valley can be added share-croppers from the Nivernais and farm-workers from the Massif Central. For this reason, the majority of land-workers who marry are the sons of a land-worker father (81 per cent), and more than two-thirds marry the daughter of a gardener, a vineyard worker or a farm-worker. Professional heredity is naturally stronger than endogamy.

The same reason – the rural exodus – makes it impossible for all farmer parents to have a son or son-in-law who is himself a farmer. The national decrease in the rural population, like the urbanization of a commune, fosters other social groups, but operating along different lines. The sons of farmers or smallholders in fact above all become day-workers or railwaymen, representing two very different sets of circumstances. Very probably, those who have received a good primary education can try their chance away from home, and go to work on the railways. Those who have not been educated hire out their muscle-power, very often close to home, since two-thirds of day-labourers were born in the Loiret. It is rare for farmers' sons to become industrial workmen: do they lack technical competence, or is Orleans industry insufficiently powerful to attract them? In any case, the rural exodus does not directly feed the ranks of trade workmen.

Then there is the world of work, of which we can grasp the complexity since we have introduced a few distinctions at its heart. This methodological approach, justified by the numerical importance of industrial workmen in both generations under consideration here, does not imply any artifice. If we merge together in a single group the day-labourers, building workers and craft workers, this group would not appear more homogeneous and would reach levels of professional heredity (2.18) and of endogamy (1.40) that would make them a more open group than most. However, an aggregate approach would have masked some significant differences.[19]

Initially, the moves from one of these worker categories to another appear simple. Each one recruits from within the other two, but a very clear hierarchy emerges: day-labourers are rarely the sons of craft workers, and vice versa, while the sons of day-labourers do become industrial workers. Similarly, day-labourers rarely marry the daughters of industrial workers, although their daughters marry industrial workers. Upward mobility within the working classes thus opens up an avenue of access for the upper ranks of the proletariat, the descendants of casual labourers.

Between the land and the workshop, the condition of day-labourer constitutes an intermediate stage, the way into the urban working population. Industrial craftsmen, in fact, appear to be relatively well integrated into the city. Their recruitment is very broad, from day-labourers to railwaymen and office employees; and although the field of their marriages is slightly smaller, it is also very broad. Urban residents over a long period, they have a more diverse network of relationships and a more complex set of social links. Building work, on the other hand, creates a separate unit, similar to that of the railwaymen. Professional heredity is strongly marked here, and the sons of bricklayers or joiners often follow their fathers. Endogamy is very limited, however; they marry the daughters of industrial workers or of office employees, not the daughters of bricklayers or joiners. Would these girls refuse them? In any case, the contrast between the strong professional heredity and the low endogamy in the construction world presents a problem. It would be useful to know if this is identifiable in other cities at the same period, or whether it is peculiar to Orleans.

We can see the contribution that marriage certificates bring to our knowledge of the internal structures and movements of a society. But this is not their true object. It is up to us to use them in particular to learn about marriage. The marriage ceremony, marking the frontier between two age-groups in life and undertaken by the mayor as representative of the civic state, marks the end of a period of youth that unfolded in different ways in different settings. It sanctions the existence of couples that have not all been created in the same way. Here is a document disclosing one of the fundamental signifying practices of a society.

Youth, Marriage and Social Groups

Between Youth and Adulthood

Marriage marks the end of a period of life that began with puberty and, generally, the end of schooldays. In this context, the age at which it occurs has social implications as well as demographic significance: the period of youth is not the same length for everyone. First, people marry at a relatively young age in Orleans: younger than in the rest of France as a whole, and younger than in Bordeaux, for example. This is surprising, for one would expect the behaviour of all young people in all cities to be the same: but this is clearly not so. The average ages for marriage in Orleans in 1911 are 26 years 8 months for men and 23 years 10 months for women. The averages for France at this time are 28 years for men and 26 years 8 months for women; and in Bordeaux in 1913, 28 years 2 months and 26 years 3 months respectively. In Bordeaux in 1938, they were established at 28 years and a little over 25 years.[20] Between the two cities the difference is appreciable; the young husbands in Orleans are on average eighteen months younger than those in Bordeaux, and their brides nearly two and a half years younger. Since this difference is indisputable – because the age records are entirely reliable in the civil state registers – we must accept it without question. This type of factor is a warning against hasty generalization: in this early twentieth-century period, cities were not at all identical.

It is in the *bourgeoisie* that youth lasts the longest. Here, the average age at marriage is over 30 years. At the other end of the social scale, metalworkers and vineyard workers do not wait until they are 25: the difference is more than five years. Between the two, divisions between the various groups are not created by chance. The sections nearest to the *bourgeoisie* are of course those of craftsmen and shop-keepers, very similar on this point to traders who, on the other hand, stand out from the rest of the *bourgeoisie,* and above all from senior office employees. Railwaymen follow shortly behind them. In these circles people marry around the age of 27 or more, and the gap between the spouses is at least three years. The common people marry younger, and the age of marriage there appears to depend on material conditions, such as stability of employment: gardeners, a group that no doubt includes a fairly large proportion of hired workers, marry later than vineyard workers, and day-labourers later than construction workers, themselves slower to marry than metalworkers.

The average age at marriage is too slight an indication to be instructive on how 'youth' comes to an end. For a clearer view we should look at a graph of the number of newly married men at each age, indicating the *bourgeoisie* (including dealers), the middleclass, from craftsmen to railwaymen via office employees of all kinds, and industrial workers, from day-labourers to domestic servants.

Table 8.6: Average age of first marriage, by occupational group.

Husband's occupation	Number	Average age				Age Difference	
		Husbands		Wives			
BGS* (without salesmen)	28	30 yrs and 2 mos		23 yrs and 10 mos		6 yrs and 4 mos	
Skilled workers	47	27	10	24	4	3	6
Craftsmen, shopkeepers	27	27	9	24	8	3	1
Railwaymen	55	27		23	4	3	8
Salesmen	8	26	10	23	9	3	1
Gardeners	18	26	10	24		2	10
Day Labourers	22	26	8	24	10	1	10
Unskilled workers	57	26	3	23	6	2	9
Building workers	36	25	8	23	6	2	2
Other workers	57	25	7	23	4	2	3
Domestic workers	17	25	2	23	9	1	5
Metal workers	45	24	10	23	7	1	3
Vineyard workers	9	24	8	22	8	2	
Total (first marriages)	436	26	8	23	10	2	10

* For the meaning of this abbreviation see Table 8.1.

The graph of industrial labourers is characterized by an extremely sharp-pointed bell-curve: here, very few men marry under the age of 23 and not many more over 17. More than two marriages in three occur when the husband is aged between 23 and 27 (68 per cent). Taking the three ages of 23, 24 and 25 alone, they represent more than half (54 per cent) of working-class marriages.

This characteristic curve is similar to that of the popular classes in Bordeaux in 1913, and even as early as 1883. However, as Pierre Guillaume notes, without explanation, the curve of 1853 showed a less steep slope at the age of 23.[21] This is undoubtedly the effect of military service, generalized since 1872, and virtually universal after the suppression in 1889 of the exemptions available to certain categories of Frenchmen. At this period, military service, which lasted for two years under the law of 1905 – the class of 1908, for example was called up in October 1909 and released in September 1911[22] – constituted a major demarcation point in the sequence of life-stages. Young men who went about together hesitated to marry beforehand and those who wished to marry during their period of military service required the authorization of a senior officer, which was only obtainable under exceptional circumstances of a pressing or serious nature: only two examples appear in our sample.[23] The patriotic republican institution of compulsory military service thus pushed back the moment for founding a family to later than the age of 22 years.

What is interesting is that after the army the workers marry without further delay. For them, the two institutional barriers separating youth from adulthood – military service and marriage – are crossed within a few months of each other. Before military service we have the young man who conforms to the social norms for his age-group – dancing, having a good time. After military service, it is time to marry and take on adult roles. There is no time for an intermediate state between the two.

The same applies to the *petite bourgeoisie*, in overall terms, and in this they are copied by office employees and railwaymen. Here, too, military service constitutes a major break-point, often closely followed by marriage. And yet between the former and the latter a gap begins to develop. The five years that follow the army represent as many marriages as among the industrial workers (68 per cent); but, within these five years, the first three figure less strongly: 43 per cent against 54 per cent. There is less rush to found a household. First of all, there is a job to settle into fully, savings to be augmented, a shop or street stall to be found, promotion, or permanent promotion to a place where one can settle down, to be attained. Since these ambitions remain modest, marriage is not put off for long: but it is long enough for the difference between the two groups to be significant.[24]

Among the true *bourgeoisie* the difference is stronger still. The break represented by military service is no longer a constraining obligation, for the law of 21 March 1905 made deferment available, and it was then possible to delay the period of service until the end of one's student years. Further, the middle-class young man often ends up among the subalterns or cadets, and he can enjoy a certain amount of freedom while in uniform. Military service occurs later than for industrial workers and the middle classes, and it does not constitute such a marked break-point. As for marriage, it often takes place at the age of 29 or 30, several years after military service: long enough, it would appear, to win and consolidate one's position. Between youth and adulthood a period of transition is thus established, a privilege of the *bourgeoisie*. While workers' youth comes to a clearly marked end with military service and marriage in quick succession, the middle classes' youth ends noticeably later and more gradually.

This analysis shows the limits of a strictly demographic approach. It is impossible in fact to analyse the evolution of age at marriage as an autonomous fact, independent of social and historic context. The age of marriage for the men of Orleans in 1911 was closely determined by the nature of military service – length of service, universality, deferment – and by the social circles to which they belonged. The pattern of the life cycle is itself social.

Profiles of Youth

But is youth the same for everyone? Does this useful word conceal a uniform reality? We must distinguish here between boys and girls. The boys appear more mobile. They are less likely to have their parents with them, as we have seen. Perhaps they are more independent in some social circles than others? The marriage certificates enable us to determine this, for they specify whether or not the spouses live with their parents.

In overall terms, two young men in five are still living at home at the time of their marriage. This significant proportion varies less than might be anticipated. For obvious reasons it is greater among farm and garden workers, but also among workers and shopkeepers or craftsmen. It is lower, on the other hand, among the groups that feed the rural exodus: unskilled employees, railwaymen, and above all day-labourers. This picture illuminates the point made above, of a later age of marriage for day-labourers and unskilled employees or railwaymen than for workers. The young men who live with their family are no doubt a little quicker to find a wife, either because they enjoy a wider range of relationships than those living alone or because, by taking care of their material needs, their family gives them more time and freedom of mind, if not independence.[25]

Two factors explain these differences. First, rootedness. Whether they live in Orleans or elsewhere, stable young married people are much more likely than migrants to live with their families, and the latter are all the more isolated if they have moved a great distance: among those who have changed commune but not *département*, 1 in 2.2 lives with his parents, as against only 1 in 4.9 for migrants who have moved from another department. The inequalities noted between social groups thus relate in part to difference in rootedness: although half the workers are stable, this applies to only one-third of day-labourers or unskilled employees, and one-sixth of railwaymen. But this is not the only factor. Even when they are settled, fewer day-labourers, office employees and railwaymen, and even fewer craftsmen and shopkeepers, live with their families than occurs with the rest of the population. They give the impression of individuals who are either undergoing downward social mobility – day-labourers – or upward social mobility – craftsmen, shopkeepers and office employees; whatever the case they appear as individuals who lie outside the norm.

The norm is still, in fact, that a young man continues to live with his parents, if they live in the same town, even when he has attained adult age and has fulfilled his military obligations. This is particularly clear for industrial workers, more than half of whom live with their families. To become independent of their parents, they must move to another town – or get married.

Table 8.7 helps us to appreciate to what extent the youth of industrial workers and that of the middle classes are diametrically opposed.[26] The young industrial worker is in employment: he has the financial means for his independence; and yet he continues to live with his family – he is always there for family meals, and we may assume with confidence that he hands over his pay to the household. The young middle-class man, on the other hand, manages to be independent of his family even while he is dependent on it in finan-

Table 8.7: Marriage partners living with their parents, by sex, occupation and geographical mobility.

Occupation	Total	Average (1 out of n)	Stable	Mobility Mobile in the Loiret	Migrants
Men					
Farm workers	27/34	1.3	18/20	7/10	2/4
Day labourers	7/29	4.1	7/11	0/8	0/10
Building workers	24/37	1.5	17/19	7/11	0/7
Other workers	59/110	1.9	39/53	11/19	9/38
Railwaymen	14/53	3.8	7/8	1/11	6/34
Unskilled labourers	27/56	2.1	14/17	7/14	6/25
Skilled workers	22/43	2	11/14	3/4	8/25
Craftsmen and shopkeepers	15/31	2	9/14	2/5	4/12
Bourgeois	15/36	2.4	13/14	1/2	1/20
Total	202/429	2.1	135/170	39/84	36/175
Women					
Farm workers	19/20	1	15/15	4/5	–
Day labourers	6/17	2.8	2/4	2/4	2/9
Seamstresses	161/200	1.2	99/104	25/36	37/60
Unskilled labourers	15/23	1.5	9/12	1/3	5/8
Skilled workers	5/7	1.4	3/4	1/2	1/1
Other workers	18/21	1.2	10/11	4/4	4/6
Shopkeepers	3/6	2	3/3	0/2	0/1
Total women active	227/294	1.3	141/153	37/56	49/85
Women without an occupation	91/105	1.15	54/56	14/16	23/33

cial terms. He begins to earn his living later, after a long period as a student and sometimes uncertain beginnings during which his father subsidizes his needs. But he lives in a different town from his family, and his daily life is independent of theirs. Independent industrial workers exist, of course: youths who have chosen this course and have moved away to pursue it, or who have been forced to seek work far away that they could not find close to home. Conversely, there are dependent *bourgeois*: those who live in the same town as their parents. It is nonetheless true that these two patterns of youth, different in duration, are also different in meaning: at the two ends of the social ladder, the relationships formed by the young man with his work and with his family are diametrically opposed. The meaning of marriage is radically modified by this factor: for the young worker, who has been working for a long time, getting married means leaving his parents; for the young *bourgeois* who left home a long time ago – more than ten years ago, sometimes – marriage means the conclusion of establishing himself in a professional life that is also a social life.

The position of young girls is more complex. For most of them, in fact, whatever the setting, independence will be either out of reach or tinged with danger: the rule is to live at home except in cases of *force majeure*, emigration or death. Table 8.7 also shows that most live at home, apart from girls born outside Orleans; and even among this category, less than half are independent. As we have seen, they often move with their family, unless they follow after. The position of young girls, in *Belle Epoque* society, makes independence from parents somewhat unusual, if not exceptional.[27]

But this uniform pattern of dependence takes on different aspects according to whether or not the young girl is employed. We must therefore look at the occupations of women who marry, and here we come up against a surprising fact: four out of ten (38.8 per cent), or 205 young women, state their occupations as dressmaker, corset-maker, waistcoat-maker, seamstress, embroiderer – they work, in fact, in the clothing sector. This considerable figure undermines the image that we had of Orleans. Would an old-style clothing industry occupy a substantial female labour-force as outworkers? Would a large number of scattered workshops, too small to attract attention, successfully sustain this specialized dressmaking activity? Should we see Orleans as a metropolis of the clothing world?

No doubt the place of the clothing industry is underestimated. Out of the 205 brides who work in this sector we find 110 'dressmakers' without further detail, but 31 corset-makers, 8 waistcoat-makers, 4 cap-makers, 4 trousers-makers, 3 tailoring cutters and one shirt-maker – a total of 51 female workers engaged in making clothes. Independent dressmakers are a very small minority, and the 6 stylists certainly do not all have their own businesses. It is true that, among the dressmakers, as among the 27 seamstresses or the four laundresses, some worked regularly in middle-class households as specialized domestic staff. In all, however, the great majority of women no doubt worked at home or in a workshop for the five clothing makers, the three corset manufacturers, the three cap manufacturers and the other five manufacturers indicated in the list of 191 commercial electors in 1911.

To understand this more fully, it is useful to find out which families these clothing worker women belonged to; this is shown in Table 8.8. This table shows only the brides whose father is living

Table 8.8: Daughters' occupations compared to that of their fathers.

Daughters' occupation	Fathers' occupation							
	AGR	JOUR	A/OUV	CHF	ENQ	EQ + ARCO	BGS	Total
No occupation	5	1	11	4	1	16	44	82
Farm labourer	17	–	–	–	–	–	–	17
Day labourer	3	4	3	–	2	2	–	14
Workers	1	6	8	–	–	–	–	15
Domestic servant	13	13	15	2	–	2	2	47
Seamstress	11	31	60	27	15	3	1	148
ENQ	–	1	4	4	2	3	2	16
EQ + ARCO	2	–	1	–	2	2	1	8
Total	52	56	102	37	22	28	50	347

Note: For occupational abbreviations see Table 8.1.

and whose occupation is known. Property-owners are treated as *bourgeois*, and retired people listed under their active occupation.

It is no surprise to see that in families of the *bourgeoisie*, young girls do not work. Nine out of ten are without occupation: a considerable proportion, if we consider that, among the fathers counted here as middle-class, some property-owners may simply be retired. The pattern of the young daughter of the house is generally followed closely among the *bourgeoisie*, but it also holds a certain attraction for the lower-middle-class world of craftsmanship, and shopkeeping, or the upper tertiary sector. In this setting, there is less than one girl in two who works: those who aspire to join the true *bourgeoisie* begin by imitating it.

At the other end of the social scale, three groups place their daughters as domestic servants: farm-workers, garden-workers and, more rarely, industrial workers. These are the settings where daughters are industrial workers or day-labourers, reflecting family patterns marked by lack of money, or even indigence, and the acceptance of dependency. As soon as a modest level of material security and social standing is achieved, as with employees or railwaymen, there is no need to let one's daughter work in a middle-class household or be taken on as a day-worker.

The dressmaker takes her place between the middle-class model of the young daughter of the house, impossible to emulate without wealth, and the humiliating model of the domestic worker or day-worker, laid off as soon as she is no longer needed. While the proportion of domestic servants is diminishing, from farm-workers to industrial workers via day-labourers (25 per cent, 23 per cent, 15 per cent), the proportion of dressmakers is increasing, from 21 to 60 per cent, reaching 73 per cent among railwaymen's families. It then decreases amongst office employees, and in the lower middle class we do not find more than one dressmaker in nine young brides.

We have here a third and heterogeneous model, which is characteristic of popular settings, where it is good that young girls should work, but where only certain occupations are seen as suitable for them. Dressmaking is highly valued, to the point of becoming typically 'feminine', because of its cleanliness and its delicacy, but also because of the possibility that it offers of remaining at home – of working at one's own pace, without any direct subordination or any hint of promiscuity.

Of course, many variations of reality are hidden behind the same label. Some dressmakers work in a workshop, others at home for an employer who pays them at piece-rates, while others again are independent and have their own small clientèle. No doubt there are even some who do not work at all, and simply indicate for official purposes that they are dressmakers because that is what they may become in case of need. Some help to keep their families existence, others are preparing their own wedding-trousseaux, or accumulating their incomes to set up their own households. As for the future, that depends on the husband: some will continue to work, others will give up work sooner or later and will be content to run their households. The large number of dressmakers among the young women of 1911 not only indicates the continuing importance of the clothing industry, but also shows the attachment of the people of Orleans, and no doubt of many other townsfolk, to a certain way of occupying their young girls before marriage; it is the sign of the popular customs of the day.[28]

Three types of girlhood can thus be defined. The young middle-class girl occupies her idleness with the arts of pleasure and social life. The young girl in the poorest class is dependent, even servile; she works under the orders of strangers. The young girl of working-class family, finally, is hard-working; young girls should not remain without anything to do, but they can avoid the most unpleasant aspects of paid employment. The first ignores work and remains under family protection. The second works, but escapes family control. The third works without leaving her family. The relationship to work and the relationship to the family thus define three sets of circumstances, and these are not without influence on the way to find a husband.

The Choice of Husband

People almost always choose a spouse from a background identical to their own. But, apart from this overall determinism, it remains for us to grasp the specific mechanisms through which it operates. How do marriages happen?

The husband's domicile gives an initial element of an answer. To know how the women, who are all living in Orleans, found their husbands, it is useful to know where they found them. This is shown in Table 8.9. Initially, the breadth of difference between the social groups is surprising. One *bourgeois* husband in two comes from outside, less than one day-worker in 36, and only one construction worker in 44. In truth, three groupings emerge. At the bottom of the social ladder, a husband is found close to home. The rule holds good almost without exception for day-labourers and construction workers; it is still generally followed by industrial workers, domestic servants and farm-workers. Curiously, although more highly placed, craftsmen and shopkeepers follow the same rule, a fact that hints at the obligations of running a shop. At the other end of the scale, only the *bourgeoisie* finds its sons-in-law outside the department as often as within it: its matrimonial market covers the whole of France and, out of 21 husbands who, for the whole sample, live outside the Loiret and departments adjacent to it or the Seine (i.e. Paris), 7 are middle-class. Between these two groups, railway workers and employees occupy an intermediate space, neither strictly local – since one husband in three comes from outside – nor truly national, because these husbands generally come from neighbouring departments or the Paris region.

These three different marriage markets are not regulated by the same customs. When two spouses live in the same street or the same Orleans district, their encounter needs no explanation: they may simply be neighbours, or meet at dances. On the other hand, when the daughter of a captain of *gendarmerie*, born in Wassy, marries the doctor at an asylum for mentally handicapped people in the Charente who was born in Montpellier, one may well wonder where they met.[29]

The answer is clear: middle-class marriages are arranged by the families and the encounters are pre-planned: the meeting of the couple-to-be was a 'presentation'. These well-known customs leave two traces in the marriage certificates. First, there is often an expression of thanks to the parent or friend who 'made' the marriage, through inviting them to act as witness. As an example, there is the daughter of an Orleans lawyer who marries the chief clerk of a Paris legal office, without an Orleans connection. The person responsible for this marriage is very probably one of the husband's witnesses, an Orleans barrister apparently unrelated to him, and who features as his 'friend' although he is 43 and the young man only 27.[30]

The existence of contracts is a second sign of the *bourgeois* family's control over marriages that are also business affairs. As the daughters in this sector generally have a dowry, almost all the middle-class marriages give rise to a marriage contract. In the minor *bourgeoisie*, one marriage in two still has a contract; at the outer limits of the *bourgeoisie*, particularly among senior office staff, middle-class customs and the desire to preserve each spouse's patrimony or capital become noticeable, and shopkeepers and craftsmen undertake

Table 8.9: Domicile of husband according to occupation.

Occupation	Number	Living beyond the Loiret		Total	Living in the Loiret	
		Total	1 out of n		Natives	Migrants
AGR	33	6	5.5	30	27	3
JOUR	36	0		36	24	12
BTP	44	1	44	43	33	10
A/OUV	126	17	7.4	109	74	35
DOM	22	6	3.7	16	4	12
CHF	68	20	3.4	48	24	24
ENQ	66	18	3.7	48	34	14
EQ	52	19	2.7	33	19	14
ARCO	36	5	7.2	31	22	9
BGS	41	20	2	21	10	11
Total	524	112	4.7	415	271	144

Note: For occupational abbreviations see Table 8.1.

guarantees to preserve their wives' possessions in the case of their own businesses turning out badly. Outside these circles, only farmers go before the lawyer, because they have land. Industrial workers and railwaymen, without land, without fortune and at no risk of bankruptcy, have no reason to pay for a contract.

The middle-class custom of a marriage arranged by the families who seek – sometimes very far away – a suitable match for their daughters, in terms of family, fortune and occupation, explains the very strong endogamy which is the norm in this social formation. But it has other consequences: in particular, it entails a major imbalance in the conjugal roles. Within the new household, each partner continues to play his or her accustomed role: the young daughter of the house becomes the mistress of the house and her husband devotes himself to the professional life he has already undertaken, sometimes retaining his taste for independence. The difference in age which separates the two is the true symbol of this imbalance.

The fact of the husband being noticeably older than his bride is still, at this early period of the twentieth century, a characteristic feature of middle-class couples. Table 6 already hinted at this, showing an average difference of 6 years and 4 months in this sector of society, with the husband the elder, against 2 – 3 years in other sectors. Table 11 offers a close analysis of this factor. It is very rare in the bourgeoisie, for the wife to be older than the husband, or even to be the same age, while in the middle classes we find 15 per cent of women who are the elder of the couple, and 25 per cent among workers. On the other hand, among the latter, 25.7 per cent of husbands are older than their wife by at least 5 years, against 33.4 per cent in the middle classes and 68 per cent in the *bourgeoisie* (25 out of 37). A quarter and one-third on one side, against two-thirds on the other: the difference is substantial.[31]

In contrast to *bourgeois* unions, marriages in other groups appear to be the result of individual affinities and spontaneous choice. The spouses are closer in age. The age difference for 68 per cent of workers and 60.8 per cent among members of the intermediate classes is less than five years, compared to 12 per cent among the *bourgeois*. Yet the absence of deliberate family strategy does not leave everything to chance. Socially determinant factors continue to operate, even though they do so in such a natural way that they may be overlooked. Three series of objective conditions affect the choice of spouse: living in the same part of town, proximity of occupation,

Table 8.10: Marriage contracts according to husbands and fathers-in-law occupations.

Husband's Occupation	Occupation of fathers-in-law								Total of husbands
	AGR	OUVR	CHF	ENQ	EQ	ARCO	BGS	Divers	
AGR	11	1	–	–	–	–	2	1	15
OUVR	4	8	2	1	–	2	–	7	24
CHF	1	2	2	–	–	–	2	4	11
ENQ	–	1	2	–	2	4	3	4	16
EQ	1	1	–	–	1	2	10	2	17
ARCO	1	–	2	1	2	5	3	3	17
BGS	–	–	1	–	–	–	32	3	36
Total	18	13	9	2	5	13	52	24	136

Note: For occupational abbreviations see Table 8.1.

Table 8.11: Age difference of marriage partners by occupational groups.

	Workers		Middle classes		Bourgeois	
	no.	%	*no.*	%	*no.*	%
Wives older						
– 5+ years	11	6.3	1	0.5	–	–
– 1–5 years	29	16.6	29	15.8	2	5
Same ages	14	8	24	13	1	3
Husband older						
– 1–5 years	76	43.4	65	35.3	9	24
– 5–10 years	44	25.1	56	30.4	17	46
– 10+ years	1	0.6	9	4.9	8	22
Total	175	100	184	100	37	100

and neighbouring family origins. People do not marry just anyone, casually. The spouse must be known, and acquaintanceship comes through living in the same neighbourhood, or because members of the two families work in the same trade, or, finally, because the family origins are the same. Calculating the exact role of these three forms of proximity is a matter of fine judgement, particularly since they may operate together. It is however rare that they cannot be guessed through the carefully written lines of the marriage certificates.

We have not studied neighbourhoods. It is possible to construct such a study, from a systematic comparison of the addresses of Orleans spouses, but we baulked at the difficulty of the undertaking. On the other hand, shared origins can sometimes be revealed through comparison of birth certificates or parental domicile for the two parties to the marriage. An example is the marriage between an ordinary labourer and a corset-maker, both born in Montargis, where their parents lived,[32] or the boiler-maker on the railways whose father is a farmer and who is marrying the dressmaker daughter of a waggoner: the point of contact becomes clear when we know that both were born in the Cher, where the husband's parents still live and from where each of the spouses invites an uncle as witness.[33] When it comes to occupation-inspired attachments, they emerge from a comparison between the occupation of the husband and that of his bride's father, but also, very substantially, those of the relatives

who feature on the certificate as witnesses. There is for example a
vehicle metal-grinder, the son of a jam-factory worker, who is marrying
a paper-worker, the daughter of a plasterer: their marriage may have
been encouraged by the young woman's witnesses, her two brothers-
in-law, who are both locksmiths.[34] Similarly for the young baker, son
of a bakery worker and the room-maid, daughter of a boiler-maker,
both of whose brothers-in-law are bakery workers.[35]

Table 8.12: Proximity of occupation and domicile of families of
marriage partners.

Husband's Occupation	Occupations in common		Domicile in common	
	no.	*1 out of*	*no.*	*1 out of*
AGR	17/36	2.1	14/36	2.6
JOUR	18/36	2	12/36	3
BTP	8/44	5.5	17/44	2.6
A/OUV	35/126	3.6	46/126	2.7
DOM	14/22	1.6	2/22	1
CHF	34/68	2	21/68	3.2
ENQ	16/66	4.1	29/66	2.6
EQ	14/53	3.8	21/53	2.5
ARCO	8/36	4	13/36	2.8
BGS	23/41	1.8	11/41	3.7
Total	187/528	2.8	186/528	2.8

Note: For occupational abbreviations see Table 8.1.

We have therefore looked carefully (Table 8.12) at the existence
of occupations and locations that are common to the two families.
Overall, occupational solidarity is a feature as much as shared
communities of origin, but we must be careful: it is possible, in fact,
when a closely shared origin is a feature for offspring from the same
region, that the marriage was in fact celebrated in the place of their
birth and not in Orleans. For this reason the *bourgeoisie*, in which
families arrange marriages, presents many cases of similar professional circumstances, while the small number with shared local
origins confirms here the national scale of the marriage market. The
same pattern, between professional solidarity and shared origins,

emerges for other groups. But on this point the *petite bourgeoisie* is noticeably different from the bourgeois model. Is this a sign of groups that are undergoing social mobility? Whatever the truth, shopkeepers and craftsmen, unlike the *bourgeoisie*, are characterized by the relatively important influence of the community of origin and not by professional traditions, which are no doubt too recent to be fully established. Construction workers show a similar pattern, which one would be tempted to explain by migrants' fidelity to their place of birth if we were looking at stone-masons from the Creuse. In the event, almost all these workers live in the Loiret (43 out of 44), and three-quarters were born there (see Table 8.9).

Conversely, certain groups create their marriages around a shared occupation. But what differences there are between them! Day-labourers, whose speciality is precisely that they have no speciality, often share the same social inferiority and the same insecurity of the morrow. Farmers often share the same attachment to the land, particularly to vines, but in their case the shared occupational solidarity is easily matched by shared community of origin. Wholly uprooted, domestic servants are too far from their home territory to sustain their attachment to it; they marry someone in their own set of attic rooms, the kitchen or the linen-room, and more than half share their future with a housemaid: 14 out of 22, to be precise. Nothing surprising in the fact that they have the lowest proportion of shared origins and the greatest of shared occupations.

There remain the railwaymen, also often uprooted from their rural origins, who find in their shared work group, even more than in their specific occupation, a powerful and enduring community. Here, marriages are strung out across the national network or the Paris–Orleans line. Among the dozens, there is an Orleans railway employee who is marrying a dressmaker. The bride's parents live in the Gironde, where they are farmers and where one of her brothers is a blacksmith. A neighbourhood encounter between a migrant and an Orléanais? Not at all. Firstly, the husband was not alone in moving into the railway culture; one of his brothers preceded him; he was a resident of Périgueux, a town where the railway company located its largest repair shop, and worked as a wheelwright on the Orleans railway. As for the bride, her father had retired from the railways, and she had two brothers, who are, respectively, district manager and head employee 'of the said railway line'. Truly, the community of railwaymen is a very large family.

Different Ceremonies

The marriage ceremony, end-point of such varying routes from one setting to another, could never be uniform, and the weddings that follow each other in front of the officiating mayor do not resemble each other. Sadly, the registers are not illustrated, and it would require lengthy research to study the costume of bride and bridegroom and wedding guests, their number, the presence or absence of bridesmaids or groomsmen, and the organization of the wedding procession and of the wedding-feast.[36]

A few details, however, are revealing. It may happen, first, that the consent of the spouses is received by the mayor in person and not by his official assistant. On the day, the first to appear in front of the mayor are modest couples: those whom he wishes to honour with a personal intervention always come last, no doubt to allow the fullest possible time to exchange congratulations. This is how we see the daughters of well-known lawyers or dealers. He also makes this arrangement for a marriage with a particularly flattering choice of witness, such as the mayor of an important town.

In contrast to these distinguished ceremonies are the others, more modest, even shameful, that are more concerned with administrative formality than family or social festive occasions. This applies, for example, to marriages accompanied by the legitimation of children already born; this sample has fifteen such cases, not one of them born to farmers or *bourgeois*. The same atmosphere also applies, fairly frequently, to marriages that take place in the absence of the parents. Normally the latter expect to take part in the ceremony and to confirm their consent even when their children have passed the age when such consent is legally required. But it may happen that their consent is given in writing, in front of a civic official or a notary, or that the parents are missing, without explanation. If they live at a great distance and are elderly and infirm, everything is clear and has no further implications; but this is not always the case. Even when matched by written consent, absence may be a sign of disapproval or indifference. We can fully appreciate the social dislocation of domestic servants by noting the frequent absence of their parents at their wedding: out of 22 male domestic servants for whom the question is applicable, only 6 (27 per cent) marry in the presence of their parents, and out of 65 female domestic servants – of whom two-thirds, as we have seen, were born in the department – only 36, or 55 per cent, are accompanied to the town hall by their parents. Among day-labourers, as with skilled workers, where the list shows

15 garrison non-commissioned officers, parents are present for barely more than one in two sons' marriages. Farmers, on the other hand, show proof on this point of a very substantial family cohesion (26 cases out of 31), while the behaviour of the *bourgeoisie* is surprising. Considering the role played by the family in the choice of a spouse, one might have expected the bride's parents always to accompany her to the town hall; in fact, when both are living, father and mother divide up on one in every three occasions and only one of them is present at the civil ceremony. This is hardly likely to be the result of marital dissention, and is more likely to be a case of the lesser importance accorded to the civil ceremony than to its religious counterpart. At this date, in fact, the *bourgeoisie* is beginning to mark itself out through the disassociation between the two ceremonies, in the town hall and in church. Although as a general rule the civil and religious marriage ceremonies are both celebrated on the same day, the second is scheduled for the next day or two days after the first on one occasion out of two among the *bourgeoisie*. Not to come to the town hall may then, for an aged parent, be a way of limiting the fatigue and costs of a journey often necessitated by the distance between Orleans and the husband's family.[37]

In any case, a major difference appears between *bourgeois* and popular marriages: they do not take place at the same time. Of course the monthly pattern of marriages in Orleans is specific.[38] The interdict of Lent, which coincides in 1911 with the month of March, is strongly respected, and even more so that of Holy Week: only 7 marriages in all in the two weeks preceding Easter, and none during Holy Week except for three on Good Friday, none of which appears to have been followed by a religious marriage. On the other hand, the fortnight following Easter is the season for weddings. With Easter Monday a public holiday, people must wait until the Tuesday, when 8 marriages are registered, or else the following Saturday (10). The curve reaches its peak the following Saturday (12), to the extent that in two weeks the month of April retrieves its low selectivity status and reaches first place. May suffers from this competition, as do June and July – the second most popular month, while a secondary minimum is noted in September (see Table 8.13).

The important factor, in this calendar, is the difference between the *bourgeoisie* and the working classes, so clearly visible that it cannot be the work of chance.[39] The *bourgeoisie* observe Lent scrupulously and marry after Easter, even more in May. Then, in July–August, they disappear – because they have left Orleans for their

Tabe 8.13: Month and Day of marriage of different occupational groups.

	Husband's Occupational Group				Total
	OUVR	CHF	ENQ+EQ	BGS	
Month					
January	11	10	8	2	34
February	22	11	6	6	54
March	17	1	7	0	27
April	26	7	16	6	62
May	14	3	13	4	40
June	25	7	5	7	53
July	23	10	16	4	60
August	26	4	9	1	45
September	11	1	10	4	30
October	17	8	13	3	46
November	17	4	6	2	34
December	19	2	10	2	43
Day					
Monday	47	13	31	9	120
Tuesday	22	10	20	10	80
Wednesday	28	10	14	10	69
Thursday	2	2	15	7	31
Friday	1	–	1	1	3
Saturday	128	33	38	4	224

Note: For occupational abbreviations see Table 8.1.

houses in the country. September and October show a modest resurgence, followed by a fresh dip in numbers, but less marked than in the summer. Industrial workers observe Lent less scrupulously, but the curve of their marriage graph drops in May. June, July and August are their months for the most marriages and, for no apparent reason, the main low point is recorded in September. To understand these clearly marked fluctuations, which do not appear in either Bordeaux or Paris, we should no doubt take account of the seasonal patterns of work. In a city where the clothing industry is important, the marriage calendar may well reflect in its own way the existence of a winter season and a summer season, separated by periods of seasonal unemployment.

The same point applies to the choice of day in the week. Saturday is outstandingly the day for popular marriages: the *bourgeoisie* avoids it, tending to select one of the first three days of the week. Friday, the day when meat was forbidden by the Church,[40] and the Thursday before it, have little attraction. As for the intermediate classes, they show affinities with the common people or with the *bourgeoisie*. Employed staff, skilled or not, show a tendency to imitate the *bourgeoisie*, with Monday taking equal place with Saturday, while on Thursdays they are almost alone in appearing at the town hall. Railwaymen, on the other hand, are closer to industrial workers, with three times more marriages on Saturday than on Monday. We can see how, right down to the calendar, the marriage ceremony is socially determined.

Implications

The first lesson to come from this survey is a warning of the need to avoid hasty generalizations. At several points the case of Orleans strikes us as unlike others, different from Bordeaux or Paris. Before establishing a statistically-based synthesis of urban social structures in the early twentieth century, it would no doubt be right to draw up a number of monographs. The interesting differences that could be elucidated in this way would show the way to more penetrating analyses. Cities, as social organizations, are too complex to make such a synthesis other than dangerous in the current state of our knowledge.

Secondly, a study of social structures implies a stance on the problem of social class. We did not wish to approach this on a theoretical basis ahead of the survey, preferring to avoid the limitations of an *a priori* analytical grid in order to remain free to adopt the social identification pattern that appeared the most appropriate. But pragmatism must come to an end, and ultimately we cannot avoid the debate.

In our survey we have not used the terminology of social classes, but of socio-professional categories. Perhaps this betrays fidelity to thinking patterns that are characteristic of French statistical thinking? Personally, I see it rather as a necessity: concerning a population of whom we are ignorant of levels of personal wealth, income and education, the occupational designation, whatever the lack of precision often warned against, is the only possible criterion on which to base a social hierarchy. The refusal to group them arbitrarily in two or three social classes gives the feeling of yielding to a certain degree of prudence and of respecting the diversity of real life. This is the advantage of socio-professional categories. This simple methodological decision immediately removes the idea of a society divided into classes with clear-cut barriers and replaces it with a hierarchical social continuum.

Faced with these two concepts, it is difficult to make a choice. In fact, social sciences have always borrowed their concepts from natural or physical sciences. Sociology grew out of a reaction against an image of the social body that transposed concepts of the life sciences (organic, cellular, functional) and the analysis of social facts. The classic representation of a society based on class, setting out distinctions between a *bourgeoisie*, a proletariat and the middle classes, the uncertain residue with fluctuating borders according to the constraints of the topic, in fact borrowed heavily from mechanics and physics. Revolutions, for example, are often thought of as the shock of a mass in movement against a resisting object, or as a combination of identifiable forces. This style of envisaging social mechanisms is no doubt adapted from political history, where constraining institutional mechanisms – the orders of the *ancien régime*, patterns of suffrage, the reality of parties – provide a structure for social reality, making it possible to identify specific forces by constructing both discontinuities and re-groupings. But this conceptual set of tools does not make it possible to imagine satisfactorily the continuum of customs and manners. In this area, more everyday and perhaps deeper, it may be legitimate to borrow the notion of a polarized field from the physics of electricity and magnetism. In this way we would think of society as an ensemble structured round two clearly recognizable poles: a kernel of *bourgeois* on the one hand, a kernel of unskilled workers on the other. Between these two poles, the various social groups would be laid out in a continuous line, according to a complex interplay of proximities and differences. This representation, in harmony with modern methods of statistical analysis such as factorial or hierarchical analysis, makes it possible to respect the internal diversity of a society while at the same time drawing out of it a pattern, an organization – that is to say, a meaning.

Notes

1. The reference studies are those of Pierre Guillaume, *La population de Bordeaux au XIXe siècle*, Paris, A. Colin, 1972, and *Permanences et mutations dans la société bordelaise contemporaine*, Bordeaux, Publications de la Maison des Sciences de l'Homme d'Aquitaine, 1978. Pierre Guillaume restricts himself, as we do, to one year of marriages, but with the population of Bordeaux exceeding that of Orleans, his sample reached or exceeded one thousand individuals.

2. The historian makes use above all of two tests. The first indicates, as a function of the size of the sample, the margin of error that affects results, taking into account the degree of approximation that is acceptable. The first table in this study shows, for example, that in a sample of 425 Orléanais of the generation of fathers of the brides of 1911, 13.4 per cent are farmers. Clearly we do not know the exact percentage, which is probably a little higher or lower. The statistical test calculates between which limits, on either side of 13.4 per cent, the exact proportion is likely to be located. Let us accept, to satisfy ourselves, a bracket such that the exact percentage has ten chances in 100 to fall outside this (one may calculate a bracket such that it would not have more than 5 chances, or 1 chance in 100, to fall outside this, but it would obviously be larger). In these circumstances, the gap of reliability in the percentage is 2.7 % on either side of 13.4 %; the exact percentage therefore has nine chances out of ten of lying between 10.7 % and 16.1 %. With a sample twice the size, the bracket would naturally be smaller, but only by 30 %. To reduce it by half would require a sample four times larger.

The second test is the $\chi2$. It makes a comparison between two distributions, i.e. the way in which two groups of individuals divide up between the given categories. This test consists of measuring, according to a complex formula, the gap between the two groups, category by category (for example, in Table 8.1, between the farmer fathers and sons, then between the day-worker fathers and sons, etc.), and then of adding up the differences thus obtained. The more numerous the categories the higher the total, and the greater the differences in each category. A table indicates, as a function of the number of categories and the degree of approximation accepted, the point from which the $\chi2$ is significant. In the simplest case, a distribution with two categories (Orléanais/non-Orléanais among the fathers and sons) with a threshold of 0.05, the $\chi2$ should exceed 3.84. If it is higher than 3.84, there are less than 5 chances in 100 that the difference between the two distributions is the effect of chance.

The $\chi2$ should always be calculated from true figures and not percentages, for if the figures are low, it would require large differences to obtain a significant $\chi2$. Take for example 20 fathers and 20 sons. There are 12 Orléanais among the fathers and 8 among the sons (pure hypothesis). Calculated on these figures, the $\chi2$ is 3.33: too small to be significant at the threshold of 0.05. There are more than 5 chances in 100 that the difference is the effect of chance. If we have unfortunately judged that there were 60 % Orléanais among the fathers and 40 % among the sons, and we performed the test for $\chi 2$, it would have arrived at 16.66 and we would have found it significant at the threshold of 0.001 (not 1 chance in 1,000).

3. The marriage rate, 146 per 10,000, is a little below the national average of 156 in 1911. One possible reason for this difference is that the total population analysed here includes soldiers in their barracks, prisoners and the sick in the hospital, thus increasing the male population in unusual ways.

4. We thank M. the Mayor of Orleans, who authorized us to analyse the register of marriages for 1911, and the heads of the *Bureau de l'État civil* and of the *Service de documentation*, who helped us greatly in this research. This survey was also the beneficiary of financial help granted by the University of Orléans. Finally, it owes a great deal to the help of the students who participated in the study with interest and tenacity. We thank them all.

5. The survey was undertaken in three phases. The first was devoted to studying the documents, analysing items of information that they were capable of supplying, formulating questions that we wished the survey to answer and, consequently, defining the tables that we wished to draw up from them, and thus the codification of data. The second phase consisted of a direct analysis of marriage certificates on data abstracts treated by computer. The third phase was the exploitation of these results: it required the construction of fresh tables to verify the hypotheses that appeared during the examination.

6. Between the two distributions in Table 8.1, the $\chi 2$ is 72.8. To be significant to a level of 0.001, with 9 degrees of freedom, it would need to exceed 27.88. Before grouping the Orleans fathers together we verified that there was no significant difference between those of the brides and those of the husbands: $\chi 2 = 14.56$ – but it would need to be greater than 14.68 to be significant at the threshold of 0.1. These two groups can therefore be considered as related and regrouped, while it would be entirely arbitrary to bring together fathers and sons.

7. The under-representation of the *bourgeoisie*, in the sons' generation, also relates to the openness of the marriage market, which brings in a number of middle-class husbands, while the young men of the Orleans middle classes probably leave to marry elsewhere.

8. We may note that in 1911 the secretary of the local CGT union was a construction worker, and that of the departmental federation of local unions a railway worker, confirming the importance of these bodies. On this point, see Guy Brucy, Catherine Hauchecorne, and Catherine Seron, 'La C.G.T. dans le Loiret des origines à la seconde guerre mondiale', D.E.S. memoir, undated (1970), typescript.

9. Orleans municipal archives, no. 2206.

10. Guillaume, *La population de Bordeaux* in the nineteenth century, indicates for 1883 (p. 277), 30.85 per cent local men and 39.68 per cent local

women. *Permances et mutations dans la société bordelaise contemporaine*, gives the local rate for Bordelais men as 44 per cent for 1913 (p. 19) and (p. 112), and for 1938, 31.06 per cent men and 35.68 per cent women of local origin.

11. Yves Lequin, *Les ouvriers de la région lyonnaise (1848–1914), I, La formation de la classe ouvrière régionale*, Lyon, Presses Universitaires de Lyon, 1977 (pp. 248–9).

12. $\chi2$ for the numbers of men/women, 2 classes (born in/outside the Loiret), giving 1 degree of freedom = 2.406 – while it would require at least 2.71 to be significant at a threshold of 0.1.

13. Given the status of women in the society of the *Belle Epoque*, the significance of their family circumstances for the fate of young women is not surprising. The fact that they may or may not be migrants has a minor effect on their marriage prospects: brides who are migrants are on average six months older than lifelong residents. On the other hand, those who have lost their father marry relatively young. The age at the time of marriage for men whose father has died is virtually the same as for those who have lost their mother: 29 years 6 months and 29 years 9 months, against 26 years 6 months for those whose father and mother are both living, and 37 years 11 months for those who no longer have either parent. This age pattern is entirely logical, and it is normal to be older when one has lost one of one's parents than when one has both of them still living. But, for girls whose parents are both alive, the average age at the time of marriage is 24 years. It is 24 years 4 months for those who have lost their father, against 27 years 3 months for those who have lost their mother, and 35 years 9 months for those who have lost both parents. That the brides who have lost their father are distinctly younger than those who have lost their mother, while this is not the case for men, implies that the loss of the father leads to an earlier marriage – proving how difficult it is at the time for a young woman to live without both a father and a husband! For men, on the other hand, the age difference at marriage between migrants and natives is greater: 10 months on average. It is particularly evident for metalworkers (1 year), construction workers (1 year 5 months) and day-labourers (2 years), but much less so for employees, craftsmen and traders. This suggests the hypothesis that workers are more likely to migrate after their military service, thus delaying their establishment in active adult life.

14. Tables 8.3 and 8.4 concern only bridegrooms for whom we know both their own professions and those of their fathers or, for Table 8.4, of the fathers-in-law. Since these items of information are not always available simultaneously for the same individuals, the totals of these two tables are different.

15. This index of proximity shows whether the numbers from boxes in Tables 8.3 and 8.4 should be seen as small or large, taking into account the overall numbers under consideration. If it were to turn out that there were no preferential link between the socio-professional categories of husbands

and those of the fathers or fathers-in-law, Table 8.5 would only show indices of proximity equal to 1. An index higher than 1 indicates a proximity, an index equal to 1 equality, and an index lower than 1 a distancing.

Table 8.3 shows, for example, that nine sons of railwaymen have become industrial workers. Is this a large number or a small one? In relation to the total of railwaymen's sons, 26, it appears substantial. In relation to the total of industrial workers in the sons' generation, 104, it is small. In percentages, this gives us 34.6 per cent of sons of railwaymen who have become industrial workers, and 8.65 per cent of industrial workers who are sons of railwaymen. Of these two percentages, which one will be more significant?

The question is insoluble. We can note, however, that in overall terms 7.65 per cent of husbands have a railwayman father. If the industrial worker husbands were recruited in line with the average of the population, we should therefore find 7.65 per cent who have a railway-worker father: yet the figure is 8.65 per cent, slightly higher: the recruitment of industrial workers among railwaymen's sons is thus moderately preferential. By dividing the true percentage, 8.65, by the average percentage, 7.65, we get 1.13: this is the index of proximity that appears in Table 8.5.

Similarly, with industrial workers making up 30.59 per cent of the population, their representation among the sons of railwaymen should reflect this level: but the figure is 34.6 per cent. Dividing 34.5 by 30.59 also yields 1.13. This index is the conditional frequency from which to undertake the factorial analysis of correspondences.

16. See for example the analysis of intergenerational mobility in R. Pohl, C. Thelot, and M.-F. Jousset, *L'enquête, formation-qualification professional de 1970*, Les Collections de l'I.N.S.E.E., series D, no. 32, and in Daniel Bertaux, *Destins personnels et structure de classe*, Paris, P.U.F., 1977, which works on the same data. See also the same author's 'Mobilité sociale biographique. Une critique de l'approche transversale', *Revue française de sociologie*, XV, 1974, pp. 329–62, and by Roger Girod, *Mobilité sociale*, Droz, 1971.

17. An obligatory marginal note on divorce settlements would enable us to study them. Out of the 528 marriages in 1911, 46 ended in divorce, 5 before the 1914–1918 war and 28 between 1916 and 1925, confirming the domestic disturbance created by the war. Divorces can be found in all social groups.

18. Study of the signatures confirms, however, what has been recognized concerning the decline of illiteracy from one generation to the next, and the inequalities that were reduced by education. All the bridegrooms except one and all the wives, except three seamstresses, signed their marriage certificate; 25 fathers and 51 mothers did not sign, confirming the greater degree of illiteracy among the women. Naturally, it is among the parents of day-labourers that illiteracy is greatest: 11 out of 40 and 15 out of 48 respectively.

19. Professional heredity can be directly appreciated by comparison between the trades of father and son. It is particularly strong among agricultural workers (1 son out of 1.3 follows the same trade as his father),

then in the *bourgeoisie* (1 in 3.4) and then the *petite bourgeoisie* of trade and craftsmanship (1 in 3.6). In the labouring world, construction comes first (1 in 4.6), followed by day-labourers (1 in 5.1) – but can we speak here of craft? – and then by the other workers (1 in 7.5) where changes are frequent from one generation to the next, as among railwaymen (1 in 6.7). New jobs, those of an unskilled employee (1 in 11) and a skilled employee (1 in 17) do not pass from father to son, for obvious reasons.

20. See Gérard Duplessis–Le Guelinel, *Les mariages en France*, Paris, A. Colin, 1954, Table p. 67; Pierre Guillaume, *La population de Bordeaux*, *op.cit.* p.265 et seq., and *Permanences et mutations*, p. 101. Following custom, we have added six months to average ages, to take into account the fact that the average age of all those who state an age of 23 years is half-way between 22 and 24 years.

21. Guillaume, *La population de Bordeaux*, pp. 98 and 268.

22. These details have been supplied by Jules Maurin. They come from his doctoral thesis: 'Armée, guerre, société: soldats languedociens (1889–1919)', Montpellier, Université Paul Valéry, vol. I, p. 457 et. seq.

23. We are not looking here at the case of officers and subalterns in the regular army, on its permanent ration strength, far more numerous in this garrison city. There authorization from the commanding officer in consultation with the *conseil d'administration* always formed part of the documentation produced and expressly consulted.

24. Between the two divisions of workers on the one hand and the middle classes on the other, in triennial age classes at the time of marriage (7 classes), the $\chi2$ is 23.24. Thus, for six degrees of freedom, it is significant to a threshold of 0.00l from 22.46.

25. As we have seen, the average age of migrants at the time of marriage is nine months older than that of spouses in stable circumstances. See Note 12 above.

26. The first figure in Table 8.7 indicates how many spouses still live with their parents, the second the number of spouses who still have at least one of their parents living. For farm-workers, for example, out of 34 who still have one of their parents living, 27 live with them. Domestic servants have been excluded from this figure. Rather than percentages, with their frequently illusory air of precision, we have calculated the converse relationship: one out of how many still living with their parents. Finally, by 'stable' we mean spouses domiciled in the commune where they were born and by 'mobile within the department' we mean those who were born in the department where they live now – but not in the same commune – and by 'migrants' those who were born in another department.

All the spouses are included in this set of figures, without reference to their domicile. One railwayman born in Fleury-les-Aubrais, where his parents are still living, while he himself lives in Vierzon, appears in this table as a migrant railwayman who does not live with his parents.

27. These comments, which confirm those already made above, in Note 12, clearly apply only to young girls. This poses the whole question of widows and divorcees, which the size of our sample has not enabled us to study. Out of 528 marriages, in fact, we have 81 remarriages: 28 widowers who are marrying a young girl, 16 widows who marry a young man, 14 marriages where both partners have been widowed, and 23 marriages of divorcees. Naturally these spouses have been excluded from calculations of the average age at marriage.

28. An initial survey in the census nominal rolls of 1911, for the most heavily populated part of Orleans, confirms this analysis. Among the unmarried women over the age of 15, it shows 44 per cent as dressmakers or in similar trades, as against 17.6 per cent among married women. Against this, 48.3 per cent of the latter are without occupation, as against 15 per cent of the young girls.

29. Certificate no. 248.

30. Certificate no. 182.

31. The $\chi 2$ calculated on the numbers in Table 8.11, by taking the extreme classes together, is significant to the threshold of 0.001: in fact it exceeds the value 12.94, threshold of significance at 0.001 for 3 degrees of freedom. Between the *bourgeois* and the middle classes, the $\chi 2$ is 17.76, and 15.85 between the middle classes and the workers, which confirms a specificity and makes it impossible to assimilate the two groups.

32. Certificate no. 174.

33. Certificate no. 38. Similarly, Certificate no. 65, for a navvy aged 23 who was born in Kerfeunteny (Finistère) and who is marrying a laundress born in Vannes (Morbihan). We can surely be confident that memories of Brittany are not without significance in this marriage.

34. Certificate no. 211

35. Certificate no. 209

36. For a more ethnological approach to these questions, see for example Martine Segalen, 'Mariage et mort à Chardonneret', *Ethnologie française*, 1974, nos.1–2, pp. 67–86.

37. A student of the University of the Third Age, Madame Barthélémy, has had the pleasing idea of completing the study of civil marriages by that of religious marriages, using the parish registers held in the diocesan records. Out of 420 religious marriages identified (37 civil marriages concern divorcees and in 71 cases there is no religious ceremony in Orleans – which does not mean that it was not celebrated in one of the suburban parishes), 387 were celebrated on the same day as the civil marriage and only 27 the following day or two days later. Out of these 27, 12 are bourgeois marriages, although there are only 41 bourgeois marriages in the total. Madame Barthélémy has also found 6 religious marriages celebrated before the civil marriage, in direct contravention of the law. Sometimes the gap lasts several days and we may have to consider a mistake by the priest. Not, however, for

a locksmith who was married on 5 July at Saint-Aignan and on 11 July at the town hall!

38. Guillaume, *La population de Bordeaux*, p. 270 and M. Dupaquier, 'Le mouvement saisonnier des mariages en France (1856–1968)', *Annales de Démographie historique*, 1977, pp.131–49, which gives, on p. 137, the shifting monthly pattern of marriages in the urban population of the Seine in 1874–1876 and 1902–1903. The Orleans pattern is different: $\chi 2 = 31.028$, significant to 0.001.

39. Despite the small number of *bourgeois*, the difference of pattern between them and workers is indisputable: $\chi 2 = 20.10$, significant to 0.05.

40. The ban on Friday is clearly religious in nature; out of three civil marriages on a Friday, no subsequent church marriage appears to have taken place.

9

Youth in France Between the Wars

Youth has not existed from the dawn of time as a stable biological state. It is a social condition: each historically determined society creates its own form, or forms, of youth. In other words, youth is the result of a social management of the life cycle that determines the timing and manner of moving from one age to another as well as age-group roles, the forms of behaviour considered normal for young people and expected as such by all members of the society, whether the same age, or younger or older. Yet in French society between the two world wars – still not far removed from the nineteenth century – the passage from childhood to adulthood, which defines youth, followed very different social patterns according to class. There were marked contrasts between middle-class and both urban and peasant working-class circles, such that there was not one but two forms of youth. To treat them as one for analytical purposes would be anachronistic. Yet for very different reasons neither working-class young people nor those of the middle classes were in opposition to French society at this time. Mechanisms for integration were very much stronger than inter-generational conflicts.

Working-class Youth: Social Definition of the Age-Group

In working-class circles, youth is an easy group to recognize. It was defined by four features: young people no longer go to school, they work, they are not yet married, they live with their parents and remain under their supervision. The dividing point between childhood and youth was clear: it came at the end of school, at the age of 13, and the start of work immediately afterwards. In the country, young people stopped going to the fields with the cows, a task kept for old people and children.[1] They played a full part in the work of the farm, respecting the gender division of tasks: the girls and their mother milked the cows, looked after the poultry and the vegetable garden and did the housework. They also helped the men with heavy work on the farm. The boys helped their fathers, cleared the manure out of the barn and the byre – Pierre-Jakez Hélias has recorded the pride of the boy who could wheel the barrow on his own[2] – scythed the hay and the corn and brought in the harvest, did the ploughing, trimmed hedges and cut wood. The value of the young peasant's labour was obvious: he took the place of the hired worker. If the paternal farm was too small to need the labour of more than one man, the youth was placed as a farmhand[3] and earned a wage for his labour. In both cases, his work had value, for it was worth money.

It was the same in town: the youth who left school was immediately either placed with a *patron* as an apprentice or began work. The case of Louis Lengrand was entirely normal: he accompanied his father, a miner, to the company offices, where he was signed on and presented himself at the mine on the following Monday. At first he worked for several weeks on the surface; then, still under 14, he went down the mine, where he pushed the coal wagons while waiting to move on to cutting the coal.[4] Similarly, the girls were very commonly placed as sales assistants in shops or went into factory work.

The move from childhood to youth was underlined, even celebrated, in several social rituals. Sometimes the end of schooling was the occasion for true festivals: in the *coron*, the typical miner's house where Louis Lengrand lived, the young boys made a bonfire of their school textbooks and exercise books. In the village the education certificate examination, taken in the central town of the canton, was the occasion for a full ceremony. A service of Solemn Communion, a great festival for the family and also for the village, often coincided with the end of the final year in school. The Solemn Communion was not an essential practice in Catholicism, since it was specific to French-speaking regions; it was not the first communion, for that takes place at the age of 7 or 8. Twentieth-century French priests invented it to support and interpret the catechism and to provide a motivation for the young people who took part in it. But the goal of the catechism reinforced that of the school: when you have 'done' your communion, you have become a young person. The specific gifts offered in these circumstances, a toilet set, an item of jewellery – like the pride of the mothers at seeing their daughters 'as beautiful as young brides', or many of the jokes that were traditional on that day – indicate clearly that it gave girls the right to 'play the young woman'.[5] Through the sacrament, the Catholic Church solemnized the passage from childhood to youth.

As proper workers, young people in working-class circles earned money, received either as wages or by sparing their parents the necessity to pay for hired staff. But this did not make them independent. They continued to live at home with their families,[6] and they owed their family the fruit of their labour until they reach their majority. The unspoken convention for youths was to continue like this until they did their military service: this was how to repay their family the cost of their childhood, as it was well expressed by Louis Lengrand. The young man who worked brought his wages back home – and what pride, when they exceeded his father's pay! This custom endured for a long time, and it was not until the beginning of the 1950s that it began to be questioned: Gaston Lucas, a locksmith in Paris – but Paris customs are ahead of provincial ways – suggested that his apprentice son should retain his own earnings, but he still continued to hand over his wages to his stepmother (Lucas, a widower, had remarried), who saved it for him and handed it back to him when he married.[7] In this way the young man, living under the family roof, remained under his father's authority.

Youth still had its own accepted rights, however: no longer a child, it was normal to see him or her 'act the young man' or young girl, finding amusements and spending free time with friends of the same age. In urban working-class circles, as in the rural peasant world, young people received sufficient pocket money for their leisure pursuits, what Louis Lengrand called 'their Sundays'. The most important of these forms of freedom was to go dancing. Dancing was a form of social life specific to young people: not to go dancing when young would be to stand apart from the group, while to continue dancing once married, on the other hand, would be to stand out. Dancing was not a strictly individual matter: people went in groups, boys on one side, girls on the other, the latter usually with their 'chaperons', who were relaxed in their attitudes.[8] Special relationships were formed here: people met their future spouses, or celebrated a wedding.[9] But all this happened in full view with the knowledge of the whole community, and traditional events were numerous, penalizing the boy or girl who failed to observe the rules or who, already 'promised', danced with another partner.[10]

Marriage marked the end of youth and the beginning of adulthood. Between the two ages, however, the frontier was much sharper for boys than for girls, for marriage came after military service.[11] This event marked a clear and substantial cut-off point: for at least eighteen months the young man was separated from his family and lived in a purely masculine community. Because this was an obligatory rite of passage, any young man would feel shamed if he did not do his military service. On his return he was a man, fully fledged as the head of a household: the authority of his own family is treated with impatience. Marriage marks his final emancipation, for married offspring almost always lived independently, separate from their own family: in the old phrase, *mariage, ménage* – 'marriage, household'.[12] Youth was over, and, to mark it clearly, a few days before the ceremony the men 'bury their boyhood life' with their friends, while the girls do the same, much more quietly. The wedding, with all its ritual festivities, sanctioned by a religious ceremony, loudly proclaims the spouses' change of status to the whole community.

Mechanisms of Integration

The strength of this social definition of the age-group explains its universal acceptance. Generational conflict was rare in this urban working-class or peasant culture, because the social roles appropriate to young people were universally known and accepted, and because they were explicitly short-lived. Revolt has no place in which to grow when status has its end fixed in advance and when in itself the status of youth constitutes a first step towards independence. Conflict, when it existed, developed at the frontiers of youth, among young girls 'ready for marriage' or young men back from their military service who aspired to independence, or perhaps among young married couples forced by circumstances to live with the parents of one or other spouse.

This pattern was all the stronger because it subsumed its own points of difference in advance. The self-affirmation of the group of young people was validated by the community, which saw it as a guarantee of its own survival. The whole village expected, for example, that military service conscripts would show group solidarity at the centre of the canton when they went for their medical examination, and it would find fault with them if they did not organize a successful dance to mark the occasion. The community also recognized specific traits among the young, including a certain level of high spirits, a tendency to create a certain degree of disturbance, to assert their presence noisily. Expressions of disagreement were allowed, recognized as both inevitable and temporary: 'Youth must have its day.' Finally, age-old tradition allowed young people to express any stronger dispute in forms that were accepted through being ritualized, at the time of noisy new-year greetings to local elected representatives, for example, or during fairs. In this way the sting was taken out of disputes, they were neutralised.

In the France of the inter-war years, two further features ensured the integration of young members of the working class. First, the republican school successfully disseminated a profoundly integrational civic culture. Democratic consensus held that progress was possible, that it was an affair of community organization, a matter of seriousness, hard work, morality. Criticism of what did not work was one of the citizen's responsibilities. In this way a radical-social wisdom developed, consisting partly of resignation and partly of a wish for change, fed by quotations taken from Victor Hugo or La Fontaine: 'Work and take trouble, money is the least of your needs.' This moral was unlikely to stir up argument, because it would show the arguer or reluctant worker as a man with a grievance, lazy, or a failure.

The second feature related to the war of 1914. In inter-war France nearly half the adult men had been through the war – they had 'done' the war of 1914. Inter-generational conflict would bring the young men face-to-face with veteran soldiers – a difficult conflict to take on. Not only because the veterans had, after all, won their war, and had thereby won an unassailable crown of honour; but because, on the contrary, they were part of a generation of sacrifice: these men had suffered, had risked their lives, one and a half million of them had died so that the young generation could live free, proud and in a world finally and for ever rid of war. How could anyone rise up against this generation? The school and the whole community constantly inculcated respect for their elders in their young people. When the schoolchildren went to the war memorial on 11 November every year, when they read the name of an uncle, an elder brother or a relative on this memorial, when they saw their father, their uncle or their brother, sometimes their grandfather, standing beside the memorial at the moment when it was their own turn to respond 'Died for France' after each name on the list of dead of the commune, how could they revolt against the generation that preceded them? Particularly because the war had reduced the weight of the generation: harsh though it may be to observe, the losses also left vacant places that had to be filled. In the villages of the inter-war years the generation of the fathers, the generation of veterans, in general terms threw less of a shadow than the one that had preceded it and that, by then, age was bearing away.

In towns, the force of tradition and the weight of the commmunity were no doubt less powerful. But the republican educational system functioned in the same way there, and the impact of the war existed there too. It was difficult, therefore, for a young person to stand out against ways of operating, speaking and thinking among the adults around him. The only way of expressing revolt was to leave. This is what unhappy farm-workers did, or maltreated apprentices, or more simply young people fed up with their situation, like the glass-worker Eugène Saulnier,[13] weary of local routines. From this point of view, the France of the inter-war years was still not very far removed from nineteenth-century France: those who revolted, the dissidents, were vagrants or itinerant workers and up to no good.

Middle-class Youth: A Different Social Formation

Although we know clearly when 'youth' began and ended in working-class circles, the same is not true of the middle classes: transitions here were more gradual and the frontiers less precise. Finishing primary education and taking the Solemn Communion did not mark a cut-off point between two age-groups here, because education lasted longer. Military service was certainly an important stage, particularly because the system of call-up deferment (1905) allowed young men to finish their studies before undertaking service. But the middle-class youth often did his military service as an officer cadet, which enabled him to preserve an independent social life outside the time spent in barracks. For him, therefore, the period in uniform did not perform the same role of initiation as for private soldiers.

In the middle classes we must take care to distinguish between the girls and the boys. For the latter, youth was characterized by features that were the opposite of those that defined working-class youth: the young middle-class male continued his education, he did not work yet, but he did not always continue to live with his parents – he escaped from their supervision and, if not already married, he was tacitly recognized as having the right to embark on sexual adventures.[14]

In this definition of male middle-class adolescence, education between the two wars played a more important role than in the past. Inflation threatened inheritance: it was no longer safe to expect to live off investment income indefinitely, and for those obliged to earn their living it was better to gain certificates. Education became more serious. True youth, moreover, did not begin until the threshold of the *baccalauréat* was passed: until then the young middle-class male was still largely a child, closely supervised; those who did not live at home were boarders in a *lycée* or college. In both cases, private life barely existed. After the *baccalauréat* a different life began. To prepare for the university-level *grandes écoles*, to train as a doctor or a lawyer, it was often necessary to leave one's home town: the great *lycées* and the universities existed in only about twenty cities. Although he continued to be financially dependent on his family, because he was not working, the middle-class youth lived far away from the family, from its supervision and its relationships; this meant that he had the advantage of true independence – quite the opposite of the manual worker or peasant who, at the same age, was working, earning his living, but still living under the watchful eye of his parents.

This privileged situation explains why young middle-class males were in no hurry to settle down. They married much later than young men in working-class circles. In 1911, the average age of marriage in Orleans for men in the middle classes was over 30, as against 25 for manual workers. More than simply a threshold between two ages of life, marriage here marked the end of a period of transition covering the end of education and military service and the beginnings of professional life: an established position was a prerequisite for taking a wife.

The situation for young girls was very different, in principle at least. Tradition held that after more or less extended secondary education – formalized, gradually but more frequently during this period, by the *baccalauréat*, as with the boys – young girls of good families returned to their mother and accompanied her in social relationships and contacts. To be 'the young girl at home' was the best apprenticeship for the profession of being mistress of a household. This is clearly visible when, in a city like Orleans, the population census on the eve of the First World War shows a striking imbalance in this area: in middle-class families we find only young girls between 18 and 25, while the boys are elsewhere, as students or doing their military service.

The family guidance imposed on young girls in this way could seem wearisome, and they hurried to escape into marriage, which for them, more than for their male counterparts, constituted a true threshold. Middle-class young girls also married at a much younger age than the young men: in Orleans in 1911 they were on average six years younger. Having to wait to the age of 24 to become mistresses of their own households could indeed seem long. The inter-war years saw an interesting development on this point: as inflation gnawed away at the dowry, it ceased to provide the same guarantee in case of widowhood, and it became prudent to be armed with a certificate of some kind. We therefore see young middle-class girls pursuing higher education: in 1930–31 we already find one young girl in five studying science or medicine, one in two studying the arts. In the end this factor was to have a radical effect in modifying the calendar of middle-class marriage. The old system of presentation, still in operation in 1940, was based on the separation of the sexes during adolescence. When young girls embarked on higher education they began to meet young men outside family supervision. The love match became the goal of student idylls. Soon, middle-class marriage would no longer wait for the moment when the husband-to-be was definitively established in adult life.[15]

Opportunities for Youthful Rebellion

Unlike working-class young people, the youthful middle classes could set out to break with the customs and opinions of earlier generations. The status of student allowed this: indeed, it encouraged it. The student opposing his family circle could criticize as much as he liked, because his family was not present to hear. He could transgress standards of dress, of language or of morals without risk, because his transgressions would be ignored. The student's financial dependence was much more likely to embarrass him: a certain excess could arise from the desire to prove to himself an independence that was recognized as radically incomplete.

Student circles might thus show generational conflicts in several domains. A certain impatience was perceptible in politics, from the young Turks of the Radical Party to the Young Communists or the students of Action Française. In other domains the inventory of generational opposition was not yet complete. In matters of dress, it might be that golfing outfits allowed young middle-class men to stand out by emphasizing their sporting side. Tennis and the clothing that it required, open sports shirts and loose-cut flannel trousers, also represented something of a challenge to stout dignitaries with their gold pocket-watch chains stretched across their waistcoats. The wristwatch, supposedly invented for pilots, was perhaps the one object that best represented the novelty of the new generation.

Literary or musical tastes that 'shocked the bourgeoisie' were another form of self-assertion: Dadaism, Surrealism, works such as the books of Louis-Ferdinand Céline, enabled the younger generation to distinguish itself from its elders. The same factor applied to jazz music and dance.

Yet we should not exaggerate the scale of this challenge. First, it was limited to students in intellectual and literary circles. Since a celebrated article by Jean Touchard, there has been a tendency to stress the originality of 1930s minds, and there is no lack of material recording the rejection of earlier generations among young intellectuals who were later drawn into notoriety.[16] But Henri Lefebvre's assertion[17] 'Never perhaps had a generational conflict been so bitter' does not authorize the historian to conclude that the youth of the 1930s was in open conflict with the older generations. Students were not the whole of the young element: there were the peasant and working-class masses. What are 80,000 students, when each year brings some 600,000 people into the age-group? And even within the category of student youth, many do not share these feelings. Within a student group already very much a minority, the challengers – no doubt the minority – may perhaps be the grain of salt that gives the period its savour; but they are scarcely more than that.

Youth Movements, a Novelty of the Inter-war Years

A closer examination of youth movements offers a more precise measure of the limits of possible dissent among young people. These movements are in fact one of the great original features of the period. Twentieth-century France was familiar with guilds or groups, like those that made up the *Association catholique de la jeunesse française*, (the Catholic association of French youth); but such organizations brought young people together in an academic way. Above all, they were closely supervised by adults, like holiday colonies. The novelty of the youth movement is the management of young people by other young people.

It appeared on the eve of the 1914 war, initially in Protestant circles, which were more open to British influence. In 1911, the *Éclaireurs unionistes* (scouts' union) was inaugurated, and shortly afterwards the *Éclaireurs de France*. More cautious, the Catholics waited until 1920 to found the Scouts, and then the Guides in 1923. A second generation of youth movements appeared at the end of the 1920s, with movements of specialized Catholic activity covering young workers, farmers and students, both male and female: *Jeunesse ouvrière chrétienne* (JOC) in 1927, followed in 1928 by its female equivalent, the JOCF, and then in 1929 the *Jeunesse agricole chrétienne* (JAC) and the *Jeunesse étudiante chrétienne* (JEC) with their female branches JACF in 1933 and JECF in 1930. A third organization was born at the same time that was not to develop fully until the time of the Popular Front, the *Auberges de jeunesse* (Youth Hostels); the (Catholic) French league of youth hostels was founded by Mark Sagnier in 1930, and a parallel secular league in 1933.

On its own the proliferation of these movements proves that they met a need, and met it with genuine success. Their numbers confirm this. Although their numbers were lower then than they would become in the 1950s, they are nonetheless worthy of consideration. In 1933 male and female scouting could count some 100,000 young people, and the JOC 50,000. The JEC had 20,000 members in 1936. On the eve of war the JAC and the JACF had 2,600 branches, and the JOC 2,350. It is an impressive record.

Youth Movements and Generation Conflict

That these movements enabled young people to assert themselves in relatively independent ways is beyond question. The simple fact of getting together among other young people indicates the wish to stand out, to affirm originality and difference. But there is more. The educational methods practised in these movements, scouting games, the investigation of Catholic action movements ('to see, to judge, to act') are marginal to traditional teaching methods. The tastes encouraged by these movements, the values that they inculcated, cut across those of adult society: exploring nature, the voluntary experience of a fairly harsh life, as in the holiday camps that proliferated at the time, the physical effort, the rejection of comfort, were all unexpected novelties. The camp is moreover symbolic, like the Youth Hostel, of a wish to establish separate locations, cut off. They are symbolic evidence of a rupture that is confirmed by their clothing: the shorts, the scarves, the armband that constitute a uniform.

Scouting gave further impetus to the creation of an enclosed community. Alone, it went so far as to develop an initiatory language in which scouts lost their civilian identity in favour of a totemic nickname, while non-scouts became 'Palefaces'. François Bloch-Lainé has spoken with humour of the pleasure that he derived from these 'incongruous' matters: wearing shorts 'when the others, miniature men, always appeared as models of adults [. . .], jostling tram passengers with rucksacks and great walking sticks. Uttering strange cries to assert profound understanding and wise resolutions. Covering oneself with mysterious signs.'[18] If this was not, properly speaking, the expression of a generational clash, it was nonetheless, and very clearly, secession.

And yet, paradoxically, scouting and the other youth movements were powerful factors of social integration in France between the wars. The affirmation of difference served to confirm solidarities. For three reasons. First, the youth movements did not challenge the status of young people in society. They accepted it, assumed it, used it; but they did not transgress it. The least confrontational was moreover the most particularistic, scouting, for the specific world in which it placed the young person related explicitly to play and not to serious matters. The style of Catholic action movements, better integrated into varied social settings, had substantial potential for more vigorous confrontations; this could be seen at the beginning of the 1960s, in the struggles of former JAC members in the *Centre national des jeunes agriculteurs*, the national centre of young farmers, against the bosses of the national federation of farmers' unions.

Going further, we can maintain – this is the second reason – that, in working-class circles, the JAC and the JOC (young Christian farmworkers and young Christian workers, respectively), far from weakening the social organization of young people, consolidated and strengthened it. The major principle of these movements was to operate on conditions as they were, in order to change them, and not to stand aside, even for the best of reasons. We thus see JAC members posing the question of the dance: given its central significance in young people's lives, it was impossible to evade it. But the JAC response was different from that of the parish priests, who condemned dancing, an occasion for sinning, and forbade young Catholics to take part – thus putting them in the position of having to choose between their priest and their friends. The JAC decided to go to the dance, but to moralize it. Their objective was to achieve an atmosphere of healthy camaraderie and to avoid any sensual abandon. The important point became to stop anyone putting out the lights.[19] This struggle to moralize dancing undeniably strengthened it.

Finally, the advance of the youth movements was deeply integrational. We should note first that, although they kept in the background, adults were not absent from these movements. Although they abstained from organizing everything themselves directly and left the young people to take on responsibilities, the influence exercised by the chaplains of the movements for Catholic action and the Scout commissioners was nonetheless decisive in the last resort, through their advice and their participation in selecting and training the young leaders. They remained an important point of reference for young people; their trust had to be earned, and what better way of showing oneself worthy of it than to take initiatives of which they would have approved? The autonomy of the youth movement was an education in responsibility that made young people interiorize the same values as those of adult society.

This process was undoubtedly dialectical: at the same time as the movement's young people interiorized the norms of the adults who acted as their points of reference, they introduced new attitudes into society, they made new values acceptable. The acknowledgement of the body, sporting, healthy, clean, vigorous and not shameful in itself, a certain feeling for nature, a way of speaking up for openness, sincerity, authenticity, of asserting personal engagement rather than speculative intelligence: all are features that would mark those who, later, would be known as managers.

Thus French society in the inter-war years succeeded in setting distinctive limits to potential generational conflicts. It benefited both from the survival of old ways of structuring working-class youth, as an age-group with specific rights, and the invention of a new way of flexible management of the aspirations to autonomy of middle-class young people, of the future elites.

Notes

1. Cf. Françoise Zonabend, *La Mémoire longue,* Paris, Éditions du Seuil, 1980.

2. Pierre-Jakez Hélias, *Le Cheval d'orgeuil*, Paris: Seuil, 1960..

3. This was the experience of the young Grenadou: cf. Éphraim Grenadou and Alain Prevost, *Grenadou, vie d'un paysan français,* Paris, Éditions du Seuil, 1966.

4. Louis Lengrand, Maria Craipeau, *Louis Lengrand, mineur du Nord*, Paris, Éditions du Seuil, 1974. The facts reported took place around 1930.

5. See the section devoted to the Solemn Communion by the ethnologist Yvonne Verdier in *Façons de dire, façons de faire*, Paris, Gallimard, 1980, and the work of Serge Bonnet and Alain Cottin, *La Communion solonnelle. Folkore païen ou fête chrétienne*, Paris, Le Centurion, 1949. An excellent literary account of the Solemn Communion can be found in *La Maison Tellier* by Guy de Maupassant (1881), depicted in film by Max Ophüls in *Le Plaisir* (1942).

6. In Orleans, in 1911, at the time of their marriage, i.e. after their military service, more than half the men still lived at home. This applied to 90 per cent of young brides. These proportions rose to 80 per cent and 95 per cent when the spouses lived in the commune where they were born (Antoine Prost, 'Mariage, jeunesse et société à Orléans en 1911', *Annales, Économies, Sociétés, Civilisations*, July–August 1981, pp. 672–701, translated as Chapter 8 in this book).

7. Adélaïde Blasquez, *Gaston Lucas, serrurier*, Paris, Plon, 1976.

8. The best analysis of the dances that I know is in Lucien Bernot and René Blancard's *Nouville, un village français* (Paris, Institut d'Ethnologie, 1953).

9. Alain Girard (*Le Choix du conjoint*, Paris PUF, 1974, new edition), shows that 17 per cent of spouses married before 1960 met at a dance.

10. Other forms of village social life, like the wake, declined between the wars. They occasionally survive, however. See, for the Burgundy village of Minot, Zonabend, *La Mémoire longue*.

11. The Orleans survey quoted above shows that boys never married before their military service.

12. Contrary to an often-repeated idea, the cohabitation of married children with their parents was rare, except in certain areas of rural France; various patterns, such as the installation of either the young couple or the parents in a smaller farm, ensured the financial independence of both households. Cf., for example, the survey at Chardonneret (*Ethnologie française*, 1–2, 1974, special issue).

13. Michel Chabot, *L'Escarbille, Histoire d'Eugène Saulnier, ouvrier verrier*, Paris, Presses de la Renaissance, 1978.

14. All the literature of the period confirms this. Scandal developed when a writer suggested extending the same freedom to women, as in Léon Blum, *Du mariage*, Paris, Ollendorf, 1907, or Victor Margueritte, *La Garçonne*, Paris, Flammarion, 1922.

15. In 1949, 12 per cent of students were married, noted Philippe Ariès in 1953 in a remarkable article: 'Familles du demi-siècle' in Robert Prigent (ed.), *Renouveau des idées sur la famille*, Paris, PUF, 1954. He sees in it the sign of the emergence of a new age-group: adolescence.

16. Jean Touchard, 'L'esprit des années 1930: une tentative de renouvellement de la pensée politique française' in *Tendances politiques dans la vie française depuis 1789*, Paris, Hachette, 1960, pp. 90–120; Henri Dubief

devoted several pages to this point in *Le Déclin de la Troisième République*, Paris, Éditions du Seuil, 1976 (p. 60 et seq.) and so did Michel Winock at the beginning of his *Histoire politique de la revue 'Esprit', 1930–1950*, Paris, Éditions du Seuil, 1975.

17. Henri Lefebvre, *La Somme et le Reste*, Paris, La Nef de Paris, 1959, quoted by Michel Winock, op.cit., p. 15.

18. François Bloch-Lainé, *Profession fonctionnaire*, Paris, Éditions du Seuil, 1976, p. 20.

19. See, on these problems of pastoral care, the book by Canon Fernand Boulard, *Problèmes missionnaires de la France rurale*, Paris, Éditions du Cerf, 1945.

III. Identities and the Discourse of Political Conflict

10

Votes and Words

One of the most venerable rhetorical *topoi,* handed down to us by the Greek and Roman orators from Demosthenes to Cicero, is the opposition of deeds and words. Indeed, they form two of the essential constituents of the human condition: men do not only act, they say what they are doing, what they have done and what they are going to do. In certain circumstances, to speak is to act, and certain political figures, such as de Gaulle, have used the spoken word to magisterial effect.

The question of deeds and words in politics is not usually posed in this guise, which the science of linguistics terms 'performative', but rather in the form of a parallel between acting and speaking: once politicians are in power, do they do what they said they would do? This is the old story of the inevitable betrayal of electoral promises not kept, of impressive promises left unfulfilled by later decisions. It would appear that the worlds of speech and of deeds do not inhabit the same universe.

Returning to the fruits of earlier research,[1] we now intend to pose a question that to some extent is a precondition of these two enquiries, by examining the respective structures of the two arenas: political decisions and speeches. To this end we will examine on the one hand the parliamentary world of votes through which the deputies declare their opinion and adopt a policy, and on the other their electoral commitments and promises. The case under consideration is that of the legislature of 1881–1885, the first under the Third Republic for which the deputies' election manifestos were officially recorded in a volume of the *Journal officiel de la République Française.*[2]

This Chamber had been elected under a system thoroughly familiar in France; it was termed the *arrondissement* ballot, which consisted of two successive votes for a single candidate, a majority being needed to win the first time around; a plurality, the second. The general election of 1881 returned a Republican majority, which had just adopted the two great laws making primary education free, obligatory and secular. After Gambetta and Freycinet, Ferry had become head of the Cabinet, and the primary leader of the majority. The new Chamber passed liberal laws on trade unions and on divorce; it established French protectorate status for Tunisia, and made the opening moves in the conquest of Tonkin with the defeat of Lang-son, which caused the fall of Jules Ferry on 30 March 1885.[3]

At this time political parties did not yet exist; there were only loosely-knit parliamentary groups. On the right were the legitimists, fervent monarchists (Albert de Mun, Freppel) hostile to the very form of republican institutions, and the bonapartists (Cassagnac), equally hostile to the Republic, but who can be distinguished from the monarchists by their more popular character, and notably their favourable attitude to universal suffrage. Next to them, the more liberal conservatives, less marked by dynastic loyalties, are characterized by their hostility to the anticlerical policy of the majority.[4] On the extreme left the radicals (Clemenceau, Lockroy, Barodet) favour laws enforcing the separation of Church and State as well as suppression of the Senate. The republicans in the government can be divided into three groups: the moderates (Ribot), the republican Left of Grévy and Ferry and, further to the left, Gambetta's Union républicaine (Steeg, Spuller, Bert, Goblet). Gambetta himself died in January 1882.

Now to the method employed in handling the evidence generated by this political system. The method used in these two enquiries is characterized by its objectivity. Actually, the factor analysis of correspondences does not prejudge the political orientation of the deputies in any way, since it places them in relation to each other exclusively as a function of their votes or their speeches, without reference to their political affiliation. Factor analysis works through large tabular grids, with the individual deputies on the lines, and on the columns the votes they cast (when dealing with political acts) or the frequency of their use of particular terms in their election manifestos (when dealing with political discourse). The underlying structure of these data is brought out in a multidimensional space, showing both how each individual is located as a function of all votes registered or expressions used and how each vote or each expression is located simultaneously, in the same space,[5] as a function of the individuals to whom they are linked. It is then the researcher's task to discover the meaning of this pattern in terms of what we know about each deputy's political orientations.

This method is particularly useful when dealing with data that lack any evident structure. Indeed, in order that two deputies be represented by two identical points, it would be necessary for their election manifestos to be absolutely identical – which is obviously impossible – or that they should have voted in exactly the same way in every roll-call ('*scrutin public*') under analysis. This kind of coincidence can be ruled out for two reasons. Firstly, on each occasion we have taken the maximum number of votes possible, within the framework of the software then available, i.e. 60 votes in each case, taken in sequence without pre-selection, and thus including votes without political importance;[6] it is highly unlikely that two deputies, even very close, would have voted identically in every case. This was particularly improbable, since – and this is the second reason – at the time the parliamentary groups did not operate any form of voting discipline, leaving everyone free to declare himself according to his own opinion. One might therefore expect the analysis of these data to produce complex configurations, clouds of points. Later, when rigorous voting discipline was in place, it might produce only one point for each party, since all deputies of a particular political group, following a three-line whip (at least in theory), would vote identically.[7]

Political Space

The Chamber elected in 1881 consisted of 481 deputies, once those who died during their terms of office are excluded, such as Gambetta. Its composition was not definitive until January 1882, after the replacement of deputies who were elected senator. The first series of votes analysed here thus begins on 16 January 1882 and covers the sixty roll-calls from that date until the following 27 May. The vote that brought about the fall of the Gambetta ministry is the third in this series. This first analysis provides a picture of the initial configuration of the Chamber. The two subsequent analyses relate to the first sixty roll-call votes of the autumn session, devoted to discussion of the budget, in 1882 and 1883 respectively. The three following diagrams (Figures 10.1–10.3) show the results obtained.[8]

The first configuration (Figure 10.1) is very clear: on the first axis, the monarchist and conservative right is set in opposition to republicans; on the second, the moderate republicans are in opposition to the radicals. Paradoxically, this overall structure accommodates considerable individual variations and gaps. Although in overall terms

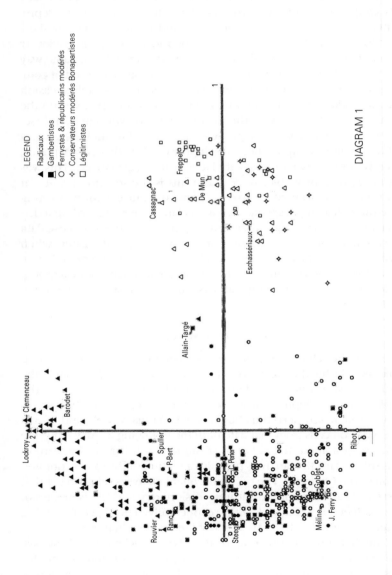

Figure 10.1: Diagram 1, The dispersal of Parliamentary space, Chamber of Deputies, votes, January–May 1882.

the legitimists are further to the right than the liberals or the bonapartists, some are less so than others. Shared opposition to the republicans often brings together deputies on the right and limits their spread. The spread of republicans in the second factorial axis is much greater. Gambetta's advocates are in general terms slightly further to the left than Ferry's supporters, and some of them vote, even quite often, with the radicals, such as Spuller. Conversely, a radical such as Rouvier is relatively close at this time to the governing republicans, but they are intermingled without any clear defining line such as the vast clear space that separates republicans from conservatives. In short, the analysis does not show us political blocs constituted inside the republican camp: the constituent groups spread out with considerable individual flexibility in a kind of spectrum or continuum.

The main advantage of the factor analysis of correspondences used here, representing deputies and votes in the same space, enables us to study exactly which votes define this political space.[9] The left/right opposition on the first factorial axis is determined by two votes on questions that touch on religion (the expulsion of Benedictines, and civil burials), by votes designed to impose on principals of private schools a state certificate of competence, and by the vote for credits for the expedition to Tunisia. The right thus asserts itself through the intransigence with which it rejects any leniency towards those involved in the 1871 Commune, during a vote on the purchase of paintings by the great artist Courbet – a notorious Communard – and during another vote releasing credits to clear up the ruins of the Tuileries palace, burnt down by the Communards. Finally, the right is alone in wanting municipal councils not to be able to vote taxes without the support of the major taxpayers.

The votes that differentiate radicals from republicans supporting Ferry's Cabinet relate to three main debates. First, the publication of the election manifestos of elected deputies: demanded by the radicals, it was resisted by the votes of the more moderate republicans, who saw in it the risk of interfering with the freedom of elected representatives. Conversely, the extreme left was defeated in two debates, on strikes and the status of foreigners. In certain cases, however, the moderate republicans voted with the right against the extreme left and a section of the Gambettists: these were technical votes of an economic nature, concerning the import of pig-meat or the regulation of drink. In addition there was a political vote: the approval of a moderate deputy, whose mandate to stand in the

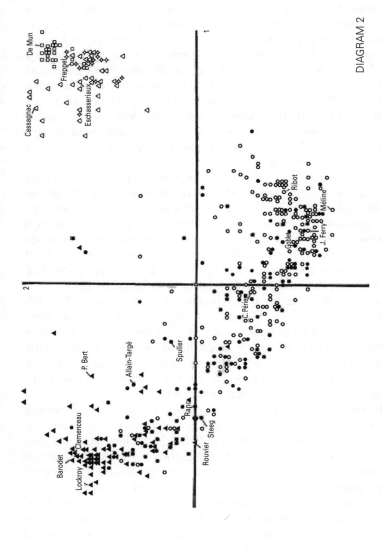

Figure 10.2: Diagram 2, The dispersal of Parliamentary space, Chamber of Deputies, votes, November–December 1882.

Chamber was opposed by the extreme left to eliminate an adversary and on which the governing republicans voted with the right because his election was effectively in order.

The second diagram (Figure 10.2) reveals a pattern of change over time, an evolution. A no-man's-land still exists between the conservative right and the republicans, but on the first factorial axis the governing republicans have moved close to the conservatives. It could perhaps be said that the floor of the Chamber of Deputies is working properly, in describing the distribution of political positions among its members. The position of Deputies in the diagram roughly coincides with their place in the Chamber, since the terms 'Left' and 'Right' indicate those who are seated on the left or the right of the hemicycle when seen from the chair. Here the centre is playing a swing game, sometimes voting with the right to repel radical claims and sometimes with the extreme left to combat clericalism. The extreme left, strongly anticlerical and in favour of the separation of Church and State, thus isolates itself by refusing, for example, to discuss funding for religious institutions,[10] or not voting credits for the ambassador to the Holy See or the salary of the Bishop of Algiers. Conversely, the extreme right marks itself out in proposing to restore grants for the great seminaries or to cut credits for the funding of teacher-training colleges, the *écoles normales*. The image thus created is of a triangular chamber in which the balancing act of the centre between the two extremes determines the configuration.

A year later (Figure 10.3), matters have changed considerably and the political configuration of the conjunction of extremes, which will lead to the fall of Jules Ferry some months later, is already in place. The first factorial axis no longer sets left against right, republicans against conservatives, but extremists against those who support the cabinet. The main opposition of the two earlier configurations now stands in second position, and henceforward structures the second factorial axis.[11] The government is forced to confront the extreme left and the extreme right across a whole series of votes: relating to colonial expansion first of all, then dealing with the Interior Minister's secret funds. Other votes repeat this new pattern, such as a reduction of taxes on paper, supported by conservatives on libertarian grounds and by the radicals for bringing down the cost of newspapers, a burdensome and somewhat demagogic proposal that the government wished to restrict. The second factorial axis describes the same classic antagonisms of the discussion on religious funding, and on schools. It also expresses the development of new

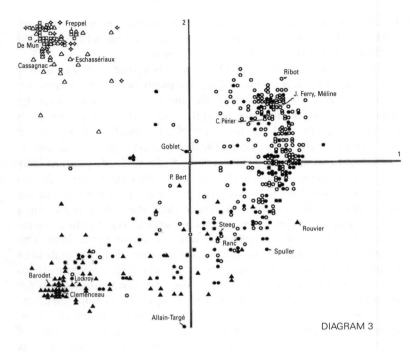

Figure 10.3: Diagram 3, The dispersal of Parliamentary space, Chamber of Deputies, votes, November–December 1883

splits: the right rejects the grant of a national funeral ceremony for the historian Henri Martin, a very moderate republican, and above all, it votes against the municipal law[12] and against municipalities' monopoly on burials, a clear threat to religious funerals.

Looking more closely at the readjustments in progress, we can see that a certain number of radicals and Gambettists, such as Spuller, Rouvier and Paul Bert, are drawing nearer to Ferry. The votes in which they distinguish themselves from the extreme left relate to the colonies. Obviously, the impulse for these developments may be found in this colonial issue. The diagram drawn up for the autumn session in 1884, not shown here, confirms this point: the conjunction of the extremes is close to becoming the majority; hence an event such as a military disaster would be enough to tip some deputies over into the opposition camp, and to overthrow the Ferry cabinet. That is what happened in March 1885.

Despite the absence of voting discipline, the parliamentary arena thus appears highly structured. The conservative right is entirely isolated; the radicals assert their identity through a group of deputies around Clemenceau who often vote in similar ways on most issues; and the republicans in support of the government often differ, but retain solidarity, despite everything, on essentials. This structured arena evolves, and we can see the conjunction of the extremes winning out over the left/right divide. However, the legibility of these configurations is unmistakable to any observer. The political topography of parliamentary decision-making is clear.

Discursive Space

The topography of speech acts is very much more complex. Where we had only a limited number of votes, we now find thousands of different words: the collected speeches of candidates in elections contain between 150,000 and 200,000 words. Such an assemblage defies exhaustive analysis: it is, therefore, essential to work on a more limited set of material.

Rather than reducing the number of deputies under scrutiny, we have chosen to look only at certain verbal expressions. Within this framework, an initial analysis of a limited sample of 54 deputies enabled us to identify some strongly contrasting terms that might come from left or right, such as *Republic, democracy, threat, family, sacred,* and, on the other side, expressions such as *policy, right, society, principle,* whose frequent use indicates that they belong to the basic political vocabulary, and suggests they were in common use by all political groups. From this study we have chosen 53 lexical items defined broadly by meaning and by their root form, and not solely in any one written form. In this way, for example, the lexical item *democracy* covers the noun *democracy*, the adjective *democratic*, the noun *democrat* and the adverb *democratically*.

We then drew up a table, with a line for each of the 554 deputies elected in 1881, and a column for each of the 53 lexical items selected. At the intersection of each line and column is indicated the particular deputy's frequency of use of the lexical item. Deputies who did not issue an election manifesto, for whatever reason, thus give rise to a line with nothing but zeros: entirely logically, factor analysis places them at zero on each axis.

This factor analysis makes it possible to establish an initial diagram locating the deputies in terms of their vocabulary (Figure 10.4)

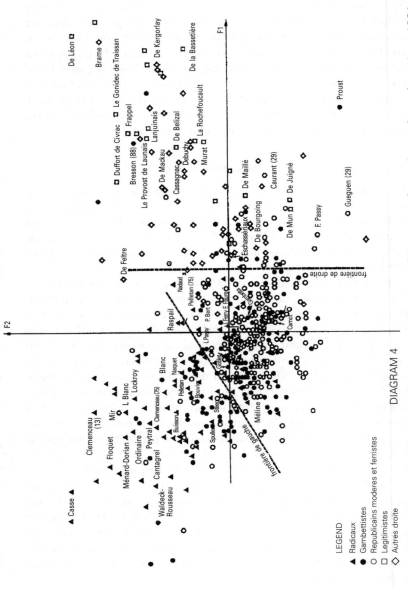

Figure 10.4: The dispersal of Parliamentary space, Chamber of Deputies, from electoral proclamations 1881.

which, for ease of reading, we here disconnect from Figure 10.5, presenting expressions used, even though they could be shown together in the same space. Here, just as anticipated, we find the configuration already indicated by the analysis of votes. On the first factorial axis left is opposed to right. It is even possible to trace a line showing that all the deputies from the right lie to the right from this 'frontier' line. Yet we note that the no-man's-land separating the republicans and the right on the voting diagrams has disappeared here. We even discover some republican deputies appearing as wanderers among those of the right. A closer study, case by case, show that these are moderates elected in very traditional rural constituencies: these deputies have spoken the language of their electors. Such is the case of the Dr Proust, the most rightist supporter of Gambetta, who was the mayor of a village of the Catholic West familiar to historians of French politics and society.[13]

The second factorial axis brings moderates into opposition to the extremes and locates radicals such as Clemenceau in an area distinct from that of the republicans in Ferry's majority. Yet the republican deputies are nonetheless far more intermingled than those of the right, and the 'frontier' that we have marked out is far less clear-cut. Again, several radicals can be found mingling with the governmental republicans, and conversely – as if the further one moves away from the centre of the diagram (the origin), the more absolute the hold of the radicals. Splits within the republican camp are not clear-cut. This is confirmed by examining the respective situation of the two groups of republicans who support the government, the 'Ferry-ites' and the 'Gambetta-ites': they are entirely intermingled. Gambetta himself (shown because having been elected he produced an election manifesto, although his death in January 1882 excludes him from the voting diagram) is immediately next to Ferry.

The topography of the speech acts appears simultaneously similar and dissimilar to that of the votes. Similar, because it presents itself according to the same factors: the two representations that we obtain represent a clear relationship. Dissimilar, because it lacks the same clarity, the same simplicity. Deputies of different political families are much more scattered on the fourth diagram (Figure 10.4) than in the first three diagrams; they are intermingled with one another. Two reasons explain this more confused configuration. On the one hand, the nature of an electoral campaign entails that the discourse of the candidates not only expresses their political stand, but also reflects the position of the electorate they are trying to seduce.

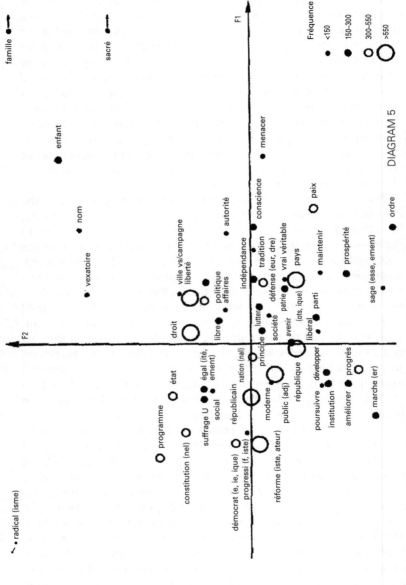

Figure 10.5: The dispersal of discursive space, from electoral proclamations, 1881

Words belong both to the speaker and to his or her audience: a moment of communication is not a moment of decision-making. On the other hand, although votes by nature reveal a dichotomy and require deputies to declare themselves For or Against, vocabulary represents a greater continuum, an element that is more supple and malleable. There are degrees in the use of words, and expressions are more or less used. In rhetorical space, differences emerge through the varying frequency of use of common expressions.

This is confirmed by the diagram of lexical items (Figure 10.5), in which we show each expression, or the group of terms derived from it (wise, wisdom, wisely, for example), by symbols that vary in size to indicate their frequency of use in the overall body of material. At first sight, in fact, it appears that certain expressions, which one would have thought highly marked in political terms, such as *republic, liberty* or *right,* are neutral: they can be found close to the origin. We must look to the 'outlyers' of the factorial axis for expressions that differentiate between right and left.

This examination reveals some unexpected results. On the right – that is, to the right of the diagram – we find the expected terms, such as *family, sacred* or *child* (on the extreme right, i.e. in the upper part of the diagram) or again, less marked, *conscience, tradition* and *authority.* Between the extreme right and moderate right, associated in their discourse with moderate republicans, the difference relates to the use of certain expressions that we still find in the right-hand part of the diagram, but low down this time: *order,* or the *wisdom* group of words. We see clearly that the assertion of willingness to work to maintain *prosperity* and *peace,* in a setting of *law* and *order,* through ruling with *wisdom,* constitutes a discourse that can be common ground for governmental republicans and a right wing that does not wish to be alarming. In this right-wing vocabulary an expression like *to threaten* is nonetheless surprising because it does not appear to belong specifically to this political vocabulary. Yet it is clear that this term is politically marked, and we can firmly identify its use as right-wing.

On the left, among the government's republicans, it is natural to *develop,* to *pursue,* to *improve institutions.* This is *progress,* which the diagram sets apart from its derivative adjectives, *progressive* or *'progressist'.* The reason for this is that the expression *'progressist'* is used pejoratively by radicals to designate their republican adversaries whom they consider too lukewarm and who, for their part, use *progressive* to emphasize their will to achieve their purpose even if they cannot realize it immediately. The lexical groups of *reform* and of *democracy* are also common to the two wings of the Republican camp, and the diagram locates them incisively close to the first factorial axis, that is virtually at point zero of the second factorial axis, which sets moderates against extremes. The same applies to a much-used adjective, *public*, which often relates to the programmatic discourse on education, and to *modern*, far less frequent, but characteristic of the society that the republicans wish to construct, as opposed to the *ancien régime*, the old order. We should note that *republican* lies further to the left than *republic*, a feature explained by its use in utterances of self-definition.

The extreme left is marked by the use of expressions from the *radical* family, in a self-definition that eliminates any need for comment. But it is also defined by the use of *programme*, of *state* and of *constitution*; this is not unexpected, for, before the Boulanger episode, radicals defined themselves through the will to reform institutions, notably through abolishing the Senate. They are equally attached to the very concept of *programme*, which they specifically set against the opportunism of Ferry's supporters. They evoke *social* questions, *equality* and *universal suffrage* more readily than do those aligned with Ferry.

There remain expressions which are important in terms of the frequency of their use, but for which the political tenor is surprising: *name* on the extreme right, *threat* on the right, *advancing* among the government republicans. To understand their meaning we must return to the actual text of electoral proclamations. The explanation is quite simple. Like *family* and *child*, which have a lower programmatical profile (protecting the family) than one might expect, *name* is used in self-defining utterances such as 'a native of the region, my family is well known to you' or 'I ask you to gather round my name'. These ways of presenting one's candidacy belong to deeply-rooted rural notables, often from the nobility, who campaign more on what they represent than on a set programme.

Threat and *to threaten* are very interesting terms: they relate to the pessimistic discourse of candidates on the right who, on the defensive, evoke the dangers that menace religion, law and order, or society. It is an expression highly characteristic of this 1881 election, held some months before the expected date and in the wake of the adoption of secular legislation, which for the right was indeed full of menace.

Advance (marcher) is also very characteristic of republican dynamism at this period. It can be found in proclamations that are apparently devoid of meaning, what we would today consider political clichés, such as to 'advance boldly along the road of progress'. Such statements resound like a banner snapping in the wind. Whoever utters such a phrase has no need to specify his programme, even if he does so: this phrase states clearly to which camp he belongs, and the electors understand this very well indeed.

These comments show the difference between the spatial array of votes and that of words. It is not merely a matter of the dichotomy between parliamentary choices, strictly aligned as 'yes, no, and maybe', as opposed to the relative freedom and latitude of discourses. The distinction lies deeper. The arena of votes is defined in advance by the questions posed: its structure lies in what it does. The verbal arena, or the discursive field, is not at all pre-structured or designated in advance: all words can, at some time or other, acquire a political connotation. The closed nature of the voting sphere contrasts with the infinitely renewable openness of the discursive sphere, because the decision that brings the debate to an end contrasts with the multiple meanings that the participants give to their choices. And yet the two different spheres come together, for we cannot give decisions just any meaning. We are dealing with but one Chamber of Deputies, with a particular array of members from radical extreme left to the conservative and monarchist extreme right; it is this closed population that generated the data displayed in the two series of factorial analyses that we have undertaken, via the same centre of governmental republicans.

Implications

At the end of this study, two sets of comments may be of more general interest. The first relates to possible extensions of this mode of analysis, and in particular, their utility in furnishing the historian with a precise and reliable account of the shift or transformation of political positions. An example of precisely this usage is to be found with respect to a factor analysis of votes in the Chamber of Deputies elected in 1936.[14] Through this procedure, we can state precisely when the Popular Front came to an end; the date is that of the formation of the Daladier cabinet in April 1938.

Another incisive instance of recourse to factor analysis as a tool to date changes in political orientation is also taken from the history of the 1930s. A study of the newspaper *L'Humanité* from January 1934 to July 1936 drew up a matrix of terms, which, when analysed, shows conclusively that a major change took place in the summer of 1935.[15] At the beginning of the period, the communist vocabulary is that of class struggle and combat, with a high frequency of terms like *bourgeois, bourgeoisie, workers, proletariat, proletarian, peasant, capitalist, class,* even *revolutionary, struggle, anger.* The political turning-point of May–June 1934, when the socialists and the communists concluded an alliance, a pact of union, has no effect on this discourse. In contrast, from the summer of 1935 on, *l'Humanité* shifts to the vocabulary of *the people,* and to a lesser degree, of *France,* with frequent resort to terms derived from the new humanism, *mankind* and *liberty,* and to terms associated with the Popular Front, *bread, peace,* and *liberty.* The vocabulary of the Nation, which emerges later on, is not yet visible.

In another domain, that of the evolution of French trade unionism between 1970 and 1990, a lexicographical analysis of the vocabulary of motions adopted by the congresses of major workers' confederations shows impressively the shift from the world of *workers* to that of *wage-earners.* This rhetorical move indicates in one way the abandonment of the traditional vocabulary of French trade unionism.[16]

Of course, discontinuity is the rule both in the trade union world and in that of the Chamber of Deputies. As time passes, the deputies are different, as are the questions on which they vote. The discontinuity of political decision here makes it impossible to move from one Chamber to the next. On the other hand, the continuity of vocabulary allows this, and we have been able to analyse the election manifestos of 1885 and 1889 in the same way as those of 1881: to some extent, in effect, we find the same words being used. It is possible, therefore, to deal simultaneously, in the same analysis, with the proclamations of several elections.

Such an extension over time becomes much more complex, since we have to extend the stock of words and phrases used to indicate political affiliation. But it may still be useful to distinguish a vocabulary peculiar to an election, to a particular configuration of issues, from a political vocabulary more enduring. The right/left dichotomy is never absent, and it has its structuring effects on ephemeral and enduring facets of political vocabulary. But over time even enduring facets evolve in such a way as to emerge in new political configurations. The factor analysis we have introduced in this essay shows that such a moment had not yet arrived in 1889: the opposition

left/right remained stronger and more structuring than the passage
of time in the 1880s. If the political configuration of the beginning
of the Third Republic shifted, it happened later. It is thus that we
see the utility of dating with precision the moment when discursive
fields shift.

Quantitative methods suffer today from a degree of disrepute,
the sources of which go beyond the idleness of some historians or
their refusal to enter into a demanding and complex mathematical
universe. Styles in historical study change, but there is a danger here
in following what is fashionable as against what is necessary. As
against quantitative arguments, we are directed to more qualitative
analyses, as the only ones considered capable of elucidating the
meaning of historic situations. I hope to have shown, from the
examples presented here, that quantitative methods, when they are
sufficiently precise and sophisticated, lead directly to qualitative
conclusions. The supposed opposition of quantitative and qualitative
has some force; but most of the time, it is purely artificial. In order
to respond to the questions that he sets himself, the historian can
deploy the same ingenuity in dreaming up quantifiable indicators as
in finding other sources or the documentary proof to which he
frequently limits himself.

The basic problem is that of knowing whether historians can
prove what they assert. In a surprising paradox, the *linguistic turn*
scarcely seems to have encouraged historians to consider carefully
the linguistic material on which they find themselves working.
Despite appeals to broaden our interest in images and objects, the
principal source of historical evidence is drawn from texts. The
words with which we speak are not innocent, and the choice of
apparently anodyne terms, such as the verbs *to threaten* or *to advance*
in 1881, reflects political or social attitudes with a clarity often
lacking when historians look to content alone. Consider these final
instances: there is much to learn from the fact that motions tabled
at congresses of the CGT, the great confederation of labour influenced by the Communists, tend to use the conjunction *and* with
greater frequency than do other confederations of labour, in particular the CFDT.[17] This emerges in expressions like 'the state *and* the
great monopolies', and clearly indicates the resort to the technique
of amalgam, a characteristic feature of communist thinking. We
ought to attend as well to the fact that, in May 1936, the head of the
Cabinet, Leon Blum, uses one set of discursive forms, marked by *I*
and *you,* whereas the Communist leader Thorez uses another, with

particular emphasis on the term *us*.[18] Out of such distinctions we can glimpse profound political differences that dwarf matters of transient policy.

Finally, the *linguistic turn* seems to have persuaded some historians that their own discursive practice is of a special kind. Wherein this particularity resides is debatable, but it surely must still relate to the time-honoured task of accounting truthfully for events that have happened in the past. This task of truthfulness is indeed proper to the historian, and distinguishes his work from that of the essayist or the novelist. It remains a task that requires us to look for proof of statements we make, to the greater or lesser degree that it is possible to do so.[19] This effort is something fundamental, something from which the historian simply cannot escape.

Notes

1. Research into the votes in the Chamber of Deputies for the 1881–1885 legislature generated two articles: Antoine Prost and Christian Rosenzveig, 'La Chambre des Députés (1881–1885). Analyse factorielle des scrutins', *Revue française de science politique*, vol. xxi, no.1, February 1971, pp. 5–50, and 'L'évolution politique des députés (1882–1884)', ibid., vol. xxiii, no. 4, August 1973, pp. 701–28, and also these two authors' contribution, 'Measurement of Attitude Changes among the Members of the French Chamber of Deputies, 1882–1884', in William O. Aydelotte (ed.), *The History of Parliamentary Behavior*, Princeton, NJ, Princeton University Press, 1977. For analysis of the political vocabulary, see: Antoine Prost, *Vocabulaire des proclamations électorales de 1881, 1885 et 1889*, Paris, PUF [Publications de la Sorbonne, nouvelle série Recherches – 9], 1974. Chapter VI in this book presents the factorial method of analysis used in terms accessible to the non-expert, having been endorsed by the promoter of the method, Professor Benzecri, who set it out himself in Jean-Paul Benzecri, *L'Analyse des données*, vol. 2, *L'Analyse des correspondances*, Paris, Dunod, 1973. Since then, the system has been extended by post-factorial methods, for which see Philippe Cibois, *L'Analyse factorielle*, Paris, PUF, 1994 [4th edn].

2. *Recueil des textes authentiques des professions de foi et engagement électoraux des députés élus en 1881, Journal officiel, documents parlementaires, Chambre de Députés*, extraordinary session, 1882, no. 808, Paris, Imprimerie nationale, 1882. This collection is referred as 'Barodet', from the name of the radical deputy who proposed its public availability in this form,

so that citizens could know if the commitments made by the candidates had been honoured. The two votes by which the Chamber adopted this proposal are, moreover, included in the first factor analysis shown here, below.

3. It is impossible to cite here the vast range of literature on the political history of the Third Republic. We would simply refer to the classic work by Jean-Marie Mayeur, *La vie politique sous la Troisième République 1870–1940*, Paris, Ed. du Seuil, 1984.

4. The classic work by René Rémond, *La droite en France de 1815 à nos jours: continuité et diversité d'une tradition politique*, Paris, Aubier, 1954, has been reissued, revised and augmented several times. Reference here is to the 1982 edition, *Les droites en France*, ibid.

5. This specificity distinguishes it from factorial analyses by principal components.

6. The software available to me at the time I conducted this research offered only 180 columns for processing. As the votes are coded across three columns, devoted respectively to votes for, votes against or abstentions ('for' is coded 1/0/0, 'against' 0/1/0, abstention 0/0/1), only 60 votes could be processed in any one analysis. We therefore took all the roll-call votes, one after another, of a given date. Some are without political significance, since the Chamber rules required a public vote for the disposition of any financial credit. The nominal results of roll-call votes are published in the *Journal official*; these data make it possible to apply factor analysis.

7. This is theoretical, since the analysis takes account of absences and abstentions. However, the voting discipline appreciably reduces the spread, as can be noted, particularly in parties that practise it, in comparing with the patterns published here those that were established by the same method for the Chamber of the Popular Front. Cf. Antoine Prost, 'L'éclatement du Front populaire. Analyse factorielle des scrutins de la Chambre des deputés, juin 1936–juin 1939', in René Rémond and Janine Bourdin (eds), *Edouard Daladier, Chef de Gouvernement*, Paris, Presses de la FNSP, 1977, pp. 25–44.

8. The analysis extracts from the total data a factorial axis that gives a summary résumé of the information contained in the initial table. It ascribes a position on each axis to each deputy. To simplify matters we reproduce here only the diagram crossing the position of deputies along the first of the two factorial axes. The study could be extended by examining the residual information carried by the third and subsequent factorial axes. In the three analyses presented in this chapter, the first two factors represent 44.8, 53.7 and 57.1 per cent respectively of the total information of the table of votes. Taking into account the third factorial axis would enhance these percentages by less than 5 per cent.

9. For editorial reasons we have not shown here the diagrams of votes corresponding to the three diagrams of deputies.

10. At the time, as a function of the Concordat, bishops and priests were paid by the State as civil servants.

11. As can be demonstrated statistically by an analysis of correlation. Cf. the statistical annexe of the article cited.

12. This law declared that mayors would be elected by the city council in large cities – with the exception of Paris – as well as in small villages.

13. Mazières-en-Gâtine. See Roger Thabault, *1848–1914. L'ascension d'un peuple. Mon village. Ses hommes, ses routes, son école.* Préface d'André Siegfried. Paris, Presses de la FNSP, 1982 [1st edn Delagrave, 1943].

14. Prost, 'L'éclatement du Front populaire'.

15. Denis Peschanski, *Et pourtant ils tournent. Vocabulaire et stratégie du P.C.F. 1934–1936*, Publications de L'InaLF, collection 'Saint-Cloud', Paris, Klincksieck, 1988. This author drew up a matrix of articles taken from the Communist daily, printed in the left-hand column of the front page. He analysed these articles printed every three days in the newspaper. He also extended his factor analysis through other linguistic methods that make it possible to determine if, and to what extent, the use of an expression is 'specific' to a given moment, through strong or weak frequency.

16. See the preface I wrote to Anne-Marie Hetzel, Josette Lefèvre, René Mouriaux and Maurice Tournier, *Le syndicalisme à mots découverts. Dictionnaire des fréquences (1971–1990)*, Paris, Syllepse, 1998, and *passim*. It is interesting to compare this study with the essay in the present volume on workers' discourse at the end of the nineteenth century: see Chapter 11.

17. Alain Bergounioux, Michel P. Launay, *et al.*, *La Parole syndicale*, Paris, PUF, 1982.

18. Lucile Courdesses, 'Blum et Thorez en mai 1936: analyse d'énoncés', *Langue francaise*, no. 9 (1971), pp. 22–33.

19. I refer here to the analysis of degrees of certainty presented, in the register of documentary proof, by Carlo Ginzburg, *Mythes, emblèmes, traces. Morphologie et histoire*, Paris, Flammarion, 1989.

11

Workers, Others and the State: A Comparison of the Discourse of the French, German and British Labour Movements at the End of the Nineteenth Century*

Comparisons between trade unionism in the major Western European countries generally emphasize the differences in their attitudes towards the state, and more generally, towards political action. Roughly speaking, we are used to juxtaposing French direct action, independent of political parties and against a dialogue with the state, with British trade unionism, determined to enter Parliament in order to defend its interests, and even more with German trade unionism, so much a part of social democracy as to appear at times as one of the party's dependencies.

These distinctions, while frequently cited, have yet to be explained. To do so requires the examination of as large as possible a set of social and political representations in which attitudes towards the state and a more general trade union discourse are expressed. Certainly, many other factors are relevant to this discussion, notably the legal framework that delimits the space in which trade unionism can operate. But it is indispensable to investigate the different forms in which British, French and German trade unionism draw upon social and political representations. We need to discover what images and ideas workers constructed about themselves, about their adversaries, their conflicts, their sense of politics. Only through such an interrogation can we clarify the assumptions that underlie workers' organizations in these three countries.

* Written jointly with Manfred Bock.

The question is how to identify the social and political represent-ations of trade unionists at the end of the nineteenth century. If we were to examine their discourse on the surface, that is, if we were to ask simply what they wanted to say and what they explicitly argued, we would only recover what we already know about their attitudes towards the state and towards politics more generally. For that reason, we have decided to abjure directly explication of trade union texts, in favour of another emphasis – on the words they used and on the constellations of associations and oppositions they created.

Surprisingly, this kind of 'linguistic turn' is rather infrequent. The interest in a linguistic approach has led American historians to deal with historians' writings and to criticize their pretensions to object-ivity.[1] They did not consider historical sources as linguistic material. Some social historians of the British working class paid attention to language and to words. Careful analysis of what people had actually said drew new perspectives on this history and eliminated earlier interpretations. But, although pointing at 'the materiality of language itself,'[2] they did not investigate the linguistic structure of historical documents with linguistic methods.

Is it possible to study languages without linguistics? It is clear that any sentence, any discourse is pre-formed and pre-determined by the structures of language. These structures are *prefigurative,* as White would say: once given a vocabulary, with all its relations of oppos-ition/substitution, with its semantical structure, grammar rules and so on, the set of sentences one can form is defined. The linguistic framework defines the limits of representations; words prefigure word-ings. Hence, to explore this lexicon, to enter these semantic fields are ways of reconstructing mental universes, of drawing into the political and social arena precise pictures of the representations that are at stake. Such methods are a quite interesting means to create new kinds of historical evidence.[3] However, before presenting the principal results of this enquiry, it is necessary to explain how it has been conducted.

Methods

Themes and Sources

The principal problem in such research is in constituting a corpus of texts for analysis. Once chosen, such texts, inevitably limited in scope and number, provide the material from which a set of conclu-sions are drawn. The assumption is that two researchers working on the same evidence and using the same methods would arrive at the same conclusion.

To make such a comparison work, the evidence chosen must be rigorously comparable. But this is unlikely, for two reasons. The first, common to all historical research, is the haphazard availability and conservation of sources. But in this instance a second problem arises. Very different trade union movements produce very different texts. The weakest of the three, the French labour movement, hardly had a labour press to speak of. For that reason, we had to search for its voice in the Republican press, in *La Petite République*, for example. The German labour movement was much richer in publications of all kinds, including a wide variety of poetry. The strong links between trade unions and the Social Democratic Party opened the party's press to our analysis. But in the French case, with the exception of the 'Guesdiste' tendency, or in the British case, where the Labour Party did not exist prior to 1900, such material is unavailable. But we can remedy this gap in the British case by reference to the literature of friendly societies, associations without direct parallels in the other two countries.

It is thus impossible to construct bodies of evidence that are strictly comparable. The differing structures of trade unions in the three countries produced different sources. Strictly speaking, a German text is only comparable to a French or British text if they are produced under similar conditions; if that is not the case, then distinctions arise from context and not from differences in social representations.

Taken to such lengths, a scrupulous methodology leads to the dead end of affirming that the comparison of differing social situations is impossible. But it is precisely because they are different that it is important to compare them. Better to defy the objection of logic than to be enslaved by it. For that reason we have tried pragmatically to constitute relatively comparable corpora of materials. We admit readily to a compromise between a scientifically rigorous enquiry and one governed by the nature of the sources produced by very different trade union movements. The justification for the compromise is to be found in the objectives of the study – to comprehend workers' social representations. With Alain Touraine, we can distinguish, in the visions of workers, a principle of identity, a principle of opposition, and a principle of totality. Working-class consciousness coheres around these notions: a self-representation, i.e. a representation of who are workers; a representation of their adversaries, employers or property-owners; and a representation of what is at stake in their conflicts. These are the clusters of representations that we need to reconstruct: workers' senses of their own identity, of that of their opponents, and of the conflict between the two. But which texts will disclose these representations? The most interesting seem to be those built into polemics, because the notions of 'us' and 'them' are built into confrontations. We therefore have sought three types of text: those centring on strikes or on working-class action; those concerning the law; and those dealing more generally with politics and society, in which we can find representations of the field of force on which workers and employers face each other.

To organize the body of texts on these three themes, we need to recognize two sets of distinctions. The first arises from situations of communication, and requires us to attend to speeches, articles, motions and tracts. Speeches and articles offer a contrast as between the spoken and the written, but they are both the products of a single voice: someone speaks, and we know who it is. Motions and tracts, in contrast, are distinguished by their collective voices: they are frequently anonymous texts, deliberately so in order better to speak for an organization. But the motion arises out of the statutory deliberations of a group, whereas the tract concerns the action it pursues. This second distinction refers to different levels of the work of organizations, national or local, professional or not. Naturally, the combination of these distinctions is not always pertinent. On the local level, it is rare to find both minutes of discussions and motions; these texts are more abundant at a higher level of labour organization. Conversely, at the higher levels, tracts are rare, since action is usually decentralized. But we were able to find calls for national action that mix the voice of the tract and the motion.

With these distinctions in mind, we searched for sources that could illuminate the three kinds of representations we have outlined above. But there the real problems emerged. Without discussing them in greater detail, it may be useful to point out the main difficulties at this point. First, it was evident that the German material was dominated by issues of organization. Around 1895, German trade unions engaged in a broad discussion of their structures, whether centralized or federal, and their functions, whether as units of struggle or as associations of aid and mutual support. Time and again they discussed their relationship with the party. The German material includes texts published in the socialist press, parallel to those found in the 'Guesdist' press, which, while not fully representative of the

French workers' movement, is one of its main components.[4] The French material is thus more heterogeneous, and must include varied materials, including those produced by Pelloutier.[5] It is both more interested in theoretical debates, on the general strike or political action, for example, and more sensitive to local political and social situations. It discusses local strikes and debates arising from the organizing commission of the London Congress of the Second International of 1896, which denied membership to those who abjured political activity, defined as action directed towards the ultimate conquest of political power by the vote. To this body of material we can add strike posters, though only in the British case can we add texts preparing strike activity and calling for solidarity before the outbreak of hostilities. The British material is more limited.[6] Aside from conference reports, there are local addresses sent for discussion by the whole trade union. The subjects treated are much more practical, many concerning the situation of the labour market.

One must not exaggerate, though, the differences among these three clusters of sources. They all address similar subjects: the 1st of May, for instance. In addition, the object of this analysis is to investigate the structure of terminology, the language employed, the vocabulary used to describe the subjects raised, not their content. Behind the vocabulary of these discourses we try to discover the organization of meaning that defines what can be said. Through the analysis of the contents of these documents, and their different thematic emphases, linguistic analysis enables us to uncover more fundamental structures of thought and meaning.

Method of Analysis

We have tried to avoid adopting a method of analysis that is either too sophisticated or too elaborate. Our objective is historical rather than linguistic.[7] Trade union or socialist discourse in France has been analysed in a substantial literature, reflecting different approaches and different methodologies. The laboratory of political lexicology at Saint-Cloud has developed techniques of scanning of texts and frequency analysis, enabling us to engage in elaborate statistical tests, factor analysis, or the study of singularities.[8] Although this laboratory has digitized a body of French texts, permitting the systematic study of particular terms, we have not engaged in such statistical work. The varied texts in our study are of such different lengths that distortions are inevitable in a strict application of these mathematical tools.

We therefore limited our study to the systematic comparison of specific terms in our texts that seem to be crucial to their semantic and lexical organization. This is what is termed in French linguistics 'analyse de discours à entrée lexicale'. For example, take a term such as *ouvrier* or *Arbeiter*. We have constructed a table listing all sentences in which this term appears, and have identified clusters of terms that are associated positively or negatively with it. We are interested both in the frequency of usage, evident from the table, and the linguistic field in which the term is included.

Unfortunately, the German and British texts have not yet been digitized. This meant that the frequency of the appearance of particular words was registered laboriously through direct reading, which reduces the systematic character of the exercise. This distinction requires us to limit any claims arising from this simple exercise in the comparative linguistic analysis of the discourse of labour movements in the past. Despite these problems, the exercise has produced some instructive results.

Workers' Self-referential Terms

The first striking finding is the greater frequency of usage of self-referential terms than of terms designating workers' adversaries. References to workers outnumber those referring to employers or the bourgeoisie in general. Many of these texts are appeals, calling on workers to unionize or to demonstrate, for example on 1 May. That is why we find a large number of salutations and direct appeals at the head of a text or in its final sentences.

Out of these forms, on both sides of the Rhine, emerged the vocabulary of camaraderie: *camarades*, in France, more frequently than *Genossen* in Germany, where the term of filiation was sometimes more precise: *Parteigenossen, Berufsgenossen*. There are national specificities. In Germany the term *Kollegen* was frequently used, whereas we have identified only three appearances of the same term in French texts, and each usage is different. Twice in the same text where this term designated members of the leading group of an organization, and once in another text, where it is associated with *citoyen*: *citoyens* and *collègues*.

'Citizen' is not used in German texts, no doubt because German workers had yet to achieve the full rights of citizenship. The German equivalent of *citoyens* and *collègues* would be *Genossen* and *Kollegen*, terms that present the two faces of a community defined both politically and professionally. In France, in contrast, 'citizen' is frequently used, notably by Pelloutier seven times in a series of articles, in the form of *citoyens délégués*. The term seems to have preserved the egalitarian connotations of citizens' address established during the French Revolution. It remained active, even though not as active as the reference to *camarade,* which features 21 times as opposed to 9 for *citoyen,* if we exclude the long text of Pelloutier that doubles the frequency of the latter.[9]

In Britain, the two equivalent terms, *comrade* and *citizen,* are not used, at least in our texts. The way one addressed trade unionists was by saying *worthy brothers,* or occasionally (and more formally) *gentlemen.* When referring to a trade union official, French workers used *citoyen* or *camarade N,* whereas the English speak of *Brother N* or in abbreviated form *bro. N.* The English term closest to *camarade* is *fellow,* often associated with other terms: *fellow man, fellow-delegates* or *fellow signalmen.*

But the real originality of French usage is the reference to *travailleur,* either singular or plural, in salutations or closing remarks. This points to clear differences among the three languages in the terms conventionally used to designate those who socially were members of the trade union.

German uses one family of terms, derived from *Arbeit,* or *work.* The most frequent term used to designate a working-class group is *Arbeiter,* employed 60 times; but we also encounter other terms derived from this noun, as in the working-class collective *Arbeiterschaft,* or more frequently (26 uses) *Arbeiterbewegung,* labour movement. Our texts refer to *Arbeiter,* either *organized* or *class-conscious, without possessions, oppressed, without rights, dominated* or *exploited.*

The English use two roots for words designating work: *labour* and *work.* The first is used more generically, and refers to all workers. It is relatively frequently used, though it is not linked to more general terms, in the way *travail* leads to *travailleur* in French. In English a labourer is someone entirely different: an unskilled labourer. Conversely, *work* is not used directly, but words derived from *work* are abundant: *workers,* the most frequent, but always in the plural; the singular *worker* is less frequent than *working man.* The collective term reserved to designate the group of workers in the same trade is *workpeople,* as in *to pay his workpeople,* while *working class* refers to a social condition *per se.* These terms are used most frequently to designate the specific working-class group, though other terms are also used, such as *men* or *hands.*

The French use two apparently synonymous terms: *ouvrier* and *travailleur*. In reality, the terms are different. The proper address among comrades or colleagues is *Travailleurs!*, and not *Ouvriers!* This latter term refers to particular workers: those employed at the arsenals, or workers *at Niort*, the *painting workers in the building trades*, unskilled workers in a particular enterprise. Of 38 usages of the term *ouvrier*, 22 referred to particular workers, and the others referred to particular situations: the workers *who had finished their day's work*, or a worker *returning home*. In contrast, *Travailleur* refers to a group, defined by its solidarity and common condition. The term *Travailleur* is much more frequently used: we noted 72 occurrences, including 9 usages of direct address already cited. This term is clearly the most widely used by workers to designate their corporate identity.

In France, the term *Classe ouvrière* is scarcely used – at least more rarely used than in Germany or in Great Britain. But simple comparisons can be misleading, since the German language permits the use of complex words that do not exist in French or in English. In German, and not in French or in English, one may speak of the state of being in a class, *Klassenstaat;* workers can be referred to as *klassenbewusst,* or being class-conscious; similar constructions in French or English about class struggle cannot be found in these texts.

The notion of class is certainly present, since we encounter here or there references to class enemies or adversaries, and the term itself is based on a notion of irreducible antagonism. And of what are *class-conscious* workers, present in France and Germany, though not in Great Britain, conscious of, if not of themselves as members of a class engaged in a class struggle?[10] Whatever the case, the expression 'class struggle' appears to be absent from the French material, and even more so from the British. In this last context it may be that the tendency to contrast 'the classes' with 'the masses' is apt to impose a further inhibition on the use of 'class' as an appropriate word to designate the workers' group.

The terms *proletarian* and *proletariat* are used relatively frequently on the Continent, but not in Britain. After *Arbeiter* in Germany and *travailleur* in France, the terms *proletarian* and *proletariat* are the most commonly used. The term *proletariat* is juxtaposed in almost every instance either to class adversaries (*patronat*) or to the state, control of which the proletariat must seize. The term has an international element, present in universalist references: *prolétariat du monde entier, universel* ou *international*.

In a way, the message of Marx's *Manifesto* of 1848 became a redundancy, a repetitive phrase: the proletariat is the body of proletarians of all countries in so far as they are united.

In French, we also find words that designate labour through substantivized adjectives: *exploited* appears seven times, as do other adjectives or past participles: *oppressed*; *suffering*; *miserable* (1 appearance each). *Victims* and *producers* appear twice each. In German the most common adjectives are *oppressed* and *poor*. British trade unionists, in contrast, rarely use adjectives. There are exceptions: *the poor and distressed* designate those they defend.

The peculiarity of British texts is the use, in the singular or the plural, of the term *trade*.[11] The French equivalent *métier*, is rare, and does not displace the term *ouvrier* in the name of *les ouvriers du métier*. In English the term *trade* is much more frequent (53 in the singular, 29 in the plural) than *workers* (10) and *labour* (28). The term has the connotation at one and the same time of profession (*engineering trade, building trade, printing trade*), and of *our trade, the trade he belongs to*, or *the state of trade*. Building workers, for instance, deplore *bad trade and inclement weather*: '. . . *we most earnestly hope for an improvement in trade*'. There are questions about '*the prospect of trade*'. The term combines not only with *union(s)* but also with *society(ies)* or organizations to designate labour associations.

The term *Union* is associational too, since it gave birth to the generic term *unionism,* which surprisingly appears 7 times in our evidence, where the word *syndicalisme* appears but once in the French material, but the *syndicat* appears 34 times. Only in English is there a word for the non-organized – *non-unionist*: 4 occurrences, but none at all in French. Is it possible to conclude that the conviction that one must create a general labour movement is weaker in France than in the other two countries?

Whatever the answer to this question, it is evident that the terms designating the world of labour as a set of labour organizations are not the same in the three countries. The terms denoting the self-designation of the group in German surround *Arbeiter* and its compound words (*Arbeiterschaft* . . .); in French, the term is *travailleur*, and in both, it is *Proletariat*; in Britain, the *proletariat* is absent, but we hear much of *trade* and *workers*. Again the differences with respect to organizations are clear: *syndicat* in France, *Arbeiterbewegung* in Germany and *trade union* in Britain, express three different social realities, the contours of which are beginning to emerge.

Designating the Enemy

Here too we are in the shadow of specificities of each language. Neither English nor German have the precise equivalent of the French term *patron*, which is the most frequent designator of the adversary in the French material (20 uses). The term refers to particular employers, those met in daily struggles: there are 12 uses in two strike posters alone. Rarely, is the term used in the singular: the *patron* refers to his class, and we can find but five occurrences when the collective term *patronat* designates the group of employers. The term *patronal* is a bit more frequent (6 occurrences, 3 of which are linked to *exploitation*). In effect when the French want to refer to employers as a class, they used the term *capital* and its derivatives.

Still, the term *capital* is not very frequent (9 uses); *capitalisme* and the substantive *capitaliste*, even less so (4 and 2 uses). The most frequent term used in this context is the adjective *capitaliste,* either as a class (5), order (2), or society (1). On this point, French and German are similar, since in both *capital* and *capitaliste* are the terms most frequently used for labour's adversary. But in our French sample, we find the phrase *grand capital* . The British case is different from the two Continental cases in having no recourse to this vocabulary. We find but one usage of the term *capitalists* and one of the conflict *between capital and labour*. The structured opposition of capital and labour in this discourse is not missing; it is just rare for this terminology to be used.

To refer to particular employers, German uses *Unternehmer*, the entrepreneur, with its variants *Unternehmertum, Unternehmerwelt,* and at times, *Fabrikant*, usually specified, for instance as manufacturer of furniture. The English usage here is to *employers* and sometimes to *industrialist*; the word *employeur* is rare in French, as is *Arbeitgeber* in German. This term has none of the connotation of the French word *patron*, with its sense of authority and paternalism.

The particularity of the German texts is the centrality of terms derived from *Besitz,* 'property': *Besitzer*, the proprietor, the owner, and less frequently, the class of owners, or the propertied class, *die besitzende Klasse, die Besitzenden.* In French texts, *possédant* is unknown, both as a noun and as an adjective, and *possesseur* appears but twice. *Propriétaire* is not used in this context. In the British texts, neither *owner* nor any other term related to property appears. (Perhaps indeed one would not expect references to 'owners' in general in such contexts: but in reality even more specific compounds, such as 'mill-owner' or 'factory-owner', that one might look for here are also absent from the texts surveyed.) Property connotes here the large domain of *landlords*. Once again we can see the evidence of a very different sensibility in Germany compared to the other two countries.

Another distinction arises when we consider expressions for domination. The German expression is to the dominant class or classes: *die Herrschenden*. In the French evidence, we find only one reference to les *classes dominantes* and six references to *dirigeant* used as an adjective or substantive. In contrast, *exploiteur* is very frequent (9 occurrences), as is *exploité* used as a substantive, to the point that we could refer to two classes: *les exploités et les exploiteurs*. There were terms used more rarely. In German, we find power holder, money holder, privileged, oppressor. We find too despot, torturer, or ironically, bread-giver. In French, we find *riches* (2), *bourreau* (1), *oppresseur* (2). In contrast, *maître* implies adversary only once; the other uses of the term assign to the workers an objective: to become masters of the state or of their destinies.

In Britain, in contrast, there is no vocabulary referring specifically to domination or to exploitation. Even the traditional word *master* appears in our texts only to connote an employers' association. Consider these distinctions: they oppose a universe where the class adversary is the possessor or the dominant class, to one in which the class adversary is the *patron* or *exploiteur,* and to a third different from the other two, where the adversary is simply an *employer*.

But the enemy is not simply the employer. In French texts, he is also the *bourgeois* and the *bourgeoisie*. We leave the terrain of the relations of production to enter the terrain of politics, at least in the French case, since in the German materials, such terms are rare, and *bourgeois* is used only as an adjective. In the British case, the term disappears completely. In France, the use of these two terms is concentrated in the two texts of Pelloutier[12] – in which there are 9 out of 10 uses of the term *bourgeois* as a noun, 2 out of 4 of the term *bourgeois* as an adjective, and 6 out of 10 denoting the *bourgeoisie*. The connotations are generally political: they refer to ministers, or to the *bourgeois* state, or the need to get rid of the power of the *bourgeoisie*; they evoke the day of the battle between the *bourgeois* capitalists and the bourgeois socialists. Sometimes, pejorative connotations become explicit: one speaks of throwing away the overstuffed carcass of the dominant *bourgeoisie*. Pelloutier quotes a text of the workers' party that declares that it will not enter into elections to win a deputy's seat, and that it will abandon these seats to the hemorrhoids of bourgeois men; such seats are not for men like themselves. The *bourgeois* is not just a class adversary owing to his domination of the state; he is also, and for the same reason, a repugnant, repulsive person. Moreover, one text states explicitly that 'what the worker aspires to is not to take the place of the *bourgeoisie*, or to create a "workers'" state, but to produce equality in standards of living'.

This political argument is not general in France. Texts with a Guesdist leaning refer positively to municipal power or state power. One text aims to force governments to regulate hours of work and wages. We can see here the significance of the composition of the evidence. If we rely on texts reflecting rank-and-file discourse, such as posters or texts produced by trade union meetings, we are struck by the way politics is held in disrepute. The state is rarely present in our texts (1 reference), and its organs, hardly more: 2 references to judges, 5 to justice and the police. The government is but lightly present (8), but often used with negative connotations: *complice, renégat, réactionnaire, aux abois.* Governments are *sans scrupules et sans conscience;* it is *la bande gouvernementale qui nous opprime.* Senators are soft. References to public powers are almost always pejorative: *il n'y a rien à attendre, rien à espérer de ce qu'on appelle pompeusement 'les Pouvoirs Publics'*, or, to cite another text: *'il n'y a rien à attendre des pouvoirs publics, quelle qu'en soit la composition, le propre du pouvoir étant d'avoir des intérêts opposés à ceux des travailleurs'.*

This disgust with politics underlies a degree of indifference towards particular politicians. The term 'party' is to be found only in Guesdist texts and in the discussion of the rules of admission to the London congress by Pelloutier. The only exception is the rejection of the conquest of power *au bénéfice d'un parti.* The adjective *politique* is used only in Guesdiste texts. Elsewhere, one motion of congress rejects all political discussion and seeks out a terrain *absolument en dehors de toute opinion politique.* The term *syndicat* is evidently more frequent, but its use is generally in reference to the identification of the signatory or particular information, such as when one speaks on a motion to be adopted by a congress. Twice the usage is related to the question of trade union liberties, and juxtaposes political division to the trade union as a site of the unity of class: *uni à tes frères dans les syndicats et les fédérations, tu peux être invincible*. But these texts are in no sense a discussion by trade unions about their identity and work.

The contrast at this point is clear with German texts, in which the troubles of organization are much more evident. This distinction arises not only from the body of evidence we have, but also from immediate German concerns. Still, the discussion of the functions of the trade union in German materials has no French equivalent. In Germany, there are discussions as to whether trade unions should limit their work to protest alone or fulfil other social functions, for instance, the maintenance of unemployment insurance funds, even though the problem of retirement pay had already found a solution in Germany unachieved for decades in France. There are discussions too about the relation between central and local trade union bodies. In effect, German trade unionists were more troubled by determining their proper forms of organization than were their French colleagues.

In addition, the representation of politics is very different. In the German material, references to public authorities are not very frequent, and they refer instead to the term *Behörde,* or authorities. There are also references to governments, states, municipalities, and sometimes even ironic references to 'the representatives of the people', in inverted commas. Invariably, the authorities are on the side of the enemies of the labour movement.

It is here that we locate another German specificity. The phrase 'labour movement' is very often qualified by one of two terms: 'socialist' or 'modern'. The French material never uses these qualifiers, and instead refers to the 'revolutionary movement', or even to the 'socialist movement'; but when its authors speak of a movement, it always means a strike movement. There is no general term to encompass the trade union or the party or parties that, we might say, worked for the same aims.

The British evidence is entirely different. There is no reference to the state, but the government of her Majesty is present. Here the question is the need to bring a question to *'the notice of Her Majesty's Government'.* The *Parliamentary Committee* of the TUC is mentioned on several occasions. There is a clear notion of the direct representation of workers in all governing bodies. These documents have a clearly deferential tone, and they abjure all pejorative terms. Annual reports soberly note whether or not approaches to the government have succeeded, and if not, there is no tone of aggressiveness over the failure. One document expresses some scepticism towards legal solutions, or *'remedial legislation'*. Of course, indignation is not appropriate to such reports. But such distinctions are precisely the ones we are looking for.

We must beware of being victims of biaises in the evidence, but it still appears clear that the British evidence is overwhelmingly factual and juridical. Steps taken are justified by reference to *trade union regulations*, the *code of rules*. The term also refers to the contractual rules governing labour in a locality, or *local rules*. For example, these refer to clauses in local rules barring non-union labour. The interests of the trade are treated as subjects to be discussed before a tribunal. The British evidence suggests that danger is to be found among employers and the judges they control rather than from the government. Here is the origin of their opposition to *judge-made law* and *the statute law of the nation*. Trade union struggles are aimed to secure *the rights and privileges of our trade*, which the government can strengthen and the courts can only weaken.

In France and Germany, the vocabulary of the law is evident, though with very different meanings. In the French evidence, the term *droit*, either in the singular or the plural, appears frequently (44 uses), but it refers to very general rights without local settings. This discourse refers to the right to strike or the *right to existence through work*. The right is the moral foundation of protest. Whereas the British texts argue about the interests of the employees, the French texts appeal to legitimacy through asserting a right undermined by the employer. There are political forms of this appeal, for instance in the text that denounces the fact that workers are *outside of common rights*, and affirms: *Nous voulons entrer en possession des droits de l'homme proclamés par la révolution française*.

The German evidence, in contrast, never ceases to pose the problem of equality of rights, both civil and trade union. They speak of 'social equality', of equal rights for all (*gleiches Recht für Jedermann*), or equality of political rights (*politische Gleichberechtigung*). They denounce privilege, or 'special rights' (*Sonderrechte*), the mention of which is practically absent in the French material. These are fundamental features of the discourse of the German labour movement in this period, arising from well-known causes described above.

The Ethical Dimension

In France as in Germany, the ethical dimension to labour discourse is very important. Protest is not formulated in terms of interests, even collective ones, but of rights and values. Here is the salient difference from British discourse, where these issues are raised, but not in the context of protest. They appear when someone wants to underline, in very general terms, the need to be generous. Thus the general secretary of the stonemasons' union ends his speech thanking his members for re-electing him by reminding them of the need to share tasks as well as benefits.[13] He adds these verses:

> He to no noble purpose lives
> Who much receives but nothing gives,
> Whom none can love, whom none can thank,
> Creation's blot, Creation's blank;
> But he who marks from day to day
> By generous acts his radiant way,
> Finds the same path the Master trod,
> The path to glory and to God.

His point is evidently to shame those non-trade unionists who refuse to join the ranks of the union.

The Continental texts are written in an entirely different vein. The most rhetorical German texts aim to present the workers as the defenders of the cause of progress, as if they were advocates for the cause of the whole of humanity. This moralist's approach led the authors of French and German texts to underscore the human qualities of the militant. Certainly, the militant was different in this respect from the rest of the workers, at least in the French texts, which tend to denounce the egoism of the masses. But both the French and the German texts evoke the tenacity, the seriousness, the spirit of sacrifice, and the openness that characterize the militant. German texts denounced indifference and suggested that trade union militancy demanded more than political militancy. The French texts insist on the *energie* of the militant (7 references, plus 2 for *énergiquement*), his capacity for struggle (15 uses, plus 2 related terms), his firm and energetic will, his courage (3 citations). One text even evokes the virility of the militant. Another shows, in contrast to the cowardice of the ruling class, how the worker would *donner héroïquement sa vie*. Militants must be *vaillants*, *patients*, *persévérants*. Above all, these texts appeal to *dignity* (4 times, plus 5 references to *dignified*). The worker, bent over, reduced to the state of a brute, relieved of his dignity, must *straighten up*, be *proud*, in effect, *be a man*, that is, a man *worthy of the name*. The defence of his rights is, in effect, a moral question. In a splendid fashion, one text wrote: *in the entire civilized world, those who abandon their rights so as to avoid hardship only merit the title of cowards.*[14]

Differences persist, despite these similarities. The German material is marked by an emphasis on the ideal of legal equality, which has as much a political as a trade union import. The employer is not subject to an irremediable condemnation. One text even argues that a rise in wages is also in the interest of employers. What is rejected absolutely in the German documents is inequality.

British texts are preoccupied about all with economic circumstances affecting the balance of forces in the labour market, and the defence of or improvement in the rules of the trade; they appear to be associations respectful of their own formal rules of functioning, which treat their claims as matters of business.

French texts are different yet again. The frequency of the term *travail* is not the least important feature (55 occurences). There are also terms designating specific conditions of work, such as *hours* or *day*, for example (13 occurrences). But what is striking is the importance of work (*travail*) *per se*, or rather the fact that the term stands for the world of labour as a whole (26 occurrences). *Travail* in French has its equivalent in the term *labour* in English, but in reality the balance of usage of the two terms is different: *travail* appears 28 times in the French texts, *labour* only 7 times as the name of a collective, once as opposed to capital, in terms such as *labour representation* or *labour programme.*[15] In the field of semantics, in French, the term *the organization of labour* combines also with *emancipation*, a term unknown in the British material. In France, it is *the army of labour marching towards its emancipation*. Elsewhere, we have the appeal *Vive l'émancipation complète, absolue du travail*. French workers' discourse is dominated by the terms *travail* and *travailleurs*.

A reader would miss the significance of these terms if he neglects the moral dimension of this discourse. Work here is not simply a constraint, a condition, a necessity: it is a positive value. Several texts illustrate this. They note that *Labour, which is all, must occupy the first level of society*; or in the same text: *Society will be based on the power of labour, which is the sole driving force of life and human activity*. Some evoked *the preponderance and the only true grandeur, of labour, creator and the unique source of wealth and of all well-being.*[16] In contrast, the class enemy, the employer in the factory or the bourgeois in politics, is an idler, a parasite. This is how they constructed the term *exploiter*, the importance of which we have already noted. One of our texts opposes the *producer* with the *employer*: that is, the employer produces nothing, since he does not work.

Under these conditions, the complete and absolute emancipation of labour is the emergence of the labour as the universal class. The trade union discourse is performative; it has as its goal the transformation of workers in the full sense of the term.[17] In the construction of this discourse, Labour as a value (the capital letter is self-evident) is absolutely central in France, as one can see in the 1895 adoption of the name of the Confédération générale du Travail. No other term would do. *Travail* sounds like the affirmation of a conviction as well as a call to arms.

Conclusion

In the terms of this comparison, and in order to provide a kind of inventory of our findings, we must first insist on the limits of our research. Still, there are clear distinctions in the languages developed in these three labour movements. The distinctions among them are evident, as are parallels arising from the condition of wage labour and moral argument. British trade unionism appears to have been configured around the rules of the trade, leading to a preoccupation with unorganized workers and with their own strength in the struggle to improve the wages of labour. Their aim is to negotiate better on the labour market; theirs is an economic syndicalism. German trade unionism is obsessed with organization, and envisions equality for the rights of labour in the whole of German society; theirs is a trade unionism of significance embedded in a political and social movement. Finally, French syndicalism appears at one and the same time like a movement of confrontation, and a movement of identity, resting on the notion of the exclusive and salient dignity of work and workers. This distinction is translated succinctly in the three general distinctions of type: *trade unions*, *Arbeiterbewegung* and *Confédération générale du Travail*.

Notes

1. The French version of this essay includes an annexe not reproduced here. This annexe gives full indications and references on how each corpus has been constituted and from what sources.

See also: Hayden White, *Metahistory. The Historical Imagination in Nineteenth-Century Europe*, Baltimore, MD and London, The Johns Hopkins University Press, 1973.

2. Gareth Stedman Jones, *Language of Class. Studies in English Working Class History 1832–1982,* Cambridge, Cambridge University Press, 1983, p. 20. This pioneering book, by taking into account seriously what the Chartists said, made obsolete and irrelevant previous assumptions about the social history of the working class. However, as Jacques Rancière points out in *La nuit des prolétaires, archives du rêve ouvrier* (Paris, Fayard, 1981), Jones does not use linguistic methods, which French linguists imported from America, mainly from Zellig S. Harris's *Discourse Analysis* translated into French in 1969. The same critique applies to Patrick Joyce, *Visions of the People. Industrial England and the Question of Class 1848-1914,* Cambridge, Cambridge University Press, 1991, especially Chapter 8 : 'The People's English', and to the collection of essays he edited: *The Historical Meanings of Work,* Cambridge, Cambridge University Press, 1987.

3. I used this linguistic approach first to analyse the electoral addresses of French deputies, in *Vocabulaires des proclamations électorales de 1881, 1885 et 1889*, (Paris, PUF, 1974), and later to discuss the patriotic and pacifist feelings of French veterans of the Great War in my book, *Les Anciens combattants et la société française, 1914–939*, tome 3, *Mentalités et idéologies*, Paris, Presses de la FNSP, 1977.

4. At this time, the French socialist movement was not unified. One of the socialist parties was led by Jules Guesde, who was a Marxist and then supported the idea of a close relationship between the party and the trade unions, and the need to achieve political power in order to realize the revolution. See Claude Willard, *Les Guesdistes*, (Paris, Ed. sociales, 1965) and Claude Willard (ed.), *La France ouvrière, tome 1, des origines à 1920,* (Paris, Ed. de l'Atelier, 1995). This faction was opposed by pure syndicalists, who were hostile to the very notion of political action and thought that the state had to be destroyed, not conquered. Fernand Pelloutier, secretary of the Federation of Labour Exchanges, was the most prominent figure in this French revolutionary syndicalist movement, emphasizing direct action. The revolution would arise from a struggle directly between workers and their capitalist exploiters, without reference to the state. Only in this way would the workers become truly free. See Jacques Julliard, *Fernand Pelloutier et le syndicalisme d'action directe* (Paris, Le Seuil, 1971).

5. I thank Stéphane Sirot for the French texts he kindly gave me.

6. Let me thank very warmly Chris Wrigley, who was kind enough to provide the texts of the British documents used in this exercise.

7. For another example of such methods applied to similar texts for more recent period, see Alain Bergounioux, Michel P. Launay, *et al. La Parole syndicale* (Paris, PUF, 1982), Anne-Marie Hetzel, Josette Lefèvre, René Mouriaux, Maurice Tournier, *Le syndicalisme à mots découverts. Dictionnaire des*

fréquences (Paris, Ed. Syllepse, 1998) and the review *Mots*, edited by the Press of the Institut des Sciences Politiques.

8. This is a sophisticated method, permitting us to see whether a word is over- or under-utilized in each of the texts compared, according to the different lengths of each text and to the linguistic rules of frequency distributions (Stoup–Zipf law).

9. This evolution of vocabulary characterizes French trade unions, in contrast to the Socialist Party, which continued to use the term *citoyen* until the Great War, when it adopted the term *camarade*, according to Jean-Louis Robert's unpublished *thèse d'état* on Parisian metalworkers during the First World War.

10. See the different formulations of Patrick Joyce and Gareth Stedman Jones on the nature of class sentiment and class consciousness. The absence or the scarcity of terms with class connotations in British texts is revealing.

11. Keith McClelland, 'Time to work, time to live: some aspects of work and the re-formation of class in Britain, 1850-1880', in Joyce, *The Historical Meanings of Work, op. cit.,* gives similar examples of the use of *trade* earlier in the century, for instance pp. 190 sq.

12. Four pages of his leaflet, *Qu'est-ce que la Grève générale* (Paris, 1895) and a series of articles in *Le Parti ouvrier,* (29-30 August, 5-6, 12-13 and 19-20 September 1895).

13. Operative stonemasons' friendly society, *Fortnightly return sheet,* 9 May–23 May 1995 (W. M. Hancock).

14. Fédération corporative des mouleurs en métaux de France, *Compte-rendu officiel du deuxième congrès, tenu les 7, 8 et 9 septembre 1895 [. . .]* Paris, Impr. J. Allemane, 1895, p. 20.

15. Tested with the chi square index, the difference between the two is significant at the level of 0.05.

16. *IV° Congrès des Bourses du travail de France et des colonies. Compte-rendu des travaux du Congrès tenu à Nîmes les 9, 10, 11 et 12 juin 1895,* Nîmes, Bourse du Travail, 1896, p. 92.

17. Robert Benoit, 'Les figures du Parti. Formation et définition du groupe (1932-1946)', *Mots,* n° 10, 1985, pp. 109-32, analyses similarly discourses from the Communist Party during the Popular Front era. In such a sentence as: 'Nous devons faire de chacun de nos adhérents un militant', those who are supposedly the object of the discourse are grammatically the subject of the action, 'We have the duty' to make militants from members. This is a clearly self-performative statement: the party is telling the party that it must become the party.

12

The French Contempt for Politics: The Case of Veterans in the Inter-war Period

History is a paradoxical profession: discussions of method rarely lead to effective practices. The linguistic turn has been hailed as a Copernican revolution that will radically enable history to attain the real, beyond mere representations, and, in France, beyond a quantitative history that has been hailed, a bit too firmly, as having dominated the historiography of the 1960s. Instead, history has been reduced to literature. Since Hayden White has inscribed in one of his books a peremptory citation of Roland Barthes, 'facts have only a linguistic existence',[1] it may not be rash to look forward to historians' discovery of linguistics. Linguists write the history of language, and some linguistic specialists write general history too. But by and large historians have refused to consider seriously texts in the setting of linguistic reality.

Nevertheless, modes of speaking are hardly innocent, and through their referential function – the reality that they aim to designate, and that a naive reader takes uncritically as it is – they disclose through their structure, through the articulation of their semantic fields, through their stereotypes and their metaphors, what French historians have termed 'mentalities' and now call 'representations'. These are the often unconscious and ignored 'prefigurations', in Hayden White's terms, that delimit and frame the field of what it is possible to say and to think in a particular period and in a particular milieu.

This detour through linguistics, which seemed to me one of the most fruitful ways of responding to historical questions before the linguistic turn and remains such after it, is in no way a contradiction of quantitative methods. The opposition between quantitative history and a new kind of history is an absurdity: why reject rigorous methods that are applicable to particular kinds of materials. Why not test them out? This is the aim of the following study: to show how a partially quantitative study, using linguistic tools, can illuminate the representations of a period. The subject in question is representations of politics in France between the two world wars.

Preliminary Remarks

One of the central problems of inter-war France is undoubtedly the poor functioning of Republican institutions. From J. Barthélémy to A. Tardieu, with stops at M. Ordinaire and G. Doumergue,[2] many advocated reform of the state. Events seemed to justify this view. The regime, blocked, operated through decrees. It was weakened by the street disturbances of 6 February 1934 and collapsed on 10 July 1940, in exceptional circumstances, no doubt, but with general public acceptance. The 80 deputies who refused on 10 July 1940 to hand power over to Marshal Pétain were isolated, and their vote did not signify approval of the regime of the Third Republic. For all that, the people in the referendum of 1946 massively refused to go back to the situation operative under pre-war institutions.

The sense of crisis went well beyond the political realm. Impotent, public opinion suffered from a sense that 'things can't go on like this'. Certainly, it was in the interest of journalists of the right and the extreme right to discredit the regime. But, in many quarters far removed from 'fascism', the crisis of the state was a preoccupation, voiced in many ways. Since 1928, in any event, veterans' associations raised this subject, and many of their reform proposals anticipated, much more than Vichy, the institutions of the Fourth and the Fifth Republic.

In this context, what was termed the 'veterans' movement' merits our attention. To reduce it, as is often done, to the folklore of its banquets and the 11 November ceremonies would be simplistic. This was a mass movement – about 3.5 million members in 1932–34 – composed of a multitude of active associations, each with its own leaders and militants and rank and file, regularly consulted. The business of local chapters was not merely social; they spoke of great problems, the problem of peace or state reform, and the events of 6 February 1934 provoked extraordinary general assemblies, which adopted argued resolutions. A flourishing press linked, usually on a monthly basis, departmental offices and branches at the local level.

These periodicals, of four pages and frequently more, dealt with more than the life of the association, its sections, the national federations and the confederation that, from Paris, attempted to govern this multiform group. There we can find articles on the burning subjects of the day. If we consider that in 1932 there were 233 local veterans' newspapers, not to mention the Parisian ones, or the national press of the national associations, then we can get a sense of the intensity of this generally unrecognized vibrant associational life.[3]

This movement is of even greater importance for the historian when it is placed in a milieu that is of central importance in the history of inter-war France, but is one that has never played a central role. We know about bourgeois opinion. We know, through trade unions, about workers' reactions. But the middling orders are by and large ignored. But these are precisely the groups that dominated the veterans' movement. Through its membership, this movement remained close enough to the mass of the population, with an over-representation of rural groups and an under-representation of working-class groups, reflecting the greater rate of membership in the countryside than in the city. On the level of the leadership, we encounter here lower-level bureaucrats and salaried workers: officials in prefectures, teachers, tax collectors, office workers, workers in commerce, accountants, shopkeepers, travelling salesmen. These are the men who formed the core of the movement on the departmental and national levels, alongside some lawyers, doctors and academics. The upper middle class of the liberal professions and business played an important role only in the right-wing Union nationale des combattants (UNC), associated with traditional elites and financial interests. Elsewhere the *petite bourgeoisie* and white-collar workers take the lead.

For these reasons, a study of the veterans' movement opens a window on the attitudes of middle-class groups, which in other countries supported authoritarian regimes. Studying this movement leads us to understand the reaction to the crisis of French political institutions. The views of veterans on constitutional problems were enmeshed in considerations of politics in general, and in a particular way of experiencing events, of feeling the effects of a political regime, of defining themselves in terms of political issues. This sense of politics, more than particular positions adopted with reference to different problems, is the object of this chapter. Our purpose is to uncover this sense of politics systematically, as in sifting the archaeological remains in a dig, through a systematic analysis of their discourse.

This kind of analysis requires some preliminary remarks on the material to be studied and the methods used to analyse them. With respect to evidence, what is needed are materials permitting both diachronic analysis and a synchronic study linking political trends and veterans. Imposing this requirement on the sources produces a wide array of materials, which need to be delimited. To this end, we have set aside books, pamphlets and congress reports, in which the views of individual authors skew the sample, and concentrated solely on articles in the movement's varied and rich set of local and national news-sheets. We have picked a sample of 147 articles that constitute a body of comparable texts, by and large of a similar nature and level of linguistic expression. These enable us to follow changes over time, differences in left/right reactions, and differences between the national and local level.

The two principal associations dividing the lion's share of the veterans' movement between 1920 and 1940 were the Union nationale des combattants (UNC) and the Union Fédérale (UF). The first was more conservative; the second was the home of Republicans, socialists, and radicals of many persuasions. The UF (925,000 members in 1932–4) was slightly more powerful than the UNC, older, and more active in helping the disabled, but also more 'provincial', in the sense that its departmental branches were to a great extent autonomous. These two associations operated a national and local press that furnished the bulk of the materials we have used. But despite the fact that the UNC, like the UF, adopted an 'apolitical' stance, we have listed those articles clearly located on the political right or left. We have also taken extracts from several articles from an ephemeral newspaper of the extreme right, *Les Étincelles, Journal des combattants,* and from several texts published by those who instigated the demonstration of 6 February 1934, published by the *UNC de Paris.* On the other side of the political divide were the Fédération nationale des combattants républicains (FNCR), which was formed to support the Cartel des gauches in 1924, and the Association républicaine des anciens combattants (ARAC), which had Communist support. Finally, we have scoured sources that escape the two categories delineated above. We then formed two groups, one of the broadly-defined political right, and the other of the independents. This last category included political extracts from the *Journal des Mutilés,* a newspaper with a circulation of 400,000 a week.[4]

In sum, this sample encompasses 147 articles written by 80 different authors, not to mention anonymous texts that arose out of collective editorial work. Some of these writers were well known: René Cassin, Jacques Duclos, Paul Vaillant-Couturier, Ernest Pezet.[5] Others were leaders of the veterans' movement who have not left much of a trace, but who at the time had a considerable audience, like Henri Pichot, the uncontested leader of the UF. Finally, some authors of articles in the local press were departmental officials and obscure militants, or even anonymous members, such as the one who signed his article 'an ex-mortar-gunner of the Argelès branch'. Even though the sample was constructed along empirical lines, this body of evidence was largely representative of the diversity of the veterans' movement, its political complexion and its levels of responsibility.

In terms of a time series, there are irregularities. In effect, the articles were selected by subject, political or civic action, and these themes naturally followed the chronology of public debate: debates about general elections, in 1919 and 1923-4, moments when the veterans' movement launched a campaign in favour of 'civic action', times of growing power in 1927-8, with the creation of the Confédération nationale, in which the majority of veterans' organizations were regrouped, with widespread attendant discussion of policy, and times of crisis of the institutions in 1932-4, with the multiplication of criticism of the regime and studies about fundamental reform of the state. The discussion was particularly vibrant in the veterans' movement, since its secretary-general, G. Rivollet, became minister of pensions in the government Doumergue formed in the aftermath of 6 February 1934. Doumergue tried to revise the constitution in order to ease the dissolution of the Chamber of Deputies.

Table 12.1 describes the full array of the evidence we have used. It is not necessary to present a detailed list of the articles that constitute the evidence.[6] Two figures indicate the year; they are followed by a letter designating the political orientation of the article: D for right-wing articles in the *Voix du Combattant*, the bi-weekly national paper of the UNC; E for the local journals of the UNC, G for left-wing, for the different national organs of the UF; H for the local papers of the same persuasion; C for the political right; F for fascist and extreme right; I for independents, and R for Republican opinion in the FNCR and ARAC, and some other left-wing individuals.[7] The last figure is a number within the designated sub-category, 33G3 designating the third article of a leader in the UF appearing in 1933.

In order to exploit all the implications of these data, we first established the frequency of these terms, and then selected the most interesting terms, which were to be investigated through lexical

Table 12.1: Distribution of political characteristics of articles in veterans' newspapers in France, 1919–39.

Year	C	D	E	F	G	H	I	R	Total
1919		1			1	1		2	5
1920									
1921									
1922			1		1				2
1923		7			2	2			11
1024		1	3		3	4			11
1925		3	1						4
1926					2	3	1		6
1927	1					1			2
1928	3	5		5	1	1	2	2	19
1929	5	1		7				5	18
1930		2		1					3
1931									
1932					1				1
1933		9	2		9			1	21
1934		3	5	3	8	5	3	5	32
1935						1	1	2	4
1936							2	2	4
1937									
1938					2			1	3
1939								1	1
Total	9	32	12	16	30	18	9	21	147

analysis of associations and oppositions in semantic fields and of tenses, syntax and usages – in effect, their rhetorical structure and force.[8] The chosen terms were words such as: *politique* (noun and adjective), *civique, parti, partisan, politicien* (and derivative words), as well as two adverbs of position: *en-dehors* and *au-dessus* (apart from and above).[9] These terms were chosen intuitively, after a first survey of the corpus – a mode of selection not entirely satisfying for social scientific research. There were other choices: emphatic turns or the use of pronouns, for instance. But our aim was not to seek a linguistic model to apply to historical research. First come the sources, and then come the methods, the utility of which depends upon their appropriateness to the materials available for analysis. Still, the tools of linguistics can provide the historian with insights into texts that do not readily afford such insights to even the most scrupulous direct and straightforward reading.

From Real Politics to Myth

Policy is a concrete subject. Everyone confronts it daily in the columns of the press. Context and timing are critical for meaning. Without both, texts float in space, literally de-contextualized. Surprisingly, the policy that the veterans discuss is not determined, has no content, and is not located either in some particular place or at some particular time; it does not happen here and now. It is a kind of policy *per se*, a Platonic idea.

There are, naturally, exceptions to this rule. The term policy sometimes brings us back to the concrete situation of a particular period. Grammatically, this usage in French is signalled by the definite article, and, after the word, by an adjective or a phrase that specifies the field or the objective of this policy. Thus we find references to *home* and *foreign policy*,[10] *financial, economic, social*,[11] or *railway policy*, or *a peace policy*, or *a policy of pacifism*, or *national economic development policy*, or *a policy of social justice*, and so on.[12] But these policies appear exclusively in writings of men on the political left, members of the UF or the FNCR or the ARAC. On the political right, they are absent, with the exception of the *policy of civic action* published in the programme of *les Étincelles*. Such a kind of policy can effectively be included in a programme.

In the same way, our authors rarely speak of actual political parties; they prefer the indeterminate reference to *parties*, or even to *party* as a generic type. This may seem odd, since it is in the nature of political parties to be concrete; but our authors avoid this specificity, or choose a general rubric, as when they speak of *party A or party B* (28F3), the *green or orange party* (24G1; but not the red, for this colour would have had a concrete political meaning), or *this or that party of your choice* (33E2). Particular political affiliations, such as to right or left, are generally absent – when they are not mocked, as in such expressions as *parties said to be right or left* (29F6, 23D2, 28F3).

The exception to the rule is a single article that deals with concrete parties, with respect to the left/right divide.[13] But, as those on the left make reference to particular parties, such references are almost exclusively made to *Republican parties* (19R1, 34R1, 34R5, 35R1), *parties of the left* (33R1, 34R6), or *those situated on the left* (35R1). Sometimes the references are more specific: *Socialist, Radical* or *Communist parties* are mentioned 19R1, 24G2, 26G2, 24G2), or oblique references are made, to *the party in the hands of the state* (33G2, the Radical Party). The Cartel of 1932 is referred to as *the two parties for which the people have voiced their support impressively* (34G2). One right-wing author does refer to the Radical Party, but it is not surprising that overall there are few references to belonging to a party, joining a party or becoming a party worker.[14] Even references to comrades who belong to a particular party are rare, although in 1926 the UF urged its members to work as individuals within the parties of their choice.

Finally, there are few direct references to political figures. They speak of *hommes politiques, hommes publics, politiciens* – a point to which we shall return – but these are generic terms, which could designate a locally elected official, an electoral agent, a minister or a deputy. *Parlementaire* is rarely used,[15] but we have no references to Deputies or Senators. Just as with respect to parties or politics, political figures are treated in these texts in general terms. Again, with some exceptions, the veterans we study here do not deal with practical politics, the politics of day-to-day affairs. And yet they constantly speak of politics. What then are they trying to say?

Paradoxically, the first essential point they are saying about politics is that *they don't engage in it, they haven't engaged in it, and they won't engage in it.*[16] Here we are dealing not with facts, but with will, with desire, with a deliberate choice, which determines their vision of the future: *the UNC, committed to avoid politics, has no intention of going back on its word.*[17] They do not want to play the political game: this is *forbidden* (34G2), or something *we do not want to do* (23D3). The consensus here is so strong that it infuses polemical exchanges: veterans' associations accuse each other of playing politics.[18] Here we confront a moral imperative, which at times becomes categorical: *No politics*, an injunction sometimes repeated for emphasis.[19]

This interdiction tells us clearly that the notion of politics is charged with strong pejorative associations. For instance, using a partitive construction, as in such frequent untranslatable expressions as *faire de la politique*, includes a strongly negative connotation. It is virtually impossible to use this expression without saying that one does not do that. From this pejorative point of view, those who should make policy are discredited for merely practising politics. Without respect for the difficulties of effective political action, Ministers, Deputies, Senators and everyone involved in political life are stigmatized by ordinary citizens, the electors, proud of their political purity. In this domain, there is substantial confusion, with which we must grapple.

When the word *politics* is used without any qualifier, the word becomes immediately pejorative. Here we enter a domain that is more emotional, even instinctive, than rational. Politics attracts a kind of general repulsion. It is *disgusting*.[20] It *puts people off* (34R1), it *upsets people* (26I1). It functions as a frightening figure, a *scarecrow* (24G2). *Les hommes de la guerre qui ont connu les marmites et les balles s'éparpillent comme une volée de moineaux dès que jaillit l'épouvantail: le mot 'politique'* (28D1): the very word *politique* works like a scarecrow frightening the veterans like a flock of sparrows. In sum, here is a major taboo, which one does not violate with impunity.

Actually, some authors follow this injunction to the letter, and don't speak about politics at all. Many precautions give the game away. For instance, the subject is raised by negation: *Far be it from my purpose to enter into a terrain that I find execrable: politics* (25E1). But it is indispensable for these writers to quarantine politics, to set boundaries around it, and they do so through two complementary processes.

The first is through denial. Whatever it is they are trying to do, it isn't politics.[21] Sometimes, this simple denial suffices. But on other occasions, it is reinforced by a supplementary emphasis: *we aren't playing politics, we are serving the country*.[22] In this context, the notion of civic action is crucial, for it allows one to speak of politics without using the word. From a linguistic point of view, civic action is the diametrical opposite of politics. They are referred to as *very different things* (29C3). *To take civic action, is not to play politics* (23D5, 29C4). And one could hear the secretary of the socialist FOP (Workers and Peasants Federation of Disabled Veterans) affirm: *Civic action, yes; politics, no.* (29R1), or like M. Dormann, the moderate Minister of Pensions, one could regret the conflation of the two (29C5).

However, as the contents of civic action are politics, it happens exceptionally that some texts work against the grain, in *identifying* civic action with politics. This is the case for Henri Rossignol, president of the UNC and secretary-general of the Confederation, at its

1929 national council meeting. Yet the way in which he put the affirmation: *civic action is politics* is highly revealing: that was not his personal opinion, but a fact independent of his personal will, such a formulation showing how aware he was that he was moving against the tide of general opinion about politics.[23] It does violence to the language of veterans to conflate the two terms *civic action* and *politics*. They are not used as synonyms. But the fact that someone tried to do it alerts us to the plasticity of the opposition. The opposition between the two is not fixed in a rigorous manner. In this context, however, Rossignol is using the term *civic action* in the same sense as those who believe it should never be confused with mere *politics*.[24] How is it that what is politics for him is not politics for them? We need to explore this question further.

The second way to quarantine politics is to distinguish two kinds of politics, a good and a bad one. In some utterances, the same word *politics* is used in two ways, with two meanings which, if the text has any sense at all, are entirely different. When Humbert Isaac, a leader of the UNC whose father was minister in the Millerand government of 1920, writes: *The fear of falling into politics and into disunity separates our common preoccupations from those things which do not appertain to politics in the full sense of the term* (24D1); it implies a divide between the *full* sense and the *ordinary* one. There are two meanings to *politics,* which must not be confused. This distinction is clarified and confirmed in other texts. There is the *ordinary usage* of the term (23D6), which is *debased, illegitimate, degraded by abuses.*[25] And there is the *true* meaning of the term (23H2), the *exact* meaning (34I2), which is the *higher* and *scientific* meaning (34F4), the *most honourable and most generous meaning* (34G3), the *etymological and proper meaning* (28D1).[26] In brief, *there is politics and politics.* (24G1, 34E5).

This opposition between two kinds of politics, however, is not always formulated identically. At a first glance, many kinds of oppositions seem possible. Some of them are neutral in value, for instance the distinction between *active* and *passive* politics (34F6). Similarly there is the distinction between *pure* politics and *economic and social* policies, which are *legitimate.*[27] Most frequently, the distinction implies very clear value judgements. On the eve of the elections of 1919, for example, an article oppose *the politics of ideas, of principles to the politics of personalities*, which is defined in extremely pejorative terms. *What is vile, shady, repugnant in politics is questions of personality, which inform base disputes, deathly hatreds, disgusting practices* (19R2). Elsewhere we find a different form of the same opposition between positive policy and electoral politics. An article opens by underscoring the ambiguity of the term: *We want to intervene in public life, that is to make policy (in the etymological and proper sense of the term) and we want to remain apart from politics.* A few lines later, the text refers to the electoral brawl, and asks: *Is this politics? Maybe kitchen boys in their electoral kitchens understand it this way . . . but undoubtedly it is not the meaning we ourselves give to this word* (28D1). Another text opposes civic action to politics, which is referred to as *electoral cooking.*[28]

By and large, negative politics is politics made by the parties, and to move far from parties is sufficient to cleanse the term politics from any pejorative associations. Several texts confirm that veterans want to enter politics, with the immediate qualification that they do not think of entering politics *in the ordinary way of political parties* (23D2), neither to *create a party* (27H1) nor to become *subordinate to any one of them* (23H2). A resolution of the UNC branch at Angers is quite clear on this point: *The UNC must not play politics. They would do so if they joined a party or if they adopted a party programme, or if they became a political party themselves. This they do not do, when they stand apart from and above political parties in order to elaborate and propose to all Frenchmen a programme that, from their point of view, seems likely to realize the veterans' war aims, that is, international peace, national independence, and at home, concord among Frenchmen with patriotism and order necessary for the country's prosperity.*[29]

At the core of this set of oppositions between different kinds of politics, there is the expression *party politics* or *partisanship*. Everyone is against it. Jacques Duclos, a prominent member of the Communist Party, wrote most seriously: *ARAC remains separate from party politics* (38R1). The UNC branch in Angers specifies: *We only prohibit party politics* (24E3). The term *party politics* is opposed to a set of positive terms: *civic action, the politics for France* (24G1 and 34F4), *national politics* or *the politics of union* (34E5). More negatively, the veterans are opposed to *this old politics of party* (26H2), this politics of *profit, vagabondage and crime* (23H2). The politics of the pig trough (*assiette au beurre*) serve well particular interests (24G1), who *exploit a situation for their own political and personal interests . . . and exploit the poverty and imbecility of others* (23H2). The only aim of politics is *to seize power for the profit of a so-called democratic oligarchy, which uses it for its own interests* (34F4).

The other kind of politics is that of reason and honesty. It is dedicated to *serving the good of each and the good of all* (24G1). It aims *to promote good finance, to find remedies for present and future problems* (23H2). This is the *art of governing the state, and every citizen has the right and the duty to interest himself in the government of public affairs* (34F4). In conclusion, let us cite a professor of law, himself a veterans' leader: *there is party politics, which produces passion and hatred, and there is policy* (Politique) *in the full meaning of the term, which consists purely and simply in creating better institutions for the country's recovery* (34H3). This is the perfect illustration of the main cleavage between *politique* and *Politique.*[30]

If politics with a lower-case 'p' is, in the evidence we cite, party politics, politics with a capital 'P', or permitted Politics,[31] is civic action, or the politics of veterans, in French, the politics of 'combattants', the word being more positive than 'veteran' which connotes ageing and tired people. They have their own point of view. *It is not party politics to say: veterans have the right and the duty to proclaim what they want France to be tomorrow* (19D1). *To enter politics is the opposite of veterans' politics . . . which is in the true sense of the term, policy made by veterans.* (23H2). *In effect, since there is a policy of veterans, there is no need to create it* (26H2). At the extreme, the use of the simple possessive establishes the distinction between a repugnant politics and permitted policy. *We must have our policy and not borrow that of others* (26H2). Or, again *We must be fair to the UF and recognize that it never placed its action, either overtly or covertly, under the sign of politics. Surely, we could say that it has its own 'politics', although it was rather a mystique of friendship and peace. But the parties that wrangle over power are always unable to influence its orientation and its decisions* (33G4)

Our body of evidence has a Manichaean Structure. On one side is evil, the parties, and politics *in the usual sense of the term* (23D6). On the other side is good, the veterans, Policy in the true sense. But neither of these entities is real. Through this dichotomy, they turn their backs on concrete policy. These texts give us a point of entry into an archetypical universe, where essences are facing each other as abstract entities. To examine their internal structure will clarify this phenomenon still further.

The World of Political Parties

Parties

The phrase *political parties* is the most frequently used in our sample of texts. But it seems useless to define what political parties are. Nothing is said about their internal structure, nothing about their membership and their operations. On the other hand, there are numerous pejorative references to them. This semantic field is vast; it is possible to structure this material around central themes: the diversity of parties and their conflicts, their narrow dogmatism, their rigidity and their senility.

The first claim against parties is that they are too numerous. *There are so many, there are too many* (33D7). *Politics is a rainbow in which every nuance demands its own autonomy* (33D7). It is *a swarming*, explicable certainly, however objectionable (34G3). *The multiplicity of parties goes down to the level of sects and clans* (34G3). *External diversity and internal diversity multiply their internal divisions* (29F6), because *they break up into hostile groups* (28F3). This discredits them: *Let me laugh about this multitude of opinions! These parties, these sub-parties, what gibberish, my goodness!* (35H1).

Too numerous, parties are *incapable of listening* (34G2). The theme of their *quarrels* (33G8, 36I2) is developed tirelessly.[32] *Party struggles* or *partisan struggles* (24D1, 19D1, 34H2), *divisions* (30F1), *competition* (34G3), *differences which appear to have their sources in partisan sentiments* (34G3), *political discord* (24E1), *political struggles* (19H1, 22G1, 24G2, 26I1, 30F1, 33E2, 34G3), *dissensions of the political rabble* (politicaillerie)[33] (34G6) return like a leitmotif. Here is the stupid *battle of parties*,[34] which is formally condemned: *these vain and annoying disputes of parties and clans necessarily lead to catastrophe for the regime and the country* (34G8); *the problems of the house are of such a nature that the political battle cannot resolve them* (34G8). *The only result of party struggles is the lowering of public morality, the disunion of the French people, and poor management of the country's interests* (38G2).

Certainly, some texts are not so severe on party conflict; but these refer to parties in principle more than to their operation and concrete modalities.[35] This more indulgent comment is not solely the monopoly of the left, just as the critique of partisan struggles is not solely the monopoly of the right. We can find on the left categorical condemnations: *the parties of the left, through their dissension, form a shaky wall* (33R1). There is criticism of *the state of con-fusion and the divergence of opinions of the different political parties* (34R1). And one rank-and-file activist declares: *What differ-ence to me and to many workers is this party rivalry, or rather rivalry of party leaders?* (34R2). The term *game* (political game or party game) signals the lack of seriousness of these quarrels; they are *childish* (33R1).

What they say is that there is no substance in these games. These authors feel that *each proposal from a party is immediately count-ered by another* (26I1); and it is reminiscent of the statement of the moderate head of government Tardieu, in his address to Radical deputies: 'Don't fire on me, I have your children in my arms.' Some-times it seemed safer that political proposals did not emerge from any political party at all, so that they could be accepted by all parties. For instance, *the first advantage of the national lottery is that the proposal to create it did not arise from a political party* (26I1); its origins are its major advantage.

Partisan struggles are seen as superficial. They arise out of the attachment of each party to its own doctrine. The extreme right put the emphasis on this point. For them, parties are *too large a set of little churches* (34F4), or *narrow chapels* (29F5). They denounce the *dogmatic narrow-mindedness* (34R1), their *narrow conceptions* (28G1), the *rigidity of their theories* (33D6), or *the dictatorship of party theses* (23D2). The solutions proposed by parties are *narrow, doctrinaire, a priori, self-interested* (28F3). Among them, *out-of-date formulae rule, narrow and parochial formulae, to which despite their failings, the partisan formations remain faithful* (29F5).

Certain texts from the left develop the same theme. One example is the article of 1919 that denounces *the doctrinaire formulae and the pattern of political chapels* (19G1). All these texts decry the sect-arian features of parties, but the term is lacking, probably because this vocabulary arose out of the debate over the separation of Church and State at the beginning of the century. However, by using words that at one and the same time refer to religion and to the limitations of religious groups, these texts denounce sectarianism. Terms such as *chapel, dogma, pontificate*, or *party pontiffs* require our attention. This is hardly surprising when someone uses the term *correligionist* for members of the same party (26G2). Another reference is to those who *excommunicate others through their dogmas* (33G1).

The dogmatic narrowness does not only divide; it also renders the parties incapable of finding solutions to contemporary problems.

They are, in the same vein, *reduced to the role of factions in an anarchic State, old, at odds, out of breath from running since their doctrines are behind the times* (33D1). A text from the left states: *To accuse the old parties of being led by the old and of being in the thrall of old ideas, is to push on an open door* (28R1). *Their economic formulae and their doctrines are equally out of date* (34I1), their doctrines are *quaint or deformed, even non-existent.*[36] In their case, old age is linked with incapacity: *the old parties are unable to solve problems* (26H1). *The old school is finished, veterans reject them, the trial is over . . . the grand old crews are worm-eaten, the parties stink of mould* (34G5). In brief, the *parties have their future behind them* (34G5), *their time is over* (34G6, 38G2), *they are sinking into the grave* (33R1).

In this way, political parties are the best scapegoat. There are differences between the extreme right and left on this matter. The extreme right takes pleasure in loudly denigrating political parties.[37] However, on the left, the formulation remains quite critical. *The old political establishment, worm-eaten, lies in groups and sub-groups that have been reduced to dust . . .* (33R1). What differs is not the judgement, but rather the tone and the field it refers to. The left says about parties on the left what the right says about all parties. This explains the similarities in language.

We must underscore this consensus about the pejorative evaluation of political parties. We never found a single defence of parties in general, or of one party in particular. All parties are seen as citadels of strife, doctrinaire narrowness, failure to adapt, and obsolescence. And it is possible to use the term party to define other terms, such as *party politics*. In this usage, *party* is generally singular and never precise.

Other terms are defined in the same way by the word *party: party men*, and *party spirit. Partisan spirit* is the very principle at the heart of parties. It sums up their noxiousness. It is the *politicians' virus* (23D5), disseminated around them by the parties, which is responsible for their *destructiveness* (34G3). Frequently this spirit is responsible for evil actions. *The party spirit destroys the will, anaesthetizes the energy, diminishes men who are forced to vote against their conscience and to support a special interest against the general interest* (33D7). *Their heads have spun so much that it is doubtful if they will ever recover morally, as we hope* (33D4). Conversely, veterans are *men uninfected by partisan spirit, and they have in mind only the country's interest* (34G6). *The strength of the veterans seems to be the national trust of the union of French people unsullied and unspoiled by the partisan spirit of the politicians* (38G1).

The party spirit is opposed to the country's interest and to veterans, who seek to expound their ideas *apart from all partisan spirit* (22G1). Just as *party politics* is opposed to *veterans' policy* and *the policy of France*, the *party spirit* is opposed to *the veterans' spirit* and the *national spirit*. The opposition is unavoidable; they cannot coexist, and must clash with each other.[38] The antithesis between *party spirit* and the *veterans' spirit* is the theme of an entire article (29F5).

Veterans and Party Men

This leads directly to the fundamental opposition of the politician and the veteran. The politician is *a party man*. As such, it is impossible for a veteran to become a politician (19H1, 23D2). The word *politician* is too negative to be linked to veterans anyway. *Afflicted by discounted political parties, we are affected by politicians too. The politician is a sad animal who is sick with fear* (Pichot, 23G3).

Politician is much more frequently used in our texts than is *political man* (59 uses to 8), and it is used almost exclusively on the right.[39] Actually, these two designations are far from equivalent. Members of the UNC would distinguish between *men of policy* and *politicians*.[40] Hence the fact that our texts prefer to use *politicians* is meaningful: *our men of policy are just politicians* (34F4).

The negative nature of politicians is frequently reinforced by adjectives. Some of them underscore their dishonesty: they are *wily* (25D2), *clever* (24G2), *sneaky* (35R2), *shady* (25E1) or *without scruples* (24D1, 34E3, 35R2). Others denounce the fact that they make a living out of politics: *partisan politicians* (21E3) which is derived from *partisan politics, politicians by trade* (34G5), or *by profession* (28F4, 29F3, 29F6). Politics is a job, the job of people who have not found any other employment; *it consists in living off of the back of the people without any worry about the truth or the public good.*[41]

There are more negative expressions about politicians. The first set of terms is derived from *politique* by adding a suffix: *politicards* (35H1) *politiqueux* (29F4), associated with *bistrot* and *boor, politicaille* (34E2), *politicailler, politicaillerie* (34G6, 36I2), *politicaillon* (23H2, 24H1).

Another set of negative expressions is formed from nouns with the addition of the word *politics* as a complement. The simplest example is *men of politics* (33G5), but there are many others. The noun can indicate a living being or a thing: *a wreck of politics*, *mostly senile* (25E1), or *stained by scandal* (34E2). When the noun itself is negative, as in the above example, we have redundant pejorative expressions: *vampires of politics* (28F5), *profiteers of politics* (26H1, 34E3), the *old stagers* (24H1, 33E2). And even *prostitutes of politics* (24H1), *the over-excited ones* (33G1), and *those who have been left out of the political fair* (19G1).

Most of these statements denote ageing, being worn out. They indicate something that has been used up and has become repugnant. It smells of the cesspit, foul. These claims are sometimes explicit: alongside their egotism and their ambition (29F5), politicians are reproached for being used up, interested only in the work of division. Politicians are *aged* (34E1), *old people* (28R1), *old-timers of the pre-war years* (29F1), old *Popes*, and so on.[42] The same reproach is implicit in several texts that accuse politicians of repeating their wrong-doing: *they return to their own vomit, he starts to lie again* (23D7). *They have learned nothing and have forgotten nothing.*[43]

On the other hand, politicians are accused of filling their pockets with the taxpayers' money. Politicians *sign receipts* (24E3). Theirs is *a trade union of profiteers* (34H4), they are a *band of thieves whose only goal is to enrich themselves through the suffering of the people* (33H2). For many of them, *the electoral competition is their only resource* (28F4). It is not the least damaging of the insults one addresses to politicians to say that they *make their living from politics* (34F4, 33D3).

Here we are in a tautological circle. Politics is reduced to parties, and parties, to politicians. They form a pejorative universe. There is no point in distinguishing between good and bad politicians. Good politicians do not belong to the world of politics, but to other worlds. For instance, they belong to the world of veterans (Tardieu, Daladier), they are men of victory (Poincaré, Clemenceau), or of peace (Briand). By this linguistic artefact, they escape from party politics and belong to veterans' policy.

Veterans' Policy

On the contrary, veterans' policy is exactly the opposite of party politics. The pejorative discourse we have surveyed has already expressed the merits of veterans' policy. It is rooted in the privileged experience of war and the solidarity of the trenches. This solidarity is not political, as when one speaks of *union sacrée* (19R1), but is a directly experienced fraternity, which leads veterans to refashion the celebrated adage of Clausewitz: *War is politics by other means* (24E3). *Veterans, during five years on the battlefields, made a certain kind of French policy.* (24E3). For them, war is the exact antithesis of politics. A cartoon illustrates this stereotype, showing a wounded man, simply dressed in his coat and cap, leaning on his crutch, facing a pot-bellied gentleman, probably a politician, dressed in a topcoat and bowler. The politician says '*To make war, the same qualities are not needed as for politics.*' '*Yes, indeed*', says the veteran, '*For politics, faults are enough*' (*Le Poilu de la Loire*, mars 1931).

However, it is difficult for veterans to develop fully the opposition between war and politics, because they are too pacifist to risk glorifying war. They adopt more general formulae: war is the triumph of the general interest over self-interest; the soldiers saved the country, which politicians are in danger of ruining. Politicians *sabotage victory* (24E3), *they never understood the lessons of war* (29F5). The political world never comprehended the mind of the veteran, and *political preoccupations quickly buried the combatants' spirit at the same time as self-interest displaced the general interest.* (25D1). Finally, and interestingly, the identity of war and true policy is confirmed by such phrases as: *war profiteers are the same as political profiteers* (26H1). Veterans would make policy the same way they made war. What does this mean?

The war was alive and remained for veterans the exceptional moment of their lives, when all political divisions vanished and were replaced by unceasing solidarity. This theme appears everywhere: on the extreme left, the Communist Vaillant-Couturier underscores *the similarity of hardships, the same obedience, the same death, the same fear. These are what made us one* (19R1). On the extreme right, the tone is more triumphant: *when they went over the top in the face of machine-guns, soldiers were not very preoccupied with the political distemper with which they had been daubed before 1914* (Marcel Bucard, 29F6). Another text asks: *Where could you find a more beautiful rosette than the croix de guerre you have won without any reference to whether you were red, green or greenish-yellow in politics?* (29F4)

French Contempt for Politics: Veterans in the Inter-War Period

Many texts develop this theme. Most of them denounced *the division of comrades in combat by the many associations and by the obscure and underhanded intrigues of low partisan politics* (34E1). The idea is expressed directly, through the verb *diviser*, by the noun *division*, or even by the noun *diviseur: politics divide and we want to speak about what unites* (28R1), *dirty politics remain unfortunately our great divisor* (34E3). Division could be imputed as well to politics or to party politics, or to parties or to politicians: *the foul politics which divides us, which lets us see people who did their duty bravely in 1914–18 quarrelling for the greater benefit of those who profit from our disunity* (25E1). *Were there parties dividing us when we made war?* (29C4). *Veterans understand at last that only politicians were interested in dividing them.*[44]

This theme is not restricted to the right. During the period of the Popular Front, when the Communist association of veterans grew, it drew upon the slogan of the well-known writer and its founder, Henri Barbusse: *Do nothing that divides; do everything that unites*, and they accuse politicians of *wanting to set veterans one against the other, those on the left against those on the right, so to weaken their capacity for action* (36R2, 35R2). There are many such statements.[45]

Conversely, such statements as *civic action divides* never appear, except as a supposed statement of mistaken adversaries, such as the following: *Let us avoid all divisive action; let us avoid civic action. . . . But we study civic action and we are not divided by it* (29R5, 28C2). Only one text argues the opposite. *It is useless to divide veterans' associations by speaking of civic action* (29C2). Another article replies: *Those who fear civic action only fear it because it may be divisive* (29R3). Veterans' policy clearly ends at the point where division begins.

However, it does not appear to be very risky. Optimistic comments on this point are explicit: *Veterans can find common ground about which civic action they will launch* (26H3). *Our union is not threatened by civic action* (23D3). This was sufficient as a defence against the manoeuvres of politicians and parties seeking to divide veterans.

Between politicians and veterans, in effect, conflict was inevitable, since they parted ways over each issue.

Veterans' civic action keeps certain politicians from sleeping; too bad. There is 'politique et politique', and we do not hide the fact that we are engaged in it. National policy, the policy of unity, policy apart from and above parties.

We still think veteranly, and we are sorry to have to say that around us too many comrades obstinately want to think politically in the bad sense of the term.

We think as veterans, and we have faith in the front generation . . . who hesitate at the crossroads where bad shopkeepers who think politically try to lead us astray and to lead them to a siding.

Too bad for the politicians and to those who chicken out ('dégonflard').

At the UNC we do not think politically, but we do think veteranly.[46]

As the title of one article indicates, it is *us or them* (29F3); *who will win – the veteran or the politician?*[47]

The relation between these two myths is not symmetrical. In these texts, politicians act on veterans, but veterans do not act on politicians. Grammatically *politicien* is used as the subject or agent, and *combattant* as the object of a verb. Action varies, but the grammatical structure remains the same. *Clever politicians have every interest in leading us out of politics* (24G2); *politicians succeeded in deflecting our good sense* (29F6); *we have been swept along, and drowned by the old stagers of politics* (24H1). In all these statements, politicians are at work against a group designated by the pronoun 'us' that includes the speaker as well as all veterans collectively. Some statements stress the politicians' actions: *The fiddlers* (combinards), *those used up types of pre-war politics* (les vieilles pipes culottées doublement de la politique d'avant-guerre) *work either to isolate us or shut us up* (nous étouffer) (29F5).

In the political Landernau[48] *some politicians try to figure out if our path heads to the left or to the right* (23D1). In any event, whatever politicians do weakens the veterans, in particular by dividing them. There are many other citations we could provide to illustrate this point: *ARAC denounces the odious manoeuvres of these wily politicians who are ready to use the name of veterans to divide them and tread on our sacred rights.* (35R2) Another political insult is the following: *Political profiteers ingeniously place us in different associations* (21H1). Politicians transform the veterans' spirit: *Political vermin have putrefied those qualities that were revealed among us during the years of the terrible war* (25E1), and *the preoccupations of politicians quickly forgot the mentality of the combatants* (25D1). Time and again we can see the dynamic opposition between the party spirit and the veterans' spirit, between the way politicians think and the way veterans think.

In the face of these baneful actions, what did the veterans do? Virtually nothing. The verbs they are using indicate subordination: *laisser, faire le jeu de, servir de tremplin à.* Their action is empty: it consists solely of *giving way to the politicians* (24E3). There are accusations: *I shall reproach veterans for having let the old political hacks back to control affairs'* (33E2), or rhetorically, *Are we meant to serve as a politicians' ramp?* (28D2) Occasionally, it is true, veterans consider action. They speak of *the offensive which veterans decided to launch against the politicians* (29F5), of *all the struggles which we wage against politicians* (23H3). *It is against the politicians that we acted on 6 February* (34F4). But, with the exception of this last instance, the actions of which they speak are indeterminate, and refer more to projects than to real action. Their orientation is negative: to act *against* politicians. At best, theirs is a counter propaganda. They speak of propaganda, but in a grammatical form that hands the initiative over to the politicians: *we understand perfectly well the hatred the politicians' spirit nurtures against us, and we denounce the dangers that it poses to the nation* (29F5).

The relationship between veterans and politicians is asymmetrical: politicians act against veterans, who in their turn hardly respond or even imagine responding. The impossibility of effective action is barely marked by their vehement and imperious tirades. For instance, in June 1934, one writer states menacingly: *For them, refuse left over from before the war, shirkers, or failures of the ill-fated post-war politics that ruins the peace, let these fucking guys leave us and get lost* [. . .] *Antiquated schemers, abandon the field and make way. That would be best for you* (34G5). With all this antithetical language about veterans and politicians, it is still unclear how the first intends to replace the second. Anathemas do not suffice to transform myths into realities.

At first view, the relationship between veterans and parties is less asymmetrical than that between veterans and politicians. There are some parallels, but they are rare: *Our associations are split, mobilized by the parties* (24H4); *We have been snatched by the parties* (29D1); *The parties inspire forgeries of our civic action* (24E1); *The parties shouldn't meddle too much in our affairs* (34G5). The *Journal des mutilés* warned veterans' associations against party activities: *We are very tempting prey, and the parties, old and new, embrace us perhaps to suffocate us* (34I3); *This force of ours, which the parties envy and of which they are jealous, we have to avoid their attempts to use it* (34I2).

However, alongside statements in which the parties refer to veterans, there are many more statements where, grammatically speaking, an inversion takes place. The veterans (*us, our association*) are the subject, and *party* is the direct object of the verb. One text imagines the transformation of the UNC into a party: *we have the aim of becoming the veterans' party* (28D3). Others imagine *submitting a programme* to all the parties. This is the intention of the UNC when it launches its programme of civic action (24D1), or the role the National Federation of Republican Combatants sets itself with respect to parties of the left (34R1). At times, the question is how to impose something on the parties – enforced retirement for certain politicians, for instance (34G7).

More numerous than positive statements are negative statements about what the veterans do not want to do. *We do not want to create a new party* (33D7), *we weren't made to become another party* (24H4), *the associations cannot undertake action in favour of a particular party* (24H4); *We are not to be incorporated into the parties* (28H1), nor even *to enter into their struggles* (19D1) or their *quarrels* (33G8).

This desire for independence was unanimous. The veterans refused to *be at the service of* (24G1) or *to tag behind* (34F4) a political party of whatever kind. They had no wish to *serve* a party (23D3, 24E1), much less to be *enslaved* (34G2) or *to pledge allegiance to* a party.[49] We must not mistake the meaning of this assertion of autonomy. It does not imply, as in the case of revolutionary syndicalism, the assertion of priority to other forms of social action, though in the priority given to direct action by syndicalists before 1914 there was a pejorative attitude towards the political realm, similar to what we describe here, that could have played a role. This attitude is not simple corporatism, designed to preserve associations from any fissiparous tendencies, even though such issues of the possibility of division were real enough. More profoundly, veterans felt that they were superior to politicians. To enter real political life would be a degradation: they were worth more than that. Their rejection grew out of a sentiment of superiority.

Two related adverbs describe this superiority in the veterans' discursive practice: *apart from* (en dehors) and *above* (au-dessus). These define the position veterans take towards politics, of left or right. *Our federation is independent and above all party politics*, declared the president of a departmental federation of the FNCR in 1939 (39R1), while in 1934, his colleagues in the Landes and

Tarn-et-Garonne wrote: *Veterans must remain above the [Republican] parties and make them hear our voice every time circumstances require* (35R1). The UF used the same discourse: *We must preserve our role of look-out and pioneer above the parties* (34G2) and *Our effort must happen apart from and above the parties* (34G3). On the right, the same rhetoric may be found, and took on the force of a slogan.[50]

Veterans demanded a privileged place: since they had once before defended the nation, they were the collective interest incarnate. Here are the words of a public school teacher from the Ardennes, departmental president of the UNC, in a speech to the local prefect: *We do not practise politics. Or more to the point, we know only one kind: that which will make France the greatest and the most human of countries. Apart from and above all the parties is not a banal formula for us* (*Le Combattant sanglier*, May 1930). In effect, *Thanks to the moral bonds created among veterans by the war, and while belonging to the most varied political groups, veterans can only act beyond the parties, on a programme of national action* (28D2), *national action apart from and above the political parties* (25D2).

Veterans placed themselves, almost physically, above the parties, in order to see the collectivity as a whole. Their moral superiority was expressed in a kind of topographical superiority. *We descend into politics and into disillusionment* (24D1), but we *rise above politics when we take civic action.*[51] Veterans *soar above political coteries* (30D1, 23D6), and their sense of superiority found its justification in the privileged position of those who had undergone their baptism of fire. It was *up there* that they found the title of nobility they placed before all others: *As for us, as in the time we were up there, we stand well above all the parties and stroll about on the summit better to find the horizon and continue our true path* (23D1). It is well to stand on the summit if one wants to realize *the union of hearts and wills, apart from and above parties, in the same ideal of social justice and love of nation* (30D2).

This *sursum corda* could give rise to a smile. It is a moral exhortation, but one based on a deep belief in the unity of the nation. The notion of a national collectivity was not an empty one; it existed and there are policies that related to it, beyond those of partisan politics that defend the particular interests of various social groups. It is *the politics of France* (La Politique France) as an article already cited had it. It is *veterans' politics, in the sense of a political practice superior to all other politics, reflecting an ensemble of ideas, principles, and sentiments common to all soldiers. That is what is clear!* (22E1). This politics, which embodies the veterans, will be denatured if they compromise in the political mêlée. Faced with real politics, that of politicians, parties, elections, governments, they cannot imagine any form of action without seeing it as an abandonment of their privileged position, a descent from their pedestal. To realize such a high political programme would approach a *deus ex machina*, or a *fiat lux*. In their discourse, we can often see a sharp disjuncture. Their texts speak of the politics of parties and its often disreputable character. Then, suddenly and without transition, the veterans appear, and everything falls into place as if by enchantment. *Such a pure cause ought to have the pleasure of being presented through men worthy of serving it.*[52] This is something of an epiphany, a transformation: to dispel the storms, to chase away the clouds; the pure essence of the combatant (the singular is more archetypical) appears in all its splendor. *The hour of the veterans is going to sound [. . .] A misunderstanding that could have been fatal is going to end. Clean ideas, a virile head, that is all that is needed to save everything* (33D1). What is meant here by *everything*? The text never specifies, because this discourse on politics ends on an act of faith, the veterans' faith. *Above all it is necessary that this work* [what work?] *be neither futile nor disappointing, that we the young and the country as a whole have faith that at the moment when everything will collapse, which cannot be long from now, the veterans, deaf to divisive calls, resistant to manoeuvres, conscious of their force and stubborn in their sense of right, will show that they are capable of building something, since they were capable of saving the country* (33D3).

Conclusion

In this discussion, one question appears in stark relief. This discourse turns its back insistently on reality. But were those who did so aware of it? Were they deluded or self-deluded? How seriously did they take their acts of faith? And did they really think that politicians and parties were as black as they said?

These questions are all the more salient since the veterans' movement did not live on the margins of the conventional political world. Numerous leaders of associations were deputies or senators. Four of the authors of the works examined here were parliamentarians. The veterans' associations lived on good terms with political men. There is no single congress of veterans' organizations without its councillors of the departmental assembly, deputies, senators, even ministers in various hierarchies. Even in the newspapers from which we have drawn elements of this discursive field, articles written by parliamentarians are not exceptional. In their practice, veterans manifest another notion of the political than in their writings.

The contradictions proliferate when political figures refer to this mythological and pejorative veterans' discourse on politics. This discourse denounces them, and yet they absorb it. Consider for instance the example of a deputy from the Ardennes, in his remarks to the departmental congress of the UNC. Just before he spoke, there was a modest uproar in the room. This is how he began his speech: *A moment ago, I was sure that I was in the Chamber of Deputies* [applause]. *And I, who have come here to find a different atmosphere, to immerse myself in the spirit of camaraderie, I was a bit unsettled (Le Combattant sanglier, avril 1933).* Who is fooling whom, when a deputy gets applause for a critique of the Chamber of Deputies?

All depends on the relation between this mythological discourse and reality. Several texts indicate an awareness of the abusive character of these generalizations about politicians: *the men who constitute our governmental teams are, individually, decent men; but once in their world of parties, they become the defenders of their own, their profits, and go through a kind of professional deformation.*[53] René Cassin, in the midst of the Stavisky affair, refers to the pressures that political men face: *no trap is evaded by their honesty, no blindfold by their clairvoyance* (34G2). But this is exceptional. More often, the generalization is self-reinforcing, and explicit: *And these are those politicians (oh, not all of them, but nine out of ten) who govern the country* (35H1).

Realistic utterances are not only rare; they also disrupt the continuity of these discourses. They are interpolations, parentheses. They do not fit in with the rest of the argument; even more, they contradict it. Insights on real politics would require in effect a renunciation, even a denunciation, of abusive generalizations and systematically pejorative statements. In no sense does the discourse of the left vary from that of the right as a realistic versus a mythological discourse. Both are fundamentally mythological in the same way, with some occasional realistic insights. The left, at moments, has elements of lucidity missing among the right; but this lucidity was useless and without any consequences. References to the realm of the real in politics were simply superimposed on the myth and did not modify it. In the common discourse of veterans on politics, reality could emerge at times, but it did not remain in a stable or fixed position.

There was simply no common point linking the history of everyday life, with its contingency, its light and shade, with the mythology structuring the confrontation of the veteran and the politician. This general discourse framed by veterans about politics in effect not only resides in the world of archetypes and allegories, but also constitutes a narrative that, for lack of a better phrase, we can call 'mythological'. Its constituent elements are not unchanging; but they do have a history that is outside time. What marks this discourse are its origins: the privileged, unique experience of the war: 'up there', the baptism of fire, which made veterans a people apart, marked by the seal of the soldiers' spirit, a people redeemed by their sacrifice, pure and disinterested, entirely devoted to the collective. Politics is the universe of others, of politicians and parties, sometimes even of ordinary citizens, who did not understand the hard lessons of the war and remained perverted by party spirit. Once the war was over, the soldiers returned home, and they were divided by politics and politicians, who had sabotaged their victory and led the nation into ruin, a ruin from which the nation had to be saved anew. But the story of this fall after redemption ends in an eschatology, and it is in this respect that this discourse differs from a myth in the strict sense, and turns into a kind of secularized Christianism. The veterans' spirit is not dead; it remains capable of saving France a second time, provided that everyone overcomes the party spirit within him, through a kind of conversion experience. If the veterans' spirit emerges, if it enables men to speak above parties, if it materializes the superior interest of the nation, then France will indeed be saved.

This analogy with conversion can be pressed further still. The generation of the trenches is like a Church: ever present, and therefore indiscernible. There are those who went through baptism, but left the Church, veterans who let themselves be retaken by the party spirit, and there are pagans who are already saved, non-combatants who grasped the lessons of the war. The health of the nation is like the Kingdom of God, already present in redemptive sacrifice, and in the fraternity and union of the trenches, but still to come, in the reconciliation of all Frenchmen, an event both impossible and foretold. The conflict of the politician and the veteran is as unforgiving as that between the devil and grace; but it is not the opposition of two social groups in history. It is rather more intimate, the conflict that takes place within every man, who is both a veteran and a citizen responsible for party politics. And the weapons of the veterans' spirit are not those that condemn and divide: instead, they are witnessing, presence, and loyalty. In the veterans' discourse on politics, the religious commemoration of a mythology ends in moral exhortation.

This analytical sketch of the common discourse among veterans on politics poses questions as to its meaning. What is the essence of the mythical antithesis between the veteran and the politician? What is the significance of the fact that veterans approach politics precisely through this mythological discourse, and not in another way?

There are three possible interpretations, relevant to most discursive forms: (1) an interpretation in terms of the speaker, which one could denominate as 'expressive', in the sense that the text expresses the author's point of view; (2) an interpretation in terms of the audience, which might be termed 'affective', or 'conative' as linguists would say, in that it provokes in the readers a sentiment, a form of reasoning, an imagery, etc.; and (3) an interpretation in terms of the context, which one might term 'referential', in that the text arises from the situation it describes.

The second interpretation, in terms of the audience, seems less important than the other two. Certainly, we can exclude a few utterances, notably by those on the extreme right, that are very emphatic, and lack sincerity in their palpable attempt to convey discontent. Their statements are propagandistic and manipulative. But these are exceptional. For the rest, the function of speech is to deepen among veterans a sentiment of fraternity. But the authors and the public share the same milieu; they are on the same side. The affective function disappears, to be replaced by an all-important 'us' (*nous*) that brings the authors of these texts and their readers together in a common sincerity.

The first interpretation, privileging the speaker, seems more convincing, and its expressive function explains its force. We have to see in these texts evidence of a certain mentality, and in consequence, a facet of collective psychology reflecting the great trauma of 1914. The generation of fire – that is how they term themselves – remained loyal to the decisive experience of the fraternity of the trenches and the profound belief in the existence of a national collectivity with respect to which political quarrels are secondary and derisory.

This interpretation stands out, but it is a bit too simple. It neglects too grossly the concrete political situation of inter-war France. It is not that the articles surveyed here had a real referential function; we have seen that they say nothing about actual political matters. But the men who wrote these texts were, themselves, in a certain political situation, and it is probable that this situation is embedded in their discourse.

What we see are the spokesmen of the middle classes, minor bureaucrats and employees, artisans and commercial travellers, an intermediate stratum of the *petite bourgeoisie*, white-collar workers, separate from the proletariat and determined to remain so, but incompletely linked to the bourgeoisie. These people do not have a real share of power. They are not rich enough, not well enough known, not sufficiently educated, nor sufficiently influential to share power with established notables. The men in power listened to them – they were after all, voters – but then did as they pleased. The press was in the hands of the business class, which cared little for these humble provincials who were at the heart of the veterans' movement. In this political system, the veterans were marginal, and had no real access to power. They had the air of frustrated men. But, in another way, in contrast with workers, veterans could not accept their marginality as part of the domination and exploitation against which a revolutionary movement could eventuate, or that a strike could contest. The middle classes in such a marginal political situation had no other choice than to reject it in theory and in principle, in the name of democracy and national unity.

Here may lie the social function of the veterans' discourse about politics. Far from being surprising, its mythical character becomes logical. Veterans' politics is the rejection and the condemnation of a political situation that alienated sections of the middle classes from effective power. The war of 1914 embedded this attitude in an intimate conviction, at the same time as it gave it its noble character. With respect to party politics, this view permitted these marginalized petty bourgeois to vent their frustration and their anger. Here a pejorative discourse fulfils its cathartic function, and permits those who adhere to it better to tolerate their political impotence.

Here, too, we confront one of the central weaknesses of the latter years of the Third Republic. Never mind marginality, it is disaffection with the regime that is the general mood, growing in the midst of general indifference. This interpretation raises a difficult problem, since the Third Republic was, in its origins, precisely the regime of these new social strata of the provincial *petite bourgeoisie*, the very same strata who found their voice in the inter-war years in the veterans' movement. How and why, at what date, under what influences and for what reasons did the regime progressively get cut off from the very social classes that had breathed life into it in its first years ? Precisely because they seem to have nothing to say, these discourses express the social and political crisis of the Third Republic in the inter-war years. Was this a consequence of the War or of the functioning of the party system? These questions deserve further investigation.

Notes

1. H. White has chosen this sentence as an epigraph to his book: *The Content of the Form. Narrative Discourse and Historical Representation,* Baltimore, MD and London, The Johns Hopkins University Press, 1987.

2. See M. Ordinaire, *La Révision de la constitution*, Paris, 1934; J. Barthélémy, *La Crise de la démocratie contemporaine*, Paris, 1931; A. Tardieu, *La Révolution à refaire*, vol. I, *Le souverain captif,* Paris, 1936; vol. II, *La Profession parlementaire*, Paris, 1937; and also, for the Doumergue attempt of 1934, J. Gicquel and L. Sfez, *Problème de la reforme de l'État en France depuis 1931*, Paris, 1965.

3. See the *Annuaire des anciens combattants et victimes de la guerre*, Paris, 1932.

4. *Journal des Mutilés*, 4 May 1930, circulation: 405,000; subscriptions: 121,204.

5. Cassin, the celebrated Resistance leader, later winner of the Nobel Peace Prize, had been a President of the UF. Duclos and Vaillant-Couturier were among the top leaders of the French Communist Party. Pezet, an influential leader of the Fédération Nationale Catholique in 1924–6, was a member of the UNC and, after the war, a member of the French Senate for the democrat–catholic Mouvement Républicain Populaire.

6. They may be consulted in Antoine Prost, *Les Anciens combattants et la société française 1919–1940,* Paris, Presses de la FNSP, vol. III, pp. 239–44.

7. This classification reflects the orientation of the newspaper on the one hand, and that of particular authors on the other. When they differ, we privilege the author's tendency, in particular with respect to the articles of leaders of national movements, such as the UNC or the UF; these we have classed in D or G, and not in category I.

8. On syntax and usages in historical research, I have discussed different methods, and have provided a bibliography of some important words in French in my essay 'Les mots' in René Rémond (ed.), *Pour une histoire politique*, Paris, Le Seuil, 1988, pp. 255–85.

9. The expressions considered overall are, for nouns, phrases (defined by a colon or semi-colon), after any necessary elimination of relative or subordinate clauses without relevance to the expression concerned (e.g., an expression relating to a previous term not under consideration here). For adjectives, the term selected is limited to the substantives to which it is attached. The syntagmata *civic action, political action, man of politics, partisan spirit* have been considered as substantives. In the case of adverbs, the expression identified is the simple phrase that it complements or, less frequently, when they introduce a verb-complement, the latter and its subject group.

In these expressions, each term has received a double analysis: grammatical and lexical. The first consists of classifying all the uses, following the grammatical function of the term (*party* subject of an active/passive verb, etc.). This was rarely productive. The second approach examined all the uses of a term as a function of the other terms with which it is set in relation (*civic action/divide, civic action/politics,* etc.) Naturally, when the same term was present in relation to several of the terms analysed (e.g. *divide*, in relation to *civic action, party, policy*) we have sought its own lexical field, and it was at this precise stage of the analysis that the limitation of the body of work becomes apparent, for hypothetical statements of the type 'France is divided by its disputes' were not listed.

10. 33G7. External only: 23D7, 34G3. Henceforth, all direct citations of veteran's language in the text will be italicized.

11. 35H1. Qualified by *généreuse* 30F1. See also, oddly in this right-wing text: *republican*.

12. Overall, determination by an adjective is more the mark of the domain in which the policy is applied, the determination by the addition of the name, of the objective to attain. A *housing policy* (28C2, 28R2) is a policy on the development of accommodation, and this comes under discussion at the time of the Loucheur Law, which finances the construction of 200,000 low-cost housing units. See policies *for wheat, for fertilizers* (30F1), *for reparations* (23D7), *for deflation* (36I1), *on national disintegration* (29F1), but also *in relation to foreign workers* (33G6).

13. 24H4 and 34R5 acknowledge this opposition. But it can be avoided even by the extreme left, as with the ARAC (36R2 quoted below).

14. *Members belonging to all the republican parties* (35R1); *Relating all political activity to the party that one has freely chosen* (32G1); *Belonging to a party* (26G2); *Joining a party* (26G2); *Being active in the parties* (26G1); *Joining the parties, subscribing to parties* (24G2); *Friends who belong to the parties* (24G2); *An attachment to the parties* (24G3).

Negative phrases should also be mentioned : *not belonging* or *not belonging to any party* (24G2, 34F3, 39R1).

15. *Parliamentary* is rare (34E4, 33G5, 34G2), but, as we have seen, we have not systematically picked up the uses of the term. For *men of politics* and *politicians*, see below.

16. 24E3, 26I1. 28I2, 33G9. The expression is most frequently found in the syntagma *to go in for politics*: 54 out of 199.

17. 33D8. Pichot uses a very categorical future tense at the opening of a series of articles on politics: *Politics? This is not what the UF will do* (23G1). See also 24H2: *Our associations have not become involved in politics and have no intention of doing so.*

18. This kind of dispute opposed the FNCR to the UNC. See 24E3, 25D2, 36H.

19. *No politics* (22G1 29F1, 34F4, 30F1), *No party politics* (23D2), *Absolutely no politics* (24E3), *Rubbish to politics* (24G1), *No more party politics* (28F4). These 8 examples are in addition to the 54 quoted above.

20. Cf. 29R2: *the repulsion which the majority of the association shows.* See also 28D1, 24G1: *Veterans are disgusted with politics, they won't take any more. 23H2. Nothing disgusts us more than politics.* 38G2 *The veterans no longer believe in politics. They have moved from disappointment to disgust and from disgust to contempt, and those among their own number who have resorted to playing politics are far from the least disgusting element.* See also 24G2, 33D3, 31F1, 36I2.

21. 23D6 : *the determination to see France united, restored, repopulated, prosperous, grateful to those who have saved her, confident of security in a world slowly becoming pacified. This is not going in for politics in the usual meaning of the word* . . . Similarly, 24E1 spells out a whole list of aims, adding after each one the phrase *that is going in for politics*, taken from the adversaries, and clearly intended ironically.

22. 34F4. See also 36R1: *we are not going in for politics in the true sense of the word. True to our ideal, we are going in for the defence of the republic.*

23. 29D1: *You are locked into an absolute error in thinking that civic action is not concerned with politics. When you begin on a plan of civic action, when you come to methods and applications, you are touching on political problems, whether you will or no [. . .] Each time that they* [our comrades] *approach a major national principle and a matter of civic action, they will, whether they intend it or do not intend it, be going in for political action* [. . .] The same form of argument may equally lead a man of the left to resist civic action (29R4).

24. From the diachronic standpoint, it will be observed that most of the statements in which *civic action* appears predate 1930. After this the expression fell out of use. After 1934 its place was taken by *veterans' action,* a phrase that would further emphasize – if that were needed – the antithesis between veteran and politician.

25. 36R1: *the word has been too blackened by ignoble compromises.*
34F4: *its exact meaning has been bastardized by the politicians.* 23H1: *it has changed meaning as a result of the misuse that has been made of it in certain circles.* 24E3: *It often happens that it suffers misuse.*

26. In French, *propre* has a double meaning: proper and clean.

27. This distinction was formulated in a motion of 1927 (not in the text). It is quite often used (29R2, for example), but also challenged (27C1).

28. 24E2: *As for us veterans, we do not go in for politics. You should understand by this that we do not want to [. . .] get involved in the electoral hothouse.*

29. *Le Poilu d'Anjou et du Maine*, April 1923 (separate from our sample).

30. An article from outside our sample perfectly formulates this opposition: 'In the true sense of the word, "Politics" – which comes from the Greek "Polis", State, city – means: the Art/science of conducting oneself, of conducting affairs in relation to one's fellow citizens, or, to be more explicit, the conduct of the individual towards the collectivity and conversely of the collectivity towards the individual.'

In its other meaning, 'politics' is almost pejorative. 'Going in for politics' in France brings to mind a mass of deeds, words, acts that are not always beneficial for their author's reputation: the struggles of parties, of classes or of religions, of which the end-point is, very often, the realization of the personal ambitions or interests of some careerists who are more devious or more fortunate than others. For us, our choice is made : none of this kind of 'politics' (L. Excoffier, *Le Mutilé savoyard*, 1 October 1919).

31. An article in *La Voix du Combattant*, 6 March 1921, entitled 'Une politique permise' [Acceptable politics]. The following is a typical extract:

To struggle for a particular form of government; to advocate a particular formula for popular representation; or to seek a particular new division of wealth; this is what politics means, which we should avoid . . .

But do you think that we do not have 'our something to say' when it is a matter of the very existence of the nation, when it is a matter of knowing if our efforts and the sacrifices of the dead will or will not be of use? This perhaps is also politics, but of a kind permitted to us and that we think we have some authority to follow [. . .].

32. See also *political disputes* (23H1), and *disputes void of passionate politics* (34G3).

33. The French text utilizes a new word, invented for polemical purposes: *politicaillerie*.

34. 34G6. The alternative expression is *partisan battle* (38G2).

35. 26G2: *Our French Republic is placed under the rule of the parties, like all democracies.* 33E2: *Parliamentary rule supposes the existence of political parties. Whether we like it or not, it is a fact* [NB: It is striking, in this statement from the right, how the writer protects himself against any possible reproach at being an apologist for political parties.] 26H1: *The party struggle is natural, it shapes the project.* 34R3: *The battle of ideas, the*

confrontation of programmes, the struggle between the parties constitutes the very essence of democracy [. . .]. *The party struggle should continue by banning forms of violence and by respecting the freedoms of others, but it is an essential element in the normal interplay of parliamentary institutions.*

36. 28D3 What is said of the parties can equally be said of party men : *Too many men remain narrowly partisan, enclosed in obsolete or worn-out formulas* (26G1).

37. See for instance 28F3.

38. See for instance, 24E1, 26G1, 28G1, 27C1, 23D2.

39. (24 uses in F, 10 and 11 in D and E, as compared to 9 and 2 in G and H and only one in R.)

40. (*La Voix du Combattant,* 14 September 1919).

41. 24G1. See also 35H1: *All these parties with their subtle variations were only set up by jokers who lack a position of authority, by parliamentarians, of course, most of them poor devils who, like you and I, need to earn their crust and who have become politicians just as one might become a barman or a bar-keeper, an unscrupulous businessman or a banker, all of them trades without special knowledge.*

42. 25E1. Other texts emphasize the age of the parties and agree with the latter. Behind the complaint of age, there is a clash of generations. The generation of defeat faces the generation of the victory. See an article in *La Voix du Combattant,* 10 July 1926 : *The old men of the generation of defeat, these old men with their defeated minds, brought up to fear Germany, hold in our plans the place that they carved out for themselves before the war, they waste our victory, victimize us, insult us, they are leading the nation to ruin* (J. Péricard).

43. *Le Poilu d'Anjou et du Maine,* July 1921.

44. *La Voix du Combattant,* 18 September 1926.

45. Apart from developments concentrating on the party struggle, we can mention: *division ascribable to politics* : 24E3, 28F4, 28I2, 33G8, 34G3, 33E2, 29R2, 26I1, 33R1; *to parties* 24H4; *to politicians* 28F4, 34F4, 34E2, 34G3, 35R2, 36R1.

46. 34 E5. We use the word 'veteranly' in order to translate the particularity of the French text, which uses the adjectives 'combattant' and 'politique' as adverbs to characterize peoples' minds: *'pensée combattante'* and *'pensée politique'.*

47. The Conclusion of an article in *La Voix du Combattant,* 23 May 1925, entirely in this vein.

48. Landernau is a small city in the remote countryside of Britanny.

49. One of the supposed characteristics of parties in effect is their tendency to impose obedience on their members. They speak of *servitude with regard to the parties* (23D2), *politicians are prisoners of their ignoble parties* (34E4). *The politicians abdicated all liberty and independence the day that, in hopes of "arriving", they descended into party formations*

(29F5). *Whoever enters into a party takes an oath of obedience. The party goes forward, he goes forward; the party retreats, he retreats; the party votes, he votes* (36F4).

50. *Outside and above the parties* (24D1, 34I3), *of all parties* (24E1, 24E2, 24E3), *of all these pernicious parties, of political discord* (24E1). *Above the parties* (28D2, 34I2), *of all the parties* (28I1), *of party politics* (33D5). *Above and beyond parties* (34D1). All these expressions come down to the same thing, as is shown in the article 33D6 entitled *Above parties* in a commentary that has an exact bearing on this expression: *The manifesto text says, very precisely, 'above party politics'. Three words fewer or three words more, this is the expression of the same idea, the declaration of the same principle. And we could have said, as elsewhere, 'beyond and above parties' – we would have removed nothing from our idea: nor would we have added anything to it.*

Outside the UNC the theme also occurs frequently, but with a search for removal of labels, to avoid an exact stereotype: *Beyond parties and above parties* (34G6), *outside parties* (33G6), *of partisan politics* (34G3). *Above all party preoccupations* (35I1). *To win acceptance by all the parties who set the welfare of France above their own aspirations* (34G7). *Beyond and above personal ambitions or political manoeuvring* (34H5, 34G7). *To serve the nation above sordid party matters* (34H5). *It is in the search for the general interest alone above political divergence and doctrinal controversy that the welfare of the nation lies* (33G8).

51. 23D6 : *To go in for civic action is not to go in for 'politics' in the usual sense of the word, it is to rise above it, taking from it what does not belong to it; it is to float above the parties which, unless they make mock of the nation, should all come together in this territory.*

52. 23G2. An analysis of the rhetorical structure of the texts in question would here be necessary to discern the precise modalities of this break in continuity. The realization, on the other hand, however banal this may seem, is irrefutable. We will supply an example below. It can be observed that the veteran's epiphany is accompanied by verbs of action used intransitively, or with an indeterminate complement (*to construct, to rescue all*).

53. 34E4. See: 38G1: *True, not all men who clutter up the political scene are corrupt; most of them are honest men; but they go round in circles, bowed down under their differences of opinion, incapable of breaking out of the vicious circle that binds them.*

13

The Strikes of 1936: The Occupation of Factories and the Decline of Deference

In French collective memory, the strikes of the Popular Front are distinctive, a founding event that affirms simultaneously the dignity of what was then called the working class, and demonstrates its power and initiates the form of social modernity symbolized by the 'conquests' of the Matignon agreements. Yet the stakes of May–June 1936 still evade us, at least in part. The abundant historiography of the strikes has evolved in the light of various concerns, primarily directed towards an analysis of the unfolding and chronology of the movement and then the identification of political or trade unions responsibilities, yet failing to draw out its full significance. To do so is the purpose of this survey, after a brief outline of the actual events.

Three Waves of Strikes and an Agreement

Beginnings

The chronology of the strikes is well known. The first two broke out at Le Havre in the Breguet factory on 11 May, and on 13 May at the Latécoère plant at Toulouse, to protest against the dismissal of workers who went on strike on 1 May.[1] The strikes were successful after one night's occupation. In the following days, two aviation factories at Courbevoie and Villacoublay experienced identical moves. The working-class press was very restrained over the strikes during this week; the following week it was less so, and, on Sunday 24 May, the issue of *L'Humanité* that was distributed throughout the vast demonstration of 600,000 people at the *Mur des Fédérés* at Père Lachaise cemetery in Paris, presented on an inside page 'a fine series of victories in the aviation factories'. Was this article influential? Did the demonstration operate as a detonating factor in itself? Whatever the answer, the following week was marked by a first wave of strikes in aviation and vehicle factories in the Paris suburbs: Nieuport, Lavalette, Hotchkiss, Sautter-Harlé, Lioré-Ollivier, Farman and, on 28 May, Renault, Fiat, Chausson, Gnome et Rhone, Talbot, Citroën, Brandt and Salmon, as well as Le Matériel Téléphonique and the Crété printing works. Immediately after this, however, the movement appeared to stop short: the Labour Minister, Frossard, arranged a meeting between the employers' association in the metalworking and mechanical industries for the Paris region and the trades unions. The return to work appeared to be settled on 30 May, while discussions continued and on Whit Monday, 1 June, only ten factories in the Paris region were still occupied.

And yet the strike broke out again with vigour. On Tuesday 2 June, 66 factories were occupied at midday, 150 in the evening. The provinces were won over: Fives-Lille in the Nord on the same day and the Batignolles factory at Nantes the next day. Renault and Citroën renewed the strike on 4 June. On 6 June came the vote of confidence in the Chamber of Deputies and on Sunday 7 June, at 15.00 h, the opening of negotiations at the Hotel Matignon, where Léon Blum – the first President of the Cabinet in history to separate his function from his responsibility for any other – had installed himself.

The history of these agreements has recently received fresh attention. Contrary to the version given by Blum himself, a first meeting between him and the negotiators selected by the CGPF (General Confederation of French Production), MM Duchemin, Dalbouze, Lambert-Ribot and Richemond, took place during the night of 4–5 June, marking the gravity of the situation, which was felt by all concerned.[2] This meeting enabled Léon Blum to confirm that the employers would not make the evacuation of factories a prerequisite for negotiations. It also established the elements of a possible negotiation: it would concern salaries and collective agreements, but not questions of the 40-hour work week and paid holidays, imposed on employers by legislation to come. Strengthened by these assurances, Blum was able to offer to negotiate with the CGT without risking an employers' rejection that would have stalled everything. Even before the ministerial council that approved his ministerial statement, he challenged the workers at midday on 5 June, 'to submit to the law over the sections of their claims that should be regulated by law, and to pursue other elements in a mood of calm, dignity and discipline'. This was the precise setting within which he established his intervention.

The 1936 Strikes: Factory Occupations and Declining Deference

The Matignon Accords, announced early on 8 June, did not prevent this second wave of strikes – indeed, the movement was extended to new occupations. Department stores went on strike on 6 June; on 8 June it was the Paris building and insurance trades, while prompt negotiations ensured that the banks did not come out on strike. By the middle of the week the number of strikers had reached 1,500,000.[3] The tide began to turn slowly at the end of the week, while the CGT, the Communist Party and the Socialist Party mobilized for a return to work. In the evening of Thursday 11 June the Communist activists, gathered together in a gymnasium – and not in a factory under occupation – listened to Thorez as he used the famous phrase: 'It is important to know how to end a strike as soon as satisfaction has been gained.' But in order for the strike to end, local negotiations must come to a conclusion, and they could be long-drawn-out. The Paris metalworking industry returned to work on 15 June. At the end of the month, with holidays and the first paid leave approaching, the strikes appeared to be coming to an end.

However, a third wave of strikes developed in late June – early July. The sectors affected this time were the peaceful or strongly unionized sectors on the one hand, where the workforce had initially chosen negotiation, and small craft enterprises where the owners could not implement wage increases on the other. In Haute-Vienne, for example, the fairly heavily unionized porcelain and shoe-making workers did not go on strike in June; the first strikes broke out in the construction sector early in July.[4] A wave of strikes even broke out in the Loiret in small businesses at the end of June.[5] The first strikes in the Finistère, essentially in Brest, broke out immediately after the Matignon Accords, and the rest of the *département* was affected at the end of June and the beginning of July, notably in the construction industry.[6] Near Le Havre, the spinning and weaving works at Graville went on strike on 25 June; their occupation of the premises did not end until 14 August.[7] This last wave of strikes was not as significant as its two predecessors, but it considerably increased the impression that the whole of France was affected. In fact only three *départements* out of 90 completely escaped strikes in May–July 1936.

More than 12,000 businesses were affected by the strikes in all, with nearly 9,000 of them experiencing occupation.[8] Although they did not affect railways, postal services, the civil service or local government, state-owned factories in the Paris region or the insurance sector, the scale of strikes in the private sector was unprecedented.

Compared with the great strikes of 1906–1910 and 1919–20 they are impressive not only for their strength but also for the coherence of their timing and even more for the new form that they took, the occupation of the place of work. It was a true 'social explosion that hit the Blum ministry at the very moment of its inception'.[9]

Strikes from Below

An explanation was already on offer in June 1936 to explain both the pattern of the movement – the factory occupations – and its concentration in the weeks when the Blum government was under construction: that of a communist plot.[10] This is not a theory that requires much consideration.[11] One point is that it is not based on any element of proof whatsoever, while there is ample evidence of the prompt wish of the PCF to limit the movement and then to bring it to an end in good order. At Renault, where the strike broke out on 28 May, the Communist section called for the resumption of work on the 29th at the cost of an agreement with the management considered derisory by F. Lehideux, member of the board of the company, while *L'Humanité* spoke of an 'enthusiastic parade'.[12] There was also the involvement of Thorez on 11 June, and over the next few days *L'Humanité* was unequivocal. Further, the communist conspiracy theory comes up against two major improbabilities. The first is strategic in nature: the PCF was far too calmly submissive to the injunctions of the Comintern to undertake destabilization in a country where, faced with Hitler's Germany, power had implications for Stalinist diplomacy. The second was tactical: if the PCF were to launch strikes, why would this occur in areas of industry in which it was relatively weak, and not in the public services, where it was much stronger?[13] The origins of the movement must be sought elsewhere.

Responsibility cannot be imputed to the extreme left: the CGT revolutionary unionism, like the Troskyites, was far too weak to have carried weight. There was still the CGT, given fresh dynamism by the unions reunification; but all witnesses describe it as caught out by the movement, as its secretary general Léon Jouhaux himself acccepted on 15 June: 'the movement broke out without anyone knowing exactly how or where'.[14] Further, the strikes here correspond even less than in the case of the PCF to the sectors of strong representation: rates of unionization were particularly low in the sectors with large-scale strikes, such as metalwork (4 per cent), textiles

(5 per cent) or the food industries (3 per cent), against 22, 44, 36 and 35 per cent in the railways, posts, public services and teaching, which escaped strikes.[15] The ultimate example is that of the department stores, which experienced a particularly spectacular strike despite having no union representation at all, nor indeed any communist cell.

It is therefore obvious that no political force or national union wanted these strikes. They came from below, from the foundations and not from the summit, from staff headquarters. This is why they can be considered spontaneous. This should not turn into a caricature showing workers responding to some sort of sudden and irrational impulse. To call the strikes spontaneous is to stress that they were responding to local initiatives; but these initiatives were often taken by militants, particularly by comunists[16] who – in some cases over several years – devoted themselves to creating the conditions for a new business power-relationship.[17] It was during this 'prehistory' of the strikes that the militant networks were established that in 1936 formed the basis of success in some large factories.[18]

At Renault the strike broke out on 28 May in the workshops that were most strongly controlled by the communist organization; national representatives – Costes, Frachon, Hénaff – immediately arrived to give support.[19] And the very first strike with factory occupation, at Breguet in Le Havre, had been carefully prepared by a well-known communist militant, Louis Eudier.[20] How could the militants have acted otherwise? The strike did not take them by surprise: they had been working on it for a long time, and they looked forward to it; they seized the favourable opportunity created by the victory of the Front populaire and the hope thereby born among the workforce.

But the success exceeded their expectations and offered proof of a new climate. To conclude from such militant initiatives that either the party or the CGT, at their central level, would have launched the strike would be to go too far; these cases are limited to a few businesses, far less numerous than those that came out on strike out of contagion, without preparing a list of claims in advance, and where one could search in vain for a single union member. No organization whatever, in fact, could have created such an extraordinary climate, where strike and factory occupation appeared to be accepted as the model of what should be done. The collective movement capable of sweeping through companies exceeded the capacity of the organizations. Proof of this lies in the difficulties that they experienced in attempting to channel and tame it and to give it a satisfactory outcome.

Causes of the Movement

The short-term political pattern

The social explosion of 1936 was an intrinsic feature of a strikingly original political climate. More relevant here than the result of the election are the conditions in which the Popular Front won it and the movement that brought the new majority to power.

Judged only by the number of votes, the 1936 election was no landslide. It is true that the centre of gravity on the left shifted: the Communist Party made great advances, while the radicals dropped back, leaving the Socialist Party as the main element of the coalition and enabling it to lead the government for the first time in French history. But although the Front Populaire led the Right by some 1,200,000 votes, the gain compared to the 1932 election – won by the cartel of left-wing parties that inclined so little to the left – was less than 300,000 votes.[21] This was no great margin, despite the clear-cut nature of the victory.

It takes on its full meaning from the popular mobilization that preceded it. The shock of the violent right-wing demonstration 6 February 1934 gave the Left as a whole the impression of a major fascist threat that required the mobilization of all democratic forces as a matter of urgent necessity. This was evident from the broad-based demonstrations of 12 February 1934: everywhere, thousands of demonstrators assembled and made it clear that they felt that action was an absolute duty; at Cognac, for example, where for the first time the socialists filed through the streets with their red banner.[22] It was truly the hour to step forward and be counted.

Work for the municipal elections of 1935, as for the legislative election of 1936, was not limited to meetings in school playing-fields. It was a period of countless parades and public meetings.[23] It was not enough for the political organizations to state their case in newspapers, tracts and posters: they showed themselves in vast processions, marching in great numbers behind streamers that announced their arrival. Mobilization operated in the street, and demonstrations became the chosen form of affirmation and propaganda, to the extent that in October 1935 the public authorities were forced to pass a decree requiring advance notice, indirectly granting them the recognition and legal status that they lacked.

These demonstrations were one of the settings for the emergence of a Front Populaire that combined the Republican heritage with class struggle, just as it combined tricolor flags and red banners. This antifascist, democratic and popular culture – popular in the sense that the entire nation was rallying against right-wing activists – 'arises from a mass education system that speaks to the group and not the individual, revalues emotions long disparaged and aestheticizes the mass movement'.[24] The demonstrations show a huge body of people in which the working-class masses are a unified element, a people pacific but strong, determined, sure of the justice of their cause and its legitimacy, for they see themselves as the descendants of the nation of the cathedrals, of Joan of Arc and of the French Revolution.[25] The films produced by trade unions or the Communist party at the time are an excellent illustration of this movement. 'France does not belong to the French, for it belongs to the 'two hundred families': France does not belong to the French, it belongs to those who are looting it', states, fairly dramatically, *La vie est à nous*, directed by Renoir in January 1936 at the request of the Communist Party. And *Les bâtisseurs*, financed by the Fédération du batiment in 1938, opens with a sequence in which two workers repairing the spire of Chartres cathedral present themselves as the descendants of the *compagnons* of the 12th century, stating that the cathedrals were 'like the houses of the people' – before the film runs through the whole of France's architectural heritage, from the Renaissance châteaux to the Eiffel Tower and the building-site of the Palais d'Iéna in Paris.[26] The 1936 election was not a poll like others; it was the culmination of this powerful political and cultural movement in which the nation as one made its wholehearted claim to the national heritage.

The social explosion of 1936 was primarily the expression of the same political culture, in the workspace. It is possible that here and there the occupations may have been a way of taking up the gauntlet at the outset of negotiations, or a guarantee against the threat of violence from outside. But it is striking how little they had been discussed: they are accepted as 'something that had to be done'. The fact is that, within the culture of the Front Populaire, factory occupations were the social equivalent of political demonstrations.

In workplaces too, it was time to show one's hand. It was not enough to stop work; the employers must be made to realize the numbers, determination and power that faced them. Although peaceful, like most of the demonstrations, factory occupation is an exercise in intimidation: to show strength, perhaps to avoid being forced to use it – and the setting ensured that it was seen as such. For this presentation, this orchestration, where should people gather together unless it be in the place of work itself? Being out in the street, a public space, was appropriate for gathering supporting opinion. But it was the boss, the managers, who must feel this power, which was now aware of itself. Factory occupation was essential to the workers as the most natural thing to do, to assert literally and symbolically both their own existence and their collective power. This was more important than the claims themselves, and that is why they often occupied the factory before discussing what they wanted of their bosses: strike and occupation first, list of demands next.

The Intermediate Term of the Economic Crisis

This cultural interpretation of the social explosion of the Front Populaire allows little space for economic causes. Yet common sense, shared by most historians, tends to view the economic crisis of the 1930s as its strongest explanation. This interpretation sees the working class, hard hit by unemployment and extreme poverty, rising up, pushing the Front Populaire to power, and expecting it to improve its fate substantially. Before looking at the role of cultural elements, would it not be easier, and more sensible, to recognize the full importance of material factors?

A first point strikes the observer: the steadiness of basic wages. Calculated on base 100 in 1930, the wage index dropped very little, staying at 94.6 from August 1935 to May 1936. Yet during the same period, retail prices dropped considerably: calculated on the same base 100 in 1930, the consumer retail prices index reached its lowest point, 74, in August 1935 and still stood at 76.4 in May 1936. This means that purchasing power, in other words the workers' standard of living, not only did not drop but actually improved appreciably during the economic crisis. According to Alfred Sauvy's calculations this represented an improvement of 23.8 per cent in May 1935, on the eve of the Front Populaire.[27]

In fact this analysis, which contradicts common sense, includes a bias that makes it unsustainable: it is based on the statistical sets of hourly rates for workers in mechanical industries in the Paris region. But the hourly wage-rate is not a sound indicator of worker income when unemployment bites. For a more precise understanding of wage-earners' standards of living, it is essential to recognize unemployment in all its forms.

First, there is complete unemployment. Its development is very difficult to trace back, for the published series concern unemployment benefit, which increased steadily, in line with the creation of council aid funds for the unemployed. The only plausible figure is that of the census for March 1936, which shows 864,000 when the crisis was at its deepest point.[28] This is high, but relatively low in relation to neighbouring countries. True, the relatively low level of complete unemployment relates to specific features of the French industry at the time. Home-working was still very significant, absorbing fluctuations in economic activity as commercial businesses sub-contracted to piece-workers at times of full activity in order to avoid laying off staff in slack periods; and home-workers without work were not seen as unemployed.[29] But the main reason was one of demography.

The labour-force available for work had dropped in size considerably between 1931 and 1936: from one census to the next the active population, unemployed included, shrank by 1,760,000, including 1,423,000 manual workers. In one way this diminution can be explained by looking back at the country of origin of many immigrants: suffering a chronic shortage of labour, Malthusian France turned instead to immigration. When the crisis struck, immigrants were sent back home in trainloads; as a result, their number dropped sharply between 1931 and 1936, from 2,715,000 to 2,198,000. Taking naturalizations into account, the total number of foreigners who left France may be evaluated at nearly 400,000. From another – and more significant – point of view, the contraction in the active population was a consequence of the war of 1914. In 1916 the number of births was less than half the pre-war rate in a normal year. In all, the deficit of births due to the war was around 1.4 million: and the generation born during the war was leaving school and starting work during the economic crisis, a factor that strongly reduced the active population, because its rate of replacement was much smaller than it should have been.[30]

A third reason explains the relatively limited scale of complete unemployment in France during the economic crisis: the arbitration of many employers in support of partial unemployment. This was partly the counterpart of paternalism: employment was not at that time the variable feature that it has become today, and many owners saw it as a moral duty to provide employment for their workers. But they also saw it as operating in their own interests. In sectors of industry that were still very craft-based, very often using old machinery, the skill of the labour-force was a major advantage: rather than dismissing good workmen who would be difficult to replace once the crisis was past, it seemed wiser to retain them and leave them without work for a day or two each week.[31]

Partial unemployment, in fact, should not be overlooked. The index of hours worked calculated by Sauvy (base 100 in 1930) falls to 90.1 in May 1932, rises over 94 in the winter of 1933–4, and then falls again to 90.8 in April 1935. At the time of the parliamentary election, it had risen again to 95.[32] The average length of the working week, established at 47.8 hours in 1930 in finishing industries, dropped by more than three hours, settling at 44.4 hours in 1935. Naturally these figures are only averages, and specific circumstances offer a contrast: alongside businesses working for six eight-hour days were others operating for less than 40 hours per week.

Overall, however, the scale of unemployment was not so severe as to force workers as a whole into destitution. To cancel out the positive effect of price cuts on the workers' standard of living on a virtually constant hourly wage-rate would have meant cutting hours by more than 20 per cent; yet at the worst moment the effect of partial unemployment appears to cut workers' income by around 10 per cent, while in the 1936 census total unemployment represented 8.6 per cent of wage-earners overall (unemployed included). The circumstances of the unemployed were insecure, but overall analysis of wages, prices and employment established that working-class destitution was not the main cause of the Front Populaire and its social explosion.

This is not to say that the economic crisis had no effect: but its effects were of another order.

The Long-term Trend of Taylorization

Comprehension of these effects requires a wider view of the business reaction to the developing crisis. It was a crisis with an external source, in the international market. In 1928 Poincaré stabilized (devalued) the franc at a level that favoured French business, giving it an exchange advantage, while *rentiers*, living off their rents and savings, would have preferred a stronger revaluation.[33] This advantage was gradually eroded by reductions in world prices, until the devaluation of the pound in 1931, and then of the dollar in 1933, reversing the situation completely. From that time on, the refusal to devalue, which favoured the *rentiers*, made French prices prohibitive on the world market. In order to retain at least some of their markets, businessmen were forced to reduce their costs; considerably. Unemployment enabled them to cut back production while sustaining the price of what they produced. The drop in wages reduced costs but, as we have seen, the drop observed did not match the scale of the problem. In order, therefore, to reduce the costs of production, another solution had to be sought.

Taylorization offered just such an alternative: to produce more for the same labour input and achieve greater productivity. This was possible because the movement had been in operation for a long time. The principles of Taylorism were introduced into France by Henry Le Chatelier, beginning in 1906, and some industrialists, such as Berliet and Renault, began to work on these principles before the war. They were introduced for limited manufacturing runs in war factories and extended at the end of the war, particularly in the automobile industry and railway repair work. The process was long and gradual: introduction of the production line was carried out in stages and not limited to chain production lines. Gradually this particular element became more precisely defined: equipment was raised to be within the worker's reach; the stopping time at each post, initially very long, was reduced. Work was gradually automated: some photographs of Renault line production in the late 1920s show screwdrivers and hammers still visible next to goods for machining.[34] But the process was in operation.[35]

It accelerated through the years of reconstruction, with the creation in 1926 of the Comité national de l'organisation francaise (CNOF), the Commission d'études générales de l'organisation scientifique du travail (CEGOS) the next year, and then the opening of a chair of Scientific Management at the Conservatoire national des Arts et Métiers. In Geneva the International Labour Office set up conferences on work organization. After founding his company in the United States, in 1927 Charles Bedaux created a subsidiary branch in France that began to foster the system of wages for productivity that bears his name. In short, when the crisis broke out, rationalization of production was being introduced and the tools for its expansion were in place. Symbols and temples of this rationalized industrial production, the great car factories designed round production-line working came to dominate the Paris landscape, with Renault at the Ile Seguin (1930) and Citroën at the Quai de Javel (1933).

Faced with the crisis, which forced down production costs, rationalization flourished. In the Anzin coal mines the Bedaux system of wages by points was introduced in 1932: timed measurements determined the value of the payment-point based on the average quantity of coal cut in one minute. The miner who 'made' 60 points in an hour received the agreed wage: if he 'made' 75 points in the hour, the 15 extra points were paid to him, minus 25 per cent. This system was widely applied in mechanical construction, and particularly in the great Taylorized factories such as Renault, Chausson, etc. Simone Weil's *Journal d'usine*[36] gives a clear description of its functioning: if the agreed production is not achieved, the worker does not 'make' the number of points necessary to win the agreed wage (bench-mark rate). This pattern of wages led not only to paying relatively less for goods produced in excess of what was forecast in the time set (the bonus); above all it forced the workers – who did not understand the detail, because the complexity of the system discouraged any analysis – to keep up their output in order not to be penalized.

This rationalization provided businesses with a gradual means of improving their productivity, and thus of reducing their unit costs by obtaining greater production for the same wages. It was a matter of increasing the pace. This was imposed on the workers by middle managers, who Simone Weil showed in operation: overseers and workshop heads were no longer the highly skilled professionals of the old workshop, and their task consisted entirely of allocating work and keeping up the pace. They became true 'sergeants' of the work army, to use a long-established metaphor: their authority, without appeal, was increasingly impossible to oppose, as unemployment became so widespread that workers feared the loss of their jobs. Prompt dismissal soon befell those who did not maintain the pace, as the frail and clumsy Simone Weil discovered several times over and as *La vie est à nous* depicts, with an old worker whose dismissal for failing to maintain the pace sparks off a strike.

Such conditions help explain the explosion of the Front Populaire. The crisis did not plunge the workforce into destitution; but it was felt as systematic overwork, an intensification of pace and an increase in disciplinary constraints. It was this set of circumstances which was wholeheartedly rejected in May–June 1936. Although the social movement took its forms of expression from the Front Populaire's cultural and political movement, the underlying cause was the overwork that Taylorization made possible and that the crisis spread far and wide.

This analysis enables us to understand many aspects of this unprecedented social confrontation – at first, the fact that it began and took root spectacularly in precisely the mechanical and automobile engineering factories where Taylorization had made the greatest progress and where the most intensive pace was set; but in other sectors, wages by result were also a direct factor – for example, in the dispatch department of La Samaritaine, where the Bedaux system was applied,[37] or in the Arthur Martin factories at Revin.[38] On all sides, arbitrary dismissals for shortfalls in production were involved.

Secondly, the main worker achievements of 1936 were specifically concerned with time: the 40–hour week and holidays with pay. To escape the constraints of paced work and the arbitrary authority of the little bosses who imposed them – this was what the Front Populaire proposed. But it was not content to create free time in this way, a time for leisure and recreation: even within the work-time, it introduced a counter-power that made it possible to limit exploitation – shop stewards.

We are not sufficiently aware of the distinct change introduced into workshops and factories by collective agreements and shop stewards. First, in a certain number of cases, the agreements concluded introduced the end of the Bedaux system as, for example, at La Samaritaine or in the coal mines of the Nord and the Pas-de-Calais.[39] And where it had not been formally abandoned, the overseers, discredited and poorly backed by the company hierarchy – the reason for the Renault overseers' strike on 22 March 1937[40] – could no longer force obedience to the pace set. As soon as they attempted to do so, the delegates elected by the workers brought the workshop out on strike. Simone Weil analysed this new situation well in her report commissioned by the CGT on the struggle in the north: 'On paper, work at piece–rate is maintained, but things happen to some extent as if it no longer existed; in any case, the rate of work has lost its obsessive nature, the workers are tending to return to the natural pace of work.'[41] The overseers are 'completely disoriented'. Far more than the forty hours, *pace* Sauvy, it was this return to a 'natural' pace that explains why industrial production did not take off as the government expected. Work picked up again after the strikes, but not as before.

The social explosion of the Front Populaire was also born out of the encounter among three temporalities that cut across each other, extended each other and resonated together like waves of different frequency: the long period of Taylorization that spread across the greater part of the twentieth century and installed new forms and conditions of workshop organization; the middle-term effects of the economic crisis, which held down production costs at the same time improving rates of payment for piecework and speeding up work-rates; and finally the short-term effects of politics, which in this case played the role of the immediate fuse or detonator that set things in motion.

And yet this explanation does not take into account the totality of the phenomenon. Although it enables us to understand that a social movement of great scale came about, it tells us nothing about the particular forms that it took. It explains the strikes, not the factory occupations.

The Meanings of the Occupations

A Revolutionary Perspective?

For many observers, the factory occupations had revolutionary significance. At the time, most owners saw them as the beginnings of sovietization,[42] an accusation sustained by an uneasy right-wing press. The textile industry employers' organization to Blum: 'It was in reality an essentially revolutionary movement, characterized by occupation of workplaces undertaken in violation of any legality.'[43] The same analysis was shared by historians on the left of the Socialist Party, who after the war reproached Léon Blum for being faint-hearted: Jacques Danos and Marcel Gibelin first of all, then Colette Audry, Daniel Guérin and, more recently, Jacques Kergoat.[44]

To a large extent the discussion is based on the meaning of words, and could begin with a long dissertation on the real meaning of 'revolution'. It is undoubtedly true that a major social movement like that of the Front Populaire (or, again, that of 1968), introduces a period of uncertainty in which the immediate future can only be foreseen with great difficulty by those involved. It is equally certain that none of the major collective activists of the time sought to develop matters towards a revolution. More than the strikers' objectives, the question posed by the factory occupations is that of their intentions. What did the strikers want to say through their factory occupations?

Historians who show them with a revolutionary vision answer this question in the same way as the employers at the time: they 'questioned the owners' right to own their business'.[45] Arguments in this direction appears regularly. The workers in the Delespaul biscuit factory, who put their factory back into work on 4 July, are quoted, or declarations such as that of Gauthier, secretary of the Paris metalworkers, on 6 June: 'On all sides, our comrades insist that we intervene with the ministries of the air and of war and the postal services.' Otherwise, declared the factory workers, we will take over production management ourselves.[46] Jacques Kergoat stresses, rightly, that such threats were not empty. But they were, after all, only simple threats, and they were rare; it would be more convincing to offer other examples rather than over-stating the 'on all sides' of this quotation to give it a degree of generality.

Conversely, the historians who contest this thesis have emphasized the strikers' total lack of concern for the company's financial records, although they were available, and their attitude towards owners, in which indifference far outweighed aggressiveness. This was noted by Jean Coutrot, a modernist engineer, employer and consultant, who visited many factories and who wrote in the heat of the action, and his account is confirmed by Henri Prouteau.[47] The strikers had no thought of getting rid of the owners. The occupation was not the onset of a movement to be expanded, it did not mark the birth of new times; it was explicitly experienced as a parenthesis as far as the owners' power was concerned. The famous article by Simone Weil is very clear on this point: 'Of course, this hard life will begin again in a few days. But we don't think about it, *we are like soldiers on leave during the war*. And then, whatever may happen afterwards, we will always have had this. In the end, for the first time, and for ever, other memories will hover round these heavy machines than silence, constraint, submission' and then, 'They know very well that despite the improvements gained, the weight of social oppression that was pushed aside for a moment will fall back on them again. They know that once again they will be submitted to rigid domination, arid and impersonal.'[48]

Other factors confirm this account, beginning with the care shown by the strikers to maintain equipment, clean machinery and organize site supervision: it was important to deny the owners any cause for complaint when work began again. The sales assistants in the department stores pushed their scrupulousness even further when they slept on the floor beside lounge chairs or sofas, to ensure that no one could charge them afterwards with having soiled or damaged the stock. Clearly, the occupation was not the opening move towards expropriation: the strikers looked ahead to the owners' return and took precautions to forestall any possible retaliation; they did not see themselves in a revolutionary setting of power in which they could replace the owners on a permanent basis. The meaning of the phenomenon must be sought elsewhere.

Struggle and Festival

For these reasons it is tempting to focus analysis not on the actual occupation itself but on its forms: and what is immediately striking is the festive aspect of the strike. Over a long period I followed the approach of many other commentators[49] in emphasizing this aspect, insisting on the break with daily life that the occupation represented: time was abolished, machines lay silent, work ceased, groups of people chatted together, space was rearranged for other purposes and parties were organized: people danced. Simone Weil's text, so often quoted, is essential here as the most explicit and pertinent account: 'Quite apart from the claims, the strike was a joy in itself. Joy, pure. Joy, unalloyed . . .'.[50] And the whole of the following page is based on a grammatical rhetoric beginning with 'Joy . . .': 'Joy at going into the factory . . . Joy at running through . . .', etc. Fifty years later, in a less literary style, a department store sales assistant echoed her words: 'It's a genuinely happy memory. We didn't have much idea of how things would turn out, but we had a very good time. There was dancing, parties . . . people sang; we were enjoying our-selves, in fact! *Even though we knew that afterwards we would be going back to work.* We had a good time together.'[51]

This view of the factory occupations has been faulted for failing to record the level of tension inside the factories. One must not forget, in fact, that the factory occupation also represented a form of blackmail, a trump card seized by the strikers both to forearm themselves against any strike-breaking attempt to get the factory working again and to make the owners more conciliatory. This tactic had already been tried here and there, at Chenard-et-Walker in 1931, provoking evacuation by the police, and then a few months later at Babcock & Wilcox.[52] They had not been forgotten, and there had been a fresh and unsuccessful attempt at Chenard-et-Walker in March 1935. In the Nord, from 13 to 18 November 1929 the Forges et Acieries du Nord et de l'Est at Trith-Saint-Léger had similarly suffered a sit-down strike, in other words a partial occupation.[53] In December 1935 the secretary of the Communist union of metal workers, Mus-meaux, reproached the Louvroil strikers with having left the factory: 'If you had held out for 24 hours inside, you would have had every-thing you wanted, and the *gendarmes mobiles* wouldn't have been able to push you out of your workshops.'[54] The first occupation, of Breguet at Le Havre, followed exactly the same pattern, and the forces of order did not risk the forcible evacuation of the workshops, where the strikers were threatening to destroy a seaplane prototype.

The 1936 Strikes: Factory Occupations and Declining Deference

Occupation, a tactical weapon, did not give strikers absolute security, even though the change of government now made it unlikely that the police would force evacuation in the future – a factor that changed everything. Tension continued. Many accounts show the occupiers on their guard, anxious to meet management attempts at regaining control, vaguely afraid of outside intervention. The occupied factory, guarded by pickets, immediately came under siege. Celebration, when it broke out, was indeed a true celebration, and the strikers' delight a true delight; but that did not disguise the fact that the celebration was not a spontaneous event: for the strike committee, it was also a way of maintaining morale and resisting both disorder and the enemy.

These comments led me to subdivide the strikes to some degree, and to say that they unfolded at two levels simultaneously: the level of claims and that of celebration.[55] One level of instrumental action, and another of symbolic expression. I compared the concept of revolution, the attempt to realize an ideal, with the strikes of 1936, which I saw as the expression of this ideal. The celebration that accompanied the strikes was not irrelevant, it did not represent merely the pleasure of being together or the wish to enjoy oneself: it had a meaning, it said something about the working-class community, its freedom, dignity and sovereignty. This led me to consider that the occupations had not become a myth, but that they were a mythic event from the beginning, and had been lived as such. In this reading, the occupation revealed men and women to themselves – which is why they never forgot it. I returned to the conclusion of J. Lhomme, who saw June 1936 as 'more a *crisis of conscience* than a crisis in the absolute meaning of the expression'.[56]

I still find this analysis accurate, but it needs to be extended in two ways. First, by making a closer link between the register of struggle and that of celebration. An affirmation of a freedom won in the hours and area of work, the celebration is a symbolic expression of what is actually at stake in the struggle. We find here the link between strike and celebration that had already structured the May Day demonstrations, when successful. The fact of not working that day represented a freedom and an emancipation embodied in the festive day in the area of emotion and symbolism, like a collective awakening of awareness and a principle of hope.[57] Secondly, it is right to give greater importance to the fact that the occupation, like the strike, was general. The general strike was an entirely original phenomenon, which gave the French worker movement a specific character. Other industrial countries have had more strikes, but none of them has seen a movement as widespread or as long as those of 1936, 1968 or 1995. In the outbreak of strikes and factory occupations, even before claims were identified, there is the intention to act in the same way as others, not to be singled out, in other words to demonstrate membership of a wider community. In its very generalization, the strike exceeded the simple struggle for a claim to confirm the existence and strength of a solidly unified group and to bring owners and management to recognize the true existence of all its elements, of legitimate needs and consideration. On a more emotional register, these acts express membership of a community, class consciousness and an acknowledgement of this condition throughout society. This set of feelings is fully heartfelt within the celebration. In fact, trade unions placed celebration at the heart of their representations of the strikes. The film shot at the time by film technicians on strike, *Grèves d'occupation*, is entirely devoted to

Figure 13.1: Striking workers inside the work-site. Some give the clenched-fist salute, others dance, most are peacefully waiting till the picture is taken. A self-representation of the 1936 strikers published by the weekly *La Vie ouvrière,* close to the communist wing of the CGT. (*Courtesy of the* Centre d'histoire sociale *of the CGT*)

them. At the core of the profound satisfaction that gave the occupations their unique and unforgettable character lies not only the sense of a dignity rediscovered and affirmed – loud and strong – but the emotion of a brotherhood and a shared destiny.

These comments do not, however, refute the fundamental contradiction around which the interpretation of 1936 has been located. It is true that the workers' factory occupations challenged the relationship with the owner and his authority, but they did not contest explicitly either his right of ownership or even his management role. And yet the owners saw the occupation as the denial of their power and the right of ownership on which it was founded. So, what was really at stake?

Private Space, Public Spaces

That property was the basis of ownership power constitutes a fact that need not detain us, except to draw consequences from it as to the very nature of this power. Property being private, the power exercised by the owner in what he often called his 'house' was for him also in the domain of the private. For the workers it implied not only submission in their work, but a form of deference or gratitude – in any case, a personal link. The owners naturally used their power to defend their economic interests – and also a specific concept of their role, their social image. The conversation reported by Simone Weil is enlightening on this point: 'The owner is the most hated person. Detested by everyone. And yet he's the one who provides everyone's living. How odd it is, this unfairness. Yes, hated by everyone – once, at least there was respect. I can remember, when I was young . . . – That's over now – Yes, even where the place is well run . . . Oh, the monsters have done all they needed to bring us to this. *But they will pay for it*.'[58] It was unfair that the owners were hated: because they 'made a living' for their workers, the latter were obligated to them and owed them a form of gratitude.

This feeling was naturally stronger among the owners of small and medium businesses than in the largest companies. The managers of the limited liability companies were less directly concerned than the owner-managers running their own industrial companies, and this difference was very widely emphasized.[59] It explains the contradictions that produced the explosion of owner organization after the Matignon accords and introduced its restructuring.[60] It was not simply a matter of economic divergence, with the small businesses encountering greater difficulty in absorbing wage rises than the big Taylorized companies, where work could be organized in several shifts. It was primarily a matter of representations: how the workers saw the owner, and how the workers were supposed to see the owner. This was what sometimes made discussion with the workers impossible. Gabriel Cognac, owner of La Samaritaine department store, agreed to receive a delegation, but he choked with anger, 'exploded, banged on the table, spoke of ingratitude: 'Work makes me ill . . .' and the meeting was cut short.'[61] A caricature of an example of this attitude, but significant, comes from the owner of three cotton factories in the Côte d'Or who, in a letter to the Prefect, spoke of 'the feelings that we would like to see predominating among our hands, so that they can earn our forgiveness for their unacceptable conduct'; before taking his workers on again after the strike, he forced them to sign an act of contrition in the following terms:

> *Regretting our bad behaviour towards you in going on strike, we beg you to forgive us and, in taking us on, to enable us to regain our place in the future through exemplary behaviour. Thanking you in advance, Monsieur Marchal, we beg you to accept our respectful greetings.*[62]

It was precisely this personal link that the strikers rejected, in large companies as well as in smaller concerns. At Sautter-Harlé, the overall boss attempted to encourage 'his workers' to return to work. The representative of the strike committee 'leaped onto the work bench, interrupted the boss and made an improvised speech in which he made the workers understand that they were not the owner's workers, and made the owner understand that the workers were not 'his' workers. The owner had to leave the scene amidst jeering.'[63] This was how June 1936 delivered the death blow to paternalism and created a profound rupture. Jean-Paul Sartre perceived it clearly, and depicted it in *L'enfance d'un chef*. His hero, Lucien Fleurier, is the son of an industrialist and expected to follow in his footsteps. When he was small, and went out for a walk with his father, 'we met papa's workers and they greeted papa', calling him Monsieur and taking off their caps as they talked, while Lucien and his father kept theirs on. At an unspecified date, but one that the context shows to be around the time of the Front Populaire, 'the attitude of M. Fleurier's workers had changed considerably . . . When Lucien went out on a little stroll with papa on Sundays, the workers barely touched their caps on seeing them, and some even crossed the road to avoid having to greet them.'[64]

What was at stake in the factory occupations was the essential nature of the link between owners and workers, that of the contract of labour. Whether or not the factory belonged to the owner was of little importance here; what counted was that the owner was not at home in the same sense as he was at home in his own house with his family. Paternalism, which for owners embodied the right way to fulfil their role, was challenged at its very foundations. The business was not a large family, and the workers were not domestic servants; they did not join the company for anything except a fixed form of work, recompensed with a set wage. They expected no kindness or personal benefaction from the owners, and owed them in return no servitude, no allegiance, no deference. The contract of labour was public in nature, and its content should be subject, not to an impossible form of personal negotiation between each wage-earner and his employer, but to negotiation between trade unions and employers as a category. The great novelty, in this respect, is the *collective* conventions, and it is revealing that they only became generalized after the Front Populaire, despite being introduced in a law of 1919.

As a collective convention, it determines the legitimate form of authority in the workshop and excludes any form of arbitrariness. This is why the question of lower-ranking managers and their power is so crucial: in a public space regulated by general rules, the arbitrary power of lesser chiefs, who at a whim can dispatch a wage-earner to unemployment, is no longer tolerable. Workshop delegates are there to see the rules respected and to give public and collective expression to staff problems. In the department stores, one of the fundamental claims was for a disciplinary council, to avoid arbitrary dismissal. The question of hiring and dismissal was posed everywhere, exasperating owners who expected to select their staff and to take into consideration criteria of behaviour outside work – which might have meaning if it was a matter of domestic staff being introduced into the intimacy of family life and to whom one's children might be handed over, but which are here displaced into the public space of the factory, the shop or the department store.

With the Front Populaire the workspace thus moved out of the private sphere and joined the public arena. The work contract did not form a personal tie of submission but a functional link for production. Wage-setting was immediately implicated; no longer related to goodwill or the owner's generosity but to collective convention,

with obligatory procedures of conciliation and arbitration established to settle disagreements on this point.[65] Private ownership of
the business existed, but the owner's power was framed in formal
regulations that defined what the owner had the right to expect of
his employees.

Nothing illustrates this central stake of the Front Populaire better
than an anecdote reported by Bénigno Cacérès. At the time he was
working for a small construction company in Toulouse. One Sunday
morning, as he was sitting outside his house and enjoying the air,
his boss happened to walk by. Greetings were exchanged, a conversation followed, and his owner requested a service of him: 'By the way,
I've left my car over there, it would be very kind if you could find a
moment to wash it this morning.' And Cacérès replied, 'I'm sorry,
Monsieur, there's no provision for that in the collective convention.'

At the end of this fresh examination, what is undoubtedly the most
striking feature in the Front Populaire is the fit between worker gains
and the economic, social and political situation. The 40-hour week
and paid holidays were a response to the overwork that followed the
economic crisis in companies that were rationalizing. They provided
more space and consistency for the private lives of wage-earners.
Symmetrically, collective conventions and workshop delegates instit-
uted a new regime of the labour contract, conceived as a contract
of public order in companies that were still the property of their
share-owners. In this sense, the Popular Front constitutes an enduring
break in French social history. Factory occupations introduced a
decisive facet of modernity into the world of work, a modernity in
which workers would achieve their dignity as free men.

Notes

1. Jacques Kergoat, *La France du Front Populaire*, Paris, La Découverte,
1986.
2. At the Riom trial, Leon Blum recounted that Lamert-Ribot had got in
touch with him through the mediation of Grunebaum-Ballin, on the Friday
morning: *L'oeuvre de Léon Blum, 1940–1945*, Paris, A. Michel, p. 261. This
version is contradicted by Adrian Rossiter, 'Popular Front economic policy
and the Matignon negotiations', *The Historical Journal*, 30, 3 (1987), pp. 663–
84, based on the account given by the President of the Paris Chamber of

Commerce, Dalbouze, to his office, in the afternoon of 8 June 1936. This article appears to be unknown to Serge Wolikow, *Le Front populaire en France*, Brussels, Ed. Complexe, 1996. Michael Torigian, *Every Factory a Fortress. The French Labor Movement in the Age of Ford and Hitler*, Athens, OH, Ohio University Press, 1999, quotes this article in its bibliography but makes no reference to it in its account, pp. 99-100.

3. The official number was 1,831,000 strikers and 12,142 strikes in June, according to the statistics of the Minister of Labour.

4. Florence Mazabraud, 'Les grèves de 1936 in Haute-Vienne', mémoire de maîtrise, Université Paris Panthéon-Sorbonne, 1980, typescript: similarly, in Clermont-Ferrand, the trades unions influence weighed in against the strike in printing and gas manufacturing. See Eric Panthou, *L'année 1936 dans le Puy-de-Dome*, Paris, FEN-UNSA, *Cahiers du Centre fédéral no. 14*, 1995

5. François Marlin, 'Pour la République, la Paix, la Liberté. Le Front populaire en terre radicale: le Loiret 1934-1939', thesis, Université de Paris VIII Saint-Denis [J.-P.Brunet], 1994, typescript.

6. 'Images du Front Populaire, Finistère 1934-1938', Morlaix, *Skol Vreizh*, no. 7, March 1987, p. 49

7. Françoise Cahier, 'La classe ouvrière havraise et le Front populaire, 1934-1938', mémoire de maîtrise, Université de Paris 1 [J.Droz, J.Girault], 1980, p. 55.

8. Jean Lhomme, 'Juin 1936', in André Siegfried (ed.), *Aspects de la société française*, Paris, Librairie générale de droit et de jurisprudence, 1954, pp. 73-93.

9. Léon Blum at the Riom trial, Blum, *L'oeuvre* p. 67, quoting here an article by Lucien Romier in *Le Figaro* on 1 September 1936.

10. Jacques Bardoux, 'Le Complot du 12 juin', *Revue de Paris*, 15 August 1936. But see also Pierre Monatte, *La Révolution prolétarienne*, 25 June 1936, who suggested that the PCF had tried to push Blum into leaving the government to a character like Edouard Herriot.

11. I have refuted it at some length in an article, 'Les grèves de juin 1936, essai d'interprétation', in *Léon Blum chef de gouvernement 1936-1937*, Paris, A. Colin, 1967, pp. 69-87. Julian Jackson, *The Popular Front in France. Defending Democracy 1934-1938*, Cambridge, Cambridge University Press, 1988, shares this assessment, pp. 87 et seq.

12. Bertrand Badie, *Stratégie de la grève*, Paris, Presses de la FNSP, 1976, p. 69; J. Kergoat, *Front Populaire*, p. 102

13. In 1934 the PCF had 80 cells in the whole of the French metalworking industry, two in the textiles industry, and 8 in chemical products, against 94, 16 and 25 in the railways, postal services and public services, which did not join the strike, respectively. Cf. R. Alloyer, 'Nos forces dans les entreprises', *Cahiers du Bolchévisme*, 1 February 1934, pp. 180 seq.

14. Declaration to the national confederal committee, quoted by J. Kergoat, *Front Populaire* p. 148. On the union permanent staff overflowing

with strikers' delegates coming to seek advice and support, see the many eye-witness accounts in Georges Lefranc, *Juin 1936, 'l'explosion sociale' du Front Populaire*, Paris, Julliard (coll. 'Archives'), 1966.

15. Antoine Prost, *La CGT à l'époque du Front populaire, essai de description numérique*, Paris, A. Colin, 1964.

16. Michael Torigian, *Every Factory*, gives several examples, pp. 99 seq.

17. Edward Shorter and Charles Tilly, *Strikes in France 1930–1968*, Cambridge, Cambridge University Press, 1974, quoting G. Lefranc, see Trotskyists, anarchists, Pivertists and strictly compliant communists as the leaders of the movement, underlining that it is a matter of political militants rather than unionists (p. 133). This is an over-hasty generalization, not confirmed by the later works of G. Lefranc nor our own researches.

18. Julian Jackson, *op. cit.*

19. Bertrand Badie, 'Les grèves du Front populaire aux usines Renault', *Le Mouvement social*, no. 81, October–December 1972, pp. 69–109, p. 82

20. F. Cahier, *'Classe ouvrière havraise'*: Louis Eudier, 'Breguet-Le Havre: première grève-occupation en 1936', *Cahiers d'histoire de l'Institut Maurice Thorez*, 1972, no. 29, pp. 67–70.

21. The radicals lost 570,000 votes in comparison to 1932 (1,745,000 compared to 2,315,000), the socialists of all shades gained 172,000 (2,203,000 against 2,034,000), and the communists gained 686,000 (1,469,000 against 783,000), a gain of 288,000 votes over the 1932 figure.

22. I have studied these demonstrations in detail: 'Les manifestations du 12 février 1934 en province', *Le Mouvement social*, Jan.–March 1966, pp. 7–27.

23. See Danielle Tartakowsky, 'Stratégies de la rue, 1934–1936', *Le Mouvement social*, no. 135, April–June 1986, pp. 31–62, and *Les Manifestations de rue en France 1918–1968*, Paris, Publications de la Sorbonne, 1997, particularly Chapters 12 and 13, pp. 307–61.

24. C. Tartakowsky, *Les Manifestations*, p. 358.

25. The partisan films of the period show this nation. 'France is not for French people, for it belongs to the two hundred families. France is not for the French, for it belongs to those who are pillaging it', according to the film directed for the PCF by Renoir in January 1936, 'La vie est a nous'.

26. Danielle Tartakowsky, 'Le cinéma militant des années trente, source pour l'histoire du Front populaire', *Les cahiers de la Cinématheque*, no. 71, December 2000, pp. 15–24.

27. Alfred Sauvy, *Histoire économique de la France entre les deux guerres, tome II (1931–1939)*, Paris, Fayard, 1967, Tables 7, 8 and 9, pp. 500, 520 and 521.

28. Against 453,000 in 1931 and 537,000 in 1926.

29. Cf. Robert Salais, 'La formation du chômage moderne dans les années trente', *Economie et statistique*, no. 155, May 1983, pp. 15–29.

30. The same purely demographic contraction in the active population was also visible in Germany and contributed considerably to the reduction

in unemployment that the Nazis attributed to their economic Policy. See Tim Mason, *Social Policy in the Third Reich. The Working Class and the 'National Community'*, Providence/Oxford, Berg, 1993.

31. Characteristic of this attitude among owners, the allocation of men to go without employment as a function of their seniority in the business was known in the metalworking and mechanial industries: although, with the prolongation of the crisis, older workers were increasingly dismissed, most of the unemployed had been employed for less than one year (55 % in 1931, 42 % in 1935). Workers with five years' seniority or more suffering dismissal represent 11 % of the total in 1931 and 25 % in 1935, still a relatively small proportion. See Charles Rist, *Les chômeurs d'après une enquête récente. Communication à la Société de Statistique de Paris*, Paris, Berger-Levrault, 1942.

32. A. Sauvy, *Histoire économique*, p. 545.

33. We may see in this fact one of the reasons for the visceral opposition in conversative circles to any devaluation that would have had a further effect on the income of *rentiers*.

34. Alain P. Michel, *L'introduction du travail à la chaîne aux usines Renault 1917-1939*, Paris, JCM Editions, 1997.

35. Aimée Moutet, 'Les origines du système de Taylor en France. Le point de vue patronal (1907-1914)', *Le Mouvement social*, October–December 1975, pp. 15-51; *Les Logiques de l'entreprise. La rationalisation dans l'industrie française de l'entre-deux-guerres*, Paris, Ed. De l'EHESS, 1997. See also Patrick Fridenson, *Histoire des usines Renault 1. Naissance de la grande entreprise, 1898-1939*, Paris, Ed. du Seuil, 1972; 'Un tournant taylorien de la société française (1904-1918)', *Annales ESC*, September–October 1987, pp. 1031-60; Sylvie Schweitzer, *Des Engrenages à la chaine. Les usines Citroën 1915-1935*, Lyon, PUL, 1982.

36. Simone Weil, *La Condition ouvrière*, Paris, Gallimard, 1968 (1st edition), pp. 45-145.

37. G. Lefranc, *Juin 1936,* p.210.

38. J. Kergoat, *Front Populaire*, p. 149, who quotes without source a song that highlights this system.

39. Raymond Hainsworth, 'Les grèves du front populaire de mai et juin 1936', *Le Mouvement social*, no. 96, July – September, 1976, pp. 3-45.

40. Antoine Prost, 'Le climat social' in René Rémond and Janine Bourdin (eds), *Edouard Daladier, chef de gouvernement*, Paris, Presses de la FNSP, 1977, pp. 99-128. These forms of resistance to the return to earlier norms of productivity have since been highlighted in the automobile industry, aviation and construction by Michael Seidman, 'The Birth of the Week-end and the Revolts against Work: The Workers of the Paris Region during the Popular Front (1936-1938)', *French Historical Studies*, vol. xii, nl. 2, autumn 1981, pp. 249-76.

41. Simone Weil, 'Enseignements à tirer des conflits du Nord', *Condition ouvrière*, pp. 267-278, quotation p.269.

42. On the owners, see J. Lhomme, 'Juin 1936', Ingo Kolboom, *La revanche des patrons. Le patronat français face au front populaire*, Paris, Flammarion, 1986 [1st edn, Rheinfelden, 1983], the anonymous contribution 'Journal d'un patron. Une collaboration de classes est-elle possible', *Etudes*, June and July 1938, pp. 332–46 and 433–46, and a letter from Simone Weil to Auguste Detoeuf reporting a conversation overhead in a train, *Condition ouvrière*, pp. 255–9.

43. Quoted by G.Lefranc, *Juin 1936*, p. 132.

44. Jacques Danos and Marcel Gibelin, *Juin 1936*, Paris, Ed. Ouvrières, 1952; Colette Audry, *Léon Blum ou la politique du juste*, Paris, Julliard, 1955; Daniel Guérin, *Front populaire, révolution manquée*, Paris, Julliard, 1963; Maurice Jaquier, *Simple militant*, Paris, Denoel, 1974; J. Kergoat, *Front Populaire*.

45. J. Kergoat, ibid. p. 155, who quotes, without giving the source, a female worker in the occupied Say refinery, as saying: 'It's no longer "that place", it's our factory'.

46. J. Danos and M. Gibelin, *Juin 1936*, p. 95; J. Kergoat, *Front Populaire*, pp. 155–6.

47. Jean Coutrot, *L'Humanisme économique. Les leçons de juin 1936*, Paris, Centre polytechnicien d'études économiques, 1936; Henri Prouteau, *Les occupations d'usine en Italie et en France*, Paris, Libraire technique et économique, 1938.

48. 'La vie et la grève des ouvrières métallos', article published under the pseudonym S. Galois in the *Revolution prolétarienne*, 10 June 1936; S.Weil, *Condition ouvrière*, pp. 218–232 and 237. My emphasis.

49. The first was surely Michel Collinet, who devoted a chapter of his book, *Esprit du syndicalisme*, Paris, Les. Ed. Ouvrières, 1951, to 'Une grève-kermesse'.

50. *Ibid.*, p. 230.

51. Account recorded by Anne Marrast, *Mémoires des grèves de 36 dans les grands magasins*, mémoire de maîtrise, Université de Paris I, Panthéon-Sorbonne, 1986, typescript, p. 101. Our emphasis.

52. Michael Torigian, *Every Factory a Fortress*, pp. 60–61.

53. Gérard Funffrock, *Les grèves ouvrières dans le Nord (1919–1935). Conjoncture économique, catégories ouvrières, organisations syndicales et partisanes*, Roubais, Edires, 1988, p. 313.

54. *Ibid.*, p. 324

55. Antoine Prost, 'Les grèves de juin 1936, essai d'interprétation', in *Léon Blum, Chef de gouvernement*, Paris, A. Colin, Presses de la FNSP, 1967, pp. 67–87.

56. J. Lhomme, *Juin 1936'*, p. 92, in italic in the text.

57. Eric J. Hobsbawm, 'Birth of a Holiday: The First of May', in Chris Wrigley and J. Shepherd (eds), *On the Move: Essays in Labour and Transport History Presented to Philip Bagwell*, London, The Hambeldon Press, 1991, pp. 104–22. See also Gita Deneckere, Marie-Louis Georgen, Inge Marssolek,

The 1936 Strikes: Factory Occupations and Declining Deference

Danielle Tartakowsky and Chris Wrigley, 'Premiers mai', in Jean-Louis Robert, Friedhelm Boll and Antoine Prost (eds), *L'invention de syndicalisme. Le syndicalisme en Europe occidentale à la fin du XIX siècle*, Paris, Publ. De la Sorbonne, 1997, pp. 199–217.

58. S. Weil, *Condition ouvrière*, p. 256. Weil's emphasis.

59. See for example an article by Jacques Bernard in the *Nouveaux cahiers*, quoted by G. Lefranc, *Juin 1936*, p. 274.

60. On this point, see I. Kolboom, *Revanche des patrons.*

61. *Ibid*, p.216.

62. Quoted by *Le Peuple*, 21 August 1936.

63. G. Lefranc, *Juin 1936*, p. 202.

64. Jean-Paul Sartre, *Le Mur*, Paris, Gallimard, 1939, pp. 147 and 159.

65. On the importance of these procedures, Joel Colton's book, *Compulsory Labor Arbitration in France, 1936–1939*, New York, King's Crown Press, 1952, remains fundamental. See also our contribution to the Daladier conference, already cited.

Index

Titles are underlined. Bold letters : persons, characters, institutions, associations. When associations or institutions are ordered according to their French initials, their meaning is explained in English between parenthesis. Italics : places, countries, towns. Capital letters : linguistic items, words analysed as such by linguistic methods.

Hence 'Republic' refers to the political regime, its institutions and ideology, '**Republic**' refers to its representations in collective imagery as a person or a myth, and 'REPUBLIC' refers to uses of the word in political discourses.

Index

APART FROM AND ABOVE : 282, 296, 298, 299

ARAC (Republican association of anciens combattants) : 40, 280, 281, 283, 296, 306

Arbeit, Arbeiter : 262, 263, 265

Arbeiterbewegung : 265, 273

Arc of Triumph : 28

Architects : 135, 138

Ardant du Picq : 94

Argelès (Pyrénées-Orientales) : 281

Argonne : 45

Ariès (Philippe) : 233

Armistice day, ceremonies : 27–33, 37, 38, 98, 225 – speeches : 34–36.

Arnoux (Jacques d') : 71

Arrondissement ballot : 237

Arthur Martin : 323

Articles : 260

Artistic occupations : 132–33, 142

Assembler : 141, 144

Attack : 96

Audin (Maurice) : 117

Audoin-Rouzeau (Stéphane) : 96, 104

Audry (Colette) : 324, 336

Auriol (Vincent) : 165

Auschwitz : 65, 121

Authority : 249

Aviation factories : 311–312

Avignon (Vaucluse) : 58

Avocourt (forest) : 52

Aydelotte (William O.) : 254

Azéma (Léon) : 58

Babcock & Wilcox : 326

Baccalauréat : 227

Badie (Bertrand) : 333, 334

Baker : 139, 143

Ballet-teacher : 134, 137

Bank of France : 151

Bank – employee : 143 – director : 143 – staff : 139, 140

Banker : 143

Banners : 11, 31

Barbusse (Henri) : 70, 295

Bardoux (Jacques) : 333

Bar-keeper : 138, 139

Bar-le-Duc (Meuse) : 50

Barodet (Désiré) : 238

Barra (soldier) : 78

Barrès (Maurice) : 63, 95, 104

Barthas (Louis) : 50, 69

Barthélémy (Joseph) : 278, 305

Barthes (Roland) : 277

Basque region : 23, 163

Bastille day 14 July° : 60

Bataille (Frédéric) : 30

Bayard : 84

Bayonet charges : 96

Bayonets (Trench of) : 54, 55, 63, 70

Bayonne (Pyrénées-Atlantiques) : 101

Bazeilles (Ardennes) : 95

Becker (Jean-Jacques) : 2

Bedaux (Charles) : 321–322

Behörde : 269

Benet (Eugène) : 19

Benoit (Robert) : 275

Benzécri (Jean-Paul) : 254

Bergounioux (Alain) : 256, 274

Bernard (Jacques) : 337

Bernier (Msgr) : 157

Bernot (Lucien) : 233

Berry : 163

Bert (Paul) : 238, 244

Bertaux (Daniel) : 217

Besitzer : 266

Billancourt : 148

Bimbenet (E.) : 158, 173

Birkenau : 121

Blancard (René) : 233

Blasquez (Adélaïde) : 233

Blavier (Yves) : 71

Bloch-Laîné (François) : 230, 234

Blum (Léon) : 233, 253, 256, 312, 314, 324, 332, 333

Index

Index

Cibois (Philippe) : 254
Citizen, citoyens : 262, 263, 275
Citroën : 148, 312, 321
Civic action : 282, 283, 285, 286, 295, 299
Civil religion : 36–37
Civil servant : 134, 143
Class struggle : 264
Class, working class, classe ouvriere, Klassen : 252, 264, 266, 311
Class-conscious : 264
Clemenceau (Georges) : 160, 161, 238, 245, 247, 293
Clergy : 157, 158, 159, 160–162, 164, 166, 167
Clerk : 131, 143
Clésinger (Jean-Baptiste) : 41
CNACVG (National confederation of Anciens combattants and War victims) : 281
CNJA (National centre of young farmers) : 231
CNOF (National committee for French organization [of work]): 321
Coal mines : 323
Cognac (Charente) : 316
Cognac (Gabriel) : 330
Colleagues, collègues, Kollegen : 262
Collective agreements : 148, 312, 323, 331, 332
Collinet (Michel) : 336
Colonel : 135
Colton (Joel) : 337
COMBATTANT : 288, 292, 293, 294, 295, 296, 297, 299, 300, 303
Comité national du Souvenir de Verdun : 61
Communication engineer : 135
Communist party : 88, 116, 252, 253, 313, 314, 315, 316, 317 – young communists : 228

Company director or manager : 131, 135, 143, 148
Comrades, camarades, Genossen : 262, 263, 275
Conan (Eric) : 124
Concierges : 141, 148
Confederation generale du travail : 273
CONFLICTS : 289
Conscience : 249
Conservatives : 238, 241, 245, 251
Constantine : 117
Constitution : 250
Contractor : 137, 138
Cooper : 158
Corbin (Alain) : 90
Corneille (Pierre) : 94, 102
Costes (Alfred) : 315
Cottin (Alain) : 233
Courbet (Gustave) : 241
Courbevoie (Hauts-de-Seine) : 311
Courdesses (Lucile) : 256
Coutrot (Jean) : 325, 336
Craftsmen : 135, 138, 142, 143, 147
Craipeau (Maria) : 232
Creuilly (Calvados) : 19
Cribier (Françoise) : 150
Cru (Jean Norton) : 55, 63, 70
Crubellier (Maurice) : 74, 89, 90
Cruchard (Abel) : 70
Cutter : 134

Daladier (Edouard) : 251, 293
Dalbouze (Pierre-Etienne) : 312, 333
Dancing : 223, 231, 233, 326, 328
Danos (Jacques) : 324, 336
Day labourer : 139, 141, 144
De Gaulle (general) : 87, 88, 95, 107, 109,113, 237
De la Bollardière (general) : 117
De Mun (Albert) : 238
De Profundis : 29
Dead Man (hill) : 46, 48, 56

Index

Index

Index

Fridenson (Patrick) : 335
Friendly societies : 259
Froideterre ravine : 52
Funffrock (Gérard) : 336
Furet (François) : 89
Furniture salesman : 130
FURR (Fédération for the unity of rapatriés) : 113, 123
Furrier : 138, 143

Gabin (Jean) : 148
Gabriel : 155
Gaillard (Jeanne) : 149
Gambetta (Léon) : 84, 238, 239, 241, 247
GAME : 290
Gardener : 158
Garnier (Albert) : 69
Garonne valley : 114
Gaudy (Georges) : 62, 71
Gaullists : 88, 113, 114
Gavoille (Jacques) : 89
Geay (Bertrand) : 91
General : 135
Geneva agreement (1954) : 109
Genevoix (Maurice) : 61
Genocide : 121–122
Gentioux (Creuse) : 25
Gentlemen : 263
Georgen (Marie-Louise) : 337
German atrocities : 95
Germans : 98, 118
Germany : 34, 60, 86, 87, 102
Gestapo : 118, 120
Giap (general) : 110
Gibelin (Marcel) : 324, 336
Gicquel (Jean) : 305
Ginisty (Msgr.) : 56, 57
Ginzburg (Carlo) : 256
Girard (Alain) : 233
Girardet (Raoul) : 104
Giraudoux (Jean) : 99, 100, 101, 102, 103, 105
Girod (Roger) : 217
Giscard d'Estaing (Mme) : 166

Givors (Rhône) : 181
Goblet (René) : 238
Goldthorpe (John H.) : 150
Good Friday : 210
Gourdon : 41
Government : 268
Greece : 82
Greengrocers : 141, 148
Grenadou (Ephraïm) : 232
Grenoble (Isère) : 11, 180
Grèves d'occupation (film) : 327
Grévy (Jules) : 238
Gribaudi (Maurizio) : 150
Grugies (Aisne) : 21
Guérin (Daniel) : 324, 336
Guesde (Jules) : 274
Guesdists : 259, 260, 268
Guides : 229, 230
Guillaume (Pierre) : 180, 194, 214, 216, 218, 219
Gutenberg : 79
Gy-l'Evêque (Yonne) : 25

Hachette (Jeanne) : 78
Hainsworth (Raymond) : 335
Hands : 263
Hargrove (June) : 39
Harkis : 111
Harris (Zellig S.) : 274
Hat-maker : 138
Hauchecorne (Catherine) : 215
Haumont (forest) : 45
Heads : 140
Hector : 102, 103
Hecuba : 100, 101
Helen : 102, 103
Hélias (Pierre-Jakez) : 222, 232
Hénaff (Eugène) : 315
Henqueville (Seine-Maritime) : 42
Héraud (Marcel) : 28
Hérold (Louis) : 18
Herriot (Edouard) : 333
Herrschenden : 267
Hetzel (Anne-Marie) : 256, 274
Hexagon : 74–75

Index

Index

Labour, labourer : 263, 265, 272
Labourer : 131, 140, 141, 142
Lalinde (Dordogne) : 90
Lamartine (Alphonse de) : 82
Lambert-Ribot (Alfred) : 312, 332
Landernau (Finistère) : 296, 309
Lang-son : 238
Launay (Michel P.) : 256, 274
Lavisse (Ernest) : 82, 91
Law, legislation : 269
Laws :
  1905 (21 mar): 195
  1919 (25 oct.) : 12
  1920 (31 jul.) : 39
  1922 (24 oct.) : 28
  1940 (10 jul.) : 87
  1968 (12 nov.): 113
Lawyers : 135, 136, 142
Le Béguec (Gilles) : 91
Le Chatelier (Henri) : 321
Le Havre (Seine-Maritime) : 61,
  311, 313
Le Pen (Jean-Marie) : 114, 115
League of Nations : 35, 87
Leather-worker : 138
Lefebvre (Henri) : 229, 234
Lefebvre (Jacques-Henri) : 55, 66,
  70
Lefèvre (Josette) : 256, 274
Lefranc (Georges) : 334, 335, 336
Legitimists : see monarchists
Lehideux (François) : 314
Leigneux (Loire) : 41
Lengrand (Louis) : 222, 223, 232
Lent : 210, 211
Lequin (Yves) : 180, 181, 216
Les bâtisseurs (film) : 317
Les croix de Bois (film) : 62
Les Etincelles : 280, 283
Levallois-Perret (Hauts-de-Seine) :
  25
Lever (Evelyne) : 122
Lewin (Christophe) : 123
Lhomme (Jean) : 327, 333, 336
Liauzu (Claude) : 123

Libera : 29
Liberal professions : 135
Liberation : 148
Liberty : 249, 252
Liebknecht (Karl) : 6
Linguistic turn, linguistic methods :
  253, 254, 258, 280–283, 306
Linville (André) : ps. for André
  L'Heureux : 42, 43.
Lockroy (Edouard Simon, dit) :
  238
Locksmith : 141
Lombard (canon) : 57
Lorette (Notre-Dame de) : 58, 116
Lorry driver : 141
Lottin (D.) : 172
Louis XIV (king) : 84
Louis XVI (king) : 82
Louvroil (Nord) : 326
Lucas (Gaston) : 223
Luirard (Monique) : 39, 40, 41, 42
Lyons (Rhône) : 40, 180, 181

Mac Orlan (Pierre) : 55, 59, 70
Maginot (André) : 80, 90
Maginot line : 97
Magistrates : 135
Magny-le-Freule (Calvados) : 16
Maingueneau (Dominique) : 90,
  91
Manent (G.) : 43
Mankind : 252
Mantelllier (P.) : 172 173
Manufacturer : 134, 135, 137, 143
Maquis : 118
Marchal : 330
Margueritte (Victor) : 233
Marlin (François) : 333
Marne battle : 53, 54
Marrast (Anne) : 336
Marriage : calendar : 210–212 –
  ceremony : 209 – certificates :
  129, 131, 175–176, 189, 195,
  202, 206, 217 – contracts : 202–
  203 – religious vs. civil : 210

347

Index

Index

Index

Sieges : 94 – of Paris : 95
Singer : 143
Sirinelli (Jean-François) : 91, 123, 124
Sirot (Stéphane) : 274
Social categories : 4, 5, 127 ff., 149 – in France and Great Britain : 128
Social classes : 212–213
Social mobility : 131
Social proximity : 187–188
Social : 250
Social-democratic Party (Germany) : 259
Socialist Party : 313, 316, 324
Societies : 265
Society : 245
Socio-professional categories : 128, 144–146, 212, 213
Solemn Communion : 222, 226, 233
Somme battle : 46, 52
Sorbias (Loire) : 41
Souilly (Meuse) : 50, 52
Souvenir français : 12
Spanish Civil War : 97
Speeches : 260
Spirit : 290, 291, 292, 296
Spuller (Eugène) : 238, 241, 244
State : 250
Statues : 14–27 – see also Joan of Arc.
Steeg (Théodore) : 238
Stora (Benjamin) : 118, 123
Strikes : 260, 311 ff. – general strike : 261, 327–328
Struggle : 252, 289, 290, 297, 298
Student : 139
Suez expedition : 109
Sullerot (Evelyne) : 98, 105
Supervisors : 140, 142
Supreme Being : 157
Susini villa : 116, 117
Syndicat, syndicalisme : 265, 268

Syndicats, syndicalism : 81, 163, 171, 252, 257 ff., 311 ff.

Taboureau (Jean) : see Jean des Vignes Rouges
Tailor : 138, 143, 145–146, 147
Tapin (sergeant) : 35
Tarde (Alfred de) : see Agathon
Tardieu (André) : 62, 278, 290, 293, 305
Tartakowsky (Danielle) : 334, 337
Taxi driver : 141
Taylorization : 320–322
Telegraphists : 141
Telephonist : 140
Thabault (Roger) : 78, 85, 90, 91, 256
Thélot (Claude) : 217
Thévenot (Laurent) : 150
Thiaumont (forest) : 64
Thorez (Maurice) : 253, 256, 313, 314
Threat, threaten : 245, 249, 250, 253
Tilly (Charles) : 334
Time-scale : 77
To the Dead (bugle call) : 30
Tonkin : 238
Toolmaker : 141, 143
Torigian (Michael) : 333, 334, 336
Torture : 117, 118, 121
Touchard (Jean) : 229, 233
Touchet (Msgr.) : 162
Toul (Meurthe-et-Moselle) : 48
Toulouse (Haute-Garonne) : 311
Touraine (Alain) : 259
Tourcoing (Nord) : 58
Tournier (Maurice) : 256, 274
Tours (Indre-et-Loire) : 180
Touvier (Paul) : 119
Tracts : 260
Trade union : 265, 273

5660